A Century of Media,
A Century of War

PETER LANG
New York • Washington, D.C./Baltimore • Bern
Frankfurt am Main • Berlin • Brussels • Vienna • Oxford

Robin Andersen

A Century of Media,
A Century of War

PETER LANG
New York • Washington, D.C./Baltimore • Bern
Frankfurt am Main • Berlin • Brussels • Vienna • Oxford

Library of Congress Cataloging-in-Publication Data

Andersen, Robin.
A century of media, a century of war / Robin Andersen.
p. cm.
Includes bibliographical references and index.
1. United States—History, Military—20th century. 2. United States—
History, Military—21st century. 3. United States—Military policy.
4. Propaganda, American—History—20th century.
5. Propaganda, American—History—21st century.
6. Mass media—Political aspects—United States. I. Title.
E745.A54   355.3'4—dc22   2006019560
ISBN 978-0-8204-7894-4 (hardcover)
ISBN 978-0-8204-7893-7 (paperback)

Bibliographic information published by **Die Deutsche Bibliothek.**
Die Deutsche Bibliothek lists this publication in the "Deutsche
Nationalbibliografie"; detailed bibliographic data is available
on the Internet at http://dnb.ddb.de/.

Cover design by Lisa Barfield
Author photo by Guy Robinson

The paper in this book meets the guidelines for permanence and durability
of the Committee on Production Guidelines for Book Longevity
of the Council of Library Resources.

To the many journalists
who have died trying to bear witness to the costs of war.

Contents

Acknowledgments

M any people have helped bring this book into print. When I first presented the idea with some early writings to Anthony Chiffolo, his
initial encouragement and sage advice led to what became a major undertaking. My good fortune continued when the book found a home with
Peter Lang through the efforts of Damon Zucca, an editor whose patience
and brilliance seems to know no bounds.

Independent artists and educators have given visual and narrative life
to some of the analysis in the videotapes *From Tragedy to War*, *Channels of
War* in the *Shocking and Awful* series, and *Beyond Good and Evil*. Some of
the video makers who worked on those productions distributed by Paper
Tiger, Deep Dish Television and the Media Education Foundation, are
Norman Cowie, Brian Drolet, Michael Eisenmenger, DeeDee Halleck,
Linda Iannacone, Joel Kovel, Carlos Pareja, Matthew Pascarella, Miguel
Picker and Chyng Sun, just to name a few.

Comments and encouragement have come from Douglas Kellner,
Jack Bratich, James Der Derian, Toby Miller, Peter Phillips, Matthew
McAllister, and Bob McChesney. I have benefited greatly from collaborat-
ing with German scholars Fabian Virchow and Tanja Thomas.

For their tireless pursuit of fair and accurate media able to live up
to First Amendment mandates, I thank my colleagues at FAIR whose
contributions have influenced the work presented here. Chats with Jim

Naureckas, editor of *EXTRA!* are always inspiring. Special help came from Janine Jackson, Jeff Cohen and Steve Rendall.

My Fordham colleagues have supported this research in many ways, and some have read and commented on parts of the manuscript in the Faculty Seminar of the Institute of International Humanitarian Affairs. They are Carlos Mejia, Jonathan Crystal, Michael Latham, Evelyn Bush and Jeannine Hill Fletcher. Special thanks also to Martin Fergus, James Marsh, Astrid O'Brien, Judith Green, Jeanne Flavin, Gwenyth Jackaway, Anahid Kassabian, Michael Tueth, Brian Glick, and Joseph Currie. Hopeton Campbell, as always, was generous with his time and expertise.

For their encouragement during the early stages of this research, I'd like to thank Paolo Carpignano, John Downing, Colin Sparks, Peter Dahlgren and Ed Herman. The continued documentation done by the National Security Archives is indispensable, and Peter Kornbluh was generous with his time. Much of the peace and justice work done by so many today is heroic, and I am grateful for time spent with Daniel Berrigan, and to Michael Ratner and Ellen Ray for their efforts against torture, among many others too numerous to list. I am grateful to the journalists who agreed to talk to me, and to Neil Hickey and Joe Wershba.

As always, I have depended on my community of friends for their intelligence and support. Michael Yellin read the work from beginning to end, and Sameh Fakhouri, Stephen Yorke and Roger Logan were there to help with computer and software and much more. For their observations, insights, support and clippings I'd like to thank, Aliza Dichter, Lourdes Font, Joan Glickman, Amelia Jones, Basia Kinglake, Jane LaTour, Kathy Leary, David Lerner, Sharon Livesey, Nancy Morris, Neil Talbot, Bill Schaap, Pamela Smorkaloff, Bruce Soloway, Kim Christensen and Susie Stulz.

I am grateful for the support of Fordham University deans Dominic Balestra and Nancy Busch, and especially the former dean of Fordham College, Jeffrey von Arx. With a topic such as this there would be rough spots, and I was helped through those times by many friends, family, and always my Fordham students, who are curious, open-minded and generous. Students in my courses, especially peace and justices classes proved to be excellent research assistants. Without their help, a weighty schedule of full-time teaching would have made completing this book impossible.

Through trying times and good, this journey would not merit the effort without the companionship of Guy Robinson.

Any errors contained in these pages are of course my own.

Preface

The nervous tension in the car hung hot and heavy, compounding the effects of the humid Salvadoran air. The car swung slowly through the winding streets of Lomas, the rich residential area on the outskirts of San Salvador. We slowed and began to turn into a driveway. The twelve-foot, chain-link fence, woven with green plastic, concealed everything behind it. The gates opened slowly. As we maneuvered through them, the guards came into view, at least half a dozen plainclothesmen armed with automatic rifles. It was too late to turn back. Kathy, the ABC correspondent, looked at me and said, "Wouldn't this make a good story? ABC News crew and graduate student kidnapped by the right-wing (paramilitary) in San Salvador."

It had not been my idea to come along. Yes, I was observing the newsgathering techniques of journalists covering Central America, and this was an important interview, but I knew it was going to be dangerous. The month before, Kathy had already been wounded by a bullet in the arm when the crew was covering a demonstration and she was hit by sniper fire. I had seen fear in their faces only yesterday, after we had been separated at another demonstration. I had fallen back to interview one of the young organizers and had inadvertently put one of their pompoms in my pocket. When she saw me with it later, Kathy yelled, "Do you want to get killed?" Carl, the cameraman, added, "That makes a great target for right-wing snipers!" We knew these were dangerous people, and so when the interview was arranged, I had said I would pass.

But here I was. We sat in the car for a few minutes not knowing what to do. The big double gates closed behind us, and the men in the lead car got out. John, the sound technician, was with them. We decided to get out, too, and Carl slipped his camera from out of the trunk. John was ahead carrying the rest of the gear. We walked along a garden path to the mansion and through the large, carved wooden doors. We were led through the foyer, and as we entered a huge patio area, we could see the shimmering blue water of the swimming pool. As John proceeded to set down the long, cylindrical carrying case, one of the guards lurched forward and aimed his rifle. John's arms shot up over his head as he declared, "It's only a tripod!" He stood for a moment looking like a character in a Western who's just been told to *reach for the sky.* The armed man finally gestured his approval, turning the gun away.

This freelance ABC News crew referred to themselves as the budget-and-bang-bang crew. They flew into Central American "hot spots" after a "coup or an earthquake" to get the pictures. It was February 1980, and El Salvador had not yet become a major concern to the architects of U.S. foreign policy. A year later the Reagan administration would "draw the line against communist intervention in the hemisphere," and the high-paid television correspondents and network staff camera crews would take the story.

But before El Salvador became famous, I watched as these freelancers, with very few resources, struggled to comprehend what was going on in the country. I wanted to know how U.S. journalists went about gathering the news in a confusing and often dangerous situation. I had learned to respect their intelligence and resourcefulness. Unlike their more highly paid counterparts at the networks, these reporters understood Spanish. We had driven through the streets of the capital listening to the radio. In fact, the radio had helped us into the present situation. We heard a program featuring a speaker with such extreme right-wing views that we knew he had to be part of the story. Carl called the organization responsible for the program and arranged an interview with Roberto D'Aubuisson. When we arrived at the office in a small shopping enclave in downtown San Salvador, I said I would wait outside. But shortly after they went in, they all came back out following several men. We were hurried into two different cars, and as we drove off, I wondered if it had been a good idea to go with these guys.

Now here we were, among armed men we knew to be dangerous, without our own car. As John began to set up the equipment on the patio, a small man with curly black hair and large, sad, brown eyes emerged from one of the rooms off the patio. His "handlers" ushered him over to the table and instructed John on how and where they wanted the interview done. As Kathy began the interview with D'Aubuisson, I stepped aside, as was my habit, and slowly struck up a conversation with two of the armed men guarding the grounds from the swimming pool terrace. They told me they were pleased to have D'Aubuisson because he was so good on camera and had a "face that women loved." Through our rambling conversation, they revealed their philosophy and plans for the country. They would eliminate the "communists" even if they had to kill 150,000 people. I learned that what they meant by "communist" was a huge proportion of the population that had taken to the streets demanding higher wages, fewer working hours, electricity in the countryside and water that they could drink.

I looked over to the men seated behind the table in front of the camera and realized that D'Aubuisson did not speak English. Kathy's questions were being answered by a tidy, pale, young man who I later found out was educated in Boston. As the interview continued, the atmosphere lightened, and we all began to relax. After the last question, we declined to stay for drinks and asked for a ride back to our car. Under protest, they agreed. On the way back they became excited about the idea of taking John and Carl up in a helicopter to view the crop damage caused by the war in the countryside. As they dropped us off, Carl said he would consider it.

Back at the hotel we let off much adrenaline as we each recounted our doubts and fears as the afternoon's events had played out. After a little while there was a knock on the door, and we all fell silent. Carl opened it, and one of the men from the mansion crowded into the small room. We acknowledged among ourselves, through eye contact, that he carried one of the typical wrist pouches that concealed a small revolver. He wanted to make arrangements for the helicopter trip, and he asked when the story would air on U.S. television. Carl told him that his work would not be complete until he finished the scheduled interview with the spokesperson for one of the largest popular organizations. Upon hearing this, the man became agitated and gestured toward Carl, yelling, "How can you talk to those people, they're communists!" Carl stood his ground, raised his hands in front of him, blocking the man's advance towards him, and said in a determined voice, "Hey, I tell both sides of the story."

Because I was not in the United States when Carl's story aired, it was over a year before I saw the ABC News story assembled from the videotape of the week's events. It bore so little resemblance to my experience that I hardly recognized it. Kathy and Carl were given one minute and thirty seconds to tell "both sides of the story." The ABC News report featured the *violence and extremism on both the left and right.* Telling "both sides of the story" had provided balance to a story that, in reality, had no balance. In El Salvador, the extremism of the left was hardly comparable to the brutality of the right. This balanced story contradicted what the journalists themselves knew all too well—that the right-wing paramilitary organizations were responsible for the bodies that appeared in the morning both in front of the hotel and carelessly thrown along the roadsides. During the twelve-year war, tens of thousands of Salvadorans, mostly civilians, would be killed by the military and paramilitary organizations. But this truth would not be "official" for another decade.

One month after our interview with Roberto D'Aubuisson, he and his organization would be implicated in the killing of the Monsignor Oscar Romero. Romero was assassinated after giving a sermon asking the military to throw down its weapons and stop the killing. D'Aubuisson would later come to be known as the "father of the death squads." By the end of 1980, these organizations would brutally rape and kill four church women who worked with the poor.

Telling both sides of the story is a professional canon promoted as a strategy to insure fairness and objectivity. Yet, stories so often have many more sides than two. Conventional news narratives that present one view, then another, all too often fail to provide enough background information so that viewers can understand the situation and evaluate both claims from an informed perspective. The short, denuded narratives of television's "balanced" coverage of El Salvador could not explain the economic and political forces that were tearing the country apart. Most stories never mentioned how the armed civil insurrection was sparked in the first place. Background on the years of failed electoral struggle, military repression and extreme conditions of poverty were not part of the exciting stories of violent demonstrations and political assassinations.

I learned watching the process of journalism from beginning to end that telling both sides of the story is a journalistic convention that often obscures more than it illuminates. This was especially disturbing to me, given the dedication and conviction with which Carl had defended the practice, even in the face of danger.

I also learned from my many trips to Central America during this time how the "pictures in our heads," to borrow Walter Lippmann's famous dictum, can justify almost any human action, including mass murder, war and conflict. This book is dedicated to understanding how our perceptions about war are formed to better find our way to peace.

Introduction

The Controlled and Uncontrollable Imagery of War

When digital photographs taken at Abu Ghraib prison outside Baghdad were aired by CBS on April 28, 2004, the images reverberated through the press, were widely reprinted and were uniformly described as shocking. The photos of nude Iraqi prisoners—some in piles, some hooded, one on a leash—showed American military personnel smugly posing in positions of domination. Possibly the most disturbing image is of a black-cloaked and hooded figure standing on what looks like a box, his arms held out from his sides at an unnatural angle, wires trailing from his hands. The posed figure is alone, attached to the instruments of torture in a bare chamber, the gray walls riddled with ugly stains. Though the pictures were released in the spring of 2004, the abuse had taken place late in 2003, and the Red Cross had been documenting the mistreatment of prisoners well before the story broke.[1] Indeed, army investigator Major General Antonio Taguba's report on conditions of Iraqi prisons had already set military court proceedings in motion. Commenting on the sequence of events, NPR's Daniel Schorr observed on May 8, 2004, that investigations were "quietly working their way up, nobody paying a whole lot of attention. Then came the pictures. It is not a crisis of prisoner abuse. It is a crisis of pictures and the effect that pictures can have." Distinguishing between war and its representation, between military conduct and its documentation, Schorr understood that the meanings made of war are distinct from war itself.

War is understood and interpreted, justified and judged through the images and narratives that tell the stories of war. Most civilians experience military conflict through the signs and symbols of its depiction, their impressions derived not from the battles in distant lands but from the manner they are rendered at home. This book retraces the history of struggle over war and its representations. Struggles over war's true meaning, its values and necessities, play out on movie and television screens and in the photographs of newspapers and magazines, the cultural outpouring influenced by commercial, political and military pressures.

War stories are constructed as complicated amalgams drawn from the bits and pieces of favored myths and stories of past battlefield heroics. The past is mined to shape new narratives able to present current conflicts in the language of old familiar ones. At the intersection of myth and memory, fictional forms mingle with those of nonfiction, as news of war is understood through cultural tropes and media formats. The politics of memory is made manifest by the fragments that are retrieved and those that are repressed, for war could not be carried out if its negative, counter-narratives of death and brutality were starkly drawn. Because a fundamental aspect of war involves destruction and death, it is at times inevitable that representations of its horrors emerge, such as the photographs from Abu Ghraib. As these uncontrollable, dark images enter the cultural sphere, they will be rhetorically reinterpreted and made culturally acceptable.

The pictures of Abu Ghraib were stunning icons impossible to ignore, because they challenged the central assumptions and standard depictions of war in American culture. On May 6, 2004 speaking from the Rose Garden in an attempt to deflect global criticism, President Bush assured King Abdullah of Jordan that "wrong-doers will be brought to justice" and that "the actions of those folks in Iraq do not represent the values of the United States of America." The values evoked when America goes to war affirm nobility and justice, not brutality and oppression. After September 11, 2001 Americans were told they were the victims of fanatics who hated freedom and American values.

WAR PROPAGANDA

Drawing a line between good and evil and between our values and theirs, George W. Bush revived classic war rhetoric from the early part of the last century. Bush returned to a world of "us and them," a crude vision invented during the First World War in which the complexities of international affairs and global relations are dismissed with sweeping generalities that condemn entire cultures, placing them on the other side of a divide between "civilization" and "barbarism." As Bush drew the world in naively stark contrasts and announced a war on terror, other countries were forced to choose as well. They were either for us or against us. The images taken at Abu Ghraib challenged the president's vision of a world drawn in black and white. Torture perpetrated by Americans shattered—at least for a moment—the simple choreography of war's justification. They confronted the rhetorical basis for the War on Terror, defined as a way to "rid the world of evil."

The naked, hooded Iraqis will forever hold a prominent position in the global catalogue of human misery documented photographically over the last one hundred and fifty years. They are arguably a visual rendering of evil itself, not as an abstract construct, but as the brutality humans inflict upon one another. Indeed, images of war comprise the largest portion of this global catalogue of pain. And here lies the greatest contradiction and challenge to war and its representations in the twenty-first century: how to make war, which at the most basic level is defined by suffering and death, an acceptable practice in contemporary democratic society.

As more pictures from the prison emerged, they began to evoke disturbing public memories from a war U.S. war planners have tried hard over the years to forget. The photographs of Abu Ghraib were being understood as part of the memory of Vietnam, a war opposed by the public. On the front page of *USA Today* (May 10, 2004), a naked Iraqi prisoner backed up against cell bars holds his hands behind his head, the fear etched plainly in his face. The photograph is part of a sequence that shows the man surrounded by uniformed Americans and being set upon by dogs. Placed to the left of the page in *USA Today* is a photograph of a North Vietnamese soldier being summarily executed on the streets of Saigon during the Tet Offensive in 1968. Photojournalist Eddie Adams captured the execution on film, and won the Pulitzer Prize for his efforts. It remains one of the most enduring images of war. The pictures of Abu Ghraib had become the twenty-first-century equivalent.

Like images of Tet, the brutality evident in the pictures from Iraq's notorious prison registered a highly negative response. A *Washington Post/ABC* poll found that by a ratio of 69 to 28 percent the American public felt that such abuse by American military personnel was unacceptable. The legitimacy of the war in Iraq had already been called into question by the failure to find the weapons of mass destruction that justified the war. In their absence, the Bush White House had argued that Iraqis would be better off on the road to democracy. The victims of Abu Ghraib presented a visual challenge to that assertion as well. Shiite cleric Sheikh al-Sadr was quoted as saying, "What sort of freedom and democracy can we expect

from you Americans when you take such joy in torturing Iraqi prisoners?"
(NPR, May 8, 2004).

Most American commentators worried less about the wounds inflicted
on individual Iraqis and more about the effects the photos were having,
especially in the Islamic world. "The effect of these pictures has been simply devastating," commented NPR's Daniel Schorr. White House officials,
including Secretary of Defense Donald Rumsfeld, issued formal apologies,
and NPR host Scott Simon asked Schorr, "Do all of these apologies succeed in blunting any of the impact of those pictures around the world?"

Long-time investigative reporter Seymour Hersh wrote detailed feature articles in the *New Yorker* about Abu Ghraib,[2] attempting to discover
the chain of command that led to what appeared to be the widespread
practice of torture in Iraq, Afghanistan and Guantanamo Bay, Cuba condoned at the highest levels of government. His articles and the continuing
release of more pictures kept the scandal in the news cycle for weeks, but
war and the manner in which it was being fought continued to take second
place to questions about the impact and meaning of the pictures.

TORTURE AND PORNOGRAPHY

Talk-show personality Rush Limbaugh began to successfully recontextual-
izes the images, diverting their meanings from war's brutality to more familiar cultural references. Limbaugh said the images "looked like standard
good old American pornography." His words were repeated and augmented across the media as the focus of debate shifted from war to sexuality
and its expression in American popular culture. Limbaugh reasoned that
soldiers "were just having a good time" and that the pictures were "just
like anything you'd see Madonna or Britney Spears do on stage...."[3] What
became the most notorious of the pictures from Abu Ghraib featured Private Lynndie England in sexually dominating poses, one with a male Iraqi
prisoner at the other end of her leash. When featured on the front page
of the *New York Post*, the headline blared: "Leash Girl in Sex Pics." The
visual representations of sexual assaults against Iraqi males merged with
pornography's imagery of sadism and *the dominatrix*. This framing easily distracted media commentary, with its commercial requirements, from
the questions of official military policy on torture. Instead, focus was directed toward the violations of gendered notions of power and sexuality in
American culture.

Speaking of war always involves a process of negotiating meanings in
a cultural context: the characterizations layered between the language and
visual spectacles common to popular media. The brutality of war was be-

ing understood as adult entertainment and the excesses of consumer/ce-
lebrity culture with Limbaugh's signature misogynist attitudes included.
The images of Lynndie England were disturbing departures from the familiar place held by women in the long conventional history of war narratives where women have occupied a set of narrowly defined roles. The
pin-up girls so iconographic of WWII, are passive visions that provide the
promise of rewards for the warriors who risk their lives. The sexualized
woman-as-sight displayed for male pleasure (not her own) is the traditional woman of war. When men go to war wielding its weaponry, their actions
are motivated by the promise of this idealized feminine mystique. Thus
contained, female sexuality is appropriated to the war effort. The pin-up
is still referenced in such films as *Black Hawk Down* and contemporary
versions include a *Talk* magazine (Lee, 2002) fashion layout with pictures
of Carmen Electra in a Versace dress. Other pages show Victoria's Secret
models standing in alluring poses for enlisted men at Fort Irwin.

When Limbaugh associated the pictures of Abu Ghraib with pornography, he was drawing attention to the violation of passive female sexuality.
The sexual deviance of Lynndie England became the news focus as criticism was directed away from investigations into the official memos and
policies that led to the detestable images. The dangers of female sexuality
took the blame for torture, not the imperiousness of an executive branch
determined to act outside long-standing legal statutes and the Uniform
Code of Military Justice that bans cruelty and inhuman treatment of any
prisoner.

The treatment of female sexuality was also quite distinct from the way
male sexuality is expressed by the valiant fighters that populate Hollywood's war hero culture. Almost exactly a year before the release of the
Abu Ghraib pictures, the president tapped into one of those masculine
narratives of war. At that time, media celebrated gendered constructs and
metaphors that tie male sexuality to the power that weapons confer.

THE *TOP GUN* PRESIDENT: MISSION ACCOMPLISHED

One of the most stunning, real-time dramas ever staged to illustrate the
glories of the victorious warrior was performed by President George
W. Bush. The visual sequences featured a triumphant president dressed
in a military flight suit in the cockpit of a fighter jet making a dramatic,
made-for-television landing onto the deck of the aircraft carrier the U.S.S.
Lincoln. A banner hung from the ship's upper deck proclaiming "Mission
Accomplished." Explaining the million-dollar pseudo-event, the administration said the jet fighter was necessary because the carrier was too far out

to sea to be reached by helicopter. In fact, the ship was so close that it had to be turned around to prevent television cameras from catching the San Diego coastline in the background.

In a culture saturated with entertainment formats purporting to be "reality," the stage-managed event was reported as news. But skillful editing by independent media makers revealed that the dramatic landing was virtually identical to visual sequences in the popular Tom Cruise film of 1986, *Top Gun*.[4] Mainstream commercial broadcasters made few critical comments that might have exposed the flight's choreography. For television broadcasters to expose the production values and fictional referencing of political events would call into question the legitimacy of the commercial media's own strategies and design. In fact, instead of questioning the legitimacy of the event, television personalities, most notably Robert Novak, pointed out how well the flight suit fit the president.

By looking good for the media in his flight suit President Bush reclaimed the Reagan era "hard body" mystique of the masculine identified by Susan Jeffords (1994). Jeffords argues that films such as *Top Gun*, *Rambo*, and *Lethal Weapon*, were cultural expressions of the Reagan revolution that associated masculine qualities such as strength and heroism with American politics. *Top Gun* is one in this genre of "spectacular narratives about characters who stand for individualism, liberty, militarism, and a mythic heroism" (16). The *Top Gun* pilot Maverick, played by Tom Cruise and imitated by President Bush, was a particular type of hero who reclaimed masculine power and sexuality through the weapons of war.

SEX AND WAR

Military hardware has long been surrounded by a symbolic culture that assigns meanings over and above its deadly purposes. Indeed, weapons designed to kill are routinely associated with male virility. Films abound that celebrate this tradition, and *Top Gun* is one of the least nuanced of the genre. The dialogue is saturated with explicit references that forge the connection between sex and war. Love and courtship run parallel to military training, and sex is discussed through the uses of combat metaphors. When Maverick enters the bar where he meets his girlfriend he exclaims, "This is a target rich environment." Words such as "approach," "engage," "maneuver," "target," "hit," and "shoot" all do double duty (Conlon 1989, 21). According to James Conlon, the movie asserts that when it comes to love and war, "the two modes of engagement aren't really distinct; warring is as erotic as loving is combative" (1989, 20).

Some of the same cultural tropes from *Top Gun* are now used as part of the arsenal of influence when leaders go to war. In a media-driven culture, presidents now change places with movie actors, and celebrities become elected officials. Stagecraft is part of media management and communication strategies essential to waging war in the twenty-first century. The new geography of culture that obscures reality from fiction, president from actor, is the same environment that creates a tie-in product of George W. Bush, the first president to become an action-adventure figure.

THE BATTLE OVER PUBLIC OPINION

The process of negotiating the meaning of war and its depictions has been on-going for centuries, but in an age of mass media and digital communication systems, that process has come to play a profound role in the history of mass conflict, and therefore the history of the contemporary world. Public interpretations of the role of war in our society and its impact on global relations are now defining factors, key elements in our ability to realize or not, a future vision for international peace and stability. Over the last century, the American public has at times expressed both favorable and disdainful opinions about war and its necessities, and those attitudes have influenced the path of conflict. They have also, of course, resulted in media management strategies and information control designed to manufacture favorable attitudes.

Over the years, elected officials and military planners have faced significant public opposition to war. Convincing the public that war is necessary, that all diplomatic channels have been exhausted, and that the call to military action justifies the inevitable loss of life in its wake requires persuasive and well-planned campaigns. Indeed, once war is waged, problems with battlefield logistics, military conduct and casualty figures can be an even greater deterrent to favorable public opinion, or what has been referred to as "homefront morale." Homefront morale and the public's resolve to continue the fight depend on a complicated equation that compares the war's justification to its destructive force. Once the public perceives that the cost in human life is too high a price to pay for the stated goals, opinion quickly turns against the war effort.

THE VIETNAM SYNDROME

One of the most significant moments in the history of war and media took place during the Vietnam War. As detailed in chapter 4, a majority of the American public turned against the fighting after the Tet Offensive of

January 1968 when television imagery revealed the escalating brutality of the war. Two months later, President Lyndon Johnson made an historic televised address to the nation announcing that he would not seek another term as president. The American government lost the battle over public perception in a stunning defeat. As we will see, interpretations of how the media depicted the Vietnam War remain contentious, and many in the military blame the press for losing the war. Presidents and generals have since called the rejection of war the "Vietnam syndrome," and as the term implies, it is viewed as a disease, a set of symptoms, a disorder. Vietnam reaffirmed that war in the information age demands a symbolic environment that hides the human costs and assures the public that accepting war is just and morally legitimate.

THE GOOD FIGHT

Unequivocally positive narratives of war are patterned after the Good Fight. World War II stands out historically as just—the most legitimate war ever fought. The enemy was rapacious, the practices of the Third Reich brutal and the consequences of losing disastrous. As examined in part 1, after the war television and film productions created what came to be the classic war genre, with distinct themes and portrayals. Since then the Good Fight has been told and retold, exemplified by *Saving Private Ryan*, a film set in World War II but released after the First Gulf War. In like fashion, media reporting of the invasion of Iraq began with numerous references to the Band of Brothers, a popularized reference to World War II and the title of an HBO miniseries. Even the Pentagon policy of embedding was understood through the tropes of World War II by referencing war reporter Ernie Pyle, who traveled with the infantry in Europe fighting the worst battles of the ground war.

World War II has become the frame of reference that confers legitimacy to war. On the other hand, when war goes wrong, it is told through the problematic narratives of brutality that characterize the popular memory of Vietnam, a memory solidified by the cultural outpouring that resulted in such post-Vietnam films as *Platoon* and *Apocalypse Now*. After the failures of the Vietnam War, a battle took place between the Pentagon and war correspondents over combat imagery and journalists were excluded from the field in subsequent conflicts. Media strategies were more carefully crafted using increasingly sophisticated techniques and information was tightly controlled.

THE WARS IN CENTRAL AMERICA IN THE 1980s

Only five years after the Vietnam War ended in 1975 with the stark images of American personnel airlifted off the roof of the American embassy in Saigon, President Ronald Reagan would come to power and attempt to convince Americans that another war against communism was necessary, this time in Central America. The leftist Sandinistas of Nicaragua were accused of funneling arms to the rebels in neighboring El Salvador, and the CIA created the contras, a clandestine army, to overthrow their government. To carry out what became known as the Reagan Doctrine, the Pentagon and the White House struggled to make war once again acceptable to the public. As we will see, advertising and marketing techniques would be adopted to sell a new product—foreign policy. A mix of fear and favor would influence press reporting and brand the Sandinistas unfit to govern their country. The contras, with well-documented human rights abuses, would be sold to the press and the public as "freedom fighters," and congressional opposition to the Reagan Doctrine would be labeled unpatriotic.

Part of the Reagan policies in Central America was to ensure that the Salvadoran government remained in power. A bloody civil war that lasted for twelve years cost American taxpayers almost 6 billion dollars and claimed the lives of ten of thousands of Salvadorans. As we will see, Salvadoran military and security forces, funded by the U.S. government, carried out massacres and horrible atrocities against the civilian population. With documentation of human rights abuses, how did American institutions, including the press, and the American public respond to the loss of life of so many innocent people? The media coverage includes stories of courage and cover-ups, of exposés and denials, of battles for things as banal as ratings in the midst of life-and-death events, all of which continue to have a legacy of influence for both the media and the possibility for peace.

The presidency of Ronald Reagan was tainted by the Iran/Contra affair and the constitutional crisis created by his policies in Central America. The day after Thanksgiving in 1986, Attorney General Edwin Meese III revealed that secret operatives had been supplying the contras in direct violation of congressional mandates. Meese also reported that those activities were part of a larger set of foreign-policy initiatives that went against the administration's own pronouncements that it would never negotiate with terrorists. Under Secretary of Defense Caspar Weinberger, sophisticated weapons systems had been sold to Iran, and money from the sales had been used to buy weapons for the contras. As a consequence of these activities, Lieutenant Colonel Oliver North and the president's national security advisor, Admiral John Poindexter, had resigned.

Operations within the executive branch were illegal, secretive and unpopular with the American public, but the Reagan White House survived the scandal, and when the former president died in June 2004, the Iran/Contra affair merited a few paragraphs of coverage. How did the media present these events at the time and in the years that followed? What images did Americans see, and what stories were they told? When the Iran/Contra story broke, how did the media portray those in its spotlight? What popular fictions interacted with real news from the war zones of Central America? As we will see, Oliver North was a key player in the scandal and became a central figure during congressional hearings in the summer of 1987. When North was questioned before Congress his chest was adorned with the icons of past battles and vanquished enemies. Just as George W. Bush would do after the invasion of Iraq almost three decades later, Oliver North assumed the role of a military hero. In the pages of this book, we will see how "Ollie" paved the way for Bush-era stagecraft and how television news reporting merged with fictional portrayals of conflict and wars past. The actual policies carried out in Central America would remain obscure and become part of the hidden history of American foreign policy. What we remember—or choose to forget—of events in this region, tirelessly referred to as our "backyard," still affects our lives and political structures.

In 1988, Reagan's vice-president, George Herbert Walker Bush, would become the 41st president and commander-in-chief. By the end of 1989, shortly before Christmas, he would send U.S. troops to invade Panama in Operation Just Cause. The press would be denied access to the initial invasion and there would be no independent documentation of the bombing and fires that claimed thousands of civilian lives in the poor neighborhood of El Chorrillo, unlucky enough to border the headquarters of the Panamanian Defense Forces that protected General Manuel Noriega. Operation Just Cause would be an historic marker in the coverage of U.S. wars, and less than a year later the First Persian Gulf War would begin.

THE GAME OF WAR

The real victory for George H.W. Bush came when he proclaimed the end to the Vietnam syndrome after Operation Desert Storm (though over time this victory like most, would prove to be fleeting). The first Persian Gulf War has been called the "Nintendo War," for the clearly identifiable graphic sensibilities and visceral thrills of high-tech weapons systems that seemed to hit their target successfully with each "sortie." Many writers have noted the role television played in promoting the stunning power of weapons through this new style of visual imagery. The war carried out from the air resulted in few American casualties, and though the media were restricted from covering the ground war, part 3 of this book details the coverage of the war, that was with rare exceptions, highly positive.

The last two decades of the century were a time of concentrated media industry restructuring, and news organizations were reeling from the effects of massive mergers, centralized corporate ownership and the intensified profit-making strategies they demanded. We will see how advertising and marketing practices influenced the language of reporting and how coverage of Desert Storm mimicked the persuasive discourse that penetrated the commercial formats of television programming. New marketing structures gave life to old war persuasions, and as the century came to an end, World War I rhetorical devices were revived and used to frame a new enemy. This period was another crucial moment in the depictions of war in American culture and another step toward the merger of entertainment and war, with amplified persuasive language an essential part of the mix.

The new visual and technological foundations for war established with Desert Storm would progress at an accelerating pace throughout the 1990s and lead to a qualitatively new set of relationships between the media industries and the industries of war. Some theorists refer to this relationship as the military/entertainment complex, and as discussed in part 4, this new nexus of digital technologies, economics and imaging is exemplified by the video game. The video-game graphic sensibility of war introduced with Desert Storm is now institutionalized within the military and games are employed for training as well as recruitment. *America's Army* was the first video game created by the military and was offered free to kids to download off the Internet on July 4, 2002. It became the number-one online action game in the country with more than three million registered players. Players are positioned as first-person shooters, and after basic training the advanced "marksmanship" is so realistic that the computer screen moves in time to the digital soldier's breathing under fire. The online actors are patterned after the actions of real soldiers. Though the weapons, graphics and settings are highly realistic, the violent consequences of killing are downplayed. The enemy is faceless, masked, and when hit releases a puff of red smoke and falls to the ground. As CNN/money.com (June 3, 2002) reported, "From a propaganda perspective the Army has seemingly hit the jackpot. (And the Army readily admits the games are a propaganda device)."[5]

As we will see in chapter 18, the visual sensibility, simplified content and excessive language of war games would come to be recognizable features of media coverage of war.

The "Reality" War

With the coverage of Operation Iraqi Freedom, the unity between the media and military messaging was evident even before the invasion started. The war was a surreal, cultural event. The meaning of "major combat operations" in Iraq was shaped and understood through a set of entertainment frameworks that made the images more convincing and compelling than the actual unpleasantness of war. The empowering perspective of looking through the camera lens with the warriors of an invasion force mimicked the excitement of video-game entertainment. War imagery also borrowed from "reality" shows as it resonated within the latest stylistic elements of television. Fit within the defining parameters of entertainment culture, we can say that a new hybrid genre was created for twenty-first century war, one best described as militainment.

But in the world of entertainment and the high-tech thrills of gaming, no one ever really dies on the other side of the screen. Such representations are necessarily dissociated from the killing of real people. What becomes of public culture and the possibilities for humanism when representations of real war, like the fictions, distance viewers from experiencing emotional empathy or responsibility for war's victims?

Chapter 17 chronicles the coverage during the months of March and April 2003, as the invasion of Iraq became a daily, serialized program, a first in television production. The initial excitement of another aerial bombardment of Baghdad gave way to treks across the sand in armored vehicles, and when the progress stopped and the narrative stalled, it was revived with a daring nighttime rescue of a female private, Jessica Lynch. As we will see, Jessica's story depicts the good-girl counterpart to Lynndie England, and the tale of her rescue and its fabrication would be fascinating if not for the escalation of propaganda design that it portends. In the words of the British Broadcasting Corporation (BBC2, May 18, 2003), "Her story is one of the most stunning pieces of news management ever conceived." The BBC went on to point out that "The Pentagon had been influenced by Hollywood producers of reality television and action movies, notably the man behind *Black Hawk Down*, Jerry Bruckheimer."

Indeed, after the 9/11 attacks *Black Hawk Down* helped readjusted the genre of war movies for a new era. The Pentagon approved and supported the movie, and the film is notable for its graphic realism, a characteristic many claim reveals what war is really like. But does it? How did *Black Hawk Down*, the story of a defeat, become the ideal cultural icon for twenty-first century war? As battles were being fought in Afghanistan, Jerry Bruckheimer, not journalists, was given access to special forces operating there. He was representing ABC Entertainment, not the news division.

The evolving design of war persuasions from recognizable rhetoric to slick military media productions was prefigured when the Bush White House called on Hollywood to help promote the War on Terror. The movies and media coverage analyzed in part 4 illustrate the results of the partnership and also shows the ways in which the military choreographed its own production of war. By examining the intermingling of war reporting and entertainment formats, this book explores the essential differences between the real and the hyperreal and argues that those differences influence public attitudes toward war and its culture.

WAR AND DEMOCRACY

With the invasion of Iraq, television culture and military messages spoke predominantly the language of visual and thematic unity. Such unity depends on excluding alternative narratives and voices. On the other side of image creation and entertainment formatting stands an older form of perception management, the blank screen, the simple elimination of the negative and the exclusion of dissent. Before the invasion, one of the few journalists to express concern for civilian casualties on a cable news program was long-time Associated Press reporter Helen Thomas. In an interview on MSNBC with Phil Donahue, shortly before the war started, Thomas said, "No one seems to be concerned that children will die." When asked to confirm rumors that the interview caused the show to be cancelled, Donahue replied, "It wasn't just that." On the program "we were opposed to the war, so they made a corporate decision" to cancel it.[6] For pointing out the human consequences of war, Helen Thomas lost her position at presidential press conferences and was not called on by the president.

Efforts to insure favorable opinions have often conflicted with the demands of open information in a democracy. The First Amendment to the U.S. Constitution is most sensitive to war's demands. Democratic participation requires an uninhibited dialogue, noisy and complicated from a profusion of perspectives. Only then can people aspire to be citizens who determine their own histories. Before the invasion of Iraq opposing voices were all but silenced on television. Even in the face of such positive media treatment, 27 percent of the public remained opposed to the invasion, but a study of network news done by FAIR (Rendall and Broughel, 2003) showed that less than 3 percent of U.S. sources on TV expressed views against the war. Real people were about ten times more likely to oppose the war than those seen on television.

War's persuasions target not citizens, but consumers and audiences, with strategic messages designed by those practiced in the art of "staying on message." Censorship, propaganda and democracy cannot exist side by side, but those who would wage war must obscure the many facts that accompany its unforgiving conduct. It comes as no surprise that attempts were made by the military to censor the pictures from Abu Ghraib prison. General Richard Myers of the Joint Chiefs of Staff reportedly called Dan Rather to urge CBS not to air the photographs, and though the *60 Minutes II* segment was delayed for two weeks, the network refused to comply. It became a major defeat in what had been almost total victory in the battle over information management since the second war on Iraq began.

WAR AND MEMORY

Each new war responds in significant ways to the ones that precede it. After the dust of war settles, memory and myth conjoin to render its meaning. Fragments of truth are mixed and remixed with mythic accounts of combat and defeat, victory and heroism, to produce an accepted cultural understanding. As battles are reworked into entertainment narratives, those are the versions committed to cultural memory. In the telling, war is transformed. But what about a war of which only the slightest fragments of memory remain?

Forgetting an *Axis of Evil*
One story of war is largely absent from American culture. The war in Korea is at best a clouded memory rarely retrieved from the American mind. When telling stories of war on film, it is rarely summoned as a reference point. It remains a repressed or occluded experience. Surprisingly, Korea was used as the background for the 1970s television series *M*A*S*H*, yet most critics believe the setting was little more than a dislocated Vietnam, always confused and mystified. Through an atmosphere of black comedy and camaraderie, the battles were portrayed as relentlessly brutal.

When films do reference Korea, they are oblique signs of unhealed wounds such as the damaged character in *The Rainmaker*. The sick boy's father never speaks, and his wife explains that he has a piece of metal in his head—he's a Korean vet. He sits all day in an old car in the driveway, drinking. One is reminded of the final episode of *M*A*S*H*, in which Hawkeye opens a bottle of cognac and toasts significantly, "We drink to forget."

What can we learn about the "axis of evil" and the legacy of a dangerous world by returning to the killing fields of Korea?

Along with the structured absences, there are cracks and fissures in the seemingly monolithic culture of war. The management and control of information is now defined as part of military planning, because revealing the horrors of war would arguably eliminate military options as an alternative to global disputes. Yet images that injure the heart and soul by telling of the brutality, humiliation and killing do break through the cracks of glorified victories' high-tech superiority. Just as the Pentagon Papers were published in the press, the images of Abu Ghraib made their way into the commercial media.

The Camera as Weapon and Mirror

At Abu Ghraib, the camera in the hands of the military was being reconfigured as a weapon of war. It acted as an instrument of torture, as prisoners at Abu Ghraib were told the images would be shown to their families and others who resisted. In addition to being assaulted, prisoners recounted the terror of hearing the sounds of the camera and knowing their humiliation was being recorded.

But the act of photography turned from weapon to critic as the pictures shattered the moral claims to war. As the military lost control, they became part of the historical record of war's documentation, whose significance is still being realized. In the midst of a bloody occupation of a foreign country, the digital imagery of Abu Ghraib acted like a mirror reflecting an image back to Americans of an identity they struggled to recognize.

War and the Presidential Campaign

As the insurgency in Iraq raged on, images of Vietnam once again splashed across television screens, this time in political attack ads aimed at presidential candidate John Kerry. A battle over the war's contested meanings was being fought once again. At a carefully choreographed presentation in Boston, fellow Vietnam veterans introduced Senator Kerry to the floor of the Democratic convention as he accepted his party's nomination with the words "John Kerry, reporting for duty." His war experience was prominently featured as a campaign strategy, his rescue of Army Lieutenant Jim Rassmann from the waters of the Bay Hap River on March 13, 1969, held center stage. By 2004, the nobility of fighting, even for an ignoble effort, seemed a strategy for winning the White House, one that Kerry had used in other campaigns. But in the midst of another contentious conflict starkly defended by an incumbent president, the Vietnam War could not be told in the simple narrative of *Black Hawk Down* or be contained within the themes of heroism and dramatic rescues. Battles over defeat and victory, patriotism and opposition, raged once again. Bitter disputes over contested details and faded memories of attacks under fire thirty-five years earlier raged again.

What angers Kerry's opponents most is his opposition to the Vietnam War, an opposition they argue discredits their sacrifice and suffering. Like a majority of the American public, Kerry had turned against the war that he defined as brutal and nihilistic. The 2004 race for the White House added another layer of complexity to the interaction between war and democracy, one that all war planners must consider. In a just cause soldiers kill for their country, but what if the cause cannot be portrayed as necessary or noble? When governments insist on fighting wars without legitimate justification and informed consent, those who fight have no way to reconcile the troubling consequences of war's disturbing conduct. Though George W. Bush was reelected, the long-term consequences of the absence of WMDs in Iraq have not been felt. Chapter 20 discusses the success of his initial attempt to downplay the false justifications for the war, but while his performance was met with little criticism at the time, given the worsening conditions in Iraq, history will not be kind to such falsifications or the media organizations that helped promote them.

WAR AND MEANING

The narratives we tell ourselves of strategic battles and heroic struggles influence the decisions we make about waging future wars and justifying their consequences. Battles over perceptions extend into the next conflict as new ways of telling old tales emerge to fit the present historical moment. The attacks and counterattacks brought on by the Swift Boat Veterans for Truth was a fundamental battle over war and its meanings. Attempts to rehabilitate the troubled memory of Vietnam will influence the waging of future wars and the means of containing present ones. Returning to those moments reveals the significance the past holds for reckoning with the present.

War's symbolic culture, its fictions and entertainments, influence public attitudes as much as on-the-spot reporting from the field of battle. As we will find in the pages of this book, the stories of war have become increasingly defined by the merger between fiction and nonfiction. By the twenty-first century, war as presented to Americans became an entertainment, essentially indistinguishable for fictional forms. As presidential stagecraft mimicked the *Top Gun* narrative of combat, the official version of war became a fiction.

We can learn much from examining the long history of rhetorical strategies and media constructions that have made sense of the battles and brutality of conflict for almost a century in a cultural landscape marked by the dominance of war. These stories of war, and the history and culture of their telling, are the subject of this book. That story begins in the modern world with the "war to end all wars" and the birth of visual and visceral media persuasions at the heart of World War I propaganda strategies that remain with us today.

Part I

From Victory to Defeat

1

The Great War and the Fight between Good and Evil

The Birth of War Propaganda

If any question why we died
Tell them, because our fathers lied.

—Rudyard Kipling wrote this poem after his son was killed, though earlier he had been a great proponent of the Great War.

John Keegan's history of the First World War, published in 1999, begins with the statement, "The First World War was a tragic and unnecessary conflict." Another writer, Niall Ferguson, ends his book *The Pity of War: Explaining World War I*, published the same year, with these lines: "It was nothing less than the greatest error of modern history." Herbert Mitgang (1999, B1) offered an equally harsh view: "The stupidity of World War I on every level—above all, the imperiousness of the monarchs and the cold-bloodedness of the generals—demands retelling." At the end of the twentieth century, historians were still coming to grips with the Great War, and their assessments were not kind. Keegan asks rhetorically, "Why did a prosperous continent, at the height of its success as a source and agent of global wealth and power and at one of the peaks of its intellectual and cultural achievement, choose to risk all it had won for itself and all it offered to the world in the lottery of vicious and local internecine conflict?" Keegan does not find compelling answers to these questions, but he and others understand that Germany and Austria were defending mutual security agreements and that Britain was concerned with its own national security and international treaties. Since so many other members of European royalty had been assassinated in the years before 1914, the killing of Archduke Ferdinand hardly seems a cause for such belligerence. Keegan suggests that if international organizations or other regional security councils were in place in 1914, a negotiated peace might have been possible.

It is a stunning proposition to look back on a conflict that transformed Europe and the Middle East, forever shaping the modern world, and assert that the motivating forces were trivial and that, with a little imagination and diplomacy, the killing of nearly ten million people could have been avoided. And later, even in the face of unprecedented slaughter, the war continued to be prosecuted. Phillip Knightley begins his discussion of World War I with these words: It "began with the promise of splendour, honour, and glory. It ended as a genocidal conflict on an unparalleled scale, a meaningless act of slaughter that continued until a state of exhaustion set in because no one knew how to stop it" (2002, 83).

Another look at the "war to end all wars," this time with a focus on the role of the communications media, will offer another layer of understanding to the folly that was World War I. By the twenty-first century, even with international organizations in place, we do not live in a global community able to resolve its disagreements through peaceful means. As we approach the centennial of the Great War, we find it is still very much with us.

The retelling must necessarily begin with the elaborate distortions and creative inventions of the public propaganda campaigns primarily responsible for perpetuating the impassioned enthusiasm for war in Britain and Europe and, a few years later, in the United States.

MODERN WAR PROPAGANDA

The length and brutality of the fighting that destroyed a generation and much of the prosperity of Europe required nurturing a public hysteria so visceral it could justify the slaughter. The propaganda born in 1914 was an explosion of messages designed to persuade on a number of different fronts. The cognitive, linguistic and visual devices that fueled the war were recognized as a qualitative leap into effective mass persuasion. This phenomenon came to be known as modern war propaganda, and it became the object of scholarly inquiry after the war. Propaganda propelled the war by fueling the public's imagination, fear and hatred. The enemy was demonized beyond all recognition, placed outside the human family and civilization itself. In Britain and France, stories of the brutality of the German "Hun" predominated, with brutish imagery of the ape-like soldiers hunched and foreboding as they attacked defenseless women and innocent children.

Of these stories none was as gruesome and horrible as the tale of the Belgian "baby without hands." In 1915, the French propaganda unit, the Bureau de la Presse, produced a photograph of the handless baby that was published in *La Rive Rouge*. The paper enhanced the story by later carrying a drawing of German soldiers eating the hands. Like most of the atrocity stories, it was not discredited until after the war, when "a series of investigations failed to find a single case of this nature" (Knightley 2002, 114). But, as we shall see throughout this study, correcting the record in the aftermath of war cannot reverse the history propelled by such narratives. The story played its role at the time. It rallied opinion and strengthened the resolution of Britain and France to continue the conflict and lowered resistance to the war in the United States.

In the period between the two world wars, propaganda became the subject of intense scrutiny. Its power over the public and the threat it posed to democracy concerned political scientists, social psychologists and First Amendment scholars as well. Harold Lasswell's 1927 study of World War I propaganda remains one of the most enduring analyses of its principles and practices. The linguistic and conceptual devices identified almost a century ago are still recognizable today. Simplicity and amplification are essential to persuasion, and ambiguity must be eliminated. Political logics and the failed practices that lead to war, including competition for economic resources, cannot be the causes of conflict, because conflict is caused by the inherent evil of the enemy. "The war must not be due to a world system of conducting international affairs…but to the rapacity of the enemy." Guilt and guilelessness must be assessed geographically, and all the guilt must be on the other side of the frontier" (Lasswell 1927, 206). The uncomplicated explanation, one that can be expressed in a simple binary of good and evil, erases shades of uncertainty and facilitates mass consensus. The world is divided between "our civilized way of life" and "their barbarism."

DEMONIZING THE ENEMY AND STATE-SANCTIONED VIOLENCE

Posters selling war bonds and recruiting GIs, first in the U.K. and then in the United States, featured brutish creatures carting away young women and bayoneting babies. The hunched, subhuman, often club-wielding Hun was a discourse of the extreme, even cartoon-like, but essential in overcoming the strong "psychological resistances" to war in modern nations. As Lasswell understood, "every war must appear to be a war of defense against a menacing, murderous aggressor" (1927, 206). Designed to appeal to visceral sensations, war rhetoric nurtures and cultivates fear and hatred, rendering reasoned discussion less compelling. Tales of such intensity enraged a population. Society normally sanctions crimes motivated by visceral hatreds. Mobilizing a collective sensibility of animosity toward an enemy requires that social inhibitions existent in peacetime be dismantled. In promoting state-sanctioned violence, the enemy's actions must be so outside the bounds of tolerance that reform and negotiation are not alternatives. The demonized enemy is no longer recognizably human, and without the quality of empathy can be killed with impunity. Such narratives of exclusion provide the necessary psycho-political context for war.

THE DRAMATIC REVERSAL

It took time for the war that began in Europe to reach the shores of America. During his reelection campaign in 1916, two years after the start of the war in Europe, Woodrow Wilson ran as a peace candidate. "So far as I can remember, this is a government of the people, and this people is not going to choose war." Nevertheless, by April 1917, he led the American people into the First World War, saying he would "make the world safe for democracy." When the American government decided to enter World War I, the American public, without a compelling reason to side with either bloc of European powers, had to be persuaded. War propaganda spilled across the Atlantic to infect the new world, and with the help of the British, Wilson the peace candidate became the new war president.

Propaganda in America

President Wilson established the Committee of Public Information under the leadership of a newspaper editor, George Creel, and the CPI came to be known as the Creel Commission. The committee enlisted public relations and advertising experts and spent millions of dollars to aggressively promote the allied cause. In addition, Creel secured millions of dollars' worth of free advertising. War promotions appeared in every possible venue, from the press to billboards, in trolley cars, and from lecture-hall podiums to movie screens. War exhibits were inserted into cultural and community events such as state fairs where, for example, inter-Allied war expositions became featured attractions. Creel documented much of his committee's work in *How We Advertised America*, pointing out the sheer quantity that resulted, such as the "thirty odd booklets" with "seventy-five million copies" circulated in the United States. In *Propaganda and Democracy*, researcher J. Michael Sproule explores archival material and historical accounts of propaganda and details the overwhelming persuasion that reached the American public on a daily basis. Enthusiasm for war was stoked by the Treasury Department's imperative to fund the war through Liberty Bonds. Hard-sell strategies were employed to separate people from their earnings, and atrocity stories were vital to that success. The quest for cash was fueled by rhetoric demanding that Germans—"the snakes of the human race"—be stamped out.

Much of the content of this "war advertising" was strikingly visual. From posters to billboards, the scenic landscapes of America became visions of patriotism and war imagery. In addition to the Treasury Department, the Creel Commission's Division of Pictorial Publicity provided graphics for the various campaigns organized through the War Department, the Department of Agriculture and the Red Cross. Chief of the division was Charles Gibson, of Gibson Girl fame, who understood that war imagery had to appeal to the emotions.

Traditional oratory and the new medium of film found a common purpose in the promotion of war, and theaters across America hosted the Four-Minute Men, who took the stage during movie intermissions to address their captive audiences. Creel commanded a volunteer army of 75,000 speakers, operating in 5,200 communities and making over 750,000 speeches to an estimated cumulative audience of 400 million. Though the bulletins introducing the Four-Minute Men emphasized the factual nature of their presentations, archival documents show that once the Four-Minute Men entered the theater, they embellished atrocity narratives that fueled outrage. University of Chicago professor Solomon Clark found that Creel's minions repeatedly invoked demonization of the Hun and other visceral content.[1]

The introduction of the Four-Minute Men into American theaters began the merger of propaganda with the entertainment industry. Soon important Hollywood directors rallied to the war effort. Carl Laemmle directed *The Kaiser, the Beast of Berlin*. Possibly the most notable American film of the period was D.W. Griffith's *Hearts of the World*, set in an occupied French village and depicting a community being set upon and victimized by marauding German troops.

ELITE OPINION, SIR GILBERT PARKER, AND LORD JAMES BRYCE

When respected leaders argue for war, they wield disproportionate influence. Much of America's intellectual and liberal elites, including John Dewey and Walter Lippmann, helped shape pro-war opinion. Many times such individuals were working through governmental divisions. An official, though secret, propaganda bureau was set up by the British government in the United States headed by Sir Gilbert Parker, a Canadian novelist who nurtured contacts with writers, teachers and prominent American opinion leaders of every profession. Parker's organization sent repeated mailings of pamphlets, interviews and speeches to colleges, libraries and newspapers.[2] In this way the official British government view that the war was simply a matter of countering German aggression was hidden under private cover.

Another prominent figure brought in to persuade the American public was James Bryce, the former British ambassador to the United States and author of a popular college textbook, *The American Commonwealth*. Under his editorship, German atrocity stories gained in status. He helped prepare a sixty-one-page *Report of the Committee on Alleged German Outrages*, which was translated into thirty languages and was said to be based on twelve hundred depositions, mostly from Belgian refugees, taken by barristers in Britain. It included gruesome and titillating details of how German soldiers publicly raped Belgian girls in the marketplace at Liege and bayoneted a two-year-old child. Yet, like the baby-without-hands tale, after the war a Belgian commission of enquiry found no evidence for any major accusation in the report. The documents had mysteriously disappeared.

The Social Psychology of Message Design

Another postwar scholar of propaganda, the psychologist Leonard Doob, articulated many of the strategies of war persuasions, ones honed over the twentieth century with increasing levels of sophistication. Well before the use of focus groups, he understood that the propagandist must consider existing public attitudes and beliefs and design messages that resonate with those values. For example,

> If people don't like to hear about babies and women who are murdered, then say that the enemy does just that sort of thing and manipulate and draw a few pictures to prove it. If the Chinese respect the dead and if you are interested in having China become sympathetic toward your cause, then inform the Chinese that Germans use corpses for soap. (1935, 305)

Indeed, Allied propagandists had made just those claims. A British intelligence officer in possession of a photograph showing dead German soldiers sent the photograph out with a caption stating that the corpses were being hauled away to a soap factory behind German lines.[3] The story circulated globally, and the version that appeared in the *Times* on April 17, 1917, attributed the story to an American diplomat in Switzerland. The

House of Commons would not formally admit that the story was false until December 1925.

German propagandists, on the other hand, were by all accounts career soldiers who were soundly defeated in the battle for hearts and minds. They adopted a military approach, and their methods corresponded to the rules of war. "Germans bungled because they were naïve: they thought the success of the war depended almost solely on military strategy and therefore they tended to neglect propaganda" (Doob 1935, 304). They had little understanding of civilian sensibilities and didn't play to them well. "To these officials with their military ideology the idea of deliberate falsehood was repugnant and unintelligible." German war propaganda was logical and tended to sound legalistic, mostly devoid of psychological strategies (Viereck 1930). Thus, when German troops shot some Allied nurses who had carried weapons, they admitted it openly. The Allies reported the incident as an atrocity and featured it in press propaganda. When French troops shot German nurses under similar circumstances, the Germans failed to exploit it.

God on "Our Side"

The effectiveness of calling upon religious beliefs held by a majority of the population is obvious in its mass appeal. Using religious language and logic has an added benefit for the propagandist. Such tactics can successfully remove the explanations for war from a political context with human agency, one characterized by a complicated set of international relationships, and reassert them into a belief system based on prescribed categories of faith. Faith-based narratives often included themes of martyrdom and religious persecution. One preacher from Baltimore claimed that the Germans had crucified Canadian soldiers. Other stories involved nurses and nuns, emphasizing the murder of innocents and altruists, making the killing all the more reprehensible.

American preachers heeded propaganda's call to arms by connecting religion to recruitment and patriotism. God was on our side, and not kindhearted to those who were against killing the enemy, such as conscientious objectors. A significant portion of the nation's clergy actively supported the conflict by blessing the spy-hunting societies, preaching against slackers, encouraging enlistment and condemning pacifists. Even those who called for peace before the war now invoked God's support for it: "Preachers adroitly shifted from pacifism to a theology of holy war in which missionary metaphors abounded as did images of redemption by sword" (Sproule 1997, 12).[4]

PROSECUTION AND COERCION

By 1918 America was in the grip of a totalizing media environment. Wilson's massive propaganda effort had succeeded in creating an atmosphere of social conformity. Less benign were the repressive legal and coercive practices that stifled opposition. Vigilant organizations such as the American Protective League, a group of three-hundred-and-fifty thousand quasi-official agitators loosely affiliated with the Justice Department, pressured individuals and communities to support recruitment and war bonds. Notable individuals who did not acquiesce, especially those holding university positions, became targets and often lost their jobs. By 1918 Nicholas Butler, the president of Columbia University, was firing professors for pacifist expressions, though he, too, had been an active member of the League to Limit Armaments before the war.

The harshest penalties were reserved for peace activists such as socialist leader Eugene Debs. In June 1917, Debs spoke at an antiwar rally in Canton, Ohio, where three of his fellow organizers were held in jail. In his hotel room shortly before his speech, Debs granted an interview to Clyde Miller, a reporter for Cleveland's *Plain Dealer*:

> Debs told Miller of his disgust at the idea of American and German youth extinguishing each other's lives so that the rich and powerful in both lands might enjoy continued prosperity. Dismissing pro-war arguments as efforts to take in vain the names of God and country, Debs affirmed his intention to "do all I can to oppose this war, to oppose our young men going over to fight in this war." (Cited in Sproule 1997, 4).

Miller, admittedly pro-war and eager to do what he could to help win it, became instrumental in Debs's prosecution, providing details of his interview in court testimony. Though initially charged with ten violations of the Espionage Act of 1917, Debs was convicted on three counts of promoting insubordination, encouraging resistance and obstructing recruiting. He was sentenced to ten years in prison. After a trip to Europe, Clyde Miller had an epiphany. Realizing that he had also been swept up in pro-war propaganda, he did what he could to help Debs, and himself became a critic of propaganda after the war.[5]

WAR FEVER

Historical accounts document an atmosphere of wartime mania. Writing about the experience in *Foreign Affairs*, Raymond Fosdick (1932, 316–23) recounts an ecstasy of hate: "We hated with a common hate that was exhilarating." He tells of a meeting in a church when a speaker demanded that upon his capture, the Kaiser should be boiled in oil. In response the audience stood on chairs "to scream its hysterical approval. This was the mood we were in. This was the kind of madness that had seized us." Other historians describe a propaganda-demented people in the grip of what has been called war fever. As in a fever, the sick person is not in his rational mind. He is not thinking clearly, and normal social inhibitions are relaxed. Similarly, when a fever is over, the revived individual often ponders the delusionary nature of his previous mental state. Journalist George Seldes, who covered the war in America, later wrote: "It wasn't until December 1918, when I came into Coblenz with the American Army that I realized how fooled I had been by all those years of poisonous propaganda" (1937, 31).

THE FAILURE OF THE PRESS

A totalizing media atmosphere characterized by the repetition of visceral appeals can only remain effective in the absence of alternative messages and information that challenges assumptions and exposes the false and constructed nature of the language. The press did not offer such alternatives. From the start of the war in Europe, Americans were subjected to a one-sided view of the belligerency. As the guns of August roared, the British Royal Navy silenced pluralistic debate by cutting the transatlantic cable lines from Germany, allowing British and French censors to filter the vast majority of news from Europe that reached America.[6] Managed news became the order of the day. The Committee of Public Information produced a weekly digest of "official" war news sent out to twelve thousand newspapers, formatted and ready for printing. Like the British press, American journalists were swept up in an atmosphere that actively discouraged independent thought. As Sproule notes, "Shedding congenial skepticism, [they] followed the lead of teachers, writers, and preachers by acquiescing in Creel's managed-news framework" (12).[7]

Propaganda from the Battlefield

When democracies go to war, a free press must serve as witness, documenting the conduct carried out in the name of the public. Only then is the rhetorical call to arms tempered by another set of values that articulates humanitarian concerns and war's social and human costs. Considering the lives of soldiers and enemy combatants (and later, with aerial bombardments, civilian victims) reminds the public that there are consequences that lie in the wake of war's glory. Unfortunately, reporters who visited the trenches of World War I failed to document or express in any meaningful way the horrible realities of the Western Front and the astonishing loss of life taking place there. A number of factors prevented the unpleasant news of war from reaching the public. Lack of access to battlefield conflict, the reliance on official briefings, blanket censorship and the war correspondents' own sense of patriotism left the public ignorant of the magnitude of human loss on all sides until the war was over.

Reporters visited the trenches by day, returning to the chateaus close to the front as evening fell. Because covering the front during actual battles was virtually impossible, correspondents relied on official dispatches. The Battle of the Somme offers a compelling example of one of the most infamous cases of the failure of war reporting. On July 1, 1916, British soldiers walked straight into German fire, and sixty thousand of them were cut down without advancing the front a single foot—twenty thousand died. Yet news coverage of the bloodiest defeat in Britain's history was placid. As Philip Gibbs wrote in his dispatch from the Somme, "It is, on balance, a good day for England and France. It is a day of promise in this war..." (1917, 17).[8] Journalists had been briefed in their quarters by the chief of intelligence as the battle started and at regular intervals throughout the day, and they reported the official military versions at face value. With no public outcry, Imperial British Commander Sir Douglas Haig refused to accept defeat and carried on. By November 1916, six hundred thousand Allied troops and four hundred fifty thousand German soldiers had died in the muddy fields along the river Somme.

Like the Europeans, Americans were not informed about the grizzly realities of war. Correspondents filed stories glorifying trench warfare and kept silent about the loss of life. The writing of seasoned war correspondent Irving Cobb describing the American Rainbow Division offers an example of the embellished prose that validated the slaughter. Soldiers advanced "like schoolboys on a lark," and those who had been left behind were "crying like babies," begging to be included (Cobb 1918, 142). H.G. Wells (who would later become known for *The War of the Worlds*) was escorted to the front lines for an eyewitness view of casualties and returned to report that they had been exaggerated.

C.E. Montague (1922, 97–98) editor of the *Manchester Guardian* wrote after the war that from that "haven of security and comfort," journalists acquired a "cheerfulness in the face of vicarious torment and danger." In his seminal book on war reporting, *The First Casualty*, it is understandable that Phillip Knightley reserves his most devastating critique of World War I for the war correspondents. They alone were in a position to know much more than others about the war of attrition on the Western Front. Yet "they identified themselves absolutely with the armies in the field; they protected the high command from criticism, wrote jauntily about life in the trenches, kept an inspired silence about the slaughter, and allowed themselves to be absorbed by the propaganda machine" (2002, 84–85). But much can also be explained about the public's ignorance and the war's momentum by looking further up the chain of news gatekeepers.

The Times *of London: Recruitment and Morale*

At the time, and even after, England's paper of record was more concerned with civilian morale and recruiting future foot soldiers than providing the public with accurate war news. Editorial policy merged with military needs, and nowhere was this more evident than with the suppression of casualty figures. Had the first battles been accurately reported, the war might never have continued. From August 14 to 25, 1914, the German army wiped out nearly three-hundred thousand French soldiers at the Battle of the Frontiers, almost 25 percent of the troops. Though a war correspondent for the *Times* was traveling with the French army at the front, the wastage went completely unreported in Britain until after the war was over. Looking back at its coverage, the *Times*'s editors continued to justify the paper's failure to inform the public. "Had it been known in England that France had lost more than a quarter of a million men from her regular army in the first month of the fighting, British determination must have been gravely weakened."[9]

Later in its historical assessment, the *Times* makes explicit the reason for the silence on the casualty figure, admitting that is was a matter of policy. "A principal aim of the war policy of Printing House Square was to increase the flow of recruits. It was an aim that would get little help from accounts of what happened to recruits once they became soldiers."[10]

LEADERS IN DENIAL

The mechanized slaughter of the machine gun was the deadliest war weapon yet conceived. At Waterloo, rifles could be fired twice a minute. By contrast, the machine gun sent out six hundred rounds a minute, creating "a zone of death that would simply saw a soldier in two if he entered it" (Gopnik, 2004). In the face of journalistic silence, the leaders who plunged into war could successfully deny the horrors of death at the front. This self-denial is evident in the words of Lloyd George, then prime minister of Britain, when, on December 28, 1917, he confided to a friend the shock he felt when listening to a rare uncensored narrative of the slaughter:

I listened last night, at a dinner given to Philip Gibbs on his return from the front, to the most impressive and moving description from him of what the war in the West really means…. If people really knew, the war would be stopped tomorrow. But of course they don't know and can't know. The correspondents don't write and the censorship would not pass the truth…. The thing is horrible beyond human nature to bear and I feel I can't go on with the bloody business.[11]

Yet he did go on with the bloody business.

WHEN MORALE WAS LOW

During World War I, the degree of evil projected onto the enemy was directly related to the immensity of the loss of life being felt at home. The casualty figures were so great that they now seem inconceivable. In the first months of World War I, the British lost more officers than in all wars of the previous hundred years put together. After assessing the war's horrors, Knightley (2002, 116) asks, "who can comprehend that half a million Frenchmen were lost in the first four months of war, one million lost by the end of 1915, and five million by 1918?" Though not accurately documented in the press, the loss was felt at the local level, in the towns and villages across Britain and France. In some places all the men from entire villages had been killed in the war, as soldiers fought from local municipalities. By 1917, as a bitter apathy set in, opposition to the war was prosecuted, and propaganda was re-employed to boost morale. Thus the suppression of the extent of the slaughter, the focus on civilian morale and recruitment together with the cycle of propaganda at key moments accounts for the war's momentum, which resulted in a loss of life of unprecedented magnitude.

THE TRUTH FROM SOLDIERS

As the war dragged on, the suffering of the soldiers in the trenches only worsened, and they began to chafe at the "jauntiness of tone" of reporting that often implied that a battle was a "jovial picnic." Their frustration and anger was amplified by "what people at home were offered as faithful accounts of what their friends in the field were thinking and suffering" (C. E. Montague 1922, 97–98). Thus did the soldier become inspired to expose the propaganda. He was on the front lines and could compare his own experiences with the alleged atrocity stories. As Knightley concludes, "the result was a deep disillusionment with his country's honesty" (2002, 111). In America, the end of propaganda also began in the trenches: "disillusionment with the propagandas of the Great War began in Europe, where the sentiment spread among American troops that atrocity stories had been false concoctions and that the Germans had behaved no worse than any other combatants" (Sproule 1997, 16). American journalist George Seldes (1937, 31–36) would later admit that anger directed toward war correspondents was justified: "We all more or less lied about the war." His retrospective insights are devastating condemnations of the press corps: "I now realize that we were told nothing but buncombe, that we were shown nothing of the realities of the war, that we were, in short, merely part of the great Allied propaganda machine whose purpose was to sustain morale at all costs and help drag unwilling America into the slaughter."

The truth of the trenches and more realistic narratives of fighting and dying would eventually emerge, many from soldiers themselves.[12] But throughout the war years the soldiers died on the Western Front without truthful witness from the press, and in the absence of public grief for their pain and acknowledgment of their sacrifice. Like George Seldes, legendary English war correspondent Philip Gibbs (1920) would express regret for his role in misrepresenting the war at the time. His books would expose the horrors of war and denounce the propaganda that emphasized atrocity stories as it sanitized the combat.

After the war, along with atrocity stories, official versions of the war fell into disrepute. As formerly secret European war documents were made available, influential proponents openly reversed their positions. By August 1919, the *Nation* magazine, which had accepted Wilson's claims that Germany was responsible, agreed that the Allies shared responsibility for the war. John Dewey, Walter Lippmann and Charles Beard were among those who were deeply disturbed by the punitive terms of the peace agreement being arranged in Paris.

REMEMBERING THE GREAT WAR

The human and economic devastation of World War I was so horrific that an entire generation of antiwar poets emerged to tell the story that could not be adequately told in simple nonfiction prose. In *The Great War and Modern Memory*, writer Paul Fussell explains that events as real as those experienced at the battle of the Somme in 1916 have been remembered through the use of literary devices. The codes of irony offered a referential framework for understanding and recounting the horrors of the First World War. It was the ironic literary structure that allowed writers to make sense of an otherwise incomprehensible human tragedy.

Central to literary irony is the elucidation of contrasts, and striking oppositions characterize the structure of World War I poetry and prose:

innocence against horror, pastoral bliss contrasted to ghostly landscapes, youthful flesh defenseless against modern weaponry. For the writer Henry James, the British entry into the war was the reversal of progress itself, a descent into barbarism; he wrote of the start of the war as "the plunge of civilization into this abyss of blood and darkness." Contained within this sensibility is the element of hope abridged, the unfulfilled potential, the surprising loss that renders the tragedy ever-more ironic and meaning-ful. The powerfully crafted writing of Siegfried Sassoon dramatizes the contrast between the idyllic, pastoral beauty of Britain's golden summer of 1914 and the unexpected shock of winter's barren landscape of war. The horrors of those scenes reflect the destruction of life, both in physical and psychic dimensions. In the traditions of Victorian poetry, writers lament the carnage visited upon the pristine bodies of youthful soldiers ripped and torn by machine-gun fire, never allowed to mature.

THE LEGACY

But before the poetic assessment, the Allied propagandists of World War I blazed the pathways of persuasion at that moment in history and suc-ceeded beyond their wildest dreams. They learned that through the use of visual media steeped in heavy doses of psychosocial techniques, entire populations could be led to madness, and that under continued rhetorical and legal controls, a horrific slaughter could continue. Newspaper editors demonstrated their willingness to hide the bodies and promote homefront morale instead of informing their readers. The alliance between religion and intellect yielded the key that allowed government imprimaturs to remain hidden from view, rendering their pronouncements all the more convincing. With attacks on activists and academics, official intelligence reports could stand unchallenged as "fact," their prevarications exposed only after the mission was accomplished. The combination of nationalism, official briefings and censorship could trump a free press and blind the wit-ness to war's conduct, conditions and casualties. The American broadcast industry was born during these years. Many who designed war persuasions became the professionals of the new advertising and public relations in-dustries closely tied to the emerging medium of radio. Edward Bernays,[13] an alumnus of CPI and the father of modern public relations, helped forge the unity between persuasion and the media landscape. They set in motion a set of media strategies and information management that would be called upon right through to the twenty-first century.

The immediate consequences of the war did lead to a reckoning dur-ing the time between the two world wars. Troubled by propaganda's efficacy, even some of its practitioners would later question its legacy for the democratic process. If a public could be so uniformly swayed, held under a totalizing atmosphere, convinced to support a conflict that should have been opposed, how could democracy remain a historical force? How would governments be kept accountable? In the years between the wars, serious evaluation of the nature of information, as opposed to propaganda, would interest many research agendas. The values of skepticism and independent thought were rearticulated, and the journalism of the 1920s returned to the hard-hitting investigative reporting practiced in the early years of the twentieth century in America.

But the damage done to the global community would not be reversed and cannot be overstated. Military analysts, historians and other scholars, writers and intellectuals of all stripes have attempted to come to terms with World War I. The Treaty of Versailles broke apart the old world and the Middle East, leaving it reconfigured in ways that would lead to some of the conflicts we live with today. The distortion that was the Third Reich emerged from the ashes of World War I, and nowhere was that more evident than in the creation of propaganda films such as *Triumph of the Will* and others that facilitated the acquiescence of the German population to Hitler's regime. In addition, the American public, after experiencing World War I, was understandably skeptical about backing another war, and propaganda became part of the structure of the military and continues to evolve with each new war.

2

The Good Fight

From the First Draft to the Grand Narrative

There is no doubt in the public mind that World War II was a just war. The battle to end the Holocaust and put a stop to the Nazi regime gave the Allied forces the noblest of causes. The Third Reich remains a fundamental historical example of social forces and values at their most destructive. Had the Nazis succeeded, Europe and other parts of the world would have struggled under a vicious regime of domination, social injustice and racial and cultural distortions. Yet vanquishing Hitler and ending the war did not result in a just social order based on equality or permanent peace. As Howard Zinn (2002, 102) points out, the "Good War" did not eliminate aggression in the world, but resulted in "two superpowers—both of which were eventually armed with nuclear weapons—fighting for control of various parts of the world." Amid the ashes of the Good Fight were the destroyed cities of Hiroshima and Nagasaki. The human cost of fighting Nazism was immense, killing an estimated sixty million people, most of them civilians. The enduring threat of nuclear annihilation gave the immediate postwar period a fearful and guarded atmosphere that tainted the budding prosperity and the potential to end tyranny. Though we continue to live with the threat of nuclear weapons, fear is called forth only occasionally, usually for political purposes during times of conflict—a point we will return to later.

Former NBC anchorman Tom Brokaw achieved note beyond his role as a television personality by celebrating what he calls "The Greatest Generation." Mr. Brokaw, as a member of the first generation to sit in front of television, was no doubt influenced by watching the war recounted in the glowing terms of a powerful collaboration between the military and broadcasters. The images, sounds and authoritative voiceovers of the documentaries and semi-documentaries that filled television screens in the 1950s told of the brilliant military maneuvers that led relentlessly to the Allied victory. A sampling of those programs reveals singularly positive images of a military ethos, with a corresponding acceptance of using force around the globe, especially against the Soviet Union. But the television fare almost pales when compared to the fictional celebration of the war and the fighting heroes who populated feature films over the next two decades. Indeed, as we shall see, by the end of the 1990s those World War II fictions would return to movie theaters and also inhabit the new technologies of war imaging and video games.

It may be fruitful here to pose a few questions whose answers may shed light on our failed quest for global peace and the role the media played during and after the war. Did the representations of the war and its aftermath help or hinder the potential for peace, both at home and abroad? What were the effects of wartime censorship on the public's understanding of the war and the military? What were the repercussions of the wartime uses of the media, and was there an open and public assessment of the costs to democracy and humanity of fighting such a war? In the crucial aftermath of World War II, how was the American victory understood, and what were the consequences for peace and democracy?

Let us begin with the first draft of history, the way the war was covered by the press.

Covering World War II

One might expect that by the twenty-first century a consensus on the relative merits of World War II journalism might have been achieved. One would be wrong. Consider the way Stephen Ambrose (2001, xv) begins his preface for the book *Reporting World War II*: "It was the greatest event of the twentieth century. It changed everything. It was also the best reported war, ever. The men and women who covered the war told Americans who was winning, and why, and who did the fighting, and how." Now consider this assessment published in the pages of *Harper's Magazine* in 1947, written by a journalist, Fletcher Pratt, who having returned from covering the war, wrote an exposé of his experiences: "The case made by military officials for the suppression of anything suggesting that our men and their officers are on a lower level than archangels is that such ideas are bad for morale. The result of this policy or set of policies has been that instead of being the best reported war in history, it was very nearly the worst reported" (Pratt 1947, 98–99).

These views seem less divergent if we consider a couple of qualifying points. Ambrose's words preface a volume hailed the *best* reporting of the war, including many now well-known dispatches from the most acclaimed war correspondents, many of whom witnessed the fighting. The selections in this anthology are not representative of overall reporting. On the other hand, Pratt reserves his harshest criticism for the more typical reporting that appeared frequently in daily newspapers around the country, reports culled mostly from official communiqués from the War Information Office. Many small papers relied on these sources on a regular basis.

Now let's consider what constitutes the *best* reporting. While lauding the "superb job the editors of the Library of America did in selecting what to reprint from the vast coverage of the war," Ambrose singles out reporting from the perspective of the individual soldiers. [1] He cares about "what the GIs were doing." According to Ambrose, the best dispatches detailed the "ordinary people from all walks of life, most of all the soldiers, marines, sailors, and airmen who did the fighting." The reporting of Ernie Pyle stands out because it "was always concerned with the ordinary soldier, especially the infantrymen" (2001, xvii). Indeed, most readers would agree that these reports are essential, offering a humanistic view told with intelligence and sensitivity. The dispatches of Ernie Pyle illuminated the living conditions of men on the frontlines as the intrepid reporter followed the battles from Tunisia to Italy, and from Omaha Beach to the Battle of Normandy. He was a dedicated war correspondent who, like many, died covering the war, killed by Japanese machine-gun fire in 1945 during the invasion of Okinawa.

Importantly for Ambrose, Pyle and others rarely wrote about the generals or officials. Pratt concurs that reporting from the "grunts-eye" view was comprehensive, and in that sense, never before had so much attention been given to the individual soldier. But the popular focus on the ground left the high command, the planning and policies of the war underreported and often out of public view. Knightley (2002, 345) recounts an amusing early example of information management. A field commander deflected interest away from a story on tactical air support by telling his public relations team to have a sergeant available to talk about his ground experience. He was brought in, "mud, beard and all," deliberately not cleaned up. Knightley also offers a more complicated understanding of the relationship between Ernie Pyle and the military. Pyle had little interest in war and knew little about battle strategy, but played an important public relations role. His celebrity status had the effect of boosting the morale of the men he traveled with. In fact, the army command had called him back from a much-needed rest so that he could cover the Pacific campaign, where he died.

CENSORSHIP

Ambrose (2001, xvi) notes that "reporters told of what they saw and learned." But correspondents were dependent on the military to be able to see the war at all. Under frontline censorship, they could not challenge official versions of events. If they did, they would lose support and access or, worse, be de-certified. War dispatches with little or no information from the command perspective certainly helped skirt issues of culpability, as censorship often concealed the names, officers and details of battles where mistakes were made. Citing Japanese torpedo attacks on two U.S. carriers, sinking one of them, Pratt observed that "the loss of the ship was not hidden, but the fact that both carriers were hit while running routine patrols in a restricted area at a speed of eight knots was hidden; and it was precisely because the Japanese had ascertained this fact that they were able to slip submarines in on the two carriers. It was never revealed whether any officer was held responsible" (1947, 98).

Ambrose (2001, xvi) claims that during World War II reporters "refused to glorify America or to repeat a propaganda line," but Pratt (1947, 98) takes a more critical view: "Our troops were surprised and defeated at Kasserine Gap in Tunisia and in the Battle of the Bulge in the Ardennes; but censorship never permitted the mention of any officer's name as responsible for either setback." Omission is a more subtle form of deception than "repeating the line." A plethora of well-documented cases reveals that on-the-spot reporting of the war from the Allied press corps bore little resemblance to what actually happened on the battlefield. Canadian war correspondent Ross Munro covered the raid on Dieppe in France on August 19, 1942, with nine other correspondents, four of whom were American. What should have been a triumph "turned into a bloody massacre." Dispatches told of fierce battles and bloody fighting, but the overall impression of the reporting was that the raid was a success. Harsh conditions and frontline censors made accurate reporting difficult, but the reporters' commitment to vanquishing the Germans resulted in a type of blanket self-censorship.[2] In addition, Munro's relationship to Canadian soldiers mirrors the relationship between Ernie Pyle and U.S. troops. He became very close to the soldiers and wrote stories about them for their home-town papers. Knightley (2002, 348–49) acknowledges that "under these circumstances, it would have been unrealistic to expect him to write the truth about Dieppe at the time (or later, to write about an incident when Canadian troops shot eight German prisoners-of-war)." Looking back on it, Munro admitted that the raid was a tactical failure "with only a gam-bler's chance of success," but field commanders and war planners were not criticized.

Ambrose cites Martha Gellhorn's reporting of the Battle of the Bulge as an example of reporting that forces us to "face the cost of victory." While Gellhorn's story is descriptive, humanistic and moving, it provides no understanding of what actually happened in the Ardennes, or what the costs of victory might actually have been. The German counterattack in December 1944 was wholly unexpected. Allied military forces thought the Germans were on the verge of defeat, yet they attacked the area and were not repulsed until the end of January 1945. In the face of censorship, the correspondents focused on episodes of bravery and troop morale.[3]

Gellhorn's piece, a fragment of the long Ardennes face-off, describes a chaotic scene of Americans holding the road to Bastogne, but the men cope in good spirits; one even grills a cheese sandwich as mortars hit their target nearby. The deaths she includes are those of Germans: "The bodies of Germans were piled on the trailer like so much ghastly firewood" (Gell-horn 2001, 586). Her piece ends in victory: "There were many dead and many wounded, but the survivors contained the fluid situation and slowly turned it into a retreat, and finally as the communiqué said, the bulge was ironed out. This was not done fast or easily; and it was not done by those anonymous things, armies, divisions, regiments. It was done by men, one by one—your men" (Gellhorn 2001, 590). World War II correspondents bore witness to the war, but witness of a particular kind. As Gellhorn's biographer commented on her 26 published war stories: "Martha, like the other war correspondents of her day, focused on the more edifying as-pects of the war. *Collier's*, like *Look* and *Life*, preferred tales of heroism and pluckiness to those of blunders, desertion, drunkenness, or cowardice" (Moorehead 2003, 213).

In the years since the war, military and civilian historians have pieced together what actually happened in the Ardennes. While it was true that many Americans fought bravely and well, panic, confusion and cowardice were also evoked by the German onslaught. In the midst of the fighting, nineteen thousand or so were absent without leave, "wandering about in bands stealing petrol, hijacking food trucks and trains on the way to the front and making fortunes on the black market" (Knightley 2002, 356).

All this complicated tragedy is vaguely referred to as a "fluid situation" in Gellhorn's piece. Just as with the Dieppe raid, the record of Ardennes has been investigated, detailed and corrected, but we choose to remember the first, more heroic versions. By the year 2006, well after the record has been set straight, we live with the myth that World War II dispatches were accurate and devoid of propaganda.

It is noteworthy that a few of the most sensational cases of military deception were exposed by commentators, not war correspondents, who were subject to having their copy examined before it was printed. The sensational story of General Patton hitting an enlisted man is a case in point. General Patton was visiting a military hospital in Sicily in August 1943 when he slapped a soldier he suspected of feigning illness. Five days later, in another hospital, he called another private "a yellow bastard" and kicked him from behind as he walked to the door. War correspondents heard General Patton shout as he came out of the hospital tent, "There's no such thing as shell shock. It's an invention of the Jews" (Knightley 2002, 350). As it turns out, the private had an excellent record, having fought throughout the Tunisian and Sicilian campaigns, and had refused to leave the front until he was finally ordered to the hospital. The incident was well known throughout the army and the press corps but was published three months later by Washington columnist Drew Pearson in an article considering whether or not Patton should be removed from his command (Koop 1946, 261).

ELIMINATE THE NEGATIVE, EMPHASIZE THE POSITIVE

Though the grunts-eye view has been celebrated as the decisive perspective on the good fight, that view was highly selective, often eliminating the negative. The military censored the private correspondence of soldiers. Pratt cites his own experience as well as those of others, "I have had my own letters home from a destroyer at sea clipped by a Navy censor when I used the forbidden phrase 'not happy' over some such minor matter as a bad breakfast egg" (1947, 99). Nor did newspapers publish stories when GIs protested frontline censorship.

Censorship blocked most information critical of the military, especially the high command, but didn't stop there. As in World War I, "morale boosting," was considered part of the legitimate war effort, and by the Second World War had become institutionalized with the United States military as public relations. On April 25, 1944, Reuters quoted supreme commander, General Eisenhower, saying before a gathering of United States newspaper editors, "Public opinion wins war." War correspondents were considered part of the larger effort to shape positive public perceptions. As correspondents grew closer to the military, some curried favor with generals and their staffs and became involved in military affairs. Military leaders became personalities, lionized as mythic heroes. According to Knightley (2002, 354) this loss of distance "had its effect on correspondents' judgment. Military successes were exaggerated to boost national pride, setbacks minimized to maintain morale."

Newspaper editors themselves certainly bear much of the responsibility for not allowing the public to understand the war. Emphasizing the positive sold papers and pleased the public, so wire service copy was often embellished. One dispatch from Okinawa described Japanese suicide bombers charging onto a bridge covered with explosives. The papers' headlines read "Japs' Human Bombs Fail to Halt Marines." In fact, the AP story reported accurately that the tactic had damaged the span enough to halt the marines for over a week.

THE EPISTEMOLOGY OF THE BATTLEFIELD

Writer Lee Sandlin (2001, 3), referring to the work of Paul Fussell and others, asserts that news reporting in general did not result in public understanding of the war. "Nobody back home has ever known much about what it was like on the battlefield. From the beginning, the actual circumstances of World War II were smothered in countless lies, evasions and distortions, like a wrecked landscape smothered by a blizzard. People all along have preferred the movie version." Even the best reporting seems to miss the point, and the war remains incomprehensible, lost in translation, unfit for the public. Ernie Pyle's writing from Tunisia includes simple prose and straightforward, even elegant, wording, but also includes "comic-book" sound effects. Pyle (2001, 295–96) wrote, "One of our half-tracks, full of ammunition, was livid red, with flames leaping and swaying. Every few seconds one of the shells would go off, and the projectile would tear into the sky with a weird whang-zing sort of noise." Reading through a compendium of war dispatches, one quickly begins to recognize qualifying descriptors that paint a picture of war as some type of supernatural, inexplicable event. Words such as "haunted," "spectral," "uncanny," "eerie" and "unearthly" remove war from the sense of the real and reposition its horrors within the realm of the surreal. Conveying the experience and its meaning in a framework of civilian experience seems to present journalists with a phenomenological block, as Edward R. Murrow told his radio audience about Buchenwald in 1945, "I have reported what I saw and heard, but only part of it. For most of it I have no words."[4]

There is no doubt that the utter destruction and futility of war is not easily imparted to those not experiencing it. Yet some of the mystifying language that surrounds the worst aspects of conflict can be attributed to censorship and the desire of journalists themselves to soften the horror. Ernie Pyle's last writing, a reflection of the end of war, found in his pocket after he was killed, expressed his frustration at witnessing sights his readers never would. As the war came to a close, he came the closest to succeeding in expressing its horrors: "These are the things you at home need not even try to understand. To you at home they are columns of figures, or he is a dear one who went away and just didn't come back. You don't see him lying so grotesque and pasty beside the gravel road in France. We saw him, saw him by the multiple thousands, that's the difference...." But Pyle's reporting two years earlier from Tunisia would have had no problem passing army censors: "As for the soldiers themselves, you need feel no shame nor concern for their ability. I have seen them in battle and afterwards and there is nothing wrong with the common American soldier. His fighting spirit is good. His morale is okay." In general, most war reporting veiled the losses and refused to describe honestly what reporters had witnessed.

War Documentaries

The filmmaker John Huston, like Frank Capra and others, was recruited by the Pentagon to produce documentaries of the war. One of Huston's films, *The Battle of San Pietro*, was made in 1944 to help the military explain why we hadn't swept over Italy as rapidly as had been expected. Erik Barnouw (1993, 162) describes the film this way: "Huston conveyed unforgettably the foot soldier's experience of battle and awareness of his expendability, in a slaughter of uncertain value." The military hierarchy "was horrified" and blocked the film's release. Cuts were ordered, and even then release of the film was delayed until the war was almost over" (Barnouw 1993, 163). What the generals seemed to dislike most was an edited sequence that Barnouw describes as "extraordinarily poignant." The film shows bodies of dead soldiers being put into sacks. The soundtrack over the images features the voices of the same dead men, recorded before battle. Huston felt he was expressing his deep feeling for the men, but for the military he had crossed the line. Huston later recounted a dialogue with one general who said: "This picture is pacifist. It's against war. Against *the* war. Against war" (Barnouw 1993, 163). He had left no justification for their deaths, and that is the essence of pacifism.

Even when a war is perceived as just, fighting can easily be perceived as unjust, and therefore subject to criticism. Military failure and purposeless slaughter can turn the public against an effort initially supported. In World War II, censorship succeeded in blocking most battlefield criticism and the public debate about it. This set the stage for postwar depictions that denied the complexities of bloody human conflict. The result for GIs is a lifetime of unacknowledged sacrifice, as Sandlin describes: "American soldiers early on grew accustomed to the idea that the truth of their experience wasn't going to be told to the folks back home." Soldiers' own stories are full of the dark humor of grim tales such as Guadalcanal, for instance, where drinking water was desperately needed, but when it arrived in used oil drums that had not been washed out, no one could drink it. The nightmare of friendly fire, one of the worst problems in World War II, was left unreported.

Battlefield honesty is a topic raised also by Paul Fussell, whose work is described as iconoclastic, even caustic. A distinguished professor of literature at the University of Pennsylvania, Fussell's writing includes the hard edges of "the Good War," where he served as an infantry lieutenant in the European theater. Nuanced and without sentimentality, his writing lays bare what is hidden in wartime glorifications. Not unfamiliar with feelings of fear and other ignoble actions of soldiers in war, he tells the story of his company coming across fifteen or twenty German soldiers caught in a crater and trying to surrender. They were shot by the men in his company "laughing and howling, hoo-ha-ing and cowboy and good-old-boy yelling," an incident that would later be remembered fondly by the soldiers as "the Great Turkey Shoot." These types of actions, so at odds with civilian life and values, place the brutalities of war outside a mythic frame. But such honesty would be buried in postwar celebrations of the Good Fight. In 1947 Pratt predicted that the political consequences would be the enduring "legends that the war was won without a single mistake, by a command consisting exclusively of geniuses, who now have asked to be rewarded by being placed in control of all scientific thought and utterance" (98).

A popular review of the war flooded television screens with programming that valorized fighting, celebrated heroism, and in general created the myths and narratives of the Good Fight, as the military dominated the cultural landscape of the 1950s.

TELEVISION AFTER THE WAR

The real story of World War II was not rendered accurately through on-the-spot reporting, nor was the record corrected in the years that followed. The vast production of film and television programming drew certain conclusions about America's victory, creating meanings and memories that shaped the latter half of the twentieth century. The military emerged as a dominating force in American society, and it exerted enormous influence over the newly emergent medium of television. As MacDonald (1985, 111) points out, "In the 1950s the American military was the mightiest armed force on Earth. The existence of that arsenal was fundamental to the conduct of American foreign policy. On television during that decade the armed forces were consistently a part of popular entertainment."

Crusade in Europe, a television series based on the memoirs of General Dwight D. Eisenhower, recounted the chronology of World War II action in the European theater. The series aired in the summer of 1949, and viewers were treated for the first time to what would become the familiar rendering of the American military/television narrative of the postwar period. Eisenhower was presented as the quintessential war hero, and the programs consistently emphasized the military's inspired battle strategies and moral rectitude. Problems that emerged on the battlefields and the heavy losses were not part of this entertainment fare. Nor were faulty command decisions and errors examined or exposed in these "documentaries."

The alliance between the military and the media forged during the war resulted in numerous programming collaborations. The military appeared in sixteen different television series from 1949 into the early 1960s. For the Pentagon's part, it provided everything from personnel to bases and weaponry for documentary productions featured as entertainment. NBC's series *Victory at Sea*, which premiered in 1952, is a case in point. Featuring authentic U.S. Navy film footage from World War II, enhanced by skillful editing and persuasive writing, the drama of the American military effort was programming that garnered mass audiences and won numerous awards, some of which came from the military itself. The U.S. Navy rewarded the producers, including Robert Sarnoff, with the Distinguished Service Medal. Though only twenty-six episodes were produced, the programs were re-run frequently and appeared at least once in 206 different television markets. It was internationally distributed as well as being turned into a ninety-minute feature film. MacDonald describes the series as one-sided and simplistic, presenting an innocent and righteous America set apart from the world's despots and imperialists. "The American cause was couched in terms of altruism, morality and international law—the enemy motive was naked aggression. There was no discussion of issues. Instead, rhetoric replaced reason and viewers had war painted in sermonizing tones" (1985, 113).

According to the television writers of the military documentaries and semi-documentaries that occupied so much programming time, America was on the march, and the inspiration was divine. Text from a *Victory at Sea* episode about Guadalcanal is illustrative: "The United States of America organizes her land, her resources, her industry, her men to answer the distant prayers. In the greatest mobilization of strength known to the world, America prepares to rescue the world. And to the rescue America marches."

Crusade in the Pacific, the sequel to the European crusade series, debuted in 1951. This series gave rise to the extension of the myths rapidly being created around World War II, into other parts of the world. As MacDonald (1985, 112) points out, the later series "went beyond World War II. Its coverage of the battle against aggression in the Far East included the Korean War, a conflagration that had begun less than a year before the series was released." As we will see in chapter 3, the Korean conflagration was viewed through the lens of World War II, a distortion of the reasons for the war that would have lasting consequences.

With a total of 828 episodes produced over a twenty-year period, *The Big Picture* was the longest-running, most elaborate and influential of television's military-genre programs. Significantly, it was filmed exclusively by the Army Signal Corps and opened weekly with these words:

> From Korea to Germany, from Alaska to Puerto Rico, all over the world the United States Army is on the alert to defend our country, you, the American people, against aggression. This is *The Big Picture*, an official television report to the nation from the United States Army.

Topics covered included historical dramatizations, the Korean War, tours of U.S. bases, displays of weaponry and defense preparation against Soviet sneak attacks.

Efforts made by the Pentagon to create a positive public image came to the attention of Senator William Fulbright, who published a book entitled *The Pentagon Propaganda Machine*. While the book focused on Vietnam and the promotion of anticommunism by the military, much of the senator's concern with the manipulation of television can be traced back to the 1950s. "The Defense Department used television to influence public opinion...the propagandistic activities of the military establishment were evident early and often in the history of video."

While television was usually on the receiving end of the Defense Department production, the flow of product between the media and the military was sometimes reversed. Episodes of *Victory at Sea* were used over the years to introduce U.S. Navy recruits to the armed services. The military's use of television programming for training and "educational" purposes recreated another equally serious set of consequences. An entire generation, many of whom would be involved in Vietnam, was influenced by programs designed as entertainment, but not without a persuasive purpose. Indeed, the attitudes, values and sensibilities of civilians as well as military personnel were shaped by this powerful media alliance.

Under the sway of a militarized foreign policy, postwar television popularized a vision of the world as a threatening place where the dangers posed by communist aggression justified extravagant military expansion. The ascendancy of the military and the corresponding development of weaponry in an increasingly dangerous global competition led President Eisenhower himself to warn, as he left office, of a country dominated by what he termed the Military-Industrial Complex.

Film

Film was part of the growing nexus between the entertainment industry and the postwar military. Financial support from the studios was available for films replete with "patriotic slogans and heroic images," as millions of people "flocked to the theatres soon after the conflict began" (Pollard 2003, 314). These new films, many produced as the war was being fought, diverged from earlier versions of war movies, which frequently contained shocking images of battlefield slaughter. Films made during and after World War II were far more battle friendly. Pollard chronicles this new genre, calling it a version of romanticized war "in which heroic men and women triumphed over brutal, sinister, semi-human villains steadfastly opposed to freedom and democracy." Defining characteristics of these movies firmly establish a unidimensional enemy with war as a necessary retaliation against demonic foes. Male-only heroes who are brave enough to gamble with life-and-death situations for a higher cause are standard depictions. Small groups of isolated men who bond under fire become a "group hero." The group is comprised of unique individuals, and the interactions, conflicts and growing unity keep audiences tied to emotional content as the action moves forward. The group invariably comes under attack from external forces. Such formulas have become stereotypical over the years. For example, individuals in these small "bands of brothers" often become recognizable cutouts of social subgroups, as in *Saving Private Ryan*. Women were mostly relegated to narrowly defined roles as the "love interest" or the pin-up girl.

Films of the Good Fight mirror news reporting in omitting any negative content about the war's conduct at home or abroad. Writers would later examine some of these issues, such as John Dower (1986) in *War Without Mercy*, a book that documents the history of race hatred in the Pacific War. But as Pollard (2003, 315) points out, post-war films presented the war in the simplified, glowing terms of mythic heroism, ignoring "any discussion of American flaws, blunders, or atrocities, including the massive relocation of Japanese Americans."

Many movies combined military weaponry with narrative plot elements, and movies such as *Flying Tigers* (1942), *Air Force* (1943), *Thirty Seconds over Tokyo* (1944) and *Flying Leathernecks* (1951) celebrate air power. These depictions would establish for years to come the rightness of dropping bombs as the most exciting, masculine and efficient method of modern warfare.

CIVILIANS AND WORLD WAR II

The cost to democracy and humanity of fighting World War II was a discussion virtually ignored in the media. Weakened by Senator Joseph McCarthy's crusade (Bayley, 1981) against an internal enemy and systematic industry blacklisting (Barnouw, 1975), the media provided little open discussion or public assessment that challenged the wisdom of militarism and the positive view of warfare. In the celebrations of war, war itself was rarely questioned, even though, for the first time in history, civilians had become the victims of modern warfare.

One of the most significant and troubling consequences of World War II was the targeting of noncombatants. British historians have documented the strategic bombing campaigns carried out by the RAF beginning in 1940, that targeted civilian populations in Germany, including densely populated neighborhoods in Berlin (Calder 1969, 286). Churchill was convinced "that raids of sufficient intensity could destroy Germany's morale, and so his War Cabinet planned a campaign that abandoned the accepted practice of attacking the enemies armed forces and, instead, made civilians the primary target" (Knightley 2002, 339). Britain officially claimed to be targeting only military facilities. In a rare broadcast on CBS radio on December 3, 1943, Edward R. Murrow described the bombing of Berlin:

> Berlin was a kind of orchestrated hell, a terrible symphony of light and flame. It isn't a pleasant kind of warfare—the men doing it speak of it as a job... The job isn't pleasant; it's terribly tiring. Men die in the sky while others are roasted alive in their cellars. Berlin last night wasn't a pretty sight. In about thirty-five minutes it was hit with about three times the amount of stuff that ever came down on London in a nightlong blitz. This is a calculated, remorseless campaign of destruction.[5]

On February 13, 1945, the RAF delivered "Thunderclap," a catastrophic blow to the city of Dresden, crowded with refugees created by the Russian advance. Three-quarters of a million incendiary bombs created a firestorm, with 100 mile an hour winds that swept every living thing into a blistering tornado that reached 1,000 degrees centigrade at its center. Between 100,000 and 130,000 people were incinerated and suffocated. Press interviews with air crews revealed that they believed they were targeting "poison gas plants" and arms dumps (Toland 1968, 157). News bulletins from Sweden and then Switzerland reported details of a horrifying raid. On February 17, the Associated Press reported the "terror bombings of German population centers as a ruthless expedient of hastening Hitler's doom." The AP dispatch was banned in Britain.

At the end of the war Allied planes firebombed other cities of the Axis powers, killing hundreds of thousands. As Brown (1982, 19) points out, "Practically no attention has been given to the moral and spiritual costs of fighting Hitler as we did. In what sense did fascism, crushed in Germany, manifest itself, Phoenix-like, in the soul of the victors because we fought 'fire with fire'?" Rare were the spiritual contemplations of such a humanitarian loss, and even more rare was discussion of the effects such actions might have on the victors in the aftermath. In the *Destruction of Dresden*, David Irving (1963) quotes Air Marshall Sir Robert Saundby who expressed, what would only later become, a full-scale global discussion about war's fundamental contradictions with civilian rights and humanitarian goals:

> It is not so much this or the other means of making war that is immoral or inhumane. What is immoral is war itself. Once full-scale war has broken out it can never be humanized or civilized, and if one side attempts to do so it would most likely be defeated. So long as we resort to war to settle differences between nations, so long will we have to endure the horrors, barbarities and excesses that war brings with it. That, to me, is the lesson of Dresden. (Irving 1963)

Critical discussion of bombing civilians seemed to fall into empty cultural spaces. In addition to the bombing of Dresden, the Allied firebombings of Hamburg, Leipzig and Tokyo and the nuclear annihilation of Hiroshima and Nagasaki were absent from media themes after the war. Hollywood combat films skipped these topics, as Pollard (2003, 315) rightly observes, "owing to their 'controversial' subject matter and, above all, to the fear they might transform a good war into something more politically and morally troublesome." The silences left by these discursive voids would magnify over the years, as civilians became ever more absent in the media frames of war. An exception was the brief historical moment during and after the Vietnam War when civilians would be seen, their presence confirming the worst fears of military planners.

Those who articulated different cultural visions and critics of a social order based on militarism were published in the pages of the alternative press or sequestered within peace institutes and policy organizations. Assessments of postwar America, such as this one published by the *Progressive*, would not have been part of the mainstream debate:

> The legacy for the Untied States is tragic: a permanently militarized conception of national security; agencies of covert action and undemocratic secrecy, prone to violation of individual rights and police-state tactics incompatible with democracy; a huge inefficient bureaucracy; militarization of foreign policy; redirection of resources away from humanitarian ends. (Brown, 1982, 19)

Not subject to popular review, the unquestioned celebrations of the Armed Forces and the attendant culture of warfare continued as the country hurtled full-speed toward becoming a permanently militarized society. The meanings made of the war greatly affected the potential for peace, both at home and abroad, and foreclosed an array of alternative visions. The meanings of the war and the way it was fought were subjects proscribed by a media inundated with television programs and films that valorized fighting, glorified military strategies and, in general, created the myths and metaphors of World War II that endure, and are often generalized to support war itself.

Those who would do the fighting in Vietnam grew up watching the Good Fight bathed in a golden light. As we will see, in the years after Vietnam, soldiers and pilots would question their own personal trajectories, seeking to understand how they believed so strongly in the mythic versions of war and the unquestioned assumptions that international conflicts should always be resolved through the use of military force. Many have argued that post-World War II media culture paved the way for, in the words of one writer, "the video road to Vietnam." But before that, just a few short years after the Good Fight, thirty-six thousand more American soldiers and two million Koreans, 70 percent of them civilians, would lose their lives in the short but terribly bloody Korean War.

3

The Korean War

Remembering the Forgotten

Fought only five years after what would become the most narrated war of the twentieth century, the Korean War barely registers in the collective catalogue of war stories and cultural references. It seems to sit in obscurity, forever occluded under the long shadow cast by the Good Fight. Though it has been called forgotten, it is hard to remember a war never really known. After attempting to reconstruct what happened in Korea for a television documentary entitled *Korea: The Unknown War*, British historian Bruce Cumings asserts that the war "symbolizes an absence, mostly a forgetting, but also a never knowing. The result is a kind of hegemony of forgetting, in which almost everything to do with the war is buried history" (Cumings 1992, 146). The struggle over memory is also a struggle over interpreting the present: North Korea, the "axis of evil," and the enduring threat of nuclear war. Shining a light on the shadow of Korea requires recounting the news stories of the war and the atmosphere of the time.

McCarthyism and the Lack of Public Debate

In June 1950, when the North Korean Army crossed into South Korea, America was in the eye of the political storm known as McCarthyism, a domestic cold war of political purges and media blacklisting. New Deal, liberal Democrats were the targets of a postwar political restructuring, with government employees, media professionals and university professors alike being called before Senator Joe McCarthy and the House Un-American Activities Committee (HUAC), accused of communist sympathizing. HUAC had fueled an atmosphere of fear in which political dissent brought accusations of subversion and guilt by association (Barnouw, 1975). The "fifth columners," domestic communist enemies in our midst, were ill defined, yet seemingly omnipresent.

The call for war against an aggressive, communist-backed North Korea in the context of McCarthyism was sufficient cause to support the war, and this inclination was magnified by the view that Korea could be understood using World War II as a model. "Official thinking of the time—Asia, 1950, viewed through the lens of Europe, 1938—South Korea seen as a sort of Asian Czechoslovakia" (Sperber 1998, 341).

THE NEWSREELS

The early days of the Korean War were also the early days of television. Networks had only just begun to move from two-dimensional graphics used as illustrations for the words of a studio anchor to constructing actual newscasts with synchronized voice and moving pictures. They were not prepared to provide the country with independent news of a distant conflict. They relied on newsreel companies and the U.S. Army Signal Corps for film footage. Motion picture photographers working in Hollywood had been drafted and recruited by the military and were given access to the front and to military sources for feature-length pieces. This material was offered free to television, but it did not meet journalistic standards. As MacDonald (1985, 31) explains, "this film presented what the military wanted Americans to see of the conflict. In this way the media became a willing conduit for preselected images flattering to the military and its commitment." In this way, news of Korea blended into the "documentary histories" of the Second World War. War reporting on American television grew up in this pro-military atmosphere of the 1950s.

When General McArthur flew to the war front, he took Signal Corps photographers with him. Such footage regularly appeared on programs like *Telenews Weekly*, a half-hour review of war news. In those first months of the Korean War, Americans saw a highly sensationalized, patriotic depiction of the conflict, complete with bold music, anticommunist rhetoric and exciting footage supplied by the government. In one program called *Front Line Camera*, President Truman warns that a free America has to be on guard against invasion and aggression. The president linked the North Korean invasion to events at Pearl Harbor a decade earlier, referring to "this kind of sneak attack." Americans, he said, must be "united in their belief in democratic freedom" and in "detesting communist slavery." Though he warned that "the cost of freedom is high," he asserted that Americans "are determined to preserve our freedom no matter what the cost." As MacDonald (1985, 32) summarizes, "In a few short unquestioned sentences from the president of the United States a civil war between strong-willed Korean governments had become a crusade to protect the freedom of all Americans."

Here we see classic war rhetoric, language designed to persuade without informing. It is impossible to be against the protection of democratic freedoms. It sounds familiar even now. But just as it did in 1950, such rhetoric closes debate by denying that any conflict is more complicated than the simple binaries of good and evil. Such language mystifies the political dimensions and complex histories that cause war.

Truman's words obscured the causes of the Korean War, while frontline censorship and McCarthyism at home prevented it from being examined and debated as it was being fought.

CENSORSHIP

The history of Korea was easily buried because, at the time, so little was known. News from the battlefield was severely restricted by the military and news organizations themselves. Military censorship blocked unwanted reporting of all kinds, such as "any derogatory comments" about U.N. troops or commanders. Journalists could not acknowledge "the effects of enemy fire," and that meant reporting U.S. troop casualties was off-limits (Hallin 1986, 38). When print and broadcast reporters did get to the front lines, they depended on the armed forces for transportation and protection, even food and housing. "Such amenities undermined the objectivity journalists preferred to have when gathering material for a story" (MacDonald 1985, 31).

From November 1950 on, General Douglas MacArthur would exert centralized control over the press. Restrictions on transportation and communication insured that the general's headquarters in Tokyo would be the focal point of newsgathering, and journalists came to rely in great measure on official army briefers and press releases called communiqués. Even before censorship was imposed, journalists could face court-martial for security breaches or unwarranted criticism, and several were expelled from Korea early on (Sperber 1998, 345–46).

From Enthusiasm to Criticism

Edward R. Murrow, having gained a reputation during World War II as the most respected broadcast commentator and war correspondent, initially threw himself behind the American effort in South Korea. "We have… risked a war and committed ourselves beyond the possibility of turning back…. If southern Korea falls, it is only reasonable to expect…that there will be other, bolder ventures" (Sperber 1998, 341). Korea was the first test of the new postwar containment strategy.

While Murrow and the mainstream press agreed with the war in principle, what they saw of the fighting in Korea dampened much of their enthusiasm within weeks. "They were unprepared, too, for the savagery of what was essentially a civil war, Korean against Korean…and by the scorched earth tactics of the forces retreating before the North Korean advance" (Sperber 1998, 342).

Early reports published before censorship was imposed had a critical edge. The *New York Times* published a dispatch by Charles Grutzner that told of U.S. troops killing Korean civilians: "Fear of infiltrators led to the slaughter of hundreds of South Korean civilians, women as well as men, by some U.S. troops and police of the Republic" (cited in Cumings 1992, 147). As early as July 1950, Keyes Beech of the Newark *Star-Ledger* reported: "It is not the time to be a Korean, for the Yankees are shooting them all." He went on, "nervous American troops are ready to fire at any Korean."

Edward R. Murrow and CBS

Murrow has received much critical acclaim for his 1952 television special *Christmas in Korea*. That historic broadcast stands out for the voices of the men fighting the war to whom Murrow and his crew had access. But his earlier CBS radio dispatches from the field were censored. Those reports were critical of the military high command and acknowledged the war's human costs. By August 1950, after several weeks in Korea observing specific battles and military actions, Murrow adopted a critical stance toward top-command decisions and wrote a blistering report quoting officers who believed that "We paid too high a price for that southern offensive. Experienced officers called it folly…. Our high command took it because…we decided we needed a victory" (Sperber 1998, 346). Though relations between Murrow and the military had become tense, his early dispatch was not censored by the military, but by the president of CBS, William Paley himself. Anticipating difficulty with the military, the network censored its star war correspondent. CBS reasoned that the piece could give comfort to the enemy or be used on Radio Moscow.[1] By Christmas 1952, as illustrated with Murrow's CBS special, journalists learned that reporting from the soldier's perspective, like Ernie Pyle's work before them, avoided military criticism and passed the censors.

THE ANTI-COMMUNISM FRAME

As Murrow learned, offering an internal context for understanding the Korean conflict was equivalent to promoting communism. In one broadcast that did air, Murrow spoke of "the surging desire for change" and the "resentment of foreign domination" as he tried to explain the appeal of communism to a population living in misery. He detailed the negative propaganda value of bombing a factory: "In Asia there is no greater crime than to destroy a man's rice bowl, and the factory is regarded as a kind of big community rice bowl" (Sperber 1998, 348). According to Murrow biographer Ann Sperber, his intention was not to promote the other side. "It was simply up to us to learn the language, the better to win friends and keep the Russians from dominating them" (Sperber 1998, 349). But anything attempting to explain why North Korea was attracted to communism, no matter what the context, "was now seen as the height of flaming liberalism, if not downright espousal of the Moscow line" (Sperber 1998, 349). When Murrow returned home, he was once again thrust into an accelerating McCarthyism, with politicians calling for tough antisubversion measures, arguing that there was no logic in waging war in Korea while allowing Communists "free rein" at home (Sperber 1998, 346).

THE COUNTER-NARRATIVE

Bruce Cumings, chief historical consultant for Thames Television, Britain's Channel 4, recounts the struggle to tell the story of Korea in his book *War and Television*. He encountered much opposition while making the documentary *Korea: The Unknown War*, because its details, even though supported with ample historical evidence, diverged from the received wisdom of war. When the WGBH version was shown on PBS, it was heavily edited for American audiences. Making the documentary proved to be a Herculean task, and the story of its production is telling.

The alternative narratives that emerged changed the conventional reading of the Korean War in significant ways. The war was not a simple case of aggression by a communist-backed regime against a democracy. According to British Historian Peter Lowe, who helped develop the documentary exposition, "At a rough guess I would assign responsibility about equally, between North and South Korea, for the provocative actions which had occurred previously" to June 1950. Declassified documentation confirmed that aggression took place on both sides. As journalists soon discovered, the Korean War bore little resemblance to World War II, the received narrative initially used for its coverage. "The origins of the war went back into the pre-1945 colonial period, back to the divisions begun in the 1920s really, and this history allows us to understand that it was fundamentally a civil war of long genesis" (Cumings 1992, 150). Because the war ended with an armistice, it cannot be understood simply as a victory; rather, it is a paradox. Interpreting that paradox remains controversial because the war can be used to confirm contending political points of view:

> For the Truman Cold War liberal, Korea was a success, "the limited war." For the MacArthur conservative, Korea was a failure: the first defeat in American history, more properly a stalemate, in any case it proved that there was "no substitute for victory." The problem for MacArthur's epitaph is that if MacArthur saw no substitute for victory, he likewise saw no limit on victory: each victory begged another war. The problem for the Truman liberal is that the limited war got rather unlimited in late 1950 [when MacArthur pushed north and was forced to retreat]. (Cumings 1992, 145)

Korea is absent, a blank spot rarely retrieved from the American mind, because it so stubbornly refuses to fit or be contained within the heroic World War II narrative of its initial telling. "The structured absence is none other than the script of World War II itself, for in Korea an American army victorious on a world scale five years earlier was fought to a standstill by rough peasant armies" (Cumings 1992, 148). So we agree to forget this war.

In addition to the controversies over interpreting the war's outcome is the assessment yet to be made of its conduct. The history of the Korean War is witness to a terrible loss of life and the devastating effects of the U.S. bombing campaigns.

THE U.S. BOMBING OF NORTH KOREA

Official statements about the extent of the U.S. bombing of North Korea were included in the British version of Cumings's documentary *Korea*, but quotes from General MacArthur himself about the devastation were deleted from the WGBH version. Editors "removed MacArthur's statement about American airpower creating 'a wasteland' in North Korea after the Chinese intervention. No substitution was included that would indicate to the viewer the true horror of this scorched earth policy." The historical consultants argued that such omissions would be like forgetting defoliation in the Vietnam War, "but it all fell on ears deaf to well-documented facts" (Cumings 1992, 255). One of the war's main architects, Dean Rusk, was also interviewed and included in the British version of the documentary. Rusk said on film that the United States bombed "everything that moved, every brick standing on top of another brick" in North Korea (Cumings 1992, 253). That was an admission the American audience would not hear.[2] As we can see, the fog that surrounds the telling of the Korean War is carefully guarded, lest that fog be lifted.

One journalist interviewed by the Thames documentary crew, Tibor Meray, a Hungarian War correspondent, traveled through North Korea after the bombing and described scenes of cities and villages in rubble, with only chimneys left standing.[3] "I saw destruction and horrible things committed by the American forces…. Everything that moved in North Korea was a military target, peasants in the fields often were machine gunned by pilots…." As Cumings summarizes, "Meray was our best eyewitness to the most awful history of the Korean War, three years of genocidal bombing by the U.S. Air Force which killed perhaps two million civilians (one-quarter of the population), dropped oceans of napalm, left barely a modern building standing, opened large dams to flood nearby rice valleys and kill thousands of peasants by denying them food, and went far beyond anything done in Vietnam in a conscious program of using air power to destroy a society…" (158). The indignation expressed by Cumings (1992, 158) when he says, "This well-documented episode merits not the slightest attention or moral qualm in the United States" was mirrored at the time by the American journalist I.F. Stone.

I.F. Stone's Hidden History

As I.F. Stone (1952) reported, the U.S. bombing and its effects were well documented by the U.S. Air Force itself, and in fact were the subject of many of General MacArthur's communiqués to the press. As Stone concluded in *The Hidden History of the Korean War*, "These communiqués must be read by anyone who wants a complete history of the Korean War. They are literally horrifying" (257). Indeed, as early as September 1950, official communiqués announced a "paucity" of targets, as everything had already been bombed. "It's hard to find good targets, for we have burned out almost everything." Stone quotes from other communiqués reporting that some bombers did manage to find targets. "The Eighth Fighter Bomber Wing F-80 jets reported large fires in villages in the western sector following attacks with rockets, napalm, and machine guns" (though, he notes, *why* was not explained). Most communiqués referred to "enemy-occupied" villages that had been bombed. Stone laments that the ratio of civilian-to-soldier dead in these raids must have been extremely high. He continues: "A complete indifference to noncombatants was reflected in the way villages were given 'saturation treatment' with napalm to dislodge a few soldiers." Stone quotes from another bombing communiqué from February 2, 1951, to the effect that after about fifty soldiers had been spotted in the area, a mass flight of twenty-four F-51 mustangs poured five thousand gallons of napalm over the area. The flight leader is named in the communiqué, and Stone adds ironically, "so as to foster individual pride in such handiwork...his flight hit every village and building in the area." Another communiqué quoted a captain: "You can kiss that group of villages good-bye" (Stone 1952, 259). Stone concludes that such communiqués "reflected, not the pity which human feeling called for, but a kind of gay moral imbecility, utterly devoid of imagination—as if the fliers were playing in a bowling alley, with villages for pins" (Stone 1952, 258).

One of the difficulties of remembering is viewing the past through the lens of a different historical moment. At least part of the reason that North Koreans could be annihilated was the dehumanizing labels that were applied to Asians. The legacy of World War II stereotyping justified Japanese internment camps and was still part of the cultural landscape. North Koreans were doubly tarred as Asians and communists; it seemed not to matter that they were civilians. It would be up to a British journalist to provide an account of some of the worst dehumanizing attitudes. In *Cry Korea*, Reginald Thompson provided an eyewitness account of the first year of the war. He saw journalists unprepared for what they saw, but few "dared to write the truth of things as they saw them" (Thompson 1951, 44). GIs "never spoke of the enemy as though they were people, but as one might speak of apes" (Thompson 1951, 84). Even among correspondents, "every man's dearest wish was to kill a Korean" or "get me a gook" (Thompson 1951, 114).

Racism also clouded the public's perception of war reporting. Stone demonstrates that the numbers of Chinese dead, at times estimated to be over five thousand a day, were widely exaggerated by the military. "These figures did not seem so strange to a newspaper-reading public in America which had been led to picture Chinese hordes 'marching abreast' and 'in human waves' against American guns, in supposed 'Oriental' disregard of their own lives.... The experts paused to wonder, but expert analysis does not make headlines" (Stone 1952, 255).

The official killing of a demonized enemy, firmly established during World War I, is acceptable conduct in war, and killing large numbers of civilians had become acceptable during the Good Fight. The firebombing of German and Japanese cities had been established as legitimate military strategy. Such bombing of civilian populations has only become unacceptable in retrospect, after years of international debate and the codification of the rules of war. Explaining how such bombing could have happened requires acknowledging that racist attitudes existed at the time and justified the loss of life.

KOREA AND THE 1980S

Cumings attributes as least part of the resistance to the making of *Korea: The Unknown War* to the 1980s. The documentary challenged the neo-Cold War assumptions of the Reagan years and the sense of "mass nostalgia" for the 1950s. "The Korean War is errant counterpoint to the rosy memories and so it vanishes" (Cumings 1992, 146). In addition, the Reagan administration was deeply involved in supporting another civil war, justified by anti-communism, resulting in a terrible loss of life. This time the war was in Central America. Hence the 1980s were not the time to revisit the Korean War, or deconstruct the anti-communist framework of justification. Reagan would evoke the same metaphor used for "swarming Asians" in his anti-communist campaign, this time referring to Central Americans. In a 1983 television address, Reagan spoke of a "tidal wave" of "feet people" that would be "swarming" into our country if the Sandinistas were "not stopped in Managua." Like the Chinese before them, "the red tide of revolution" would be on the move, this time marching north to Mexico and across the Rio Grande.

The best historical documentaries seek to reframe questions, open debate, jar the received interpretations and offer new perspectives through the lens of history. But as long as war remains the solution to global problems, there will never be a time for reassessing. When will the record be set straight?

There was a moment under the Clinton presidency when it appeared that negotiations between North and South Korea might result in a new era of peace and reconciliation. Negotiations involved finding answers to long-simmering accusations of war crimes in Korea and healing old wounds. In the fall of 1999, a group of AP reporters won a Pulitzer Prize for their investigation into the massacre at No Gun Ri in South Korea. Roughly three hundred civilians, many of them women and children, were bombed and strafed from the air by U.S. gunner pilots under direct military command to do so.

But the revelations did not come without a price. *U.S. News & World Report* and other major news organizations challenged the authenticity of the sources.[4] The controversy made it all the way to television's *Dateline*, when Tom Brokaw interviewed a U.S. veteran who testified to the massacre but could not have been in No Gun Ri at the time. But the truth of the incident did not rely on one faulty memory of war. Other evidence and testimony provided ample proof that a massacre took place. Only later was it revealed that the attempt to discredit the story came from the military affairs reporter at *U.S. News & World Report*, Joseph Galloway, a member of the veterans group opposed to the story.

The report led to an official U.S. government investigation and confirmation of the incident. In January 2001, just before Clinton left office, peace negotiations were creating a context for reconciliation. An important memory was retrieved and a first step taken. The United States became a signatory to a Statement of Mutual Understanding (2001) and admitted: "2.a.(1): In the early period of the conflict, many of the U.S. soldiers deployed to Korea were young, under-trained, under-equipped and new to combat. Units operating in the vicinity of No Gun Ri were under the command and control of leaders with limited proven experience in combat." The conclusion of the official report on No Gun Ri reads in part:

> In the desperate opening weeks of defensive combat in the Korean War, U.S. soldiers killed or injured an unconfirmed number of Korean refugees in the last week of July 1950 during a withdrawal under pressure in the vicinity of No Gun Ri. Bearing in mind the long-lasting sorrow of victims as well as the sacrifice of U.S. soldiers during the Korean War, the ROK and U.S. teams firmly believe that this investigation…will not only help maintain a more stable ROK-U.S. alliance but also is an example of two nations working together to realize the value of democracy and recognize the importance of human rights.

The power of the press to influence the military in matters of human rights violations is evident in the No Gun Ri investigation. Early press reports by Murrow and others critical of military directives and the human consequences of the war clearly needed to be heard and acted upon by American citizens and their leaders. Instead, journalists were silenced by military censors and their own editors and news organizations, actions which no doubt facilitated the continuation of a bloody war.

AMERICAN PRISONERS OF WAR: A BITTER PILL TO SWALLOW

The official number of American deaths in Korea is thirty-six thousand—a toll taken in three short years. By the year 2000, more than eight thousand U.S. personnel were still "missing" and unaccounted for. In 2000, Philip

Chinnery, the historian for the National Ex-Prisoners of War Association, wrote *Korean Atrocity!* a book based on declassified files on the Korean War. Published by the Naval Institute Press, the book documents death marches, war crimes and atrocities against U.S. soldiers that took place after the first year of the war. Chinnery describes the material he discovered in the Public Records Office as "horrific," and the book includes pictures of Americans soldiers as young as age seventeen shown sitting in groups as their captors look on. So disturbing is this material that the documents were originally closed for seventy-five years, not to be declassified until 2028. Contemplation of the fate of young prisoners at the hands of the enemy gives many Americans pause, and keeping those horrors secret is part of a necessary forgetting. Without such secrecy and censorship, peaceful solutions to conflicts would be far more in demand.

FORESHADOWING VIETNAM

Following Nietzsche, Cumings (1992, 148) refers to Korea as "*historia abscondita*," or a structured absence. It remains a repressed or hidden experience. Ironically, Korea was used as the background for the popular 1970s television series *M*A*S*H*, yet the setting has always been understood as a dislocated Vietnam. But in that final episode, when Hawkeye offers a toast to forgetting, the reference more accurately captures the Korean War.

Fighting the Vietnam War depended on forgetting Korea. Some of the most difficult lessons of Vietnam had already occurred in Korea, yet they had gone relatively unnoticed: scorched-earth bombing and the use of napalm, massacres of civilians, and the result, was a bloody stalemate. How might history have been different had the American public known what was going on in Korea in the way that it became aware of what was going on in Vietnam by the late 1960s? As Walter Goodman, television critic for the *New York Times*, mused after seeing *Korea: The Unknown War*, "Viewers with a memory of television's treatment of the Vietnam War may find themselves wondering how matters might have turned out if Americans at home had been a nightly audience to scenes from the bitter battlefield of Korea" (Goodman, 1990).

Korea was a watershed in the American position in the world. Retrieving the lost history of the Korean War not only sets the record straight, but it seeks to understand how Korea set in motion so many policy decisions that influenced the course of war in Vietnam. As Cumings (1992, 148) argues, "The amnesia masks a reality in which we all are a product of Korea whether we know it or not; it was the Korean War...that inaugurated big defense budgets and the national security state, that transformed a limited containment doctrine into a global crusade, that ignited McCarthyism just as it seemed to fizzle, and thereby gave the Cold War its long run." Fighting the Korean War committed the United States to an enormous military buildup and inaugurated the military-industrial complex that President Eisenhower would later warn against.

Today North Korea poses a dangerous threat to America and the globe. Its distorted nuclear priorities exist in a country whose young population is remarkably smaller than its South Korean counterpart because of chronic malnutrition. Remembering the history of a bombing campaign that killed nearly two million people and leveled the country a little over fifty years ago would be the first step in understanding and negotiating an end to this threat. The George W. Bush administration's failure to successfully negotiate with North Korea is tied to its commitment to a costly nuclear defense system that continued testing has proven to be unworkable. If negotiations with North Korea were begun in earnest, a major justification for the nuclear option would disappear.

4

Vietnam

Shattered Illusions

The Vietnam War remains a contentious, troubling episode in American history, one that weaves in and out of popular culture and media debates and in recent years is increasingly surrounded by an array of transmuting interpretations. Re-remembering the war in Indochina remains a project for the ongoing political culture of war and its story. Along its trajectory from experience to expression, the war in Vietnam resulted in a genre of antiwar films and alternative documentary narratives attempting to come to terms with what was then considered, even to many governing elites, a significant moment of American infamy. Such a stunning experience required new ways of telling the story, and "Nam" challenged the basic assumptions of war and the military and rendered obsolete (at least for most of a generation) the privileged narratives of combat and heroism. Indeed, the cataclysmic nature of the war seemed to defy any kind of coherent representation, because reality itself, especially to American GIs, seemed to stop making sense. How could American democracy, the valiant salvation for Europe's descent into barbarism, create its own legacy of human suffering such a short time later?

As a moment in the grand sweep of history, the war has been termed "postmodernist." Theorists grappling to understand a society able to carry out atrocities in the name of modernity and progress have also used the term "posthumanist." William Spanos (1993) underscores the paradox that created a brutal spectacle of intervention in the affairs of non-European people in the name of European freedom. The war and its remembering shredded the legitimacy of the received assumptions both of American idealism and more generally transcendent Enlightenment values.

Those who identify the war in Indochina as a key moment in the episodic shift from modernism into a fragmented, postmodern, world use as illustration a key journalistic text of the war, Michael Herr's acclaimed *Dispatches*. Fredric Jameson (1991) points to *Dispatches* when he asserts, "This first terrible postmodernist war cannot be told in any of the traditional paradigms of the war novel or movie—indeed, that breakdown of all previous narrative paradigms, along with the breakdown of a shared language through which a veteran might convey such experiences…may be said to open up the place of a whole new reflexivity." *Dispatches* broke the narrative mold and conveyed the experience of Vietnam through a series of staccato shots that could only allude to the actual violence, nihilistic chaos and futility of the war itself. As the war shattered the received world from which it emerged, it ended the elevated status enjoyed by the military in American society and popular culture. Over the decade of the 1960s the war's tenacious grip displaced television images of victorious battles narrated by authoritative voices and replaced them with scenes of burning villages, grief-stricken civilians and a bloody Saigon street where a summary execution was caught live on film. The images bore witness to a conduct and sensibility utterly at odds with the familiar features of the Good Fight. The sense of betrayal and rage felt by those who fought were reflected in the shattered narratives recounted both during and after the war. Engelhardt referred to this episodic shift in attitude toward war as The End of Victory Culture in his 1995 book of the same title.

The cultural spaces that opened in response to the failure of the war in Indochina marked an important transformation and rejection of war and its celebration. The rebellion against the war took place over a period of time. To understand this cultural dislocation and the historical lessons it teaches, we must return to the media atmosphere created as the war was perpetrated. Key moments and texts mark sequences in the flow of the ongoing story of the Television War. In re-covering that story, it is best to begin in the middle.

THE TET OFFENSIVE

On January 31, 1968, in a surprise attack during the Chinese New Year, North Vietnamese troops invaded every major city in South Vietnam in what came to be known as the Tet Offensive. When fierce street fighting brought the war into previously secure urban areas, it shook American war planners, the press and the public alike. Herr describes in *Dispatches* what it felt like to be under attack during Tet:

> Almost as much as the grunts and the Vietnamese, Tet was pushing correspondents closer to the wall than they'd ever wanted to go. I realized later that however childish I might remain, actual youth had been pressed out of me in just the three days that it took me to cross the sixty miles between Can Tho and Saigon. In Saigon, I saw friends flipping out almost completely; a few left, some took to their beds for days with the exhaustion of deep depression. I went the other way, hyper and agitated, until I was only doing three hours of sleep a night. A friend on the *Times* said he didn't mind his nightmares so much as the waking impulse to file on them. (1977, 206–7)

Journalists not incapacitated from fear or depression could step out of their hotel rooms and into the midst of combat. The war had come to them. Photographers captured images of battles being fought in the streets of Saigon, including wounded U.S. soldiers, and television brought those pictures into American living rooms during dinnertime. New satellite technology allowed immediate uplinks that made airtime with very little editing: "Network producers in control rooms in New York had neither the time nor the opportunity to shield American viewers from the grisly close-ups of wounded Americans, body bags, and death" (Epstein 1975, 221).

One of the most disturbing sequences of the war was caught on film during Tet: the summary execution of a Vietcong officer by a South Vietnamese general. Though the final sequence of the soldier's death was edited for television, NBC producer Robert J. Northfield described the footage as "the strongest stuff American viewers had ever seen" (cited in Epstein 1975, 221). Photojournalist Eddie Adams also took stills of the street execution, and the images became known as "the shot seen around the world."

For the next few months the public would be exposed to graphic images of fighting, including footage of wounded civilians in addition to American soldiers. As Hallin's (1986) research shows, from January 31 to March 31, 1968, film of civilian casualties and urban destruction in South Vietnam increased four-fold on television, and footage of military casualties jumped from 2.4 to 6.8 times a week. Hallin concludes, "Tet was the first sustained period during which it could be said that the war appeared on television as a really brutal affair" (1986, 171). The pictures and coverage began to drive home the collective realization that thousands of American soldiers had already been killed, and the American viewing public began to recoil from the war's brutality.

SHATTERING THE FRAME

Media coverage of the war in Indochina can best be understood along a historical trajectory, not as a consistent set of frames, themes or images. The Tet Offensive was a defining moment in the chronology of reporting and marks a turning point, with both a distinct "before" and "after." Indeed, it was the divergent themes of coverage pre- and post-Tet, and the striking contradictions in those narratives, that amplified the effects of the graphic coverage. Epstein (1975, 220) describes pre-Tet reporting as a "carefully edited view of an orderly, controlled war." For years public affairs officers directed and escorted journalists, even offering free airlifts to the battlefield. They took reporters on routine "search and destroy" missions, from which pictures of successful operations aired on nightly news. Aronson (1970, 233) recounts the effectiveness of Pentagon public relations efforts, quoting Richard West of the *New Statesman* as saying that reporters felt "overwhelmed by the help and hospitality they receive from the American propaganda machine." He understood that journalists were "bound to be grateful" and in danger of becoming a part of the official military version of the conflict.

Other journalists, mostly freelancers traveling on their own and often working for alternative media, were telling a different, far less positive story about the war. But in the mainstream media, defeated enemies and official body counts were the order of the day, as reporters frequently quoted military officials who claimed they could "see the light at the end of the tunnel." The war was winnable, and progress was being made. Over time the daily Saigon press briefing would come to be known as the "five o'clock follies," but before Tet the interpretations they offered were reported as legitimate information. Critical reports rarely saw the light of day. A censored eyewitness account by *Newsweek* reporter Mert Perry from the Mekong Delta in the summer of 1966 is a case in point. Perry concluded that "the much heralded progress in the delta was arrant nonsense; that things had, rather, gone from bad to worse in almost every category."[1] *Newsweek* refused to print the story.

News reporting assumed that given the superiority of American weapons, a constant feature of coverage, the enemy would surely be defeated. With each new shipment of Huey helicopters, television brought pictures of increased firepower into American homes. Weapons superiority mirrored the moral superiority conveyed in news coverage. "Television painted an almost perfectly one-dimensional image of the North Vietnamese and Vietcong as cruel, ruthless and fanatical" (Hallin 1986, 148). Cast in a classic mold of the godless enemy ready to enslave its own people and beyond redemption, the Vietcong were what Hallin describes as beyond the bounds of "legitimate controversy." Though peace negotiations ultimately ended the war, before Tet they were unthinkable. When in December 1966 *New York Times* reporter Harrison Salisbury sent dispatches from North Vietnam that articulated the aspirations and positions of the National Liberation Front, he was heavily criticized by many of his colleagues.

COGNITIVE DISSONANCE

In the midst of these frames of a noble war that America must and surely would win came the images of Tet. It was the shock caused by the divergent depictions of the war before and after the Tet Offensive that rendered the coverage so iconoclastic. A war that had for years been characterized as "winnable," clean" and "just" had suddenly become brutal, messy and costly. As Epstein remarked in 1975, after years of television portraying a "continuous series of putative American military successes…the American public was unable to digest the unprecedented violence and gore they saw during Tet" (222). Suddenly Americans saw for the first time that the years of official pronouncements about the war amounted to little more than wishful thinking. Tet resulted in a kind of cognitive dissonance that created in the public mind a crisis of credibility toward the military and the government.

CRITICAL COVERAGE

Once the framework for a just and winnable war was shattered, the significance of Tet was amplified by the silence from the Johnson administration. For the next few months, no plausible alternative interpretations emanated from the White House. As the media responded to these new coordinates, coverage shifted palpably through February and March of 1968. Without a strong message from the executive branch, debate and criticism escalated in the media. Editorial comments and opinions on television news jumped from a pre-Tet average of 5.9 percent to 20 percent during the two months following Tet (Hallin 1986, 169). Amid continuing controversy, public confidence in the military was further eroded by a significant leak to the *New York Times* on March 10, 1968. The Joint Chiefs of Staff, planning to send another huge contingent to Vietnam, were asking for an additional

206,000 troops. Yet the Pentagon refused to discuss its planning publicly. The leak to the press indicated significant internal opposition to the war.

Critical information about failed military strategies and images documenting the human costs of the war circulated widely for the first time. The imagery of a brutal, mismanaged war solidified in the public mind in the weeks to come. In the midst of this sea change, CBS anchorman Walter Cronkite decided to fly to Vietnam to personally assess the war effort. Reporting from Vietnam in a special broadcast that aired on February 27, he characterized the war as a "bloody stalemate." Cronkite seemed to change his opinion of the war on the air. After his brief witness, he determined that the anti-communist rationale for the war was no longer being served. Cronkite concluded his report with the statement that "It is increasingly clear to this reporter that the only rational way out then will be to negotiate, not as victors but as honorable people." These words—from the most trusted anchorman in America—confirmed that the war was an ignoble effort. To continue its escalation would only amplify American culpability.

THE PUBLIC OPPOSES THE WAR

By the end of March 1968, a majority of Americans was opposed to the war for the first time. On Sunday, March 31, Lyndon Johnson made an historic televised address to the nation, announcing that he would halt the bombing of North Vietnam. He also said he would not seek another term in office. Epstein rightly points out that Johnson's withdrawal from the presidential campaign was in a response to public sentiment against the war. "President Johnson, always responsive to public opinion, announced in a moment of high drama that he would not seek a second term as President" (1975, 224). In his 2002 memoir *Secrets*, Daniel Ellsberg concurs that Johnson's decision to step down was based on the public's opposition to the war. A week earlier he had told a gathering of officials at the White House: "The country is demoralized. I will have overwhelming disapproval in the polls and elections. I will go down the drain.... We have no support for the war" (Ellsberg 2002, 209).[2]

In the days following Johnson's abdication speech, *Time* magazine (April 5, 1968, p. 19) gave this explanation: "His popularity hit an all-time low in a Gallup poll released this week. Only 36 percent of those questioned approved of his conduct of the Presidency (versus 48 percent in January): only 26 percent approved of his conduct of the war (versus 39 percent). *Obviously, the Tet offensive had much to do with Johnson's slide*" (cited in Braestrup 1978, 501; emphasis added by Braestrup). Political scientists Reiter and Stam also write in *Democracies at War* (2002, 175) that the American public's support for the war was quite "high at the outset, 78 percent of Americans expressing approval of the administration's handling of the war in October 1965. This figure dwindled slowly but steadily over the next two years. After the January 1968 Tet Offensive, public support collapsed; a March 1968 poll revealed that only 30 percent still approved of the administration's handling of the war."

Of course the war would not end until 1975, even in the face of public opposition. With the help of Henry Kissinger, President Richard Nixon would go on to bomb Cambodia in 1969, and though Nixon campaigned as a peace candidate in 1972, he continued to escalate the war.

BLAMING THE MEDIA FOR THE CONSEQUENCES OF TET

The stunning visuals that rang in the Chinese New Year in 1968 and the transformation in media coverage they foreshadowed have long been the basis for the charge that the media, not the military, lost the war in Vietnam. The story follows this narrative: The media turned the public against the war by leaving the impression that Tet was a defeat for the American and South Vietnamese forces. But the Tet Offensive was not a victory for the North Vietnamese. They held no territory when the battle was over, and they suffered many more losses than the South and the American forces. The North could never have sustained such attacks. Tet greatly depleted their resources. But with the public against the war because of press coverage, the military could no longer fight to victory and instead had to end the war in defeat.

Over time, more vituperative charges of disloyalty have been leveled against the opposition movement and antiwar government officials for opposing the war. This narrative of a military betrayed, unable to unleash the firepower necessary for "total victory" in the wake of media coverage of Tet, has long been used to support claims that the media were disloyal and unpatriotic during the "uncensored" war, and worse, that the media are "liberal," biased against the military and the powers that be. These have become the unspoken yet fundamental assumptions that have served to justify the curtailment of First-Amendment guarantees and to block journalistic access to the battlefield in subsequent conflicts.

Coming to terms with charges of media bias during Vietnam is central to issues of war and imagery in the twenty-first century. To the charge that the media deliberately misrepresented the facts of the battle, Reiter and Stam (2002, 175) point out: "Despite the essential veracity of claims that Tet was a military victory for the American and Southvietnamese forces, the simple fact that it occurred dashed any hopes the American people might have entertained that the North vietnamese military had been broken and that the end was near." Tet also confirmed in the public mind that since the war was not about to end, the cost in human life would continue to escalate.

Media analysts often attribute the public's disenchantment to the length of the war. They argue that the public's taste soured from battle fatigue as the war dragged on. But it was more than that. Tet made it clear that the government and the military were not telling the truth about the war. Many Americans, especially young people in the antiwar movement, were well aware that the war on the ground bore little resemblance to official pronouncements. But the unusual circumstances of Tet resulted in a relatively "unedited" version of an ugly war breaking out on broadcasts in primetime, when only a clean one had been seen before. As the alternative narrative became the dominant one, it exposed the years of deception and false official versions of the war.

A now-disillusioned public was more critical of the military, and resentment over the draft continued to grow. The war was certainly not worth more American lives, though the draft continued. GIs returned home to inadequate medical and emotional care and with rates of addiction to heroin higher than 15 percent. Fighting the war had become virtually impossible, and commanding officers were also being killed on the battlefield by their own soldiers. Veterans came home to tell stories of a hellish world of ignoble conduct and increasing chaos.

Yet the military continued to define the war in its own, more positive, terms, and that war looked nothing like the incoherent reality on the ground. "Official discourse functioned in its own linguistic sphere, radically at odds with the experience of the troops and the more enquiring members of the press" (Kellner 1999, 200). As Kellner argues, the Vietnam War challenged the familiar vernacular of military speech: "It appears that the distance between language and reality grew in the Vietnam War where the military discourse clearly did not correspond to the disturbing actuality of the war" (200).

MILITARY LANGUAGE, BRIEFINGS AND BODY COUNTS

Vietnam was a counterinsurgency war where an "enemy" was indistinguishable from the people. North Vietnamese forces moved among the villages and hamlets where the war was fought. Civilian noncombatants often gave them food and shelter. Americans were frequently killed in night ambushes, surprise attacks and by land mines. The enemy seemed to be everywhere and nowhere at the same time. American military strategy focused on clearing the countryside, and throughout the course of the war relocation strategies displaced entire villages and created millions of refugees. Under these circumstances, the American military perpetrated enormous hardships on the people of Vietnam, and American troops killed many civilians.

The body count was one of the many ways in which the Vietnam War laid bare the worst of war's dehumanizing consequences. As territory was gained and then lost again, and as superior weaponry failed to deter North Vietnamese forces, finding a discursive measure of victory became ever more illusory. The military began to proclaim its measure of success in Vietnam with an ongoing count of the death toll. Numbers of dead Americans were compared to those of the enemy. The higher the number of enemy dead, the closer to victory. Attributing value to the greater number of dead human beings began to dismantle a system based on humanitarian values. As war historian James William Gibson (1986) argues, this "production model of war," the input and output of integers, is based on a corporate model of performativity.[3] In this mechanized, bureaucratic format, "information" about the war, with victory assigned by comparative numerical calculations, no longer made sense. The winning number, though a smaller one, still added up to death.

As the lives of American soldiers were transmuted into dehumanized integers, those numbers became indicators not of victory but of a war going terribly wrong. As the war continued to be prosecuted with few clear political goals articulated or achieved, such abstract calculations revealed a posthumanist dilemma that began to sound surreal. Take, for example, the reporting of Bernard Weinraub in *Times Talk*, the *New York Times*'s in-house newsletter of January 1968. He describes a briefing by JUSPAO (Joint United States Public Affairs Office) at its office building in Saigon:

> In some cases there is also a rather brutal and remarkable insensitivity to death. At a Wednesday briefing a few months ago—one of those "deep Background" sessions—a brigadier general said with a smile:
>
> "Well, I'm happy to say that the Army's casualties finally caught up with the Marines last week."
>
> There was a gasp. A civilian U.S. mission officer, sitting next to the general, turned and said incredulously: "You don't mean you're *happy*."
>
> The general was adamant. "Well, the Army should be doing their job too," he said.
>
> Jim Pringle, the bureau chief of Reuters, turned to me and whispered: "My God, this is straight out of *Catch-22*." (Cited in Aronson 1970, 244).

But critical reporting of this type was reserved for the journalistic family, and in most cases it never made it into the pages of daily newspapers. As Aronson (1970, 243) points out: "The difference between public and private writing about Vietnam was sharply apparent to anyone who had access to both." The press briefing did find its way into the pages of the *Village Voice*, and, as noted above, those reading alternative media were exposed to a different, more brutal war, long before coverage of Tet hit the mainstream media.

Vietnam created fear and frustration in American soldiers, who were forced to fight in a place where life had become cheap and where the whole population seemed to be the enemy. Jonathan Schell (1968, 14–15) was an early critic of American policy, which was to bomb entire villages without warning if American troops took fire from them. This killing also took its toll on American GIs. In addition to veterans who returned to the United States from Vietnam addicted to heroin, a drug easily available there, shell-shock became a common feature in the military.[4] Many returning GIs could not reconcile the conduct of the war with civilian life. They were unable to come to terms with the brutality they either experienced or knew about. One of those soldiers was Ron Ridenhour.

My Lai

On November 13, 1969, newspapers around the country picked up a story from a little-known news agency, Dispatch News Service, written by Seymour Hersh. The story described twenty-six-year-old Lieutenant William L. Calley, Jr., as "a mild-mannered, boyish-looking Vietnam combat veteran with the nickname of 'Rusty.'[5] The Army says he deliberately murdered at least 109 Vietnamese civilians during a search and destroy mission in March, 1968, in a Vietcong stronghold known as 'Pinkville.'" News of the massacre at My Lai, which took place in March 1968, had taken twenty months to reach the American public. The road to discovery was a long one. Ron Ridenhour had served with soldiers who had witnessed—and some who had participated in—the massacre. When he got home from Vietnam, he could not forget the disturbing accounts, and in April 1969 he wrote a letter saying he believed that something "dark and bloody" had occurred in "Pinkville." He sent it to the Army, the DOD, the Joint Chiefs, the White House, legislators and individuals. An investigation was begun in September 1969, and charges were brought against Calley. Seymour Hersh was working on a book about the Pentagon when he found out about My Lai.

Within weeks of Hersh breaking the story, details of the massacre, including shocking photographs, were published in the Cleveland *Plain Dealer* and soon after in *Life, Time* and *Newsweek*. They told of the early morning hours of March 16, 1968, when William Calley's platoon, one of three in Charlie Company, entered My Lai 4, a subhamlet of Son My village (known to Americans as Pinkville) located on the Battambang Peninsula in Quangngai Province, South Vietnam. Charlie Company had been told to expect an engagement with enemy Vietcong. Instead they found only unarmed women with infants and children and old men, all finishing breakfast. Though no one resisted, the area had been declared a free-fire zone, and after pounding the hamlet from the air, eleven helicopters dropped soldiers on the ground shooting.

On December 5, 1969, in an issue of *Life* magazine that carried the picture of an African antelope on its cover and promised more "great action pictures," ten pages of images from My Lai were published in what Engelhardt described as a "photo album from hell." Taken by military cameraman Ronald Haeberle, the pictures tell "a story of indisputable horror," of gruesome scenes of people covered in blood, of the burned village and mutilated corpses. Captions tell of the deliberate slaughter of men, women and children, including the story of a rape. GIs stripped a thirteen-year-old girl, yelling "VC boom-boom," and calling her a whore for the Vietcong.

The December exposé in *Life* magazine is particularly chilling, especially compared with the front-page story carried by the *New York Times* the morning after the massacre. No independent journalists went into Pinkville with Charlie Company that morning in March 1968, and the *Times* reported the story straight from an Army press release: "American troops caught a North Vietnamese force in a pincer movement on the central coastal plain yesterday, killing 128 enemy soldiers in day-long fighting." For the mainstream press it was a "significant success" and an "impressive victory." United Press International added, "The Vietcong broke and ran for their hide-out tunnels. Six and a half hours later, 'Pink Ville' had become 'Red, White and Blue Village.'"

Ridenhour's letter and the investigation into what happened at My Lai, including the trial of Lieutenant Calley, culminated in the reporting of the massacre in great detail, including confessional statements by participants on nightly news broadcasts. For Engelhardt, My Lai was a significant marker in the protracted struggle in Indochina that ended "victory culture." America lost the mantle of nobility as civilians were slaughtered. The victim narrative told by the Vietnamese was virtually the same story that eventually reached the American people. The massacre seemed "to rise inexorably through layers of official cover-up and denial, through what was left of victory culture, without losing the look of a horror as seen through the eyes of the massacred" (Engelhardt 1995, 217). Consider this Vietnamese narrative of My Lai:

> Vo Thi Phu, mother of a 12-month-old baby, was shot dead.... The baby, which tried to suck at its mother's breast, cried when it found only blood instead of milk. The Yankees got angry and shouted "Viet Cong, Viet Cong," and heaped straw on mother and baby and set fire to it.... After raping to death Mrs. Sam, a sexagenarian, the aggressors made a deep slash in her body with a bayonet.... Mui, 14, was raped and shut in her hut. The GIs set fire to it, guarded the door and pushed back the poor little girl who tried to run from the fire.... (Engelhardt 1995, 216).

The story goes on to detail the way over 100 people were lined up and shot with machine guns and thrown into a canal. In one day, 502 people, including 170 children, were massacred, all the houses burned and over 870 cattle slaughtered. "Our coastal village so green with coconut palms, bamboos and willows is now but heaps of ashes."

After the story of My Lai, the war itself had implicitly taken on the aura of an atrocity.

THE COST OF THE WAR: LIVES AND NAPALM

A little more than four years after the Tet Offensive and the massacre at My Lai, the image of a 9-year-old Vietnamese girl who stripped off her clothes trying to rid herself of flaming napalm jelly would be seen around the world. Nick Ut's photograph of Kim Phuc running from the attack, her body a patchwork of burns was published long after the majority of Americans had turned against the war. In 1973, when Ut won the Pulitzer Prize for the photograph, Phan Thi Kim Phuc was one of millions, but she became the most recognizable face that expressed the horrors of the Vietnam War.

The crisis of humanitarian values would be well documented after the war. "U.S. intervention involved the use of 15.5 million tons of bombs and munitions in Vietnam, and the spraying of 18 million gallons of poisonous chemical herbicides (including Agent Orange) over the country's forests and farmlands" (Bibby 1999, 153).

Kim Phuc became the visual icon of the human cost of the Vietnam War, and over the years her image has evoked grief, pain, sorrow and guilt, but also interpretation and revision. In the years that followed, much has been made of the fact that the incident was an "accident." The plane that bombed Kim and killed her two cousins on June 8, 1972, was flown by a Vietnamese pilot in support of South Vietnamese troops. They were fighting the North Vietnamese Army after it occupied the village of Trang Bang. The pilot bombed the South Vietnamese children "in error." Though it was widely reported that an American commander in Saigon ordered the air strike, many in the U.S. military maintain that no Americans were involved in the incident.

Debate over the details of the photograph and its taking are motivated by a desire for absolution as much as a need for accuracy. The deliberation also invites a type of intellectual distance from the initial emotional response to the image. If the burning of Kim was "unintentional," carried out in error, then the call to war can somehow gain back some of its "cruel legitimacy."[6] If death is "accidental," it becomes acceptable. In these terms, war can be planned and justified, relied on and perpetuated, as it continues to be. But the death toll resulting from the force and effectiveness with which the United States battled the Vietnamese, is staggering and cannot be considered an unintended consequence.

> The years of U.S. military intervention witnessed the deaths of over 1.9 million Vietnamese, 200,000 Cambodians, and 100,000 Laotians. The war left 3.2 million Vietnamese, Cambodians, and Laotians wounded and made more than 14.3 million more refugees by its end. According to one account, between 1965 and 1973 about one out of every thirty Indochinese was killed by the war." (Bibby 1999, 153)

The war also took a heavy toll in American lives. "By 1975 the Vietnam War had involved 2.5 million U.S. soldiers. It killed 58,135 of those soldiers in combat along with 35,000 noncombatant U.S. civilians. It wounded 303,616 more soldiers, 33,000 of whom were paralyzed. According to a 1982 report, 110,000 more died from 'war-related' problems after returning to the U.S.—of those, 60,000 were suicides" (Bibby 1999, 152–53).

POSING THE QUESTION OF PRESS LOYALTY

The public's resolve to continue a war depends on a complicated equation that balances war's justification with its destructive force. Once the public perceives that the cost in human life is too high a price to pay for the stated goals, opinion quickly turns against the war effort. Graphic images of death and wounded soldiers have, over the years, become identified as the most egregious case of media excess, and this is to be avoided at all costs. The specter of that fundamental shift remains the greatest fear to those who would wage war. Within the highest ranks of the military these perceptions endure, and media management strategies have been designed to prevent a recurrence of such coverage.

On numerous occasions, military officers and elected officials have openly blamed the press for losing the Vietnam War. As we will see, the press was barred from covering the invasions of Grenada and Panama, and they were highly restricted during the First Gulf War. Over the years, the military has routinely raised questions about the loyalty of the press corps during times of war.[7] The highly charged political nature of this question has long placed journalists (and a free press) at a disadvantage. How can journalists position themselves as independent reporters able to fulfill their obligation to the First Amendment if they must prove that they will, in principle, be loyal to any war effort? And how will they gain access to the battlefield, soldiers and military sources if they are not? By placing the media in a defensive position through the charge of disloyalty, the military has succeeded in justifying the information-control strategies adopted in subsequent wars. As we will see, by the twenty-first century, reporters have learned that they do not gain access unless they demonstrate sympathetic attitudes toward war.

AFTER THE VIETNAM WAR

The Documentary: Shattering the Grand Narrative

Vietnam documentaries, many made with the help of veterans or produced by them, confronted the once-unquestioned culture that presented war as righteous, rational and technically proficient. Some of the most important of those works juxtaposed the firsthand experiences of those who fought with mythic renderings. Veterans themselves gave birth to another way of talking about war.

One of the strongest video treatments to shatter the grand narrative of war is the experimental documentary *Smothering Dreams*, done by Vietnam veteran Dan Reeves. Wounded on his tour of duty in Vietnam in 1969, and with his hearing almost gone, Reeves worked through the video not to heal his physical wounds but his psychic ones. "What I learned about myself, morality, mortality and responsibility during my year in combat has been the focus of most of my life and life's work" (Reeves, 2004).

Like many Vietnam veterans, he believed in the war—at first. He dropped out of school to enlist in the marines. In *Smothering Dreams*, he explores the reasons why. Reeves grew up playing war games, pretending to fight like the brave D-Day heroes at Normandy, imitating the classic imagery of John Wayne masculinity. But he ended up in the jungles of Vietnam, not in a black-and-white fantasy of oppression versus freedom. Dreaming of being an elite member of a brotherly team, he became instead just one more expendable life, forced to live with the memories of doing horrible things not because someone ordered him to, but to stay alive.

Through cropping, changing image size and slow-motion techniques, Reeves creates an atmosphere of confusion, loss and grief by alternating between reenactments of his "childhood dreams of battle and adult nightmares of the atrocities of war" (Zimmerman, 2000). The documentary throws together fragments of these mixed emotions, jumps in time and leaps in space, creating a montage of startling contrasts, visually punctuated by images of shattering glass. Patty Zimmerman (2000) argues that the video "shatters the smothering and numbing of war through shards of images that cut into emotional paralysis." Disrupting causal sequencing, image fragments hit the senses, engaging the viewer in a psychic process. *Smothering Dreams* reverses the emotional alienation of dehumanizing body counts in a world defined through the distance of geopolitics, logocentrism, government and nations. Foregrounding the soldier's experience of horror reverses the point of view from macro-abstraction to the interior spaces of war's attack on psychic well-being.

Chilling interviews with American pilots describing what it was like to bomb Vietnamese villages is a feature few will forget after seeing the well-known documentary *Hearts and Minds*. As one of the best testaments to the inhumanity of war carried out from the air, those who bomb from their elevated distance see control panels and feel the power of technology, not its consequences. Vietnam is seen as a sweeping historical catastrophe of irreparable loss, deception and guilt. General Westmoreland delivers his famous line that life is cheap in Asia: "The Oriental doesn't put the same high price on life as does the Westerner." His words are contradicted by footage of a heartbreaking funeral where a Vietnamese boy cries hysterically from grief as a member of his family is buried. The film was delayed, but then widely shown across the country. It is a devastating montage of official justifications of the war juxtaposed to horrific footage of brutality. The film left a lasting impression on the collective conscience of the American public.

The Post-Vietnam Film Genre

After Vietnam, war depicted in the singular vernacular of the Good Fight no longer resonated as a popular fictional site for American nationhood. War, the military, MIAs and Vietnam veterans remained too complicated a set of contradictory national and personal symbols of sorrow, grief, pride and conscience to be rendered in uni-dimensional stories of bravery and heroism. The war film genre so popular after World War II gave way to

critical expressions of war. Television and film dramatized America's igno-
minies and defeat in an outpouring of cultural narratives that challenged
military motivations and practices.

A Huey helicopter rattles the windows of a hotel room in Saigon where
Captain Benjamin Willard (Martin Sheen) awaits his up-river journey into
the heart of darkness in *Apocalypse Now* (1979). His assignment: follow the
highly decorated, but now entirely mad, renegade Colonel Kurtz (Mar-
lon Brando) into forbidden territory in Cambodia and "terminate with
extreme prejudice." Willard's mission is an odyssey of pain, cruelty, chaos
and suffering. Along the way, Jim Morrison's voice from the Doors' song
"The End" can be heard from another Huey as it flies low over a burning
tree line. In another scene of war and madness, the iconic Huey is used in
an air assault to clear a beach of civilians so that one of the soldiers can surf.
Kurtz's compound is the embodiment of evil, the grounds strewn with a
hideous display of decapitated heads and the terror of insanity. As a profound filmic depiction of hell on earth, and written by Michael Herr in the
same fragmented style as *Dispatches*, the final scene of *Apocalypse Now* is of
total destruction, as Kurtz utters, "The horror, the horror!"

In *Platoon* (1986), written and directed by Vietnam veteran Oliver
Stone, a linear structure is again abandoned, and the film is disorienting
as it jumps in sequences without warning. The GIs in *Platoon* also seem to
occupy a living hell "at the point of physical collapse, bedeviled by long
marches, no sleep, ants, snakes, cuts, bruises and constant gnawing fear"
(Ebert, 1986). American soldiers use drugs, fight with each other, and
through fear, anger and madness, kill civilians. As Rita Kemply (1987) says
of one of the main characters, Barnes, "killing is no longer an ugly necessity: It's a living." Auster and Quart (1988, 137) call the film iconic of the
post-Vietnam genre: "Stone succeeds in creating a richly textured portrait
of the war. His talent for remembering how Vietnam looked and felt gave
the film an affecting shock of recognition to vets and nonvets alike, making
Platoon, despite its soporific narration and over-the-top mythologizing, the
first real cinematic step taken by Hollywood in coming to terms with the
truth about Vietnam." The realism of *Platoon* highlights the reality of the
"grunts-eye view," but that portrayal caused some to criticize the refusal
to abandon the myth of the super-hero. Though as Kempley (1987) points
out, these heroes are not used to glorify war: "Stone doesn't preach. He
just remembers. He explodes the Rambo myth, like one of Stallone's fool
arrows, to remind us that war is hell." War in Vietnam was also unwinnable
and by setting the action around the time of the Tet Offensive, "Platoon
deals with the war at the moment when the notion of a winnable war had

rapidly receded down a dark hole of despair and defeat" (Auster and Quart 1988, 137).

Stanley Kubrick's *Full Metal Jacket* (1987) is a chilling illustration of the post-Vietnam treatment of the military. From training to battle, it is a scathing indictment of war's brutality and futility.[8] Though *Jacket* does not depict the lush, fetid jungles of Vietnam, it is one of the most forceful examples of the post-Vietnam attitude toward fighting, combat and killing. In *Full Metal Jacket*, Kubrick deals specifically with how humanity is challenged by such dehumanized training. As Auster and Quart (1988, 142) point out, *Full Metal Jacket* offers a damning view of "the military as an institution that breeds killers." As Pollard (2003, 323) notes, "This bleak portrait of the Vietnam conflict…demonstrates the force of disillusionment with what had come to be recognized as America's first military defeat."

John Irvin's *Hamburger Hill,* a brutal Vietnam battle chronicle with a powerful anti-war statement, would also come out in 1987. And in 1989 Oliver Stone would relate another grueling tale from the perspective of a veteran, this time the story of Ron Kovic, played by Tom Cruise, in *Born on the Fourth of July.* The brutal dialogue about war between the wounded, disillusioned vet and his mother speaks to a generation who turned against a war promoted by their guardians. Cynthia Fuchs (1999) offers the most critical and insightful reading of Stone's film when she recalls the empty Mexican landscape where the two drunk, paraplegic veterans, played by Cruise and Willem Dafoe, scream "Fuck you!" at each other: "At stake for each character is the authenticity of his war-induced emotional damage." The issues of damage and identity revolve around the question of who was forced to commit the worst atrocity in Vietnam, who is the real baby killer. Though critical of what she refers to as the most brilliant "hysterical collapse of Vietnam War memory onto masculine identity ever put to celluloid," she identifies the moment of recognition the sequence offers. For America, "the baby-killer identity was entrenched in U.S. popular culture—as a cogent distillation of U.S. atrocities and amorality—these two dying-with-guilt veterans feel compelled to remember it, internalize it, be it" (53).

The films of Stone, Kubrick, Coppola and others represent a significant break for the normal combat film of heroic deeds and just causes. As Pollard (2003, 325) notes, they reached large audiences and "articulated a generation's anti-war yearnings" by depicting the brutality, futility and grim realities of war. "By dwelling upon more critical images of the Indochina debacle, they helped educate audiences concerning wartime atrocities and the gross failures of the American military and foreign policy spanning the JFK, Johnson, and Nixon years" (Pollard 2003, 325). These and other films of Vietnam constitute an important record of one of the most tragic and tumultuous periods in American history.

It would not be until Steven Spielberg's portrayal of the compassionate and competent Captain Miller (Tom Hanks) in *Saving Private Ryan* (1998) that military legitimacy would once again be reasserted through the use of a World War II narrative. By stepping back from the memory of Vietnam, cultural constructions of war could more easily return to depictions of patriotism and military legitimacy characteristic of the Good Fight.

POSTMODERNIST WAR?

Many argue that the Vietnam War was, if not the first or last blow to the modernist canon, then at least a significant blast that helped rupture modernist historical coherence and the legitimacy of Western humanist assumptions. As the meaning of war and culture changes over time, their historical significance must also be reassessed. In the midst of continuing wars in the twenty-first century, with few cultural expressions of the horrors experienced by those on the receiving end of American weaponry, it could be argued that far from being posthumanist, Vietnam and its aftermath may mark a significant moment when humanism was ascendant, displacing the usual themes of victory and glory. A human perspective, one of subjectivity—though admittedly damaged and gendered in problematic ways—displaced abstract ideals whose cynical use justified the slaughter. As we have seen, for a moment in American culture, the story of war was told from the victim's point of view, as America openly admitted the atrocities at My Lai.

Postmodern Culture

The term postmodern might best be applied to American culture, especially during the 1980s. Even as post-Vietnam films dismantled the old myths of the Good Fight and exposed war's worst conduct, that same cultural firmament was busy reinventing a new mythic hero in the character of Rambo, who successfully transmuted war's critique into the superhero. Though Fuchs and others would argue that the seeds of the superhero were firmly embedded in post-Vietnam genres, it might also be said that the postmodernist cultural marvel may be the ability of both genres to occupy the same cultural space. As political culture was reinvented, "hard bodies" served to remasculinize American culture. During the Reagan/Bush years, Rambo emerged as a symbol of patriotic, betrayed manhood (Kellner, 1995). In *First Blood* (1982), "Rambo embodied not merely the forgotten warrior, but also the self-disciplined macho character with awesome mental and physical powers—with the capacity to kill any number of human beings" (Pollard 2003, 322). Susan Jeffords (1994) argues that this Vietnam-veteran superhero, along with Schwarzenegger's Terminator, became an integral part of the neo-Cold War imagination: "these hard bodies came to stand not only for a type of national character—heroic, aggressive, and determined—but for the nation itself" (25).

Ronald Reagan, Oliver North and, much later, George W. Bush, would all benefit from the "hard body" mold as they fashioned themselves according to the reinvented heroes of their day. In addition, the post-Vietnam film genre itself would solidify into a cardboard cutout, one easy to yank out of context and reinsert into another with deadly consequences for the meaning of war. The significations for key codes of the genre, such as the iconic helicopter, rock-and-roll music and GI helmets with "born to kill," would transmute into positive meanings, utterly detached from their original significations as critique. They would become the new cultural practices of war itself, most stunningly illustrated in the fact (as noted by Jeffords [1989] and Beidler [1999]) that American helicopters invading Grenada played Wagner as they imitated *Apocalypse Now*. Innumerable television movies feature hip soldiers landing in choppers over thundering rock-guitar sequences, and Jerry Bruckheimer would refer to rock and roll as hip war genre itself in his revisionist film for the twenty-first century, *Black Hawk Down*.

Part II

Eyes Wide Shut

The Not-So-Secret Wars of
Central America and the Caribbean

5

Visions of Instability

Telling Stories on Television News

During the 1980s, America would fight another counterinsurgency war, this time in Central America. This would be a proxy war, funded by the United States but fought by Central Americans trained in the business of counterinsurgency by U.S. advisors. The helicopter would remain a visual icon, its cultural tenacity a testament to the enduring reality of conflict. This time the gunships would carry brown-skinned soldiers pointing automatic weapons down on rebel-held territory in the northern mountains of El Salvador. On the ground along the mountain ridges that separate Honduras from Nicaragua, *contras* would slip across the border into Nicaragua. Their attacks were mostly against civilians, but the Reagan administration said it was funding them to overthrow the Sandinista government. Ronald Reagan would call them freedom fighters, the equivalent of our founding fathers, and proclaim them America's only hope against the invading influences of Soviet communism. In the face of opposition from Congress and the American people, officials in the Reagan White House would resort to illegal means to finance the proxy war, and during the Iran/Contra hearings, Oliver North would grieve the deaths of the brave men he called heroes. Along the way the American military would unleash Urgent Fury on the tiny island of Grenada, and television correspondents would use helicopters to fly over the island, barred from covering the battle. The decade would end with the invasion of Panama, another battle carried out without journalistic witness to the initial combat.

In 1981 the Sandinistas were accused of funneling arms to the rebels in neighboring El Salvador, the ones trying to take power from the military. The conflict in El Salvador, the tiny but populous country, would take the form of a bloody, twelve-year civil war that would cost American taxpayers almost $6 billion and end in a negotiated peace brokered by the United Nations in 1992. Horrible atrocities against the civilian population would be carried out by the Salvadoran military and security forces, and funded by the U.S. government.

What did Americans know of these events at the time, and what did they think about them? What images did they see, and what stories were they told? How was information about these conflicts managed, and what kinds of official interpretations were constructed as legitimate? Which arguments, claims and positions were considered credible, and which were not? How did popular fictions available in the 1980s interact with real news from the war zones of Central America and the Caribbean? And when a scandal broke, how did the media portray those in its spotlight? With documentation of human rights abuses, how did American institutions, including the press, and the American public respond to the loss of life of so many innocent people?

An appropriate place to begin recounting this history is the coup in El Salvador in 1979. The interruption it caused intermingled with another set of confounding images shown on television from a different part of the world, the disturbing pictures of Americans held hostage in Iran. As the decade pressed on, Central America and Iran would be surprisingly paired as unlikely cohorts united by their geopolitical importance to the neo-Cold Warriors of the 1980s, who—as it would be revealed—sold weapons to the regime responsible for kidnapping Americans and used the money to arm the contras. But the Iran/Contra scandal would come later.

The 1979 coup in El Salvador caught the attention of the media, especially television, and the sense they made of it was the result of a particular combination of television's disdain for historical context, its fascination with drama and its willingness, if not to believe, then to repeat a convenient, journalistically plausible version of events. Such stories were usually hastily constructed during conversations at the Intercontinental Hotel in San Salvador, which often took place after embassy briefings.

U.S. Television Coverage of the Salvadoran Coup of October 15, 1979

Action and drama characterized the television news coverage of El Salvador during and following the coup in 1979. Violent civil disorder exploded on the television screen. Stories featured fast-moving footage of people running in the streets, some wounded, along with soldiers, tanks and crossfire, with accompanying audio of screams and gunshots. The anchorman had to explain that "tiny" El Salvador, a country hardly known to North American audiences, was part of Central America, and that San Salvador was the capital city. Tiny foreign countries do not usually become the focus of news stories unless there is a coup or an earthquake.[1]

The foreign press corps was unprepared. Television correspondents were not chosen on the basis of their knowledge of the region they were sent to cover. Nor did they have the firsthand experience that would have given them at least some background knowledge of El Salvador, because it had only just become the story. During the Carter presidency, Central America was not the geopolitical focus for foreign policy, or the theater for a new Cold War. That era would be ushered in a year later when Ronald Reagan came to power. For many reporters in 1979, it was their first time in Central America, and most did not speak Spanish. Nonetheless, they had to make a story out of seemingly incomprehensible events. It had to fit within a framework of understanding and interpretation that editors would accept and that the North American public would recognize. It had to fit, and be fit for, television.

FOREIGN VIOLENCE AS INFOTAINMENT

The freelance network-news crew based in Mexico City covering Central America called themselves the "budget bang-bang crew."[2] They went to El Salvador when demonstrations were planned or if they had information on a major disturbance. They were well aware that the main value of coverage from El Salvador was entertainment-violence.[3] Action coverage was the most likely to be aired, and stories that did not include violence of some sort were not considered newsworthy. The crew hoped to capture exciting and disturbing visuals of the social conflict spilling into the streets of San Salvador.

THE LAW-AND-ORDER FRAME

With very little background knowledge of the region, journalists relied on a standard media framework, one that could accommodate such dramatic visual footage. They would focus on chaos as the theme and feature those who promised to restore law and order. British theorists identified such conventional treatment by the BBC in reporting crime and urban riots and described the framework as "dangerously pre-emptive and frequently mythical" (Wren-Lewis 1981–82, 15).

Not surprisingly, the most important structural element of the law-and-order frame is violence. Conflict usually begins the news report, either in the anchorman's introduction, or at the beginning of the story itself. A few examples from news stories about El Salvador during this period illustrate the common opening lines:

> In other foreign news today, the military junta in El Salvador is but three days old, but has already fought off one leftist attempt to overthrow it.... (ABC, October 17, 1979)

> In the Central American country of El Salvador the leftist fight against the new military junta there intensified.... (ABC, November 4, 1979)

> In El Salvador more turmoil, leftist demonstrators in the capital city of San Salvador attacked the American embassy.... (NBC, October 30, 1979)

The conflict in El Salvador is portrayed as having been initiated by leftists and/or demonstrators. Other stories use labels such as guerrillas, extremists, students or some variation thereof. The leftists are always attacking, fighting or rebelling against the newly established government. The impression is that the legitimate government is continually under a state of siege, a state that threatens the fundamental social order.

The disruption of social order is a recurring theme of news stories, identified by Herbert Gans (1979) as an important value in the news. That value is underscored on television. Opening with attack and disruption is the beginning of a good story. Dramatic conflict, especially visually depicted, is exciting and gains the attention of the viewer. As the crisis unfolds, the viewer remains engaged, waiting to see how it will be resolved. Crisis is made to order for television news reporting of the developing world, because little or no background knowledge is needed to encapsulate an exciting story.

Opening footage presents a situation of chaos, and as the story unfolds, a solution is sought. The disruption poses a problem for *those in power,* and it calls upon authorities to react. It is they who must develop strategies for the restoration of order. In the news stories of El Salvador, the agents of law and order are the army and the security forces directed by the new junta. It is they who react to leftist violence and, after a battle, restore order. The "leftists" cause the problem and are set in dramatic conflict with legitimate force, as these stories illustrate:

...The army also wants the leftists to put down their weapons, but despite that call for peace, a leftist group early this morning took over a neighborhood in San Salvador, the capital. The National Guard *had to be brought in* to get them out.... (emphasis added; ABC, October 16, 1979)

El Salvador's new government today made its first get-tough *reply* to protesting leftists.... (emphasis added; CBS, October 28, 1979)

Strengthening of the agents of law and order is always presented as defensive, reactive and necessary. They "had to be" called in, and they "had to get tough." In acting out this drama between leftists and security forces, the scales are always tilted in favor of those in positions of state-sanctioned power. As Wren-Lewis (1981–82, 16) points out, their social positions are strictly pre-defined within the law-and-order frame: "The policeman signifies within the sacred realm of "the law"—the policeman represents the law and therefore is the law—while the demonstrator/rioter is entrenched within the realm of the arrested or arrestable."

When the law-and-order frame is used to cover a country such as El Salvador, where the status quo is maintained by force, the leftist demonstrator/rioter is not only within the realm of the arrestable, but within that of the killable, as this CBS story shows: "But so far leftist uprisings have failed, seventeen people were killed in San Marcos when the army quashed a guerrilla takeover of that city" (CBS, October 18, 1979).

The information that seventeen people were killed is placed within a sequence that establishes the leftists as violent, and the fact that people were killed is portrayed merely as a consequence of the army's obligation to restore order. The added use of the word "quashed" makes it also seem to have been somehow gentle, as if brute force were not really exerted, even though seventeen people died. Within the law-and-order context, putting down uprisings is something the army is supposed to do, a positive act. The consequence of the frame, then, is to make the killing of leftists, and even "innocent" people, a palatable event: a necessary, if lamentable, by-product of maintaining order.

After giving the body count and other related details, the Salvador stories of law and order end. The restoration of order, or at least a temporary calm, closes the narrative, as do these ending lines:

Late reports say students have now begun to leave the University campus and that the city is quiet.... (ABC, January 23, 1980)

Or, as in this story, in which an action taken by the government promises order in the near future:

The new junta has suspended constitutional rights until the crisis is under control.... (ABC, October 16, 1979)

Many times the temporary restoration of order prefigures more violence to come. In situations such as these, it is not at all easy for the correspondent to "wrap it up." Different visual images are used to signify calm, or at least pseudo-normality: an empty city street, people who look "relieved that it's all over." One story ends with a funeral, the finality of burying the dead signifying calm, if only for the time being. Speculation as to whether the junta will be able to survive future onslaughts signifies order at present and serves the added function of setting the stage for future stories:

Everyone expects more killing. The four-month-old government may not be able to survive either.... (ABC, January 23, 1980)

Video news from little-known countries that emphasize action-drama contain almost no context, and the little information offered distorts the viewers' understanding of events. The narrative introduced a crisis, pitted characters against one another, was filled in with how many shots were fired, what part of town it was in and how many people died. The drama of leftists battling with security forces was fast-paced and exciting and therefore entertaining. Closure was effected when calm returned and the forces of law and order were once again in control, if only temporarily. Such contained, rushed stories never seem to pause to ask why demonstrations and attacks have occurred. These actions appear to be totally without history, motivation or political purpose. They appear out of a mysterious void—as if from nowhere.[4] Journalism critic W. Lance Bennett identifies the frequent loss of context in news this way: "In place of seeing a coherent world anchored in clear historical, economic and political tendencies, the public is exposed to a world made chaotic by seemingly arbitrary and mysterious forces" (2003, 24). In stories of law and order, those killed by military force are dangerous, yet unknown. This combination of features is historically consistent in stories of conflict. As Herbert Schiller observed about the Vietnam War, media stories made the conflict "appear random, senseless and totally irrational. The NLF fighters (Vietcong) where portrayed as vague ill defined menacing figures whose motivations were hard to comprehend" (Schiller 1973, 91). In place of explanation comes the familiar assertion that those who cause violence, usually leftist, are simply extremists by nature. "Notions of causality are tautological in the mythic sense—a criminal is criminal is criminal" (Wren-Lewis 1981–82, 16). For other explanations to come into play, the site of the problem would need to shift from the focus on violence to the world of *conditions that precipitated* such startling events.

THE "MODERATE" JUNTA THAT NEVER WAS

The coup of October 15, 1979, reportedly brought to power a moderate government composed of civilian and military officials willing to make structural changes within Salvadoran society. This premise formed the foundation of media coverage and conferred legitimacy on the Salvadoran Army. Brutality in the person of General Romero had been overthrown, and a just society was in the making. Official statements from the U.S. government and the new ruling junta went like this: Young progressive military officers had ousted Romero, a right-wing general and the perpetrator of brutal repression, who had ruled the country with an iron fist. The corrupt system of social and economic injustice maintained through force by police and military would stop. Right-wing oligarchs, who up to that point had kept the wealth of the country to themselves, were to relinquish a small fraction of their privilege. From this more equitable arrangement, a middle class would emerge, creating a corresponding politically moderate center. A fledgling, lawful democracy would replace revolution. The "left" would be appeased with reforms, and "extremists" would be controlled. Most important, the status quo would be preserved, and U.S. interests would be safe.

Credibility for this position assumed that reforms were taking place and that a more equitable society was in the making. This gave the security forces the right to "get tough." However, the junta never lived up to this characterization, even though news coverage consistently made that claim. It was true that reform-minded officers were among those who led the coup. They did promise to begin the process that would abolish injustice, and they asked civilians to join them in the task of restructuring Salvadoran society. Armstrong and Shenk (1982, 122) characterized these civilians as "men of impeccable democratic credentials." In the beginning, then, the junta was a coalition of military and civilian progressives willing to work for change. It also included, however, military conservatives such as Jose Guillermo Garcia and Jaime Abdule Gutierrez, who led the right-wing faction of the military. During this time leaders representing a more progressive military, together with civilian officials, would struggle to gain control over security forces for the three months that followed the coup, a battle they would lose against right-wing influences.

From the beginning, television news reports characterized the junta as centrist and moderate:

> The State Department in Washington said the leadership appeared centrist and moderate.... (NBC, October 16, 1979)

> The State Department said today the new military government in El Salvador appears to be moderate and its first statements are encouraging.... (ABC, October 16, 1979)

> On October 18, 1979, CBS reported the appointment of civilians to the new government:

> Three civilians considered sympathizers of the moderate opposition party were appointed to serve on the junta....

This CBS report goes on to describe the "moderate" credentials of Roman Mayorga, a former university president educated at M.I.T. This would be the last report on the structure and nature of the junta. From this time on, it is labeled "reform-minded," "moderate," "centrist" or "civilian/military." Although the "moderate" label stuck, the "centrist" description did not, but television viewers would not be privy to this information. Almost immediately the progressive officers and civilians found it impossible to control the actions of the right-wing elements within the military. The human-rights report confirms that abuses continued: "The Majano-led wing soon found its influence over the army was limited or in the case of the National Guard and the Treasury Police, virtually non-existent. Members of the latter two branches of the Security Forces also belonged to various paramilitary groups that played an ever-more-violent role in the last months of 1979."[5]

On December 29, 1979, Salvador Samayoa, then Minister of Education, and Enrique Alvarez Cordova, Minister of Agriculture, along with three other civilian members from the first junta, resigned in protest. After three months of internal struggles, neither Majano, a military man, nor the civilians were able to control the army and stop the brutality. Their letter of resignation read in part: "We see now that this political project was, from the very beginning, a maneuver against the people. But we do not regret having participated in this government, having put all our efforts and skills toward a different outcome. But now that everything is clear, we should regret for the rest of our lives any further collaboration."[6] Then, on January 3, 1980, Guillermo Ungo and Roman Mayorga resigned along with virtually the entire cabinet and all high-ranking officials. In the words of Armstrong and Shenk (1982, 130), "the center had collapsed." This interpretation is corroborated in the report on human rights, which states that: "With the fall of the 'First Junta' the centrist alternative was effectively closed, and the conservatives were back in unquestioned control."[7]

None of the networks reported any of these events, nor the final resignation of the junta members. Even though the collapse of the first junta did not make headline news in the United States, the resignation letter of Ungo and Samayoa was carried on the front page of *Le Monde*. Even CBS, which had reported at length on the appointment of Roman Mayorga, failed to report his resignation or any of the others. For television news viewers, these political developments never happened, and the government continued to be labeled "moderate." A report aired on NBC never mentioned that any of these struggles were taking place: "The leftists oppose the moderate junta which took power here last October." Even after the resignations, as late as February 19, 1980, NBC reported: "The Carter Administration is considering proposals to send military advisors to help bolster the moderate government now in power." The government was labeled moderate even when it seemed to be a contradiction in terms: "The ruling moderate junta clamped a news blackout on radio stations" (CBS, January 23, 1980).

Though the final blow to the centrist position came at the beginning of 1980, it must be remembered that the junta was never in control of the security forces. The army never acted in a moderate way. The civilians finally resigned because they realized that they were the democratic face that shielded the military from criticism. In spite of continuing demands for reform, and contrary to what television news reported, repression actually increased after the coup, as the human-rights report documents: "Popular pressure for reform, including an end to repression, intensified, but the level of repression actually increased." Security forces acted with the same brutality as those under Romero. "Within a week, the government was held responsible for more than 100 killings of demonstrators and striking workers." (Americas Watch Committee and the American Civil Liberties Union 1982, xxxiii).

Independent sources describe continued and escalating military abuses against major sectors of the population. But this might not have been so surprising to viewers had they known the long history of political inequality, army repression and economic disparities in El Salvador.

The Historical Void

Explaining even a little of the uncontested history of El Salvador would have provided a context for understanding the internal power struggles tearing the new government apart. The legacy of colonialism had left most Central American countries controlled by economic elites, but nowhere, with the possible exception of Guatemala, was their power as complete and long reigning as in El Salvador. The Salvadoran oligarchy—the small group of families who controlled the country's wealth—survived and grew richer because of their willingness to make alliances with the armed forces. While the wealthy made money, the colonels and generals kept the poor, the workers and the peasants under control, too terrified to rebel. Decades of social and economic injustice were maintained by security forces and their unofficial paramilitary death squads. Such entrenched economic and military structures are not easily relinquished by those who have enjoyed power and privilege. Democratic elections over the years had been stolen; when progressives had been voted in, they were either killed or forced to flee. The political arena had been effectively closed as a mechanism for reform. Amid this background, the coup of 1979 took place.

That moderate civilians within the junta were not able to end the years of military repression was most clearly evidenced by the continued military and paramilitary attacks on demonstrators. The rights to peaceful assembly and to organize unions, which had been declared illegal in the past, were to have been ushered in with the new junta. But instead of fulfilling its promise of reform, the new regime followed in the footsteps of the previous dictatorship. The continuing attacks were documented by the Americas Watch Committee and the American Civil Liberties Union report (1982, 135), which states: "Although the Proclamation issued following the coup guaranteed the establishment of (political) parties of all ideologies" and recognized "the right to unionize, in all labor sectors," attacks on unionists continued to take place almost from the outset. The report (1982, 135) included the documentation of security force and paramilitary attacks on demonstrations called by organizations pressing for reform: "A demonstration on October 19, 1979, left 30 civilians dead, all killed by government troops."

Shortly after the coup, television news condoned government brutality against peaceful demonstrators with these words:

> El Salvador's new government today made its first get tough reply to protesting
> leftists since the coup there two weeks ago…. Troops fired into a crowd of about

200 demonstrators in the capital, they wounded twenty two. (CBS, October 30, 1979)

Demonstrations were a frequent topic of news stories during this period and resulted in some of the most distorted and misleading news coverage. As demonstrators became the victims of army attacks, the resulting images of chaos had entertainment value. An exciting story of disruption could be told, complete with people running from sniper fire, in jerky, "documentary" camera-style, with corpses in the streets, pierced by the screams both of Red Cross ambulance sirens and of the wounded in the background.

THE JANUARY MARCH

On January 22, 1980, a mass march of unprecedented historic significance took place in San Salvador. The largest mass demonstration in the history of the country, it represented a broad coalition of popular organizations in a country whose majority population was unified against a repressive government. Armstrong and Shenk write:

> Thousands and yet again thousands of shabbily dressed Salvadorans surged toward the crossroads and…took their places behind the standard bearers of the different popular organizations. At 1:00 a.m., the demonstration stretched…twenty blocks from the crossroads and out to the nearest hill slopes on either side of the Avenida Guerrero. There were columns of state employees, organized slum dwellers, factory workers, electricians, teachers and, endlessly, the farmworkers and peasants who had slipped through the roadblocks to enter the capital before dawn. (1982, 134)

It took this mass of people a considerable amount of time to march to the center of the city. It is impossible for the television viewer to understand the significance of a mass opposition movement of this magnitude in a thirty-second television news report that focuses on the few seconds of gunfire. Hours of massive protest characterized by orderliness, discipline and diversity were reduced to these words:

> An anti-government march through San Salvador today by 50,000 leftists turned into a shooting match with unidentified snipers on rooftops. At least twenty persons were reported killed and twenty-seven wounded. (CBS, January 22, 1980)

Armstrong and Shenk (1982) blame the attack on the military, not "unidentified" gunmen. As the march moved toward the downtown square, shots rang out, "the thudding booms characteristic of the military's regulation G-3 machine gun, a combat weapon thoroughly inappropriate for routine urban police needs, yet carried by all security forces as well as the army" (135).

The army was creating not order but chaos out of what would otherwise have been a peaceful demonstration. Armstrong and Shenk (1982, 135) conclude their account of the day at the point at which the television drama would begin: "The first bodies slumped to the ground in front of the cathedral, and as the now terrified crowd broke ranks and scattered down the side streets and into nearby buildings."

> "Very wild" is how a Western diplomat describes the situation in San Salvador tonight. Government troops there surrounded an estimated 20,000 rebelling leftists…. (CBS Evening News, January 23, 1980)

If news reports had begun with the first part of the demonstration, the orderliness and vast numbers of participants, it would be impossible to blame the violence on the demonstrators. The two other network-news stories of the march were very much the same. NBC referred to the march as an "anti-government parade" and used more mystifying rhetoric for the violence, referring to those killed as "victims of the latest political slaughter in El Salvador." They also referred to the army attack as "unidentified gunmen on rooftops."

If the focal point of news coverage were shifted from violence to problems of political, social, economic and repressive realities, an entirely different set of solutions and outcomes responding to questions of social causality would necessarily come into play. Issues would emerge such as whether attempts were being made to resolve existing social inequities within the country, namely improvements in working and living conditions. Resolutions would consist of, for example, agreeing to fair wages and safe working conditions, allowing for better housing and nutrition, providing public services such as potable water, electric power and sanitation, just to list a very few. It would mean, in essence, pointing out the necessity for economic reform, which was the alleged objective for the October 15 coup. Above all, it would mean solving the problem of military abuses. Security forces would fall well within the realm of problems, instead of being looked to for solutions.

This restructuring and re-emphasis would help the viewer understand the real problems and social realities that exist within the country, and a different kind of narrative would emerge. Instead of looking to the military to maintain the status quo, the new problems presented would demand dramatic changes of the status quo.

Events that took place up to January 1980 changed the direction that El Salvador would take. The country began its descent into a full-blown civil war as the period of open political struggle came to an end. Unable to protect themselves against paramilitary violence and from army fire in the face of legal, peaceful actions, and unable to achieve social and economic justice in the political arena, many people left San Salvador and retreated to rural areas. Violence by the military and paramilitary security forces escalated, but it was harder to document in the countryside than it had been in the more open, urban context of San Salvador. The rebels took up arms and formed the FMLN, the Farabundo Marti National Liberation Front. The Carter administration sent more military aid to the army, now led by the hard-right-wing General Garcia, and failed to enter into diplomatic negotiations that could have resulted in real reform and a negotiated peace. Intensive diplomatic pressure from the United States might well have ended the war before it gained momentum, but at that point it could not be achieved without those who controlled the country agreeing to economic-military reform. This they were unwilling to do.

By the end of 1980, the brutality of the security forces was already well documented, yet the United States continued to fund the Salvadoran military. The war would personally confront U.S. Ambassador Robert White when he peered down into the shallow graves of four American churchwomen in December. Catholics who worked in poor and underserved neighborhoods in San Salvador were not exempt from right-wing death squads. The nuns had been kidnapped on the way back from the airport, returning to the poor communities they served. Raped and murdered, their bodies were thrown into hastily dug graves along the road.

They were not the first from the religious community to die. From the pulpit of his church in San Salvador, Archbishop Oscar Romero criticized the military for brutality and asked them to lay down their guns. He was killed shortly after, while giving a sermon in church in March 1980. An outspoken critic of right-wing violence, he argued:

> There is an institutionalized violence that provokes the anger of the people. It is a violence that comes from the right. They want to maintain their privileges through oppressive means. The oppressed, on the other hand, react to this violence and are labeled leftist. But as long as the violence from the right continues, then the right is to blame for this situation.[8]

Investigations of the army to find those responsible for the murders of the churchwomen were begun, but another U.S. president had just been elected. Ronald Reagan would pursue the military option in earnest, Carter having let slip the moment when war could have been prevented.

CONCLUSION

The real world, constituted through the movement of social forces and historical imperatives, is reduced to fragments, broken into bits and pieces. Fragmented glimpses, ripped out of context, are unintelligible—a baffling morass of "random violence"—then reconstituted into a familiar view, one that does make sense: the news story. Media images of chaos and instability in El Salvador confirmed the public's worst fears of disorder and instability in the Third World, and it was happening in our own backyard. This message was constructed through the use of a media frame applied equally to fictional stories, especially crime dramas. With the application of law and order, news and entertainment would mingle in ways that would increasingly blur fact from fiction, and entertainment from news, especially problematic for news from countries little known and understood.

The logical directions for a foreign policy based on law-and-order precepts are obvious: the continued bolstering of "moderate" governments and the use of military strategies to eliminate the "radical" opposition rather than diplomacy. This was achieved through constant increases in U.S. military aid to El Salvador.

The mystification of violence continued and reached levels of absurdity by the end of the Carter years. The incredible loss of human life at the hands of the death-squads and security forces was always "caused by extremists on both the left and the right." The moderate label affixed to the government held tight through numerous reshufflings, even in the face of executions and murders tied to the armed forces. And the belittling of the mass opposition movement allowed subsequent coverage to discount the importance of the internal political dynamic of the country. In this way a national movement born out of military repression and social injustice could be explained by the new president, Ronald Reagan, as an external contest between two superpowers—Democracy versus the Evil Empire. Because television is a system of internal references, the constellation of a fictional law and order genre has itself become, for the U.S. media, the history of El Salvador.

6

The Problem of
Seeing and Believing

Empathy, Denial and War's Human Costs

The end of the war in Vietnam marked the end of an era in which anticommunism could easily evoke public support for war. The American people had lived through a nightly war, brought into their homes on television screens, and experienced the war coming home to their streets. Flag-draped boxes of young draftees returned to Dover Air Force Base as college campuses erupted in protest. The war truly came home in 1970 when National Guardsmen killed four students on the campus of Kent State University in Ohio. The country was torn apart. The losses soured their taste for ridding the world of communism at any cost.

Yet Ronald Reagan would come to power in 1980 and within a matter of months begin to sell the public on a new Cold War. This time American troops would not be sent to a foreign country; others would do the fighting and dying. But this proxy war would result in another wave of human rights violations and another period of American infamy, buried and forgotten in America, but remembered certainly by its victims, and now understood globally as part of America's history. While many of those in power would prefer to forget, it continues to tarnish America's place in the world community, even though many Americans may not be aware of these events or appreciate their full significance.

THE WHITE PAPER

In March 1981, the new Reagan White House released a "White Paper," a document that would come to define the Reagan Doctrine and its strategy to reinvigorate a pre-Vietnam, Cold War atmosphere. The policy paper "drew the line" against communism in the Western Hemisphere. In Nicaragua, the Sandinistas had successfully taken power from the U.S.-backed Somoza dictatorship, and the White Paper claimed to include evidence that the Sandinistas were arming the rebels in El Salvador. It was "the funnel" through which communism was being spread into our hemisphere. Other countries would fall like dominos, and only force could stop the collapse of democratic governments one by one. The Reagan Doctrine called for escalating military support to the Salvadoran military, now headed by the hard-line General Jose Guillermo Garcia, who led the right-wing faction of the military and successfully consolidated his power after the 1979 coup. The architects of the Reagan Doctrine would assert that negotiations with the Sandinistas and the rebels in El Salvador were impossible, and only military solutions could be advanced. Thus was the Cold War reborn in the early 1980s as Reagan popularized his favorite term for the Soviet Union; a phrase borrowed from the movie *Star Wars*, the Evil Empire.

Television news reported the allegations contained in the White Paper almost verbatim. One ABC anchorman held before the cameras what he called a "phone-book" size report containing "evidence" of communist interference in Central America. Only later would it be acknowledged that the White Paper contained no evidence for such claims. Not one shipment of arms from Nicaragua to El Salvador was ever found. Major news media reported on the White Paper after reading only the executive summary; the complete documents were not released until after the initial news cycle. It was left to the alternative press and media critics to demonstrate the inaccuracies of news reporting and the lack of credible evidence in the White Paper.

Press coverage of the region increased exponentially as it became the geopolitical focus of Ronald Reagan's foreign policy. The agenda for what would be considered newsworthy emanated from Washington, and the policy debate about El Salvador shifted from an internal focus to concern about external communist meddling in "our" hemisphere. The axis of discussion was now framed around a simple choice between supporting the Salvadoran military and U.S. national security interests, or letting the country fall to communists. U.S. embassy personnel were replaced, and almost overnight this new language of national security dominated policy discussions and became the lens through which El Salvador was viewed.

Yet human rights remained the stumbling block for Reagan's new policies. So many people had already been killed, and human rights had been on the press agenda while Carter was in office. The accelerating abuses kept it there. The foreign press corps was well aware that the dead bodies carelessly thrown along the roadsides most mornings and left in front of their own hotels[1] were the work of the paramilitary death squads. Reagan replaced Carter's U.S. Ambassador, Robert White, with Dean Hinton, but the deaths of the nuns and the lay worker had affected White in a profound way. He understood the nature of the Salvadoran military and became a significant critic of increased military aid to the generals. Human rights organizations, church leaders, policy critics and solidarity groups all lined up against these new policies, which they understood would lead to increased brutality against civilians. This, combined with considerable opposition from lawmakers, led Congress to pass an amendment to the Foreign Assistance Act of 1961. The language required the president to certify that the Salvadoran government was "making a concerted and significant effort to comply with internationally recognized human rights." Congress wanted to see the military and "elements in its own armed forces" brought under control "so as to bring to an end the indiscriminate torture and murder of Salvadoran citizens by these forces." Certification would be required periodically as a condition of continued funding for the Salvadoran military. The continuous certification process would have the effect of keeping critical comments about Central American policy, mostly by congressional Democrats, an aspect of mainstream media coverage. It provided the press with an opening for publishing articles that included documentation of human rights abuses. But by the end of Reagan's first year in office, the humanitarian costs of this new Cold War would prove to be greater than almost anyone had imagined.

REQUEST FOR CONFIRMATION OF A MASSACRE

On December 15, 1981, Reverend William Wipfler, director of the human rights office of the National Council of Churches in New York, wrote a telegram to Ambassador Dean Hinton at the embassy in San Salvador asking him "for confirmation or otherwise" about "reliable reports" that indicate "that between December 10 and 13 joint military and security forces operation took place in Morazan Department which resulted in over 900 civilian deaths." Reverend Wipfler had received a call from Roberto Cuellar at Socorro Juridico, the human-rights organization of the Archbishopric of San Salvador, who heard from members and friends of the church who lived in the zone that the American-trained-and-outfitted Atlacatl Brigade had carried out a massacre at El Mozote and in the neighboring village of La Joya. Survivors of the army's "limpieza" of the rural hamlets, roughly translated as "cleaning," had notified Cuellar, and he told Wipfler that eyewitnesses had been to the site and that evidence of the killings remained intact.

GETTING THE STORY

By January 3, photojournalist Susan Meiselas and *New York Times* correspondent Raymond Bonner were peering through the darkness, trying to follow their guide down a rocky trail in the mountains of Morazan. They reached the bank of a small river, and in the moonlight, they took off their clothes, put them in their backpacks and held them above their heads to cross the cold rushing water and follow the trail beyond that led to El Mozote. "I was scared shitless," Bonner admitted.[2] Ray Bonner had had a standing request with the main rebel group, FMLN (Farabundo Marti National Liberation Front) to visit guerrilla-held territory. After many delays, they contacted him in late December and arranged this trip for early January. Bonner then called Meiselas, whose documentation of the region's conflict was already extensive.

Bonner and Meiselas hiked all night through the mountains and reached the rebels' camp at dawn, where scattered tents among the trees housed about thirty people. At daybreak on January 6, three days after leaving the Honduran border area on foot, the two Americans walked into what had been the town of El Mozote, almost a month after the massacre. There they saw bodies and parts of bodies, destroyed houses and total destruction. Meiselas remembers a group of fourteen bodies in a cornfield on the outskirts of the village, and she could "see on their faces the horrors of what had happened to them."[3]

Before leaving New York, Bonner had also called freelancer Alma Guillermoprieto, who was writing for the *Washington Post*. After frantic negotiations with her own FMLN contacts, she took the same journey through Morazan several days later. She recounts the journey as arduous, that her rebel guides were irritable and tense and that she was terrified. Her camera was ruined at the river crossing, and an accident had forced her to complete the journey with a swollen leg. Because of security reasons, none of the three journalists had known their exact locations during the trip. Guillermoprieto would later recall the traumatizing sensation as she walked through the nearby town of Arambala, with its pretty, white-washed adobe houses, where "whole families had been blown away—these recognizable human beings, in their little dresses, just lying there mummifying in the sun.[4] Forty-five minutes away she started to smell El Mozote. As she entered there, she would later write in the *Washington Post* (January 27, 1983), "The overwhelming initial impression was of the sickly sweet smell of decomposing bodies."

On January 27, 1982, the *New York Times* published Ray Bonner's report describing what he found in El Mozote and the surrounding area, and Alma Guillermoprieto's story appeared the same day in the *Washington Post* (in fact, in an earlier edition). Both papers carried the stories on the front page. Bonner's story begins, "From interviews with people who live in this small mountain village and surrounding hamlets, it is clear that a massacre of major proportions occurred here last month." He describes "the charred skulls and bones of dozens of bodies buried under burned out roofs, beams and shattered tiles." He interviewed the survivor, 38-year-old Rufina Amaya, whose husband was killed along with "her 9-year-old son and three daughters, ages 5 years, 3 years, and 8 months." (For years Rufina would continue to tell her eyewitness account, but only after the war ended and the site was exhumed would her story be considered credible.) Bonner's story continues: "Many of the peasants were shot in their homes, but the soldiers dragged others from their houses and the church and put them in lines, women in one and men in another." During this confusion Rufina had managed to escape. In El Mozote, Guillermoprieto was shown the ruin of the little church in the central square. "The smaller sacristy beside it also appeared to have had its adobe walls pushed in. Inside, the stench was overpowering, and countless bits of bones—skulls, rib cages, femurs, a spinal column—poked out of the rubble."

Both journalists included numerous testimonials from people in the surrounding area who had fled their villages to hide in the mountains, only to return to find their families killed, their houses destroyed and their animals slaughtered. Both journalistic accounts included statements of denial from the military.[5]

These stories represent independent investigative reporting at its best and are one of the most courageous examples of newsgathering in a war zone documenting one of the worst cases of twentieth-century war crimes in the New World. They included corroborating victim testimony, a stunning eyewitness account of what had happened from a survivor, on-site descriptive reporting from an undisturbed scene of mass murder by three correspondents working for different organizations, and two rolls of film shot by an experienced photojournalist. Yet these stories were discredited, the massacre denied and the sources attacked. The story of El Mozote would linger in a twilight of uncertainty for a decade.

The day after the stories appeared in the mainstream press, President Ronald Reagan signed and sent to Congress the certification that the Salvadoran government was gaining control of the military and that the human rights situation was improving. Throughout the certification process, which included congressional hearings, administration officials would deny the massacre by designing successful interpretive strategies for seemingly irrefutable evidence. The denial and the process by which the massacre was finally admitted offer lessons about how the horrors of war can be buried, even in plain sight. They also provide a blueprint for defining the tactics of news management and the consequences such strategies have on war reporting, humanitarian considerations and democratic practices in general.

Much of what we know about what embassy officials and the U.S. government knew at the time comes from documents released later to journalists and the National Security Archives, and from interviews with most of the principles done in the early 1990s by Mark Danner and documented in his fine book, *The Massacre at El Mozote*.

THE PROCESS OF DISCREDITING THE STORY

AS ENEMY PROPAGANDA: Before reports of the massacre were published in the U.S. press, news of El Mozote was first broadcast on Christmas Eve, 1981, over a portable transmitter by Radio Venceremos. From a ravine near the town of El Zapotal in the liberated zone of Jucuaran, the world was told of the "great killing." The report was delayed because the Atlacatl Battalion had accomplished one of its main objectives—to stop news from the liberated zones being broadcast by rebels across El Salvador. Determined to capture the broadcasting equipment, Lieutenant Colonel Domingo Monterroso, in charge of Operation Rescue, had bagged his main prize—the radio transmitter. It took time for the radio crew to locate and set up another one. In addition, as the army moved out and the guerrillas returned with civilians[6] who had hidden in the mountains, the horrors they described seemed unbelievable. Leaders of the rebel groups were incredulous. After all, most of the residents of the village were neutral evangelical Christians who accommodated the military and were not rebel supporters. The comandantes demanded a further accounting. It took days to assemble a record. They listed the corpses they could see and estimated the number of missing based on surviving friends and relatives. The leaders were finally "forced to believe that many hundreds had died, and they had apparently settled on the round number of a thousand" (Danner 1994, 87). The story of surviving the attack and returning to broadcast the horrors is also told by Jose Lopez Vigil (1994) in *Rebel Radio*. President Duarte went on Salvadoran television claiming that news of the massacre was propaganda designed to discredit his government. In the days that followed, a priest, Father Rogelio, made the journey to the rebel camp outside El Mozote. Lopez Vigil writes, "Who would have thought that the only station to broadcast a mass for the dead would be Venceremos" (80).

On January 8, 1982, Dean Hinton replied to Reverend Wipfler's request for information by saying the only information he had came from clandestine Radio Venceremos, which he did not consider "to be a reliable source." Much was made subsequently about the FMLN using the massacre as propaganda. Indeed, that assertion became the official White House position during congressional hearings. Then-assistant secretary of state for inter-American affairs, Elliott Abrams, told a Senate committee on February 8 that reports of the massacre were not credible and that "it appears to be an incident that is at least being significantly misused, at the very best, by the guerrillas."

The timing, also—with major news of a massacre coming just before certification hearings—must certainly confirm that the story was political propaganda. Why wasn't it broadcast earlier in December, if these events were true?

MILITARY STONEWALLING: Though at least ten American advisors were working in El Salvador with the Atlacatl Brigade during this time, they failed to make definitive information about the massacre a requirement for continued military aid. When told by Special Forces to come in and answer questions, Domingo Monterroso reportedly said, as he climbed into his helicopter, "If they want to talk to me I'll be out with my troops." And the attitude of General Garcia, now Minister of Defense,[7] was equally recalcitrant. When asked about the massacre by Dean Hinton, he dismissed the charges by calling it a "novela," a "pack of lies" and Marxist propaganda.

THE INVESTIGATION: Though the American embassy is charged with the considerable task of being the eyes and ears of Washington, the two investigators sent by Dean Hinton, Todd Greentree, the junior recording officer at the embassy, and Major John McKay, a marine from the defense attaché's office and a Vietnam veteran, did not visit the site of the massacre or conduct successful interviews with survivors. They flew in Alouette helicopters with Salvadoran army officers to Morazan and the camps outside

San Francisco Gotera that housed the refugees. Those they talked to were traumatized, too terrified to talk, as McKay would later admit to Mark Danner: "You had a bunch of very intimidated, scared people, and now the army presence further intimidated them" (1994, 107). They continued to travel by road to surrounding hamlets, and though no one would give them an exact account, after their trip Greentree was convinced "that there probably had been a massacre, that they had lined people up and shot them" (108). When they approached the turnoff to El Mozote—now less than an hour away and where they could have seen for themselves the crumbled sacristy, the charred buildings and the bodies—their army escorts, who served as their guides and protectors, refused to go on. Faced with having to travel alone through guerrilla-held territory,[8] they turned back toward the safety of San Salvador, and the investigation was over. "In the end, we went up there and we didn't want to find that anything horrible had happened," Colonel McKay later admitted to Mark Danner. "And the fact that we didn't get to the site turned out to be very detrimental to our reporting—the Salvadorans, you know, were not very good about cleaning up their shell casings" (124).

On January 31, 1982, the report of the official investigation was cabled to Washington. The linguistic strategies employed to report what they did not find ("it is not possible to prove or disprove excesses of violence against the civilian population of El Mozote by government troops") and to characterize what they did know ("Civilians did die during Operation Rescate but no evidence could be found to confirm that government forces systematically massacred civilians in the operation zone") resulted in the United States denying allegations of a massacre, when officials were well aware at the time that it had occurred. As Ambassador Hinton admitted in a confidential cable dated February 1, 1982, "evidence strongly suggests that something happened that should not have happened and that it is quite possible Salvadoran military did commit excesses."

DISPUTING THE NUMBERS: Though the Reagan administration said it accepted human rights as a goal, it contested the certification process by continually disputing details, most importantly, the numbers of dead. Confronted with the impossibility of precise documentation of casualties in a war zone, this remains an effective strategy. Greentree's January 31 report, cabled from the embassy, gave Washington the strategy it needed to deny the murders, as it contended that the number of civilians killed does not "even remotely approach numbers being cited in other reports circulating internationally." Before Congress, Elliott Abrams repeatedly contested the numbers, saying only three hundred people could have been in El Mozote at the time.[9]

DISCREDITING THE SOURCE—INDEPENDENT NEWS AS BIASED: Reagan officials were vocal about their displeasure with Raymond Bonner's reporting from El Salvador, and other mainstream news outlets joined the criticism, the harshest coming from the editorial page of the *Wall Street Journal* (February 10, 1982), charging Ray Bonner as "overly credulous." In particular it challenged his wording, claiming "it is clear" that a massacre had occurred was not good journalism. Asserting that the report of a massacre was a "propaganda exercise," the *Journal* mirrored the objections of the White House. It quoted Thomas O. Enders, assistant secretary of state for inter-American affairs, saying that there was no systematic killing of civilians, "and anyway" there were only three hundred people in the village "in which 926 people supposedly died." One *Times* reporter told Mark Danner that the *Journal*'s criticism of Bonner resonated with *New York Times* editor A. M. Rosenthal, who thought the reporter was "too willing to accept the Communist side of the story" (1994, 139).

SUCCESSFULLY INTIMIDATING THE PRESS: The controversy compelled *New York Times* editor A. M. Rosenthal to travel to San Salvador for an unusual meeting with Ambassador Hinton. According to one reporter on the *Times*, Hinton "became hysterical" about Bonner's critical reporting and flagrant disregard for the official news briefings (Bennett 2003, 154). Although Rosenthal denied being influenced by the embassy, he recalled Bonner from El Salvador and replaced him with a young reporter who had no experience or contacts in the region. Journalism historian W. Lance Bennett lists Raymond Bonner's expulsion from El Salvador as a significant case in the annals of press intimidation. "The successful attack on an organization as prestigious as the *New York Times* sent shock waves through the rest of the media" (2003, 154). If a paper as prestigious as the *Times* could be compelled to withdraw support for its own reporter, how could other journalists feel safe? Bonner's transfer left American reporters painfully aware of their increased vulnerability. As a *Newsweek* photographer complained, "When they pulled Bonner they hung the rest of us out to dry."[10] The messages to journalists stuffed in the mouths of corpses now seemed more threatening. Bonner's removal marked a significant loss in independent reporting and prevented more serious news investigations.

With a carrot-and-stick process described by Michael Massing (1983), the embassy warmed up to the press corps,[11] changing its strategy to one of cooperation with more frequent briefings which "were warm, witty, and filled with newsworthy quotes" (Bennett 2003, 154). The public relations approach adopted by the embassy, together with the intimidation that the Bonner episode bespoke, successfully prevented most journalistic attempts to cover the war outside the framework defined by the embassy.

THE POSITION—THE SECURITY ARGUMENT: During this period, American diplomats were urged to support a "grit your teeth" policy. A memo was sent in Secretary of State Alexander Haig's name requesting support for "a reformist junta, with a lot of bad eggs in it," or El Salvador would go the Cuban way (Danner 1994, 92). This simple dichotomy replaced more complicated formulations that could have led to a diplomatic option. Though "negotiation" was a dirty word under the Reagan administration,[12] it was ultimately diplomacy that brought the war to an end, but only after the death toll had reached staggering proportions.

THE FINAL OFFENSIVE

As the war went on, so did the killing. By the end of the decade, under a renewed and fierce attack by the FMLN, an offensive that brought the war back into the streets of the capital, the Salvadoran army realized it would not be able to win a military victory. In desperation, security forces responded in their usual way, with atrocities and terror against civilians. But this time they would go too far.

KILLING THE JESUITS

Once again soldiers of the Atlacatl Brigade would take action. Not able to win militarily, they would strike terror into the hearts of the "enemy." On November 16, 1989, dressed not in uniform but in all black with stocking caps, they crept through the lush gardens of the campus of the Central American University and into the bedrooms of the sleeping Jesuit priests. They would leave behind on the lawn outside the residence a scene of horrifying brutality. The bodies of six Jesuits, their cook and her daughter lie on the blood-soaked grass where they had been dragged and shot execution-style, but with so many bullets that little remained of their heads.

After a decade of violence, this event would be the beginning of the end of the civil war. Defending further military aid to El Salvador at a press conference in early 1990, President Bush was forced to respond to a woman from the audience who shouted, "The question is why are we killing priests in El Salvador?" This time, justifying more money for the generals would require an investigation. The U.S. Congress sent a team to El Salvador headed by Representative Joseph Moakley, a long-time congressman from Massachusetts. Initial press reports adhered to what had become, through years of repetition, the entrenched convention, and statements by then-U.S. Ambassador William Walker stated that it was not known who killed the priests, because "the history of atrocious death in El Salvador has come from extremes of both right and left." Yet on their first fact-finding trip, the congressman and his team quickly understood that the Salvadoran security forces had to be responsible for the murders. Top military personnel lived in the same neighborhood where the Jesuits were killed, and security forces had the area under constant surveillance. In the course of his investigation, and through his refusal to allow security forces to stonewall, Moakley and his task force discovered that the highest level of the Salvadoran military had been involved in the murders and had tried to cover up their actions.[13] Moakley reported the findings of the task force on the floor of the U.S. House of Representatives.

The United Nations helped broker a negotiated settlement that brought the war to an end in January 1992, after Salvadoran President Alfredo Christiani met with the comandantes of the FMLN. They signed a peace agreement called the Chapultepec Accords that ended the twelve-year civil war and provided for a *commission on the truth* that would investigate "serious acts of violence that have occurred since 1980 and whose impact on society urgently demands that the public should know the truth."[14] The army would be reduced by half and purged of known human rights violators, and the FMLN would disarm, while some of their members would join the police force. Most important, the Atlacatl Battalion and other "rapid-reaction" forces would be disbanded.

THE EXHUMATION AND THE TRUTH COMMISSION REPORT

The small convent that stood beside the church in the central square of El Mozote, the one that Alma Guillermoprieto referred to as the sacristy in the *Washington Post* a decade earlier, was exhumed in October and November 1992. Experienced forensic anthropologists, who first worked on finding and identifying the remains of those who disappeared under the Argentine dictatorship, began their careful exhumation. They separated the splintered beams of the burned building from the small bones and human fragments left of the children who had been gathered there and shot. In the laboratory, the skeletal remains of 143 bodies were identified, including 131 children under the age of 12, 5 adolescents and 7 adults. The experts noted in addition that the average age of the children was approximately 6.

Though only one of the sites where killings took place during the massacre, this location would offer exact and irrefutable evidence. At the same level where the children's remains were found were the empty shell casings of the Atlacatl Brigade, carelessly left behind and easy to discover—had authorities been interested. Ballistic analysts found 245 cartridge cases, of which 184 had discernable headstamps "identifying the ammunition as having been manufactured for the United States government at Lake City, Missouri." At least twenty-four people did the shooting with M-16 rifles, also manufactured in the United States. They stood inside and at the doors and windows, shooting in, and at least nine times in a downward angle, indicating that the victims were on the floor. The evidence offers "full proof that the victims were summarily executed, as the witnesses have testified," and confirms the allegations that they were the intentional victims of an extra-judicial mass murder.

The Truth Commission also summarized the pattern of conduct by the military and its U.S. advisors. Counterinsurgency warfare, as in Vietnam, was the most murderous on the civilian population. The Atlacatl, the Rapid Deployment Infantry Battalion, carried out the massacre and was the first unit of its kind to be specially trained under the supervision of U.S. military advisers in early 1981. El Mozote was only one village that took the brunt of this deliberate strategy of eliminating or terrifying the peasant population in areas where the guerrillas were active, the purpose being to deprive the guerrilla forces of this source of supplies and information and of the possibility of hiding or concealing themselves among the population.

Highly critical of the lack of prior investigation, the report states that the evidence shows "the collusion of senior commanders of the armed forces, for they show that the evidence of the unburied bodies was there for a long time for anyone who wanted to investigate the facts."[15] They rebuked the military for allowing the "deliberate, systematic and indiscriminate violence against the peasant population" that "went on for years." Indeed, had U.S. government officials such as Elliott Abrams, ordered a thorough investigating instead of facilitating a cover up, thousands of Salvadorans murdered during the 1980s might have been saved. As a consequence of the Iran/Contra hearings, Elliott Abrams would be convicted of lying to Congress, but in 1992 Abrams would be pardoned by George H.W. Bush as he left office. By 2001, George W. Bush would rehire Abrams as senior director for democracy, human rights and international operations at the National Security Council. Later he would be transferred to become the director of Middle Eastern affairs at the NSC.

In addition to confirming the massacre at El Mozote, the Truth Commission also confirmed what journalists knew all along, that the paramilitary death squads aligned with the Salvadoran military were responsible for 85 percent of the killings during the war.

Mark Danner published the definitive English language account of the incident at El Mozote in his 1994 book *The Massacre at El Mozote*. The work stands as a reckoning and tribute to the victims, told through the eyes of those who were killed, giving them a voice even long after their deaths. The story of El Mozote is also a testament to the failure of the American press to provide empathy and compassion when official policy failed to do so. What lessons does this episode teach about war and humanity?

THE QUESTION OF EMPATHY

Susan Meiselas took photographs at the massacre site in El Mozote, and those pictures, quite graphic in their presentation of the bodies of the victims, were published in the *New York Times Magazine* in February 1982. How could such stunning visual documentation of the horrors of a war being aided by American tax dollars be forgotten, pushed to the back of the public's awareness? Even now there is no easily evoked public memory about the massacre that took place in a small village in the mountains of El Salvador. Looking back at the visual record of this war might offer insights into that elusive quality of empathy and awareness, and the struggle to create meaning and memories of war through its reporting and documentation.

THE PHOTOGRAPHS

Many dedicated photojournalists took pictures of the civilian victims of the war in El Salvador, and those images were printed in the U.S. press and viewed by many throughout the 1980s. Photojournalists risked their lives to document the war, and some died in the process. They thought their work would make a difference. But what effect did the photographic record of such terrible—almost unthinkable—atrocities have?[16]

SEEING AND BELIEVING

Many war photographers consider themselves the eyes of the world's conscience. As expressed by photojournalist Murry Sills, "It's the only way to get the attention of those in political power to make them realize the horrors of war and make them work harder to prevent it" (1981, 30). In his book *Eyewitness* (1980), Harold Evans reasons that the power of the image stems from its credibility, and that "believability" moves the public with "its compelling authority in description, documentation and corroboration. We believe what we see; and only what we believe can become a public issue" (24). He goes on to assert that understanding certain historic events, particularly war, "can only be understood through photography" (91).

The idea of recording the truth of war's horror motivated photojournalists who covered the Central American conflict.[17] Margaret Bourke-White, an American photojournalist who recorded many events of World War II, was an influential proponent of what she viewed as the camera's unique abilities to present reality as essential truth:

> Sometimes I come away from what I am photographing sick at heart, with the faces of people in pain etched as sharply in my mind as on my negatives. But I go back because I feel it is my place to make such pictures. Utter truth is essential, and that is what stirs me when I look through the camera. (cited in Berger and Mohr 1982, 97)

Bourke-White's sentiments echo in the words of contemporary war photographers who capture the most disturbing pictures to bring home the "truth."

Pronouncements of the photograph's ability to convey accurate, truthful information about the physical world coincided with positivism and the quest for scientific progress that marked the late nineteenth century.[18] These assumptions underpin the use of the camera for news and documentary photography. It is said that photographs provide certainty, a type of knowledge that can otherwise be gained only through firsthand experience. These somewhat more sophisticated pronouncements are simply other ways of assigning truth to the old adages "the camera never lies" and "a picture is worth a thousand words." But is it?

PHOTOGRAPHS AND CONTEXT

What kind of knowledge or truth is contained within an image? The photograph is a powerful emotive, but it does not convey significance or help us to understand world events. It offers no explanation. We can feel shock or sorrow for those pictured as they lie dead, but the image cannot reveal what happened before or after their deaths, nor can it tell us who did the killing. It offers no political context, much less an analysis. Both John Berger and Susan Sontag have written eloquently about what we can know from photographs of horror and what range of emotional response is possible.[19] As time frozen, the photograph remains a moment yanked from the historical flow that produced it. The news photograph circulates through time and place, yet it is a moment frozen in temporal space. Time captured by the camera as a single image can then be placed into some other context: a news page, an art gallery, an antiwar pamphlet or an assassin's hand for identification purposes. This quality of the photograph enables it to be used to make a number of abstract points and convey a variety of meanings.

During the 1980s the helicopter became the icon of counterinsurgency war. The efficacy of its destructive power, forever immortalized in *Apocalypse Now*, still fascinates and terrifies at the same time. The image was used extensively in news, films, documentaries, newsletters and informational bulletins on Central America. It made the covers of both *Time* and *Newsweek*. A large, color close-up of a helicopter in flight looms over two pages of *Time* magazine (March 15, 1982, 20–21) as the headline proclaims, "We Can Move Anywhere." Within the mainstream news context the helicopter signifies the primary weapon, the pragmatic tool that is needed to maintain hemispheric dominance by the United States.[20] On the other hand, the same image of the helicopter gunship on the cover of an informational bulletin published by the American Friends Service Committee is used to illustrate quite a different political point. It was argued in the latter that the war was an unnecessary military response, substituting belligerent policies where political ones were needed. There is possibly no better example of the inability of the image to explain than the helicopter. A soldier aiming out of a helicopter gunship tells us what one small part of the conflict *looks like*. It is a convenient, one-way image that does not show the results of strafing by air, so it can be used as corroboration for different points of view. At the same time, it offers the illusion of understanding. We think we understand because we come to recognize the image. When we see the image, we know the subject is counterinsurgency war. But it is recognition without knowledge. In most cases the photograph is dependent upon a context if the viewer is to understand the "why" of any conflict.

IMAGES OF WAR'S HUMAN COSTS

In the early 1980s, in addition to the pictures of El Mozote published in the *Times*, numerous pictures in the U.S. press graphically detailed the human cost of the conflict in El Salvador. Photographs of corpses lying in the street, and even piles of corpses, were published, but articles and captions rarely included adequate explanations as to who had done the killing. As discussed in chapter 5, death-squad violence was consistently attributed to "extremists on both the left and the right." This frequently resulted in a type of reporting that made very little sense. For example, when leaders of the leftist group Revolutionary Democratic Front (Frente Democritico Revolucionario) were kidnapped from a press conference by plainclothesmen accompanied by soldiers in uniform, *Time* (December 8, 1980) began its article with: "The junta that took over El Salvador's government more than a year ago, ending the repressive reign of Dictator Carlos Humberto Romero, *has proved powerless against the wave of terror loosed by both the left and the right.*" In this way, responsibility for paramilitary terror was assigned equally to both sides.

The Unknown Killers?

As death-squad atrocities became harder to deny, news reporting of the human toll became more rhetorical and mystified. *Newsweek* (April 14, 1980) captioned images of the wounded as "bloody bedlam" breaking out of nowhere. Death was attributed to "political violence" and "senseless mayhem." Individuals were "victims of random violence" from "strife-torn El Salvador." A situation of baffling chaos was portrayed. Pictures published in *Time* and *Newsweek* show people dodging bullets and running in the streets, and civilians shooting handguns in city streets. Under one picture of corpses being carried away in a truck, the caption reads: "Carting away the corpses; 'Change is coming'" (*Newsweek*, April 14, 1980). In this story, change itself causes chaos and death, not the brutal atrocities of death squads and security forces. Change is presented as destructive and pathological, even if the vast majority of Salvadorans would benefit from a change to a more equitable economic and social order.

El Salvador as Other

In the face of unexplained political violence, the problems in El Salvador came to be understood as some inherent evil in the *country itself*. The people and country seemed prone to brutality and violence. As *Newsweek* (April 14, 1980) proclaimed, there is "Something Vile in This Land." The bold print on the cover of the *New York Times Magazine* of February 22, 1981, declared that El Salvador was "A Nation at War with Itself." The cover photo pictured armed soldiers on a flatbed truck standing over the bodies of civilians. The caption points away from the soldier's responsibility for the deaths and instead funnels the meaning toward the interpretation that El Salvador itself is rotten from the inside. Here we see the discourse of Otherness, as the country is excluded from a global community of civilized nations. Unexplained political violence indicts the culture itself and repeatedly confirms that *this is part of their culture, not ours*. Yet the problems in El Salvador were not contained within its own borders. U.S. military aid to El Salvador was paying for the weapons used against the people of El Salvador.

HOPELESSNESS

A particularly disturbing type of photograph came to characterize Salvadoran reality. News photographs featured in national magazines imaged piles of bodies, severed heads and gruesome cadavers. To a passive spectator looking at such pictures of dead and mutilated corpses, the impression is one of finality, even disgust. The act exists in the past by the time it reaches the eyes of the magazine reader. There is nothing to be done at present. Such images proclaim forcefully that *the worst has already happened.*[21] Dead, unidentified individuals will always remain anonymous. Viewers will never know these people. Such brutal images stand in contrast to a *Newsweek* cover of June 6, 1983, featuring a photograph of the first American advisor killed there. It is altogether different from the Salvadoran cadavers. The *Newsweek* cover photo of Lieutenant Commander Albert Schaufelberger III is very specific. His name is spelled out in full, and the photograph was taken when he was very much alive. As he stands at a dignified three-quarter pose in uniform, the aura of his humanity and individuality is still present. The bold print announces: *"Central America, The First Casualty."* To the U.S. press, all those pictures of corpses for three years before this one American's death were not considered with the same humanity as the American military casualty. This point is sadly confirmed by the photographic treatment.

THE LOSS OF MORAL ENGAGEMENT

The portrayal of human suffering without a rational explanation or cause has a particular effect on the viewer. It often leaves those asked to look upon the violence in a state of bewilderment, an emotional blank. Instead of being able to take action to alleviate the suffering, the viewer is frozen. Susan Sontag argued that the possibility of being "affected morally" by the photograph requires a relevant political consciousness. "Without a politics, photographs of the slaughter-bench of history will most likely be experienced as simply unreal or as a demoralizing emotional blow."[22] John Berger (1980) also points out that without a sociopolitical understanding, the viewer cannot act in a way that would prevent further suffering. Because the image accuses no one and everyone in the country, the sense of moral obligation that would lead to a commitment to act is not elicited. The assumed effects of concerned photojournalism are nullified. Instead, when we look at a photograph of agony without taking an action to stop it, we become complicit with the violence. As we lay the magazine down, the image has become a corruption, a distancing, an acceptance of the way things are. Each new photo layout positions the viewer now as a voyeur. The images offer only glimpses of the type of brutality considered taboo in a "civilized" country.

JUSTIFICATION

Feelings of disgust, confusion, and helplessness aroused in the viewer by the presentation of horrific images are unpleasant, but the news text usually offers the reader a way out. The roots of war may not be apparent in the photographs or in the text, but what is usually present is a discussion of U.S. interests in the region. Arguments include what would happen if the wrong people came to power and the overriding concern—to justify the slaughter—that the country would "fall" into the hands of the wrong people, though one could hardly imagine how things might have been worse. This was the logic of many photographic presentations. As soldiers stand over a corpse in a truck, the caption reads: "Another casualty: As civilians die, the rebels win converts." This is most disturbing, not for the sheer impact of the image, but because the caption admits that the army is responsible for the death of this civilian. But the reader is asked to focus on the political interests as defined by the U.S. government rather than to feel concern for the dead. In doing so, the viewer is drawn away from the responsibility of the consequences of U.S. military aid to a security force out of democratic control.

Within the media discourse, the deceased or living lose their humanity and become pawns of the great game of strategy of U.S. interests, in whatever way those interests are articulated at the time. "Innocent victims caught in the crossfire" becomes an unfortunate but "necessary consequence" of fighting for abstract principles such as "hemispheric security." Another picture of a pile of human bodies from El Salvador carries the caption "Carnage in San Salvador's Square: Is Cuba Playing Out a Grand Design to Spread Marxist Revolution?" (Newsweek, April 14, 1980, 38). Again "U.S. interests" and the fear of "communism" have been used to minimize the impact of real people dying. Indeed, the horror prevents people from further inquiry that might lead them to question the need for war and their own assessment of their government's policies.

DANGEROUS REBELS

Rebels who fight the army look straight back at the viewer; stern and un-smiling, they *confront* the viewer. In almost every picture in the national press, rebels were shown holding up rifles. The rifle is not down to one side, or back over the shoulder, but purposely held in front of the body, coming between the guerrilla and the viewer. Adding the rifle to the fron-tal stare adds to the aggressiveness of the subject, who can then best be described as *threatening*.[23] In one particular shot, flames can be seen in the background coming from a car that the guerrilla has just set on fire. The image presents a complete picture of armed lawlessness (*Time*, February 15, 1982, 24; see also *Newsweek*, March 1, 1982, 22).

PEACEFUL SOLDIERS

The headline "To Save El Salvador" published in *Time* (February 15, 1982, 22) included a photograph of Salvadoran soldiers. The soldiers are sitting down, and their rifles are off to the side. They wear short sleeves. They do not look straight into the camera but gaze off to the side in a three-quar-ter pose that looks past the viewer, past the present and into the future. As Sontag (1977, 116) remarks, the three-quarter gaze "soars rather than confronts, suggesting instead of the relation to the viewer, to the present, the more ennobling abstract relation to the future." They appear *unthreat-ening*, indeed thoughtful. Sitting high atop a hill, they are the hope, the future of El Salvador.

ALTERNATIVE IMAGES

Alternative magazines and newsletters, books by photojournalists and photography exhibitions contain a vast catalogue of images, few of which resemble those published in the mainstream press.[24] During the civil war, areas outside of the control of the army show children and adults engaged in different activities: fishing, learning and caring for the sick. Though undoubtedly part of the story, none of these images was common to any of the mainstream publications.[25] The lack of visual balance in the main-stream press is particularly interesting, since media critics argued that war coverage improved with the Salvadoran conflict because the press covered the insurgent forces. Yet the alternative social practices encouraged in the liberated zones in El Salvador were all but ignored in the media. Just as we will see, this was the case in Nicaragua.

The Quality of Empathy

Consider one alternative image of death that does evoke empathy. A woman is shown kneeling over the body of a boy. She is crying. We see loss, grief and sorrow through her eyes, and the death is human, not the abstract lens of political strategies. We are beseeched by the living. The picture evokes compassion as the viewer sees the death through a human sensibility.[26] There is nothing that beautifies this image, yet it is not a scene of utter hopelessness and horror like severed heads and body piles.

Conclusion

The presentations of death, violence and the brutal images that visually characterize war have not always called forth its end. Instead, both the fluid nature of photographic meaning and the selection of images and their context allow pictures to be used to confirm policies that many times have created the human toll themselves. Looking at such pictures with detachment and justification robs the viewing public of its humanity. Another piece of compassion is lost with the acceptance of war's brutality and the willingness to believe even questionable polices as justification for the deaths of civilians. Without the presence of a humanitarian perspective, military conflict and war can always be prosecuted in the place of political diplomacy and policies that would lead to global cooperation.

We see but we don't believe. Or, put more accurately, we see but we can be convinced not to believe. And in the worst case for the possibility of any future humanitarianism, we see, but we do not (or cannot) care, because we accept the currently articulated justifications.

7

The Office of Public Diplomacy

Creating Fear and Favor

The military program carried out in El Salvador, which led to a "grit your teeth" policy on atrocities, was part of the Reagan Doctrine's vision for Central America as a whole, and included attempts to overthrow—through clandestine means—the Sandinista government that held power in Nicaragua. Through the lens of the revived Cold War, Nicaragua was charged with being a Cuban satellite, and both were pawns of the Soviet Union. The American media's emphasis on the present, with so little attention paid to history and context, certainly facilitated official claims of an "external threat." This explanation for policy would have sounded far less plausible if it were widely known that the ideology of Sandinismo was based firmly on the figure of Sandino, a legendary Nicaraguan figure who fought for independence in the 1930s. The Sandinistas had fought an internal struggle against the Somoza dictatorship and won, and that regime had been supported for generations by the United States. Now the new government was under attack by a counterrevolutionary, or contra, army made up former national guardsmen, the most brutal of Somoza's security forces.

THE CONTRA WAR

Basing their operation in Costa Rica and Honduras, the U.S. administration set up the contras in December 1981. What started as a secret war with fighters organized by the CIA became an illegal one a year later, after an act of Congress prohibited further military aid to the contras. In the face of controversy and congressional opposition, the policy of clandestine war was also unpopular with the American public, and the way the White House chose to respond to unfavorable public opinion would have severe consequences for American democratic institutions. To carry out the Reagan Doctrine, information management became key. A battle of words shaped public discourse as the White House struggled to bring American public opinion into line with its policies. Like the contra war, the information war would also be a battle that made use of clandestine and illegal means.

The composition of the contra army would pose a huge public relations problem and required a Herculean effort at image management. The CIA created the contra fighters out of a group of former national guardsmen loyal to ousted dictator Anastasio Somoza. By establishing the contras as a proxy force to overthrow the Sandinistas, the administration hoped to overcome the public's objection to direct U.S. intervention. That seemed to solve the problem of American casualties, an outcome the administration feared most. But it created another, formidable difficulty. The conduct of the contras was creating an "image problem" for the Reagan administration. From the start, the contra war as a war of terror. As former contra leader, Edgar Chamorro (1987), would later explain, "During my four years as a contra director, it was premeditated policy to terrorize civilian noncombatants to prevent them from cooperating with the Government. Hundreds of civilian murders, tortures and rapes were committed in pursuit of this policy, of which the 'contra' leaders and their CIA superiors were well aware." *Washington Post* correspondent Christopher Dickey (1985) wrote a compelling account entitled *With the Contras* that offers a description of their ideology and tactics. Dickey also points out that the CIA was well aware of the contras' reputation for cruelty, and that the former guardsmen had been charged with human rights abuses and atrocities. From the start, the contras demonstrated to their U.S. supporters in the CIA that they were not about to change. The war of terror against the civilian population was especially targeted toward medical personnel who worked at rural clinics.

Another obstacle to the designers of military intervention came when the press revealed the secret role being played by the CIA in organizing the contra army. The timing could not have been worse, coming as it did during certification hearings on El Salvador, as White House officials struggled to justify their policies in the midst of reports of a massacre. These public struggles over policy led Congress to pass the first Boland

Amendment in December 1982, denying military support for the contras based on their human rights record. That forced the Reagan White House to find other, more creative funding streams. The Central American RIG (Restricted Interagency Group) would make newspaper headlines in the summer of 1987 during the Iran/Contra Scandal when its connection to former General Richard Secord's "Enterprise" was exposed. Under the direction of the RIG—made up of Oliver North, Elliott Abrams and CIA Central American Task Force Director Alan Fiers—Secord's Enterprise illegally funneled arms to the contras.

But the year was 1982, and Reagan pressed on with his doctrinaire policies.

OPINION POLLS

The president's passionate rhetoric against Nicaragua, Cuba and the Soviet Union achieved a significant amount of cultural currency but fell short of its goal to reunite the public in favor of military intervention. As policy analyst Peter Kornbluh (1987, 188) noted:

> The electorate remained unconvinced by the Reagan/Bush incantation of the "Communist Threat." Fifty-five percent believed that becoming entangled in Central America was a "greater danger" to the United States than the spread of communism there.

Opinion polls reflected a consistent pattern of public opposition to war in El Salvador, and the public continued to register its disapproval to the contra war sometimes by a margin of two to one, sometimes by a margin of three to one. According to Kornbluh (1987, 188):

> In March 1982, just after the media had exposed CIA support for the contras, an ABC/*Washington Post* survey found that by a margin of three to one (66 to 22 percent) the American public felt there "were no circumstances" in which "the United States should secretly get involved in overthrowing a Latin American government." Fourteen months later, when the same pollster asked whether the U.S. should "secretly try to overthrow the government of Nicaragua" that margin had expanded to six to one (78 to 13 percent).[1]

The public's disagreement with Reagan's military policy in Central America presented the executive branch with the formidable task of reestablishing public consensus among an increasingly skeptical public. How could the American public be convinced to support the Reagan Doctrine?

THE PUBLIC RELATIONS CAMPAIGN

Reagan's unpopular Central American policies presented a major challenge to his newly assembled public relations team. The task of opinion management went to a group of men who, according to Mark Hertsgaard (1988), formed the best public relations team to inhabit the White House to that point. The president and his men established an extensive, well-organized and well-funded public diplomacy apparatus.

THE OFFICE OF PUBLIC DIPLOMACY

In the spring of 1983, the Office of Public Diplomacy for Latin America and the Caribbean (S/LPD) was set in motion. This domestic propaganda bureaucracy was made possible by a National Security Decision Directive, number 77, signed by the president in January of that year. The base of operations for the group was the National Security Council, which had successfully wrested control away from the State Department (Committee on Foreign Affairs 1988, 18). It included personnel from the CIA, DOD, USIA and State Department, and NSC staff including Oliver North. CIA director William Casey brought company operatives into this public diplomacy effort. One of them, Walter Raymond, Jr., a long-time veteran of overseas propaganda work, headed up what came to be called the Thursday morning planning group.[2] Cuban exile and former USAID administrator, Otto J. Reich, headed the Office of Public Diplomacy. The seemingly benign term "public diplomacy" was a euphemism, as one public diplomacy official would later admit to the *Miami Herald*: "The Office of Public Diplomacy was carrying out a huge psychological operation, the kind the military conduct to influence the population in denied or enemy territory" (*Miami Herald*, July 19, 1987).

CLASSIC PROPAGANDA STRATEGIES

The use of public diplomacy to sell the Reagan Doctrine mirrored many of the propaganda strategies first initiated by the Creel Commission during World War I and was reminiscent of the Four-Minute Men who demonized the Hun. In its first year alone, OPD booked more than 1,500 speaking engagements, including radio, television and editorial board interviews; published three booklets on Nicaragua; and distributed materials to 1,600 college libraries, 520 political science faculties, 122 editorial writers and 107 religious organizations. Special attention was given to prominent journalists (Parry and Kornbluh 1988, 17).

Marshalling elite opinion makers in much the same way that Sir Gilbert Parker was enlisted during World War I, Reagan's Office of Public Diplomacy used private groups, individuals and think tanks for disseminating their message. The OPD hired outside consultants and gave encouragement, support and direction to groups of private citizens outside the government. In addition to raising money for contra weapons, these groups lobbied Congress, ran sophisticated media campaigns in targeted congressional districts and worked with the OPD to influence American public opinion through the U.S. media (Committee on Foreign Affairs, 1988). In this regard, the OPD used classic clandestine propaganda tactics, presenting articles, research, ideas and individuals as independent sources, concealing their government sponsorship. The twofold purpose of these methods was to shield the illegal government involvement and to enhance their credibility with the public, the media and Congress by presenting themselves as "neutral."

New Marketing Strategies

In attempting to engineer consensus around the unpopular war in Central America, the White House set in motion the media and marketing techniques developed over the last twenty years in the American culture industry. In an NSC memo dated January 25, 1983, Walter Raymond expressed the need to develop a "new art form" (Parry and Kornbluh 1988, 9). The new art form was the application of marketing principles so successful in persuading consumers. Why couldn't they be applied to ideas, and thereby persuade Americans to change their minds? Casey is said to have long admired the advertising industry, and documents reveal that he hosted meetings with marketing executives at the White House. There was talk of "selling the product of Central America" (*Newsweek*, October 12, 1987, p. 36).

Finding the Hot Buttons

The first phase of sophisticated marketing always involves polling. Under the public diplomacy umbrella, the Reagan administration had begun to employ computer models and attitudinal surveys to shape foreign policy messages. The pollster Richard Wirthlin, who had worked on Governor Reagan's presidential campaign, was now invited to apply campaign techniques to promoting government foreign policy. Wirthlin continued ceaselessly to poll the American public, tapping into the vital signs of the body politic.[3] Though the approximately twenty thousand polls a year were kept secret from the public, Wirthlin shared his findings with the president "approximately every three weeks, and within a few months of [Donald] Regan's arrival [at the White House] he was consulting with either Regan or his staff almost daily" (Mayer and McManus 1988, 43).

Policy justifications responded to the findings of opinion surveys, and speeches and official statements uniformly repeated the themes derived from polling data. These procedures were laid out in a March 1985 memo[4] from Oliver North to Robert McFarlane revealing that the strategic use of opinion polls was central to their program:

> March 1–8,1985: Conduct public opinion poll of America [sic] attitudes toward Sandinistas, freedom fighters.

> March 16–22,1985: Results due on public opinion survey to see what turns Americans against Sandinistas.

> Review and restate themes based on results of public opinion poll.

DESIGNING THE MESSAGE

Opinion surveys on Central America asked open-ended attitudinal questions such as "What turns the American public against the Sandinistas?" One of these probes, conducted in 1983, turned up a deep-seated domestic fear that was to become the foundation for one of the main themes the Reagan administration would develop. The White House found that Americans were afraid of an influx of Latin American refugees along the U.S.-Mexican border. This "hot-button" fear was quickly incorporated into a foreign policy narrative. In a June 1983 speech, President Reagan warned that unless a tough stand were taken against communism in Nicaragua, "a 'tidal wave' of 'feetpeople' would be 'swarming into our country.'" Reagan argued that only by crushing leftist movements could such a "flood be stopped" (Parry and Kornbluh 1988, 7).

This theme resonated with one particular quasi-private group connected to the OPD, the Gulf & Caribbean Foundation. Together with the Texas business community, they helped promote the theme of illegal immigration. The G&C was founded by a former Republican congressman from Tennessee, Daniel Kuykendall, working with contra fundraiser Carl (Spitz) Channell. It was listed on the flow chart found by Iran/Contra investigators in Oliver North's safe (Cockburn 1987, 350). Though this foundation did not have letterhead or a mailing address, it produced pamphlets and raised money for the contras. Promoting fears that hordes of Central Americans would come through Mexico and across the Rio Grande resonated in the region and was an effective "selling" strategy.[5] Themes, language and ominous references from rhetorical techniques from the past made a toxic mix. If the Sandinistas were not stopped in Managua, the red tide of revolution would roll north, spilling illegal feetpeople into Texas.

The New Cold War

What were the strategies set in motion by 1980s public diplomacy? President Reagan was called "The Great Communicator," a term that usually referred to his effective use of television, a medium employed on many occasions to get his message across. Few who saw it could forget the televised speech of March 16, 1986, in which a map of Central America was transformed visually, each country consecutively turning red under the malignancy of the communist threat emanating from Managua. This graphic technique was borrowed directly from early Cold War propaganda films from the 1950s, wherein the map depicted an Eastern European "red menace." But there was more to the public relations strategies of the White House than simply recycled Cold War rhetoric.

A memo from North to McFarlane entitled "Timing and the Nicaraguan Resistance Vote" also listed Mr. Kuykendall as a private supporter helping efforts aimed "at securing Congressional approval for renewed support of the Nicaraguan Resistance Forces" (NSC Intelligence Document 1985). Kuykendall's Gulf & Caribbean Foundation also provided what members of Congress believed to be an independent analysis of Central America and the Sandinistas. For example, the office of then-Speaker of the House, Thomas P. O'Neill, a contra opponent, unsuspectingly "sought the advice of an academic whose critical report on Nicaragua had been sponsored by the Gulf & Caribbean Foundation" (Parry and Kornbluh 1988, 7).

THE APPEARANCE OF INTELLECTUAL OBJECTIVITY

Academics and intellectuals often wield discursive power in the public sphere because journalists perceive them as detached, disinterested and apolitical. As we have seen since World War I, intellectuals have played a key role in justifying war. Under the Reagan administration, academics were often used, promoting a political agenda disguised as legitimate research and documentation. A case in point is Robert Leiken. As a writer with ties to academic institutions, Leiken claimed intellectual disinterest, but a declassified memorandum from Walter Raymond to then-National Security Advisor Robert McFarlane in January 1985 reveled his connection to the OPD (*The Nation*, May 7, 1988, 628). Raymond wrote that Leiken had approached him and "wanted to help sell the contras." Raymond knew he would be particularly useful in lobbying Democratic congressmen: "He believes we have a pretty good chance of winning the contras' fight on the hill if we play our cards right." Leiken's suggestions were to

> [b]uild a positive image of the F.D.N. [Nicaraguan Democratic Force]. To do this we should send down one or more key journalists to start developing major positive stories for the U.S. He thought [Southern Illinois University professor] Richard Millett might be willing. (*The Nation*, May 7, 1988, 628)

While helping plan contra public diplomacy, Leiken presented himself to international journalists as a nonpartisan intellectual. Six months after Raymond wrote the memo, Leiken was the keynote speaker at an Annual Briefing Session for Professional Journalists held at the Center for U.S./Mexican Studies at the University of California, San Diego. He opened his remarks by establishing his intellectual independence and claiming that each side (left and right) tries to use his academic "research" to their own ends.[6]

INTEREST GROUPS AND MARKETING SEGMENTATION

Other strategies were used to lobby Congress by bringing pressure to bear on certain constituencies. The memo written by Oliver North, "Timing and the Nicaraguan Resistance Votes," laid out the "public diplomacy" plan of action to take place from the first of March to the end of April 1985, when Congress was to vote on military aid to the contras. The following example reveals the use of market segmentation and the way in which the OPD disseminated information without acknowledging its role:

> Supervise preparation and assignment of articles directed to special interest groups at the rate of one per week beginning March 18 (example: article on Nicaragua educational system for NEA [apparently the National Education Association]).

THE OUTREACH PROGRAM

Edgar Chamorro explained how the CIA targeted certain sectors of the population with false information specifically designed to "win them over to the contra cause."[7] Chamorro was told that the Jewish community was an important voting constituency in the United States, so he supplied the names of two Jewish businessmen who had been living in Miami. The men left Nicaragua because of their association with the dictator Somoza. They were invited to attend a three-day White House "Outreach Program" organized to provide the media and Congress with "evidence" of Sandinista abuses. Even though they had not been recent victims of anti-Semitism, they claimed that persecution and anti-Semitism were repressive features of the Sandinista regime. In fact, the CIA had earlier advised the contras to claim that there was anti-Semitism, without any proof, for the effect it could have in the United States (Chamorro 1987, 47). Native Americans were also included in the three-day program, introduced to Miskito Indians.[8]

CONTRAS VS. SANDINISTAS

Much of the public diplomacy effort focused on this issue, and over time, the Reagan administration was largely successful in transforming the political debate. Alleged Sandinista abuses dominated media discourse, making it virtually impossible to criticize the contras without "balancing" such charges with Sandinista "atrocities." For example, a major strategy of the OPD was to censor and discredit critics of Reagan's Central American policy, particularly those who documented human rights abuses of the contras. Otto Reich reported to Walter Raymond in March 1986 that his office generally did not give the critics of the policy any quarter in the debate (Committee on Foreign Affairs 1988, 20). The clearly defined goal of public diplomacy was, in Raymond's words, to pin black hats on the Sandinistas and white hats on the contras. Determined to create headlines and images that were pro-contra and anti-Sandinista, they embarked on a campaign to make the Sandinistas brutal dictators and the contras the "moral equivalent of the Founding Fathers." Those who did not agree with the administration became targets of McCarthyesque charges of being soft on communism. Congressional opponents who voted against contra aid were labeled unpatriotic and un-American. Charges leveled against the Sandinistas gained credibility in the media, as they were increasingly uncontested. Pinning black hats on the Sandinistas with claims of a communist conspiracy diverted criticism away from the U.S.-backed counterinsurgency war and contra human rights abuses.

The effects such strategies had are best exemplified by a *Christian Science Monitor* news analysis citing an Americas Watch human rights report. Responding to questions raised in the debate surrounding the contra aid bill, Charlotte Sailowski wrote on March 19, 1986:

QUESTION: Do the contras commit atrocities?
ANSWER: Reports by human rights organizations, including Americas Watch, show that both the Sandinistas and the contras engage in violence and brutality against the Nicaraguan people.

Juan Mendez, head of the Nicaraguan mission for Americas Watch, asserted at the time that the *Monitor* article "is a bad misreading of the report," which reveals the abuses of the contras to be much more serious than those of the Sandinistas.[9] To compare them is like trying to compare apples and oranges, but he added, "we would like researchers to understand through facts.... Anyone with an intelligent mind can compare what we say about Nicaragua with Turkey or Guatemala and make their own judgments."

Divisions within the Catholic Church in Nicaragua were also exploited. A Catholic intellectual, Humberto Belli, "had his quarrels with the Sandinistas" and was funded by the CIA to write a book entitled *Nicaragua: Christians Under Fire*. With CIA financing, Belli founded the Puebla Institute and went on to produce "neither thorough nor accurate reports on Nicaraguan government human rights abuses. These reports were used to counter independent documentation of contra atrocities" (Chamorro 1987, 51). Articles appeared in the press supporting the Reagan characterization of Nicaragua as a totalitarian dungeon. Nina Shea, director of the Puebla Institute's Washington, DC, office, used this "information" for articles placed in the *New Republic* ("Human Rights in Nicaragua: The Sandinista Way of Repression," September 1, 1986) and the *Wall Street Journal* ("Systematic Destruction of Faith in Nicaragua," May 22, 1987). Another contra supporter named Tom Dowling, dressed in the garb of a Roman Catholic priest, testified before the House Foreign Affairs Subcommittee on Western Hemisphere Affairs in April 1985 and denounced the Sandinistas for religious persecution:

> Committee members did not discover until later that Dowling...was not an ordained Roman Catholic priest, but belonged instead to an unrecognized sect called the Old Catholic Church. (Parry and Kornbluh 1988, 15)

A staff report issued by the House Foreign Affairs Committee lists Dowling as a recipient of monies distributed "at [Oliver] North's request to other persons and entities engaged in activities relating to the contras" (Committee on Foreign Affairs 1988, 26).

MEDIA CREDIBILITY

The media responded to the congressional investigation into domestic propaganda either by ignoring or downplaying the revelations. After five years of covert domestic propaganda, the Government Accounting Office Legal Opinion stated that the OPD had engaged in illegal covert propaganda activities to influence the media but received little press coverage (Comptroller General of the United States, 1987). Yet the report detailed a number of documented cases of media manipulation. Clearly of front-page news value, the *New York Times* story (October 4, 1987) appeared on page 3 with the headline "State Department Linked to Contra Publicity." In an atmosphere where "publicity" carries little negative connotation, the headline downplays the significance of the issue.

The most damaging piece of evidence provided by the GAO report was a confidential memo written to then-Director of Communications at the White House Patrick J. Buchanan by OPD staffer Jonathan Miller (1985). The memo boasts of the success at media manipulation, referring to the operation as "White Propaganda." It offers "Five illustrative examples," one being the manipulation of television news:

> In case you missed last night's NBC News with Tom Brokaw...the Fred Francis story on the "Contras"...was prepared by Francis after he consulted two of our contractors.... It was a positive piece.

Miller goes on to explain in the memo that NBC's Pentagon correspondent, Fred Francis, had gone with the "OPD contractors" on a "clandestine trip" to the "Freedom Fighter camp" along the Honduras border. According to Miller, the purpose of the trip was for "many selected journalists" to get a "true flavor" of what the "freedom fighters" were doing—"not killing babies."

What should be treated as a startling revelation with major significance for network newsgathering practices is instead discounted in the *Times* by the following two sentences: "Mr. Francis said he made the trip with several other United States journalists. 'I don't feel like I was ever duped,' he said, calling the public policy [sic] office 'ineffective.'" No follow-up description or attempt to evaluate the content or truthfulness of the story was offered by the *Times*. However, the network's description of the Francis story reveals much about OPD's effectiveness:

> John Singlaub inspects contra platoon. Addressing contras, Singlaub says he represents thousands of Americans sympathetic to their cause that want to help.... Contra military leader Enrique Bermudez points to map. In an interview he says rebels have been supplied with food, information, and medical aid, by the civilian population. Rebels play baseball as armed comrades look on.

The story included all the information objectives important to the political agenda of the White House. The contras play baseball and are reportedly helped by civilians, the very people who, documentation shows, were repeated victims of abuses by the contras. John Singlaub, a colleague of General Secord, was an important operative in illegally supplying the contras with weapons in spite of congressional restrictions, yet the story emphasizes humanitarian aid. Singlaub was featured prominently in the Iran/Contra hearings, yet these connections are not part of the *Times* story.

The *Times* piece follows with the most disingenuous claim, "There was no explicit evidence that the *Times* or the *Post* had published articles resulting from the operation." But by then it had been well documented that Robert Leiken had been the pen behind the Op-Ed pieces signed by Arturo Cruz in the papers of record by Otto Reich.[10]

Publicity or Propaganda?

It is interesting to compare such denials by the press of their own manipulation of the actual news reporting in question. A content analysis of press coverage in the first months of 1986 reveals the effectiveness of public diplomacy. The most important dimension of evaluation, the actual language used to describe Nicaragua, the Sandinistas and the contras was severely circumscribed in the *Christian Science Monitor* and the *New York Times*:

> ...with respect to both Nicaragua and the Sandinistas, scarcely a positive descriptor can be found. Moreover, although the Contras could hardly be described as the "darlings" of the press, they were in fact portrayed in language that was positive twice as often as negative. The war of actual words, the raw material that shape meaning, was clearly won by the supporters of Contra aid. (Soderlund et al. 1988, 7)[11]

The *New York Times* coverage followed the administration's lead, often reporting on key claims such as the repressive policies of the Nicaraguan government. In a count of items defined as major issues tied to the aid vote, Nicaraguan repression appeared 15 percent of the time. This can be compared to contra atrocities included significantly less—8 percent of the time. Nicaraguan subversion and Cuban expansion were discussed 22 percent and 15 percent of the time, respectively, while the problematic issues of contra leadership and military capabilities were placed on the agenda 7 percent and 9 percent respectively.

Reagan's framing of the Sandinistas as repressive communists achieved consensus in the U.S. media. This finding is borne out in Noam Chomsky's (1987, 27) examination of editorials during the same period. He found that in the *Times*:

The debate included...nothing that could be construed as sympathetic to the Sandinistas. It is particularly impressive that the two most striking features of their rule were almost entirely ignored: the fact that in sharp contrast to U.S. clients (Nicaragua under Somoza, Duarte in El Salvador, etc.), the government has not engaged in mass slaughter and torture (unmentioned), and the constructive social programs....

Chomsky was disturbed by the highly controlled nature of news reports. Even though no one was featured in mainstream debates supporting the Sandinistas, would-be supporters are anonymously vilified to circumscribe the possibility of response: "In this practice, we see clearly exhibited some essential features of the totalitarian mentality" (Chomsky 1987, 29).

Confirming this estimation after the Iran/Contra scandal, the General Accounting Office (the investigative wing of Congress) released a Legal Opinion stating that the "prohibited, covert" activities of the OPD "constituted propaganda within the common understanding of that term" (Comptroller General of the United States, 1987). The Comptroller General, a Republican appointee, also concluded that the OPD's efforts were "beyond the range of acceptable agency public information activities." Exposing the American public to the same types of propaganda usually reserved for foreign populations was of course illegal.[12] One of the best measures of the administration's propaganda success was demonstrated, ironically, by its critics. The report issued by Congress after its investigation into the Iran/Contra affair (Committee on Foreign Affairs, 1988) refers to the contras as the "democratic resistance in Nicaragua." But there was nothing democratic about the contras, and they bore little resemblance to President Reagan's "founding fathers" designation for them. Their former leader (Chamorro, 1987) wrote, "It is a gross fabrication to claim that the contras are composed of democratic groups." He went on to say "This is how murder and torture were justified, how the destruction of property and the sabotage of the economy and the social fabric of a nation were excused, all in the name of patriotism and anticommunism" (59). Nor was there anything democratic about they way the contras were supplied and trained in secret, even as the American people and their congressional representatives opposed it.

In 1986, the International Court of Justice, part of the World Court in The Hague, found the United States guilty of terrorism, and ordered it to desist from its hostile activities. Not surprisingly, the Reagan administration disregarded international law and continued to support the contras, and the illegal attack on the nation of Nicaragua.

In 2005, a *New York Times* (April 5) story on Nicaragua repeated 1980s inaccuracies as history itself. Ginger Thompson refers to the U.S. covert attempts to overthrow the Nicaraguan government as part of the "global struggle against communism," though under the Sandinistas, Nicaragua had a mixed economy, multiple political parties and a highly critical opposition press. Thompson claimed "the armies fought each other to a standstill, until both sides agreed to elections in 1990." In fact, the contras never fought the Sandinista army; theirs was a war of terror against civilians. Thompson implies that contra pressure resulted in elections, but the country's constitution called for elections every six years. Daniel Ortega referred to as a "strongman," won 67 percent of the popular vote in 1984, not 1990. So inaccurate was the story that the media watch group FAIR requested that the paper print a retraction.[13]

CONCLUSION

Though described as public diplomacy, only the passing of time separates these techniques from the more classic practices of propaganda developed during World War I. Those in the government did refer to such press manipulation as propaganda, but the media preferred the term publicity. Used no doubt to conjure fewer negative connotations, the term publicity is at least partly accurate, as some of the new media strategies were based on a marketing model, especially target segmentation and polling for message design. Whatever term we choose to use for (dis)information strategies, the fact remains that the practices were effective propaganda. Distorted news about the contra war and the misrepresentations of Sandinista government policies corresponded to the terms and themes promoted by the Office of Public Diplomacy.

Even though the Reagan administration sold major portions of the country on the fear of communism in the 1980s, it was not able to overcome the American experience of the Vietnam War. Vietnam continued to float through the culture, remembered and relived, in devastatingly critical films such as *Platoon* and *Full Metal Jacket*, released in 1986 and 1987, respectively. This is why the administration needed a proxy fighting force and why it undertook such an extensive propaganda effort. Over the course of the decade, the Reagan White House became so effective at media manipulation that the press failed to break the story of the Iran/Contra scandal—the constitutional crisis created by the illegal implementation of the Reagan Doctrine. In chapter 9, we will return to the sordid history of the contra war and its unraveling, and also examine the meteoric rise of Lieutenant Colonel Oliver North as a television phenomenon.

But in the next chapter, we will direct our attention to a tiny island battlefield where the U.S. press was denied access to the fighting. Grenada would be an important step in the long-term Pentagon strategy to gain media compliance for coverage in the theater of war. In the midst of Ronald Reagan's presidency, so dominated by his neo-Cold War view, the tiny island of Grenada would be the first military intervention since Vietnam. It was indeed short, with few American casualties. Looking back on the arguments offered for the need to go to war, we find many points of convergence between what was said then and what the forty-third president, George W. Bush, would say two decades later. As Reagan's words attempted to rework Cold War history, he and his advisors would help ground a new rhetorical moment for future wars.

8

Invading Grenada

Entebbe-Style Rescue, or the First Preemptive Strike?

It isn't nutmeg that's at stake in the Caribbean and Central America; it is the United States' national security.
—President Ronald Reagan, March 10, 1983

On October 23, 1983, U.S. combat troops began Operation Urgent Fury in the Eastern Caribbean, invading the sovereign state of Grenada, an island of 113 square miles with approximately 110,000 inhabitants. It was the first time the U.S. military had committed troops since Vietnam. Over the course of a year the Reagan administration had argued vigorously that Grenada posed a threat to U.S. national security.

Unlike the unlimited access journalists had in Vietnam, the media were barred from covering Urgent Fury. Admiral Wesley McDonald banned reporters for "operational reasons." Nightly news broadcasts showed images of journalists in helicopters circling the island in a futile attempt to cover the combat. After three days of heated charges by media organizations of Pentagon censorship and pressure from some members of Congress, Joints Chiefs of Staff Chairman General John W. Vessey directed McDonald to allow reporters on the island by October 28.

Urgent Fury, carried out twenty years before Operation Iraqi Freedom, has faded from public and political memory. Indeed, during the commemoration of the death of Ronald Reagan in the summer of 2004, Grenada was all but forgotten. Few heralded the former president for saving the country from what he characterized at the time as an imminent threat. Yet there is much to be remembered, and there are many cogent parallels between Grenada and Iraq. Certainly there are numerous points of departure, not least of which are the geographic, religious and political differences between the two countries. Also, Urgent Fury was quickly completed and considered a success at the time. But on that small island can be found the precursors to much of what would happen two decades later. Though contentious, it was the first time the formulation of "preemption" for security reasons was posed as a justification for military intervention. The invasion of Grenada, it was argued, was a defense against communism; that of Iraq was called a defense against terror. But in the aftermath of both operations, flawed intelligence would be the common theme. In denouncing enemies quite distinct from one another, the rhetorical similarities between two activist Republican presidents are nonetheless striking. Finally, in implementing new and historically divergent policies restricting media access, the military learned important lessons about the press and the public, lessons they would later apply to the Middle East.

URGENT FURY

Because the press corps was kept off the island, no independent footage of the first three days of Urgent Fury was available to the news media. Pentagon camera crews supplied the first pictures from Grenada of warehouses that appeared to be stacked with automatic weapons. The footage was used to verify Reagan's claim that there were enough weapons to "supply thousands of terrorists." When reporters were finally allowed onto the island, the warehouses they found were half empty. Some contained cases of sardines, and most of the weapons were antiquated. Writing in the *Columbia Journalism Review*, *Newsday* editor Anthony Marro (1985, 39) suggested, the weapons were "more suited for defense by an island militia than for the export of terrorism and revolutions." Stuart Taylor, Jr., writing in the *New York Times* about U.S. intelligence, reported that initial claims of the numbers of Cubans on the island were greatly inflated. "Over three days the Pentagon estimate of the number of Cuban fighters who had met the invading force seems to have plunged from more than 1,000 to fewer than 200, including the estimated 30 to 70 Cubans who were killed" (cited in Marro 1985, 38). In the wake of the invasion, reporters criticized the inaccuracies that had been used to justify it. "The inflation of the number of Cubans, and the initial characterization of them as a military force, was part of the data that were used by the Reagan administration to argue that a Cuban takeover was at hand, and that American students were in danger"

(Marro 1985, 38). In addition, since journalists did not accompany troops, there was little independent documentation to refute or confirm administration assertions.

Taking a closer look at claims made by the Reagan White House about the dangers posed by Grenada will help illustrate the enduring language and logic of war. Recognizable at the time as classic Cold War rhetoric, Ronald Reagan's oratory also heralded speeches yet to be given by President George W. Bush.

OUR VALUES AND THEIRS

As early as February 1982, when introducing the Caribbean Basin Initiative (CBI), President Reagan drew a line between democratic governments in the hemisphere and the New Jewel Movement headed by Prime Minister Maurice Bishop.

> Nowhere in its whole sordid history have the promises of communism been redeemed. Everywhere it has exploited and aggravated temporary economic suffering to seize power and then to institutionalize economic deprivation and suppress human rights.... In the Caribbean we above all seek to protect those values and principles that shape the proud heritage of this hemisphere. Some, however, have turned from their American neighbors and their heritage. Let them return to the traditions and common values of the hemisphere and we all will welcome them. The choice is theirs. (Cited in Beck, 2004, 75–76)

We recognize in these words, as detailed in chapter 1, the fundamentals of war rhetoric, with the clearly drawn dividing line between "us" and "them." In a speech two months later, the president added another dimension to the basic binary structure by assigning a geopolitical context that emphasized the dangers posed by what he argued was a small but formidable enemy. While speaking in Barbados, Reagan included Grenada in the spreading communist threat he saw in Central America. "El Salvador isn't the only country that's being threatened with Marxism, and I think all of us are concerned with the overturn of Westminster parliamentary democracy in Grenada. That country now bears the Soviet and Cuban trademark, which means that it will attempt to spread the virus among its neighbors" (1982, 18).

The metaphor of viral disease evokes fear and offers few avenues of approach consistent with diplomatic or even rational solutions to foreign disputes. The metaphor can only be extended in certain proscribed ways. Since it is a "spreading virus," not some bacteria, a simple antibiotic cannot restore health. Interventions far more drastic need to be taken. We see here the linguistic logic of such military euphemisms as "surgical strike."

By the spring of 1983, the president escalated his rhetoric about the dangers Grenada posed to the United States. As Robert Beck (2004, 75) has argued, "Just like that which preceded the March 2003 U.S. attack on Iraq, the Grenada invasion was preceded by maximalist administration rhetoric about regional and strategic threat." On March 23, in a "National Security Address to the Nation," Ronald Reagan delivered what Beck (2004, 76) calls a "rhetorical coup de grace" on Grenada. The president showed television viewers reconnaissance photographs that he said provided evidence that a suspicious airfield was being constructed on the island. Reagan asserted, "On the small Island of Grenada...the Cubans with Soviet financing and backing, are in the process of building an airfield with a 10,000-foot runway. Grenada doesn't even have an air force. Who is it intended for?" Explaining that American oil imports pass through the Caribbean, he continued, "The Soviet-Cuban militarization of Grenada, in short, can only be seen as power projection into the region."

But the new airstrip at Point Salines was no military secret. American students attending St. George Medical School had frequently jogged around it as it was being built. In fact, the Soviet Union did not financially support building the airfield, while development money did come from other members of the Organization of Eastern Caribbean States. The project was consistent with the development of a tourism industry and other Caribbean business ventures. But satellite imaging creates meanings over and above what it purports to depict. The strong visual rhetoric communicates a sense of danger and urgency that demands timely response. The need to use a spy satellite to reveal a construction project asserts that the project is secret, and therefore a threat to those it is hidden from. Taken from such distances, the visual technology produces a blurred, grainy scene, making spy images difficult to decode. With details hard to define, they are not recognized as familiar landscapes. A high degree of interpretive analysis assigns meaning to them. These characteristics render such imagery extremely suitable as persuasion. As we will see, these same strategies would be used two decades later on February 5, 2003, this time by Secretary of State Colin Powell, on the floor of the United Nations, as he argued the need for preemptive war against Iraq.

THE CARIBBEAN TRIANGLE AND THE AXIS OF EVIL

As detailed in the last chapter, President Reagan was unable to garner public support for a U.S. invasion of Nicaragua. But a small island, Grenada, would be an easier target, more quickly subdued. And the cumulative criticism of Nicaragua played an important role in the president's pre-invasion rhetoric characterizing Grenada. Grenada, Cuba and Nicaragua were coined the "Caribbean Triangle." Reagan's words are familiar now in retrospect. The words exhibit a distinct rhetorical similarity to the "axis of evil." And like the "axis of evil" phrase, "Caribbean Triangle" implies a crucial connection without having to articulate or defend accusations that influential economic or political ties exist and have resulted in significant threat.

The defining moment for the invasion of Grenada came when the government of Maurice Bishop was deposed and the prime minister was assassinated on March 19, 1983. Though the Reagan White House was predisposed to military intervention with increasingly escalating rhetoric, the final plan for Urgent Fury followed the coup. The coup provided an incident that could be responded to, just as the terrorist attacks of September 11, 2001, provided the context for the war on Iraq. The invasion was set in motion in the days following, and the White House was careful to launch diplomatic efforts garnering regional support from the Organization of Eastern Caribbean States, the same group that had helped finance the new airport.

A RESCUE MISSION?

In the absence of combat coverage, the military did offer other photo opportunities that were very effective in justifying their mission. Members of the press were escorted to Charleston Air Force Base, where returning medical students kissed the ground, exhilarated to be out of harm's way. Highly positive television and newspaper reports repeated the assertion of President Reagan that "we got there just in time." The invasion in retrospect became justified as a rescue mission of American nationals—an evacuation of the approximately one thousand students attending St. George Medical School.

With few negative images to cast a dark eye over Urgent Fury, the American public responded favorably to assertions that the mission had to be carried out to save the American students on the island. An ABC/*Washington Post* poll found 71 percent of the public in favor of the invasion, and only 22 percent opposed.

CENSORSHIP: BENEFITS AND RISKS

Without independent real-time coverage, "There were no on-the-spot reports of the inter-service snafus that bedeviled the operation, of the high incidence of U.S. casualties from 'friendly fire' or of the 30 inmates killed in an air strike on the local mental hospital" (*Los Angeles Times*, January 13, 1991). Even though no television footage was aired in a timely manner of the bombing of a civilian psychiatric hospital, two journalists who managed to slip ashore the night before the assault recorded the story. Four other members of the press were captured by the military and held incommunicado for two days.

The government said that it prevented reporters from accompanying the troops because of concern for their safety. But this had never been a deterrent to journalists, fifty of whom died in Vietnam covering that war. Part of the credentialing required to cover combat were forms releasing the government from responsibility. Subsequent comments by Secretary of State George Shultz reveal some sense of what the real motivations were. "These days in the advocacy journalism that's been adopted, it seems as though the reporters are always against us and so they are always trying to screw things up. And when you're trying to conduct a military operation, you don't need that." And in the midst of the controversy following the press embargo, President Reagan explained at a press conference that the media had not been on "our side militarily" in Vietnam. However, former President Jimmy Carter would later comment that the military's handling of journalists in Grenada was "much more repressive in nature than anything I remember in the history of our country" (*Los Angeles Time*, February 13, 1989).

"Flawed Intelligence"

Numerous government investigations over the years have demonstrated a disturbing lack of evidence behind the claims that Grenada was a threat to the United States and other islands in the Caribbean. Beck cites a Senate Armed Services Committee staff report from February 1986 and a Department of Defense assessment from July 1986 that both discuss the "almost total lack of accurate intelligence." These reports were later confirmed in the memoir of General Norman Schwarzkopf (1992, 258), who admitted to "an abysmal lack of accurate intelligence" before the Grenada invasion. Beck (2004, 77) notes that the Reagan White House had an "exaggerated perception of threat posed by a Cuba-backed Grenada." In a PBS Frontline documentary, *Operation Urgent Fury*, Francis McNeil, President Reagan's Special Emissary during the Grenada intervention, told journalist Seymour Hersh: "Wishful thinking is a problem that afflicts any government...but it seemed to me that the ideological component of the Reagan Administration harkened back to almost the McCarthy period."

And as Beck (2004, 78) points out, "The extent to which the Soviet Union would or could have strategically exploited Grenada seems in retrospect rather slight."

THE FIRST PREEMPTIVE STRIKE?

Though a staunch anticommunist and friend of President Reagan, then-British Prime Minister Margaret Thatcher did not approve of the U.S. action, commenting on BBC radio, "If you are going to pronounce a new law that wherever there is communism imposed against the will of the people then the U.S. shall enter, then we are going to have really terrible wars in the world" (Beck 2004, 82).

Though the administration had secured an invitation from OECS, the United Nations Security Council passed a resolution on November 2 condemning the invasion as a "violation of international law." The vote had a greater majority than the resolution condemning the Soviet invasion of Afghanistan. Article 51 of the U.N. Charter bars military actions against another country unless it is defensive in nature. As we will see, in 2003 the United States argued that the invasion of Iraq was a defensive action against the imminent threat of weapons of mass destruction. Subsequently, that claim, too, was shown to be based on faulty, exaggerated and planted evidence. As we can see, similar arguments were made about Grenada twenty years earlier. The lack of adequate public examination in the aftermath of Urgent Fury and in the years that followed have no doubt contributed to the loss of critical perspective on war rhetoric of preemptive strikes.

Preparing the legal argument that justified Urgent Fury for U.N. Ambassador Jeane Kirkpatrick's October 27 address to the Security Council was a contentious affair. Allan Gerson, a member of the U.S. Mission to the U.N., advocated that the invasion should be justified as an anticipatory "collective self-defense action." But Department of State representative Michael Kozak objected, saying that Grenada posed no imminent threat of "armed attack." In heated discussions, Kozak argued that a U.S. self-defense rationale under the circumstances would extend an exception to the U.N. Charter prohibiting the use of force "to the point that armies could march through it. And any such future armies might not be those of the United States and its allies" (Beck 2004, 80). Instead, he urged the legal justification to be restricted to the "protection of nationals." But Allan Gerson explained his disagreement with Kozak in his 1991 book *The Kirkpatrick Mission: Diplomacy Without Apology, America at the United Nations 1981–1985* this way: "The whole world knows that that's not what the operation was really about. If it was it would have been much more limited, without the need for OECS involvement. If protection of nationals is what we were truly interested in, we would have done an Entebbe-style rescue. Here U.S. national security interests in the region were involved…. Isn't that why we did what we did? If so, why not say it?" (227)

Ambassador Kirkpatrick's speech represented a compromise between the two positions, and strong references to the preemptive rationale remained in her statement to the U.N. "The United States, whose own nationals and vital interests were independently affected, joined the effort to restore minimal conditions of law and order in Grenada and eliminate the threat posed to the security of the entire region."[1]

CONCLUSION

While historians recognize the challenges to the U.N. Charter posed by the U.S. invasion of Grenada, it did not become a major international incident, nor did it pose the problems for the United States that rose in the wake of the invasion of Iraq. The subdued post-invasion situation in Grenada left the justifications for Urgent Fury intact, and one can only surmise that the outcome emboldened those who would propose a preemptive strike in the future. Operation Iraqi Freedom, however, did not enjoy such success. While images of the toppling of the statue of Saddam Hussein made it appear initially that Iraqis would accept U.S. forces in Baghdad, the year that followed the invasion showed that occupying troops (though the Pentagon preferred the term "coalition forces") could not stabilize the country, and reconstruction efforts were thwarted by the lack of security. The death toll for Iraqis and hostility toward the American occupation resulted in constant attacks.

In addition adequate international support will not be forthcoming without adherence to the spirit of international law. As Beck and others, including the Center for Constitutional Rights have pointed out, the U.S. doctrine of preemption departs from the common understandings of the legal argument that supports a state's right to self-protection under the U.N. Charter. Taking the exceptional step to military action, without it being an unquestioned response in self-defense to an attack, depends on the reliable assessment of a given threat's imminence. In evaluating the need for both Urgent Fury and Iraqi Freedom, such claims of imminent threat seem easy to assert as war rhetoric designed to persuade, but harder to verify as a justification for war.

The Pentagon did learn important lessons of media management by implementing such restrictive policies during Urgent Fury. Without on-the-spot reportage, few unpleasant images found their way onto television screens. Yet the military paid a price for creating such ill will among network reporters and the international press corps. Negative coverage and complaints did follow in subsequent reporting, and pressure was brought to bear from current and ex-government officials. The controversy over the press lockout resulted in a review by a special Department of Defense panel. The Sidle Commission recommended, among other things, the press pool arrangement (Kirtley 2001, 42). Selected journalists accredited and assembled by the military were to go in with the fighting forces next time. Clearly the press would have to be managed in a different way in future conflicts. But the impact of the images of students kissing the tarmac could not be underestimated. They would become iconographic of Urgent Fury, confirming the dominant narrative of a rescue mission, erasing the more complicated nature of the invasion. Here, too, at the time, media management seemed a great success. Belief in the power of the image to confer meaning onto military conflict no doubt influenced the staging of future visual representations such as the toppling of Hussein's statue.

As we will see, by the end of the decade the United States would invade Panama, and the post-Vietnam military management of press access to the battlefield would continue to evolve. Before that, however, the zealousness with which Ronald Reagan pushed his anticommunist campaign in Central America would lead to a scandal born of determination to carry out a proxy war against Nicaragua, even if it meant negotiating with Iran, an officially designated terrorist state.

9

Oliver North

The War Hero and the Scandal

As Eugene Hasenfus and his three compatriots flew over the green Nicaraguan countryside on a Sunday afternoon in 1986, they must have been surprised when Sandinista soldiers shot them out of the early October sky. After all, they had flown that route regularly for the last few years. Only Eugene survived the crash of the C-123 cargo plane, and at a press conference in Managua four days later, he revealed significant details of the clandestine operation to supply the contras headed by Lieutenant Colonel Oliver North and retired air force Major General Richard Secord. The soldiers of fortune had taken off from a small airfield in Miami, a favorite of the CIA. Hasenfus's contact was a man he knew as Max Gomez, who, he assumed, worked for the CIA. It was Gomez who organized the transshipment of arms across Central America, and the American public would come to find out that Max Gomez was really Felix Rodriguez, a veteran of the Bay of Pigs invasion of Cuba in 1961 and an ex-CIA employee who had close ties to then-Vice-President George Bush, with whom he had met on at least three occasions at the White House.

The Reagan administration denied any connection to the supply mission, claiming that those who owned and operated the planes being used were private individuals. But now the press had finally started tracking a major story that came to be known as the Iran/Contra scandal. In the midst of mounting evidence of secret supply operations, the White

House held a news conference the day after Thanksgiving, and Attorney General Edwin Meese III revealed—to the astonishment of the press and the public—that supplying the contras was only part of a larger set of foreign-policy initiatives carried out in secret and in direct conflict with congressional mandates. Against the administration's own, often-repeated pronouncements that it would never negotiate with terrorists, Meese revealed that sophisticated weapons systems had been sold to Iran, and that money from the sales had been diverted to buy weapons for the contras. As a consequence of these activities, Lieutenant Colonel Oliver North and the president's National Security Advisor, Admiral John Poindexter, had resigned.

The Iran/Contra affair was the most significant political news story of the 1980s, and yet as *Washington Post* editors Leonard Downie and Robert Kaiser admitted in 2002, the American press establishment missed the story. "What a story! Defiance of Congress, trading missiles with the enemy, ransoming hostages, senior officials' heads rolling—an amazing sequence of events. Yet the *Post* and the rest of the American news media had missed nearly all of it. We didn't get one of the biggest stories of the Reagan years until it was handed to us on a platter" (2002, 54).

The years of press management and "public diplomacy" had been effective. The charge of bias leveled against journalists who reported news deemed unfavorable to the White House, together with the successful shaping of favorable coverage of the contras, had diverted the press from independent investigation. The revelations by the White House about its own activities were startling in their severity. The executive branch had subverted the Constitution as it bypassed the separation of powers and carried out an undeclared war. From a public relations standpoint, it was a disaster. After repeated declarations that it would never negotiate with terrorists, the Reagan White House had done just that. Congress called hearings to investigate the scandal, and during the summer of 1987 television provided live coverage of the biggest story of the decade. The key figure in the scandal would come to be identified as a former marine, Oliver North, the same man who had been involved with the Office of Public Diplomacy, helping to shape positive news coverage.

The Congressional Hearings

As the story of the secret supply operation unfolded during congressional hearings in the summer of 1987, Oliver North rose from obscurity to become a national figure. The media spotlight cast an unusual (and what for many must have been a surprising) warm and favorable glow over a man who, just as easily, could have been cast in the role of villain. In the words of former President Ronald Reagan, "Ollie" was a national hero. From the first day of his testimony, "Ollie" successfully deflected criticism and justified his actions with the power of his own self-image, shaped as it was in the mold of a battle-weary soldier. Media professionals themselves were struck by his appearance in front of the camera: "He made for a story journalists and news executives alike describe as 'fascinating'" *(Broadcasting*, 1987, 23). The *New York Times* could not help but notice that from "his first appearance, the signals came to us like an artillery burst—the marine uniform, the clump of medals, the shoulders-back-head-high bearing, the boyish grin" (Goodman, 1987, 27). *Electronic Media* reported that it was "good enough soap opera" for the ratings to compete with their regular daytime schedules (Tedesco, 1987, 1). In fact, North's appearances attracted five times the number of viewers as the most popular daytime soap, *General Hospital* (Boyer, 1987). It was clear that people wanted to watch Oliver North defend himself. But Emily Prager (1987, 43–44) of the *Village Voice* described North thusly: "Part TV preacher, part bad TV actor, North is exactly the kind of mediocrity that American TV audiences adore. A pretty boy oozing false sincerity, you see him all the time on soaps, sitcoms, TV movies."

Commentators recognized that the televised congressional hearings were intertextual and that their meanings would best be understood within the landscape of popular fiction. Walter Goodman (1987) of the *New York Times* reasoned that, "As television drama or vaudeville, the Iran/Contra hearings send forth signals we have been trained to recognize in popular entertainment" (27). Because the hearings were aired during regular soap-opera scheduling, they were offhandedly dismissed as the "soap opera hearings." But the chord North was able to strike in the hearts of American viewers was not the stuff of soap opera. He portrayed himself as far too prudish to titillate that audience: "I've been faithful to my wife since the day I married her."

Though many dismissed his popularity as bad melodrama, Oliver North hit the bedrock of fundamentally masculine mythologies quite removed from soap opera. He tapped into the various codes of the action/adventurers and war heroes deeply etched in the genres of popular culture. His presentation also borrowed from classic film mythology, his performance at times reminiscent of Jimmy Stewart speaking truth to compromised politicians in *Mr. Smith Goes to Washington*. However, North did not succeed in doing this entirely on his own. When the going got tough, the various news media were there to facilitate evocative cultural representations. North's television appearances and the edited sequences that appeared as news reports are testimony to a form of media construction that mixes fragments of fictional genres inherited from the past. They are assemblages of a variety of elements that forge cultural understandings of the news event. In this way news stories are inserted into the fabric of shared cultural knowledge that understands current events within familiar fictional and mythical realms.

OLIVER NORTH IN THE SPOTLIGHT

As the tension mounted through the testimony of those before him, it became clear that North was defined by the media as the individual most responsible for the Iran/Contra scandal and that he was being set up to take the fall. Television relies on the personalities of those it presents to provide intrigue and empathy. Investigators asked personal questions, and news coverage followed suit by featuring the actions of "the little-known staff member on the NSC." The day before his appearance, ABC News declared (July 6, 1987): "Almost from the opening gavel these hearings have pounded home one point. In the Iran arms sales and the efforts to arm the contras, all roads led to and from Oliver North."

The discourse of character was pivotal, and North's personal behavior was defined as a major problem. A CBS report (June 23, 1987) began the story of ex-CIA agent Glen Robinette with "Phil Jones reports today key testimony was about the money trail, not cash for contras, but secret thousands for Oliver North and his main man Richard Secord."

> *Phil Jones:* An ex-CIA agent, Glen Robinette, put today's focus on Ollie-gate and elaborate efforts to conceal this apparent gift received by Lt. Col. Oliver North. Robinette was asked by retired General Richard Secord to install this security gate and $16,000 security system at North's home after North complained of harassment.

CBS further damaged North's character: "But the committees have turned up evidence North spent some of the contra money on himself. Specifically travelers checks used for purchases including snow tires." The following exchange between the congressional lawyer and contra leader Adolfo Calero was repeated several times on various television reports:

> *Counsel:* When was the last time it snowed in Nicaragua?
> *Calero:* It does not snow in Nicaragua.

In an example of the marked standardization of news coverage, out of an entire day of hearings ABC used the same segment of testimony that was aired on CBS. Peter Jennings reported the scandal, not from the "White House," but from the "security fence around his own house." And Brit Hume (ABC, June 23, 1987) reported from Capitol Hill that "the spotlight again is on Colonel North's personal behavior."

> *Brit Hume:* Security consultant and retired CIA man Glen Robinette told of installing a $14,000 security system at the home of Oliver North, and being paid for it in cash, not by North but by General Richard Secord....

Reporter Hume then went on to recount the "cover up." "But much later after the scandal broke, Robinette got a call from North, who wanted to be billed for the system. So Robinette billed him for about half of what the whole thing actually cost."

THE POLITICS OF PERSONALITY

Focusing on character and personality is a convenient substitute for explaining a complicated and deliberately obscure political process. News coverage of the testimony of Colonel Oliver North emphasized the military man as a personality, while the most damaging and serious of his actions remain secrets kept from the American public. An example of questions that were not followed up and testimony that did not make the nightly news illustrates the extent to which Congress and the media ignored the wider political context. Glen Robinette also testified that Secord had paid him to "dig up some dirt" on journalists Tony Avergan and Martha Honey in Costa Rica, and he admitted trying to discredit the Christic Institute, an organization that had filed an important lawsuit against the secret actions of the executive branch.[1] Following up on Robinette's activities in Costa Rica would have revealed information about government involvement in covert operations that involved drug trafficking and illegally supplying the contras. But counsel did not pursue that line of questioning, and nightly news ignored that portion of the testimony altogether. Instead they included the sequence of testimony referring to "phony bills and phony letters" that damaged North's personal character and judgment.

THE EVIL GENIUS

One ABC report (July 6, 1987) presented selected sequences of people referring to North in their testimony: a collage of voices from Secord, Owen, Calero, Tambs and, lastly, his attractive secretary, Fawn Hall. He is portrayed as the evil genius in control of everything. He alone is implicated in all actions, while the degree of involvement of other members of the U.S. government is ignored. This was, of course, no accident. The *New York Times* would later report that part of the administration's attempt at damage control involved turning Oliver North into a "scapegoat" (Engelberg, 1987). That plan had been in place as early as November 1986, and the hearings demonstrated that the media were more than willing to adopt the personality angle as an intriguing substitute for the actual intrigue. While North was a key figure in the scandal, the CIA, FBI, DEA, USIA, DOD, Justice Department and the Pentagon were also involved. With few exceptions, during his entire testimony the mainstream media failed to reveal in any coherent form North's involvement in the broader picture of covert actions and their meaning for U.S. policy.

Coverage by the print media was consistent with that of television. A *Newsweek* article appearing before North's testimony entitled "North: 'Felon or Fall Guy?'" asked, "Did…North personally profit from the deal?" (Morganthau and Sandza, 1987). The report foregrounds a "bellybutton" account that Albert Hakim set up in a Swiss bank allegedly to support North's wife, Betsy. The critical story ends with, "For the moment, however, North stood accused in…a soap opera of…greed; part James Bond and part Jimmy Durante."

The other Oliver North was an American patriot with a strong character—an admirable man. ABC's (July 6, 1987) coverage referred to Reagan's hero statement: "To his partners in all this, and others too, North was, to use the President's phrase, an American hero." The report goes on to quote former National Security Advisor Robert McFarlane: "A very solid determined energetic officer," and from others: "A man of very high integrity," and "An honest man and an honorable one." The ABC news crew traveled to upstate New York and the small town where Ollie was raised to visit the people who knew him then. ABC's Betsy Aaron went on "Special Assignment" to Philmont, New York (July 6, 1987). She describes Philmont as a "picture-perfect postcard little American town," evoking images and emotions of Americana. "Everybody seems to like the boy they called Larry." He is described as polite, friendly and outgoing; he "had it all," and was handsome and courteous. "He came from the kind of family where values and morals and obligations were not taken lightly." That night CBS (July 6, 1987) broadcast a similar story using many of ABC's sources and the very same photographs that came from Ollie's high school yearbook.

On the eve of North's testimony, the media set the stage for a character drama. CBS (July 6, 1987) warned, "The most difficult questions for North will be about his personal conduct." CBS's Phil Jones went on to assert that congressional investigators "feel that Col. North let the President and the Administration down." ABC's (July 6, 1987) Peter Jennings reported that three former marines were overheard in a restaurant "saying what a disgrace it was that he wore his uniform before the Iran/Contra committee." It would be up to Oliver North to prove himself either a loyal American patriot or a malicious zealot upon whom all blame could be thrust. His uniform would prove to be an essential part of his defense.

THE REVERSAL: NORTH AS WAR HERO

From the moment Ollie was sworn in, he easily defended his actions. The security fence was so easy to explain. In a long story beginning with the FBI informing him of a threat from "the Fatah Revolutionary council, the Abu Nidal group," North testified that this brutal murderer "targeted me for assassination." North told of attempting to get the U.S. government to provide protection, but when it refused (the U.S. government later released a statement that received little coverage, claiming that no request had been made), General Secord hired Robinette. North then evoked a decidedly implausible scenario: "Now I want you to know that I'd be more than willing. I'd be glad to meet Abu Nidal on equal terms anywhere in the world, OK, as an even deal for him. But I'm not willing to have my wife and four children meet Abu Nidal or his organization on his terms." His self presentation through the codes of the tough-guy war hero inspired *Newsweek* (July 20, 1987) to do an abrupt about-face, with the headline, "The Fall Guy Becomes a Folk Hero: Ollie Takes the Hill."

His loyalty to his family and his commitment to be paternally protective added to the picture being painted of a combative, gung-ho fighter, ready to take on the most formidable rival in hand-to-hand combat. It was easy for North to fit into this classic character construction, because that was one of the options provided on nightly newscasts.

Television's trip to Ollie's hometown of Philmont, New York, gathered quotes from friends and family confirming that North was the quintessential example of a patriotic, red-blooded American war hero. We saw black-and-white stills of Ollie in Vietnam and heard from Randall Herrod, an old war buddy who provided the needed quotes to establish Ollie as mythic hero. The ABC (July 6, 1987) narrative referred to him as a "can-do guy, this Oliver North." In Vietnam he commanded fierce respect from his men. Testimony was provided that "He's a compassionate man. He's a loyal man, he's patriotic, and he's a marine. I'd follow him to Hell if he'd lead the way cause I figure we could get back."

One of North's legendary exploits in Vietnam was "leading his men" across the forbidden DMZ line by night and capturing a North Vietnamese soldier. This tale was published in a special edition of *U.S. News and World Report* (1987, 12), a glossy five-dollar magazine entitled, "The Story of Lieutenant Colonel Oliver North," with full-color photos of his "life story." Even as the editors admit that most of it is fictional, it is still celebrated. The editors quote marine historian Ret. Lieutenant General Victor H. Krulak, who says that "His combat exploits in Vietnam are romanticized, like the Sunday-supplement tale of his valiant single-handed midnight foray across the DMZ to capture and bring back a North Vietnamese prisoner. It is an exciting story, but like many others, it never happened" (*U.S. News and World Report*, 1987, 12).

MYTH AND WAR

Doing hand-to-hand combat with Abu Nidal and taking his men to Hell and back evoke strong images and masculine sensations, but they do not fare well with the realities of modern warfare. Vietnam veteran Leo Cawley, reviewing the movie *Platoon*, discussed such fictional representations as he challenged the myth that the tough guy has a better chance of getting back from Hell than, say, a lucky one. "As everyone in combat soon learns, modern war kills very, very tough guys much like it kills everybody else.... It would go something like this: a black belt in Karate is standing near a tank. The tank trips a mine. Sorry about that" (Cawley 1987, 15). "A grunt may come to this knowledge reluctantly. After all, he probably bought some part of the cowboy, tough-guy ethos, every American boy does" (Cawley 1987, 15). Through his war experience as a marine in Vietnam, Cawley realized that the gung-ho super achiever is more often than not a liability rather than an asset, and his actions may well subject an entire group to even more danger.

The gung-ho, tough-guy hero who makes it by virtue of his ability, mythic as it may be, was the appeal of Oliver North to the American public. Cawley believes that this fiction will also appeal to infantry veterans who have not been able to come to terms with the failure of Vietnam. "Many infantry veterans will feel the sense that there was another war that they didn't get to fight, one where skill and courage would have decided things, not carpet bombings and politics, where they could have met capable opponents man to man. But in reality there was no other war, only this one where skill and courage didn't count for much" (Cawley 1987, 16–17).[2] But it was clear that Oliver North never came to terms with the Vietnam War, and continued to fight it in Central America. He lectured congressional counsel Nields, "We didn't lose the war in Vietnam, counsel, we lost it in this city."

THE HERO GENRE

In the 1980s, film culture also battled the memory and legacy of Vietnam, releasing movies devastatingly critical of the military such as *Platoon* (1986) and *Full Metal Jacket* (1987). At the same time Hollywood was reinventing another hero, one who had been betrayed by the war and was dead set on reclaiming American masculinity. Rambo and Maverick, the pilot in *Top Gun*, are identified by Susan Jeffords (1994) as Reagan era "hard body" characters who were busy recovering the lost mystique of the masculine in popular culture. The militarism and mythic heroism evident in *Top Gun* would be called upon seventeen years later by George W. Bush when he donned a form-fitting flight suit to proclaim "mission accomplished" in Iraq.

Hand-to-hand combat and trips to Hell and back, so recognizable in *Rambo* films, are mythic representations of modern war used effectively by North in his testimony, but these are not the only ones. In *What a Man's Gotta Do: The Masculine Myth in Popular Culture*, Antony Easthope (1986) points out that there are four key moments in the masculine representation of war in popular culture: defeat, combat, victory and comradeship. In addition to his many references to combat, defeat and victory—and especially comradeship—were also essential elements of North's television appearance, providing powerful images with maximum effects to television audiences.

DEFEAT AND VICTORY

For Ollie, defeat propelled his narrative. It began with the end—his defeat. He failed to carry out his mission and he was fired. The drama of the hearings will tell us how he got there. The country will base its final judgment on how Ollie plays the hand dealt him by the Select Committee and the quality of his performance in front of the cameras.

In addition, North's past victories were the subjects of many news stories. His involvement in the "successes" of Grenada, Libya and the capture of the *Achille Lauro* hijackers were inserted into stories wherever possible, usually with the phrase "derring-do" or "can-do guy." Every soldier worth his medals has to have the recognition of his victories. Ollie's uniform, especially the large patch of medals, was a constant reminder.

COMRADESHIP

Comradeship was established through the testimony of those who went before him. Media emphasis on Ollie-the-individual included repeating edited sequences of endearing statements made by those who worked (conspired) with him.

> *Owen:*I'm proud to be a friend of Col. North's.
> *Hakim:* And I really love this man.

The theme of comradeship was a markedly important one for North himself. It is here that he offered some of his most notable performances. Ollie had a slide show that he used for fundraising to illegally buy weapons for the contras at a time when that activity was banned by Congress. His lawyer requested that he be able to show the slides at the hearing. Presenting his slide show would have filled in the remaining visual gaps needed to complete the picture of combat and comradeship. The request was refused, but North held the slides and voiced his text anyway. Most importantly CBS (July 14, 1987) focused on North's description of the last slide—the grave of a dead contra. Ollie pauses here, and demonstrates a truly remarkable ability to emote. His voice cracks as he describes (after a pause apparently to hold back emotion) the slide of the grave of a dead "freedom fighter." This powerful image is a crucial element for a complete picture of the war hero, for it signals "the moment of comradeship, the picture of the soldier weeping for the fallen, comforting his wounded buddy" (Easthope 1986, 63).

ABC (July 14, 1987) went further in cooperating with Oliver North's defense by broadcasting a video of North giving his slide show some time in the past. ABC provided the pictures of Soviet Sandinista helicopters that Ollie was not able to present at the hearings. At the end of the report they show President Reagan shaking hands with the rich Americans who have been solicited to give money to this cause, but we are assured that no funds were raised at this meeting, leaving Reagan in the clear.

THE HERO AGAINST THE BUREAUCRATS

Oliver North told congressional investigators, "I came…to tell the truth, the good the bad and the ugly." The movie phrase was often used subsequently to refer to his testimony. CBS (July 9, 1987) treated its audience to visual juxtapositions of Ollie with other fictional heroes. They chose Rambo and Dirty Harry, the quintessential action figures who take the law into their own hands but only because they are forced to do so in the name of justice. Both characters have been forced by circumstance to go beyond formal justice to achieve substantive justice. The bureaucracy of the criminal justice system hinders Dirty Harry in his quest to rid the world of criminality. Rambo is in conflict with the military bureaucrats who are attempting to prevent him from finally winning the Vietnam War. North's testimony revealed his utter conviction that he had to circumvent Congress in order to achieve his substantive goal of "keeping the contras alive." North's loyal secretary, Fawn Hall, when testifying on his behalf, stated that it is sometimes necessary to go "beyond the written law." But it was *U.S. News and World Report* (Hersey, 1987) that explicitly merged Dirty Harry with the war hero to create a truly modern military hero now embodied in the person of Oliver North. "With his can-do attitude and contempt for the career bureaucrats around him, the young officer with shrapnel still buried in him from his Vietnam wounds seems to have stepped into a kind of vacuum on the NSC staff."

Oliver North and Dirty Harry meet at the intersection of myth and ideology. The state in 1980s America was thrown into crisis as Ronald Reagan articulated an anti-state ideology. This position was used to support broad cuts in all social programs in American society. Ollie became the hero of the Iran/Contra scandal because he set himself apart from the state and unscrupulous bureaucrats. He stood in contradistinction from, as the media called them, "his interrogators." The message might not have been so effective had the Democrats been able to challenge the Reagan Doctrine. While North and the Republicans repeatedly asserted that the Nicaraguan "resistance" were "freedom fighters" and honorable men, and our only hope against Soviet-inspired destruction of our "way of life," no Democrat challenged that position. They refused to object to arguments that the contras were freedom fighters. Though, as detailed in chapter 7, the contras were criminals and former National Guardsmen who terrorized civilians, the Reagan administration successfully intimidated legislators by labeling anyone who did not vote for the contras disloyal, and most importantly, dupes of communism. Long before the hearings, Congress had capitulated to the White House when in 1986, it once again allowed aid to be given to the contras. With legislators unable to articulate an alternative argument, contra war crimes and brutality did not become part of the debate.

The points that legislators Lee Hamilton and Daniel Inouye emphasized in their closing statements at the end of the investigation were that the means did not justify the ends, and it was really the Constitution that was more important than getting funds by whatever means for the contras.

But the disingenuousness of their position was hard to miss. Why had they allowed North to act alone for so long? Calling on the Constitution appeared to be simply to prevent North from acting on purely procedural grounds. North effectively argued in his own behalf by centering the blame squarely on the shoulders of those who looked down on him from their elevated positions. They were the ones who could not "make up their minds" as to whether or not to fund the contras and constantly generated mixed signals. North's position was not ambiguous. Like the heroes of fictional dramas, he was true to his convictions in the face of the confusion and disorder of the state. He would fight to the end against unjust laws, for his "good intentions" and his fellow soldiers.

It also became clear that his superiors in the Reagan administration, and Reagan himself, were "hanging Ollie out to dry." But North refused to take the blame for the debacle and continually claimed that his superiors knew what he was doing. By the third day of his testimony, CBS News (July 9, 1987) remarked that an "enormous number of people knew about all this," and thought it was "a good idea," though they never said who, and that North didn't "dream it up on his own," though again, we never found out who did. Blaming Ollie began to look extremely unfair. This underdog status endeared him to the American public even more.

MR. NORTH GOES TO WASHINGTON

Oliver North was a truly postmodern composite character, an assemblage of intertextual references to the self-made rebels at the bedrock of American cultural formations. North's television presence seemed an uncanny parallel to Jefferson Smith, the classic idealist of Frank Capra's *Mr. Smith Goes to Washington*. Like the young Jimmy Stewart, North's boyish demeanor and stubborn determination are endearing. Sitting alone with his counsel, he looked up at his inquisitors, maintaining a defiant pose. He was questioned by not one, but two rows of elevated politicians. The visual and iconographic similarities between North at the hearings and Jefferson Smith's filibuster on the Senate floor are striking. The intentions of Capra's project were unmistakably those of Oliver North's as well. Fighting against a corrupted political process, Smith perseveres, undaunted by the fact that popular opinion is against him. As the narrative of Oliver North unfolded, he, too, was forced to persevere, even though his covert operations had been decidedly unpopular and the media had set him up as the target. It was up to North, as it was the Smith character, to speak his mind and give voice to an ideology that could justify his actions by evoking American idealism.[3] In the shadow of James Stewart, North, too, successfully used his impassioned speech to animate a dying unpopular policy. Ollie renewed the debate for the contras by reasserting the alignment between them (freedom fighters) and American idealism. His former boss, Robert McFarlane, was truly awed by North's disclosure, having of course failed to articulate support for the cause in such a manner himself. At the hearings he pointed out the efficacy of North's vision:

> Perhaps as never before in this administration the nation has [been] treated to a comprehensive explanation of just what United States interests are in Central America, how those interests are threatened, and why our support for the contras was and is in my judgment still justified. It was a superb performance passionate in delivery and persuasive in argument, and for it all of us I think are deeply indebted to Colonel North.[4]

North averted a real constitutional crisis by articulating his justifications at a level of patriotism that transcended what had come to be perceived as bureaucratic red tape. The culturally literate viewer recognized these particularly American character traits, primarily from their fictional constructions. The force of North's testimony lies with its fit into these American heroes who will act on the power of their convictions even if lesser men—bureaucrats—try to get in their way. This was the overriding sentiment of those interviewed on television who showed their support for him. He represented the essence of the American spirit, one willing to take risks to fight for what he felt was right.

STAR WARS

The defining characteristic of North was his individuality, his lonely fight against the burden of state bureaucracy. His fight resonated with another hero, Luke Skywalker, leader of his "plucky band of rebels" fighting for "freedom and democracy" against the Imperial Storm Troopers of the Empire. In Reagan's words, the Evil Empire was the Soviet Union. In the *Star Wars* trilogy the audience identifies with a position that opposes a cruel and dominant power:

> The Hero, along with his companions, is struggling against a technocratic dictatorship, the Empire, which is faceless, unconcerned with the needs of the individual. The representation of the Empire in the films can be taken to be representative of any oppressive bureaucracy in modern society...the modern individual in the audience can vicariously experience what it is like to fight back against the bureaucracy and win. (Wise 1989, 12–13)

In *The Empire Strikes Back*, Luke and his companions fight the unknown "collective mask" of the Imperial Storm troopers, and the audience reads the film in opposition to the forces of oppression. This was also the appeal of Oliver North's battle against Congress. From his initial positioning as scapegoat and underdog, he must battle the forces of injustice at home and abroad by taking a stand against oppressive bureaucracies cloaked in obscurity and indifference.

The process of tapping into popular fictions is a process of inviting interpretations that are most often incongruous. Oliver North and Luke Skywalker are far removed from one another, even diametrically opposed. North is part of a complex set of powerful governmental (and para-governmental) relationships and policies. North's position was not that of the underdog, and the consequences of his actions for the people of Nicaragua were enormous. Ollie organized the contras, whose attacks were carried out in rural areas against civilians, a deliberate strategy of terror. Those were the real victims of a faceless bureaucracy. Indeed, he led an organization with no democratic accountability, acting without representative mandate.

The Power of Resonating with Popular Fictions

Why did the American public fall for this "pretty boy oozing false sincerity?" And fall they did. From the first day of his appearance, his image filled the pages and screens of the national media. CBS (July 9, 1987) discovered that North spoke "the language of middle America," right down to the "cadence of his voice." Dan Rather told Democratic Congressman Louis Stokes of Ohio that he "overwhelmingly has majority opinion of the country behind him, and that he has in military terms put you and the other investigators in chaotic and disorderly retreat." One *National Enquirer* headline (August 18, 1987) claimed that their readers voted 15 to 1 in favor of "Ollie for President," and they traced his "Hero's Roots Back 500 Years." Of course he would be popular, as Hersey (1987) observed. "He lived out a real-life version of the plots that dominate half our movies and three-quarters of our TV scripts."

In the six days of testimony before the Iran/Contra hearings, Lieutenant Colonel Oliver North moved the American public closer to supporting the contras than President Reagan had been able to do since entering office. It was a dramatic accomplishment considering the enormous energy and rhetoric the Reagan administration had directed toward an unwavering American public, an average of 70 percent of whom had opposed support for the contras. Oliver North's testimony changed that figure to a bare majority.[5] The administration scrambled to capitalize on North's performance and push through increases in contra aid. This, and discussions of his surprising popularity, became the media tie-in stories to the Iran/Contra hearings. Almost forgotten in news reporting was the fact that North had lied to Congress, and for that he would receive a felony conviction. North's boss, Admiral John Poindexter, the National Security Advisor, would also be convicted of lying to Congress, and to conspiracy, defrauding the government, and destroying evidence in the Iran/Contra scandal. However, neither would serve time in jail for their criminal activities. Their convictions were overturned on a technicality when it was ruled that their testimony should not have been used against them because they had been granted immunity. North would go on to become an embedded journalist for Fox news during the 2003 invasion of Iraq. John Poindexter would go on to develop computer software applications for spying, and contract with the Pentagon agency DARPA, discussed in chapter 18. In 2002, George W. Bush rehired Poindexter to head the Orwellian, Total Information Awareness Office of DARPA, and there he helped develop a plan for super-computer surveillance of the nation's Internet, phone and fax lines, a system able to collect the credit, financial, medical and travel records of American citizens. In 2003, the U.S. Congress barred the office from spying on Americans, but the program continued under the Pentagon, retiled, Terrorism Information Awareness.

FICTIONAL MYTHOLOGIES AND THE CULTURE OF WAR

It is no accident that Oliver North presented his case with such efficacy. His own self-coding as war hero was an art in which he had become well versed as an integral part of the public diplomacy campaign.[6] The domestic side of the scandal, in fact, was the manipulation of the press by means reserved only for overseas propaganda. That was to be the last chapter of the congressional report on the hearings, but it was judged to be too damaging and was repressed. Out of that silence rose the myth of Oliver North.

American hero mythologies helped hide the human cost of the contra war. The war was understood within the terrain of myth, transformed into a fictional spectacle of American entertainment. By forging new associations with heroes as diverse as Dirty Harry, Rambo, Jefferson Smith and Luke Skywalker, the American public was presented a social construction recognizable at the level of culture, but one which has no relationship to actual reasons for and conduct of war. As those who write of their own experiences in war, such as Cawley (1987) and Fussell (1989) among many others, such myths rarely ring true to the behaviors of real soldiers. Recall John McKay, the former marine who fought in Vietnam, the one who investigated the El Mozote massacre with Todd Greentree for Ambassador Hinton in 1982. He admitted to Mark Danner why he decided not to continue on to the site of the massacre, to see for himself. "What made me decide—me, the big tough marine? I was scared shitless" (Danner 1994, 109). Sadly, when the Atlacatl Brigade, armed and trained with American tax dollars, slaughtered innocent peasants, our military representatives were too scared to see for themselves the corpses of peasants they had put in harm's way.

A news context can be transformed by the memories of past fictions in ways that preserve present conceptions, no matter how problematic the present has become. The North episode was a surreal drama in which myth appeared more reasonable than the black world of covert policies and cynical motivations and the real lack of values. North as mythic hero is a symptom of the crisis of public discourse, but also a crisis of democratic governance. The White House carried out a secret war because, in the political arena, Americans and their congressional representatives had rejected the Reagan Doctrine. In defiance of the American democratic state, the policy could only be articulated through a transcendent rhetoric of idealism and patriotism. Increasingly that idealism has come to be understood through a free-floating body of fictional texts. The actual practice of the American government, especially with regard to military intervention, has become increasingly difficult to explain, and equally hard to defend at the level of non-fiction. Unable to defend in the terms of democratic values, much of it remains hidden, part of the black world of clandestine operations involving murder, assassination and cover up. Though George H.W. Bush had met with clandestine operatives at the White House, his role in arming the contras and selling missiles to Iran was never revealed. When President Bush pardoned Elliott Abrams and Caper Weinberger, the Secretary of Defense, as he left office in 1992, Iran/Contra prosecutor Lawrence Walsh understood that the truth would not be unearthed, "the Iran/Contra cover-up, which has continued for more than six years, has now been complete" (Scheer, 2001). In pardoning Weinberger, Bush insured that he would not be called to testify at a trial, and that Weinberger's notes, which "contained evidence of a conspiracy among the highest-ranking Reagan administration officials," according to Walsh, would not be made public (Scheer, 2001). Bush's daily diary entry about Iran/Contra from November 5, 1986 read: "I'm one of the few people that know fully the details...This is one operation that has been held very, very tight, and I hope it will not leak" (Brouwer 2004, 176). To date, it has not leaked.

Vice President Bush went on to become President Bush in 1988, and 2 years later he would preside over the invasion of Panama and continue the militarization of Central American policy. Like Grenada, the invasion would be carried out without journalistic witness, and the brutal combat in urban neighborhoods that took the lives of many civilians would not be televised.

10

Dover Air Force Base, Press Pools and the Panama Invasion

THE INVASION OF PANAMA

Micah Ian Wright describes parachuting into Panama in the early hours of December 20, 1989, from a C-130 cargo plane, 500 feet from the ground going 300 miles per hour. He describes the fear, sweat and "panckiy acid stomach belching" of the men as they prepare to jump while under fire from the Panamanians below:

> The light turns green. The jump chalk surges forward. Sixty-four men stream toward two three-foot-wide doors, all of us burdened with two parachutes, weapons, and a rucksack the size of a large child. One by one everyone leaps from the doorway. My turn. I experience a moment of panic as the image of my static line not disengaging from my parachute runs through my head—no one wants to become a towed jumper, repeatedly smacking into the plane's fuselage at 350 miles per hour until you're a puddle of goo. Before I have time to freeze, though, someone shoves me from behind and I plunge out into the blackness below. (Wright 2003, 16-17)

As part of Charlie Company's Second Ranger Battalion/75th Ranger Regiment, Wright was part of the "vanguard," of Operation Just Cause and the "Liberation" of Panama from the Dictator Manuel Noriega. He says of his participation, "Unbeknownst to us, we're about to participate in the twelfth U.S. invasion of Panama since 1903" (15). Many of those who jumped that night didn't make it. They were dropped off target into shark-infested waters. Wright's Ranger Battalion was going into Rio Hato Military Base, 65 miles west of Panama City, home of the Seventh Rifle Company, "an elite counterinsurgency force, known to be loyal to Noriega and trained by Uncle Sam at the School of the Americas (the college to which every self-respecting Third World dictator sends his troops in order for them to learn how to torture and kill their own citizen)." The 400 Rangers would do battle with over 500 members of the Panamanian Defense Force (PDF). Once on the ground they headed for Noriega's beach house to hopefully capture the "pineapple-faced" dictator. "We do a hell of a job. No one will ever again use that beach house once we finish with it." But Noriega had escaped to the Vatican embassy. Wright continues, "The Rangers kicked ass; we did what we were trained to do and we did it well. We jumped into direct fire and we survived. We were proud of ourselves and our unit." The next day his unit was assigned to guard PDF's military headquarters, the Commandencia. And then Wright says, "everything in my life changed. Forever."

The Commandencia was situated in the middle of Panama City, in the poor neighborhood of Chorrillo. The crowded slum, constructed of old wooden buildings, was home to over 20,000 of the cities poorest residents. During the initial airborne assault by the U.S. Air Force, several bombs fell on El Chorrillo, exploding in the densely populated neighborhood, setting fire to nearby buildings. The fire spread and raged for 2 days. Wright continues:

> When it finally burned itself out, no one knew how many dead innocents lay in the ruins. What was startlingly apparent were the thousands of newly homeless poor people wandering the ashes, desperately looking for some shred of their previous lives or burnt loved ones. I never shot at anyone who didn't shoot at me first—I didn't bury anyone in mass graves or burn their houses down—and yet, I share the guilt of those who did those things, because I was there. And guess what? So do you. Because it was your government that did it. (Wright 2003, 18)

Media coverage of Operation Just Cause portrayed the invasion in a most positive light. As Doug Ireland (1990, 8) put it, "In the first 48 hours, most of TV's talking heads psychologically identified themselves with the administration." The loss of independence between the media and the military intervention was best illustrated by the words of anchorman Tom Brokaw, when he told NBC (December 20, 1989) viewers, "*We* haven't got [Noriega] yet." PBS's Judy Woodruff concluded the next day, "Not only have *we* done away with the [Panamanian army], *we've* done away with the police force." Micah Wright would later note, "Strange, I never saw

Tom Brokaw humping an M-60 down the Rio Hato runway next to me. Perhaps I was distracted by the sight of Judy Woodruff providing covering fire on the runway control tower" (2003, 21). CNN (December 21, 1989) followed suit the next day when Mary Ann Loughlin asked an ex-CIA official, "Noriega has stayed one step ahead of *us*—do you think *we'll* be able to find him?"

Television personalities worried about American casualties, but some helped deaden public compassion for them, such as NBC's John Chancellor who intoned, "*We* lose numbers like that in large training exercises" (December 21, 1989). No mention was made of civilian casualties. In the print media reporting, some editorial pages offered more nuanced reporting, but the *New York Times* and *Washington Post* supported the invasion. The rare exception of New York's *Newsday* (December 21, 1989), which questioned Just Cause: "Bush seems to have acted more to serve his own political needs than those of national security... His stated reasons for the action just don't hold up scrutiny of International Law." The rare exception to television coverage was NBC's John Dancy who pointed out that while the U.S. claimed that the Organization of American States (OAS) charter gave it the right to intervene in protection of American lives, the administration "had nothing to say about Article 20 of that same charter, which states the territory of a state is inviolable" (cited in Ireland 1990, 8).

In language that would sound similar to that of his son's 14 years later, President George Herbert Walker Bush said his reasons for invading Panama were to depose a murderous dictator who was a threat to Americans. Manuel Noriega was also a convicted drug dealer. Against the wishes of the Reagan administration, Noriega had been indicted for drug dealing in a federal court in Miami. Hi excesses had become an embarrassment to the United States. Noriega was once a trusted asset of the CIA, and a partner of the American military. As Hodding Carter (1990) wrote, "The Panamanian Defense Forces (PDF) that he ran is our creation, too, a confederacy of goons trained by the U.S. that has been routinely stealing elections for more than 20 years while we either averted our gaze or applauded." And similar to the rhetoric that would be used to describe Saddam Hussein, Noriega would be demonized in ways that reached levels of absurdity. Revelations of his perversions saturated media stories, such as his propensity to wear women's clothes. In the press, Noriega was the thug of thugs, the top narco-criminal of the hemisphere, and the perverted, depraved friend of communist regimes. He had to be deposed.

The United States set up a government headed by Guillermo Endara, but background on the new president was hard to find in press reports. In his Oxford book, *The Panama Canal*, Walter LaFebre details some of

Endara's history, most notably his ten-year term as top aide to former Panamanian president Arnulfo Arias Madrid. Arias promulgated race laws and his support came from the new anti-black class and oligarchies with fascist tendencies.

In the weeks following the invasion, the Pentagon refused to provide documentation to human rights groups or international media investigators. An Independent Commission of Inquiry (1990) was formed in New York by individuals, lawyers and public advocates acting on behalf of the people of Panama. The group sent investigators who collected testimony, visited hospitals, and sought out evidence and documentation of the invasion. The commission estimated the death toll to be three to four thousand and found that many people had been killed by shrapnel and exploding bullets. U.S. tanks had flattened cars, homes and bodies in the streets. Residents reported soldiers collecting bodies in plastic bags and transporting them elsewhere. The offices of opposition political parties were broken into and their records destroyed. U.S. troops blew up the government radio station with broadcasters still inside. The U.S. occupation, called Operation Promote Liberty, was constructing a new state and government apparatus free of nationalist or anti-U.S. organizations. On January 25, 1990, the Commission reported that Dr. Romulo Escobar Betancourt, the chief negotiator of the Panama Canal Treaty and a former delegate to the OAS, was arrested at his home and held at Fort Clayton.

No Independent Documentation

In the aftermath of the invasion of Grenada called Urgent Fury, the Sidle Commission criticized the policy of military press restrictions during the Grenada invasion and recommended that "press pools" accompany U.S. combat troops the next time. The "next time" was Panama, but even though there had been "dress rehearsals" of the pools in previous years, all journalists were excluded from accompanying invasion forces. The pool was not activated in time. In fact, pool reporters were excluded from all military activity until the second day of the invasion. Five hundred other U.S. journalists were restricted to a military base and barred from on-the-scene coverage of the invasion and its aftermath.

Very little is known of what happened during the invasion in the shantytown of El Chorrillo, where so many civilians were killed when their neighborhood was leveled and destroyed by fire. On January 11, 1990, the U.S. Southern Command issued a casualty count of 202 civilians. However, subsequent investigative reporting, including a September 1990 segment on the CBS program *60 Minutes*, discovered the existence of "mass graves indicating far higher casualties of perhaps thousands of civilians during the period of the exclusion of the press." Because reporters were not present, firsthand accounts that would have provided independent documentary evidence were not available.

The military handling of the press in Panama led to another Defense Department report. Released on March 20, 1991, and entitled "Review of Panama Pool Deployment, December 1991," it addressed the complaints from journalists and news organizations, and—like the Sidle Commission—evaluated the press coverage of the invasion. Referred to as the Hoffman Report, it concluded that because of the events surrounding the failure of the pool arrangement, news reports produced stories and pictures of secondary value (MacArthur 1992, 143). In another report by the Pentagon, then Secretary of Defense Dick Cheney was "lambasted" for his handling of information about Panama because of his "excessive" secrecy (Kirtely 2001, 42).

Excluding journalists from the invasion of Panama, like Grenada, was an effective strategy for preventing public opposition to the actions. There were no bloody pictures of the worst fighting or of the lost, homeless burned civilians of El Chorrillo. Nor was there any evidence or footage that could have criticized or questioned the military action.

As in Grenada, journalists were directed to photo opportunities in Panama that served positive public relations purposes far more than public information about the invasion. Coverage consisted of pictures of groups of grateful Panamanians cheering the arrival of U.S. troops. Directing the press to images of cheering crowds welcoming the arrival of U.S. invasion forces would become a staple of managed war coverage, culminating in the toppling of the statue of Saddam Hussein, one of the most repeated filmic sequences of Operation Iraqi Freedom.

If the coverage of Panama failed to be independent and informative, it was nonetheless, in the words of the Republican National Chairman, a "political jackpot." There was, however, one moment when the president and the Pentagon lost significant control of the television image.

CLOSING DOVER AIR FORCE BASE

On the second day of the invasion of Panama, President Bush began a press conference only minutes before the bodies of dead Americans arrived at Dover Air Force Base in Delaware. As he cajoled the press corps, complaining about having a stiff neck, CBS, ABC and CNN used a "two box" or split screen technique to show simultaneous live images of the honor guard carrying the first coffins from the belly of the military transport plane across the tarmac. NBC did not use the technique "because of fears that the coverage might cast the President in a negative light." Even though ABC News president Roone Arledge "called the broadcast room and ordered a return to the full picture of the president," CBS and CNN continued to air the coffins' return to Dover.

At his next press conference, on January 5, 1990, President Bush attempted to reverse the public relations damage done during the invasion and openly attacked the press. Live on national television, he complained about the coverage, saying that he had received letters and calls from viewers who "thought their President, at a solemn moment like that, didn't give a damn." Attempting to reverse the negative public response, he provided emotional reassurance: "I do. I do. I feel it so strongly." The president asked the networks for advanced warning the next time they were planning to use the technique.

In a *New York Times* (January 8, 1990) op-ed piece, Tom Wicker noted that editorial judgment "under the First Amendment is not to be submitted for government approval." But the CBS network response to the suggestion of government prior restraint was compliant. They found the president's words and request "beneficial not only to news organizations but to the workings of our free society" (January 6, 1990). As we will see, this statement by CBS did not bode well for a free press and the accuracy of future war reporting. This incident marked a significant, uncontested step in the control of the press. Even if the battlefield were restricted, the military realized that images of those killed in battle would still remind the public that war leads to the deaths of young Americans. The Pentagon would close the doors to Dover permanently. Though Pentagon spokesman Pete Williams would later claim that blocking images of the traditional ceremonies in honor of the dead was "to show sensitivity to the families," the families had no way of knowing if the coffins shown on television were those of family members.

After working as a Pentagon Public Relations officer, Williams would be hired by NBC news and report on the Pentagon as an independent journalist in future wars. During the First Gulf War, the American Civil Liberties Union would file suit against he government to lift the ban imposed on ceremonies at Dover, but no national news segment about the legal suit would air on network television. Solemn images of flag draped coffins reminding the public that death is the ultimate outcome of war would not impose such dreadful realities on the wars of the twenty-first century. The press would remain permanently blocked from military bases.

Part III

The First Persian Gulf War

*The Battle Over Access,
Video Game Imagery and Smart Bombs*

11

Trading the First Amendment to Defeat the "Vietnam Syndrome"

Throughout the fall of 1990, numerous Pentagon restrictions blocked media access to military planners as well as troops deployed along the Saudi border. Only after several thousand air "sorties" turned Desert Shield into Desert Storm did journalists openly criticize restrictions that prevented them from moving freely through the theater of operations. One reporter explained that media organizations had not complained noisily about the problem of access before the war because "the press gauges its freedom to cover the military by how much fighting it gets to see" (Nathan, 1991). Reporters were eager to be part of the action, and the Pentagon had promised at least limited access through "press pools" when combat began. After the war started, their frustrations were underscored by the lack of timely and accurate information from the military. Only after the war would the extent of army control of information and its consequences be more fully understood.

Complicating the problem of access for reporters in the Gulf was the remote, inhospitable nature of the desert border area. In addition, the Saudi government did not give visitor or tourist visas, making it virtually impossible for journalists to get visas without U.S. military sponsorship. Reporters visited troops and units only when escorted by public affairs officers. No independent freedom of access was allowed. Journalists were organized by the military into pools, and pool reporters were assembled and activated at the behest of the military, taken to locations designated by the military, and accompanied by escorts at all times. Those who ventured out on their own were detained or told to leave when they arrived at bases without escorts.

The disappearance in the Saudi desert of CBS correspondent Bob Simon and his crew while trying to get to the front lines underscores the determination journalists have to be part of the action.

PRESS ACCESS IN PREVIOUS WARS

Up to the invasion of Grenada, and with the exception of Korea, journalists enjoyed unrestricted access to combat and military deployments. As discussed in chapter 2, during World War II, even though formal censorship was imposed, the press still had freedom of access. Journalists were among the first waves of forces landing on the Normandy beaches on D-Day. As stated in the federal lawsuit discussed below, brought against the Pentagon in 1991, during the Second World War "correspondents flew on bombing missions, rode destroyers, went on patrols, accompanied assault troops in the first stages of battle in numerous invasions."

During Vietnam anyone could take a commercial flight to Saigon, and even freelancers could go with relative ease. It was common practice for journalists to sleep in the barracks, eat in mess halls with the troops and talk to the commanding officers as well as local officials and peasants, all of this without public affairs escorts. During the Vietnam War, journalists routinely hitched rides on military transport planes going into areas of combat. Journalists' eyewitness accounts of Vietnam documented the war on the ground in copious detail. If their reports did not come out in a timely manner, they provided a historical record. As detailed in chapter 4, the graphic images of fighting from Vietnam caused the media and the public to reassess their commitment to the war. The military learned to distain the pictures of war's human cost.

In the Persian Gulf, one of the main reasons for denying access to the field was to foreclose the possibility of combat footage and its negative impact on the public. The Pentagon was especially afraid of, and attempted to ban, pictures of American soldiers wounded in combat. Graphic pictures of wounded "personnel in agony or severe shock" or "imagery of patients suffering from severe disfigurement" were defined as the most damaging. They said it was to protect the privacy of wounded troops, but video technology can do that much more easily by simply blacking out portions of the picture. Even though the final draft of the Pentagon restrictions excluded those words, the concern resulted in the near-total absence of disturbing images from the ground, and an overall depiction of a war as being without cost. As the war neared its end, news reports of the Scud attack on the barracks near Dhahran showed pictures of the press being blocked from taking photographs of the wounded. Perhaps the most revealing comment came from a military officer quoted in the *Washington Post*: there will be no discussion of the costs of the war, he said, "So the natural tendency in any democracy, which is to debate…can't work against us" (*Los Angeles Times*, January 13, 1991). The first ground combat in the Gulf illustrates these points.

THE BATTLE OF KHAFJI

The greatest fear for the military was the possibility of a ground war and the resulting images of American casualties. The first engagement of troops was the battle of Khafji, where eleven marines were killed. General Norman Schwarzkopf personally appeared before the press. Analysis of this press conference reveals the role played by the graphic imagery of superior weapons technology and its use as a distraction from the human cost of war. For twenty-three minutes the general focused on spectacular videotape of smart bombs obliterating their targets and described Iraqi losses as "rather sensational." Only toward the end did he announce that the marines had eleven "KIAs." The media followed his lead, and the high-tech video became the emphasis. No imagery of a bloody battle was included, and no bodies of the dead were visible. Fallen soldiers referred to as numbers and acronyms allowed the military to distance the public from comprehending the loss in emotional and human terms.

In addition, television viewers were shown pictures and interviews with two marines who had been wounded but said they would die for their country if they had to. The coverage directed the emotions of the public toward feelings of patriotism, blocking the sense of grief, sadness and loss for those killed. Ted Koppel's guest on *Nightline* that evening was David Halberstam, who expressed concern that the country was "extraordinarily ill-prepared emotionally for this war."

LACK OF DEBATE DURING DESERT SHIELD

Considering Halberstam's observation about the lack of emotional preparedness on the part of the public, let's consider the comments of another writer at the time, George Black. Commenting on the press restrictions imposed on Gulf coverage, Black (1991) pointed out that "the broader intent of the new reporting rules is to tighten control over news of a war that already lacks informed public consent." The prerequisite to informed consent is a public debate from numerous perspectives that results in a shared consensus. Without such a commitment based on a compelling purpose, the public is ill-prepared to deal with the consequences of war.

During the fall of 1990, the crucial period of Desert Shield when the country should have been engaged in a thorough and uninhibited debate about the need for war, studies of television coverage demonstrate a lack of diverse voices in the media. One study shows that during five months of television coverage, from the first commitment of U.S. troops on August 8, 1990, until January 3, 1991, few critical or opposing views were presented on television. ABC offered only 0.7 percent of its total Gulf coverage to opposition to the military buildup. CBS delivered 0.8 percent, and NBC made the greatest impact with a total of 1.5 percent, 13.3 minutes, devoted to all stories about protests, peace organizations, conscientious objectors, religious dissenters, antiwar veterans and the like. Missing was not only footage of protest, but "none of the foreign policy experts associated with the peace movement—such as Edward Said, Noam Chomsky or the scholars of the Institute of Policy Studies appeared on any nightly news program."[1]

As we will see in the following chapter, television news was dominated by footage provided by public relations professionals. These persuasive messages were designed to look like news reporting. They emphasized human rights abuses from Kuwait and featured plenty of graphic images of "wounded" people. Though funded by a foreign government and proven false after the war, such visceral fare was effective. Even confronted with such media managment, the public recognized and disapproved of the lack of broad public debate. A *Times Mirror* (1991) poll recorded in September 1990 and January 1991 found "pluralities of the public saying they wished to hear more about the views of Americans who oppose sending forces to the Gulf."

Legislators in support of the war reportedly encouraged President Bush to call a special session of Congress to help produce popular support for the war effort. Instead, the White House and the Democratic leadership postponed such a debate until the momentum of the military operation left armed conflict the primary option. With half a million troops in the desert, a U.N. resolution and a deadline, other diplomatic efforts were foreclosed.

A Just Cause?

Even amid press restrictions, and with little public opposition acknowledged, the White House was unable to articulate extraordinarily compelling reasons to go to war. During the fall of 1990, a variety of "objectives" for the war were formulated by the administration. As each of these failed to resonate with the public, another was launched. First was the need for oil, which changed to American responsibility to save Kuwait. The simple abstraction of democracy and "our way of life" was another. But none of these compelled strong acquiescence to sending American troops. One assertion by James Baker, that American jobs were at stake in the Gulf, became the object of ridicule in a national news magazine. A short piece in *Newsweek* illustrates the tone: "Baker's Joe Sixpack pander was patronizing and cynical." *Newsweek's* (December 3, 1990, 6) chiding of the White House included "Who wants to die defending the Saudis' right to treat their women like camels?" The demonization of Saddam Hussein as the embodiment of evil and equivalent to Hitler was of course a theme, but none of this rhetoric seemed to have any impact on the polls or offer an extraordinarily compelling need to begin the war. The need to risk American lives had not been convincingly articulated. As one military analyst, Colonel Harry G. Summers (1991), noted, "True, the media and television in particular, are good at showing the cost of war, but cost only has meaning in relation to value…it is the objective of a war that determines its value."

Manufacturing Consent?

On November 22, 1990, three months after Desert Shield was launched, one explanation for war was found to be widely accepted by the public. A CBS/*New York Times* poll found that the public would support a war to stop an Iraqi nuclear bomb. "In the days that followed, reporters led their stories with official assertions that new evidence had prompted a reassessment of Iraqi nuclear capabilities" (Hibbs 1991, 5). But as Mark Hibbs, editor of *Nuckonics Week*, pointed out at the time, Iraqi nuclear weapons capabilities "are still measured in years not months" (Hibbs 1991, 6). Here we see the first use of weapons of mass destruction as a justification for invading Iraq. Used again over a decade later as the primary reason for regime change, as we will see, this charge seems far more potent as a persuasive strategy than it ever was as a plausible explanation for war. Designing messages found to be persuasive through the use of focus groups and opinion data constitutes a cynical use of media discourse, one antithetical to democratic debate. Effective in the short term, its long-term consequences are stunning in their destructiveness, not only to the democratic process, but to actions that such "manufactured consent" allows.

A Moment of Questioning

Toward the end of 1990, as Congress took up the issue of war, a few stories critical of the deployment of troops appeared in the print media. An article published in the *Washington Post* on December 9, 1990, provided an alternative view of the troop deployment. The article documented a growing number of troops expressing "reservations over U.S. involvement in what they see as an internal Arab conflict." During the president's Thanksgiving Day visit to troops in Saudi Arabia, "a truckload of soldiers drove past television cameras and reporters shouting, 'We're not supposed to be here! This isn't our war! Why are we over here?'" Army Lieutenant Alexander Dumas said, "This is not worth one American losing his life. If they [Iraqis] were threatening us, I'd be ready to lay down my life in a minute—but this is different." Lieutenant Dumas was told that he could "get in trouble" for telling his opinions to a reporter. The American public had not previously heard such criticism from the troops, which the article asserted "continues nightly." Many troops were impatient with a "mission they feel has not been clearly articulated by political leaders."

As November and December wore on, public confusion and anxiety about the war was reflected in polls showing that support for the deployment stood at a bare majority. The close vote in the Senate, 52 to 46, demonstrated a country deeply divided and nowhere near a consensus on the need to go to war. The swiftness with which the bombing of Baghdad occurred after the U.N. deadline was at least in part to forestall any further decline in public support for Operation Desert Shield. Indeed, the lack of meaningful public debate, especially on television, resulted in a fatalistic acceptance of the inevitable rather than a commitment based on reasoned opinion. This is why the public was so "ill-prepared emotionally."

Psy-ops and Censorship

Psychological operations strategists were deployed to boost the morale of American soldiers. Cards were distributed to U.S. soldiers entitled "Why We Are Here." They offered familiar abstract justifications with little explanation as to the need to fight in the Persian Gulf, such as "If history teaches us anything, it is that we must resist aggression, or it will destroy our freedoms." In addition to persuasive strategies, other measures reminiscent of World War II V-mail censorship were also instituted. National Public Radio reported that letters from an air force reservist from Michigan were being published in his local paper, but the military ordered *The*

Bay Voice to stop publishing them. The contents of the letters were critical of living conditions, and the reservist complained that bathroom facilities were inadequate, that there were too few showers, and that the smell was terrible.

Human Interest and "Hometowners"
As censorship was imposed on the troops, information management strategies were also deployed to actively encourage and facilitate positive stories. Reporters from local television stations were allowed much freer access to the field, and many had their trips to Saudi Arabia paid for by the Pentagon. A Pentagon "Media Support Program" invited about 450 reporters to travel to the Persian Gulf at military expense (Nathan, 1991). Journalists complained that national and print reporters were squeezed out by the local television crews the military referred to as "hometowners." The "hometowners" were allowed to spend as long as four days visiting the units from their cities. The emphasis on local news promoted coverage far more likely to be soft, morale-boosting coverage, sending words and pictures of the boys in the field to the folks back home. Joint Information Bureau director Captain Michael Sherman in Saudi Arabia admitted that he favored this type of human interest coverage.

In addition, public affairs officers escorted journalists, who met with hand-selected soldiers and officers who had been coached on ways to respond to the press. Desert Storm veteran Anthony Swofford would later recount such an incident in his acclaimed memoir, *Jarhead*. When journalists visited his marine sniper unit in the Saudi desert, his sergeant told his men to take off their shirts, show their muscles and say they believed in the mission. The managed imagery included "photo ops" that allowed reporters access to the magnificent aircraft and planned desert maneuvers. These sessions usually took place against the setting sun, providing excellent backdrops to news stories. Graphic imagery of weapons systems and training videos from tanks and targeting were also supplied to news organizations, filling the news frame left open by the lack of diverse debate.

COVERING CENSORSHIP

After the bombing of Baghdad began, even fewer stories questioned Desert Storm. One report by James LeMoyne of the *New York Times* (February 17, 1991) about military management practices in the field stands out. LeMoyne reported that Pentagon public affairs officers made journalists keenly aware that their stories were being monitored. For nearly two months, LeMoyne had a standing request for an interview with General

Norman Schwarzkopf. A Pentagon official admitted to LeMoyne that if his "articles were not 'liked' the interview would probably be denied." After writing "a story which included quotes from soldiers who criticized President Bush and "emotionally questioned the purpose of their being sent to fight and perhaps die in Saudi Arabia," he was told they "definitely did not like" it.

But the military's disdain for political debate was articulated by their spokesman. It was Pete Williams who repeated the comments of one military commander: "I don't know what side (the media) are on…. I see them interview [Iraqi Foreign Minister] Tariq Aziz in Baghdad and the next day interview Secretary of State Jim Baker as if they were the same, as if this is some kind of big political debate."[2]

LeMoyne's experience was not unique. Many journalists were forced to play a waiting game for access. It could take weeks and even months for the Joint Information Bureau to honor requests to visit troops and units, which some journalists simply never received. ABC's John Laurence was refused access to the troops. He felt he was blacklisted for his role in producing a segment during Desert Shield that detailed heat and sand problems with equipment and also described ammunition shortages. Laurence had provoked the ire of the military in Vietnam when *CBS Reports* aired his footage of soldiers refusing orders in 1970. The difference during Vietnam was that he continued to cover the war. A *Newsday* journalist who covered the war later said about then Secretary of Defense Dick Cheney: "He effectively shredded the First Amendment by imposing censorship on U.S. journalists covering the confrontation" (Sloyan 2001, 59).

As mentioned above, in Desert Storm the issue of press restrictions did become a theme in the war coverage. However, the military successfully framed the debate around issues of security. First Amendment rights and the role of democratic involvement in deciding issues of war were rarely voiced. Much of the debate was restricted to official claims that issues of security were at stake. Journalists did not challenge statements justifying the censorship on military grounds, such as Norman Schwarzkopf's comment presented at face value on NBC, "I don't think our public out there would ever say they were willing to risk one life so that they know more." Indeed polls show that a majority of the public believed that the restrictions were necessary. But this belief was based on the assumption that press restrictions were required for security reasons, not to shape public opinion. A full 78 percent of the public did not believe that the military was hiding bad news from them, but rather thought that they were "telling as much as they can under the circumstances." And a large majority, 61 percent of the public, believed the coverage was "accurate" (*Times Mirror*, 1991).

The Legal Suit

The New York-based public law firm, the Center for Constitutional Rights, filed a federal lawsuit against the Pentagon in an attempt to block press restrictions. The suit asserted that public affairs "escorts engaged in arbitrary censorship of interviews, photography, and altered the activities of soldiers when reporters come into their presence, not for security reasons, but to ensure favorable coverage of the military presence" (Federal Lawsuit, 1991).

In addition to First Amendment issues, the lawsuit also contended that the "press pools" assembled and escorted by the military were violations of the Fifth Amendment guarantee of equal protection under the law, because the pool system gave preferential treatment to select news organizations. In addition to paid travel expenses, the military intervened with Saudi government officials to expedite visas and transit papers for some correspondents "anticipated to favor the U.S. military." The suit argued that the press rules were not undertaken for bona fide reasons, but to "restrict, control and manipulate the content and character of information reported to the American public."

Neither the *Washington Post*, the *New York Times* or any major television broadcast organization signed on to the suit, nor did they feature news reports about the federal lawsuit that might have drawn attention to the public relations nature of the press restriction. To do so without being part of the legal challenge would have cast suspicions over their press coverage. The Pentagon's continuing promise of access to the ground war, and the desire not to be excluded as they were in Grenada and Panama, kept the main news outlets from pursuing legal means to guarantee their First Amendment rights. The hope of following troops into the ground war when it began, even if only in press pools, discouraged critical stories and shaped positive media coverage for the most part. Commenting on the list of press restrictions, CNN's Ed Turner said, "Sure, we'll abide by it...because we're not about to be banned from the theater of operation just because we disagree with some of the points on the list."[3]

THE MADE-FOR-TELEVISION WAR

When the war started during evening news broadcasts on January 16, 1991, the general excitement of live broadcasting turned into unbridled optimism as initial reports of the success of the bombing came in. On CBS, the bombing of a highly populated urban area was described enthusiastically as "staggering" and "fantastic." It was "rolling thunder air war." Television aired cruise missile footage supplied by the Pentagon, with one pilot boasting, "We dropped some excellent bombs." The night footage of the bombing of Baghdad was an aesthetic spectacle, the visual reference of fireworks symbolizing the destruction of the city. High-technology weaponry became the answer to issues once raised about the moral and ethical—or even economic—problems of war.

War Without Consequence

While the media engaged in endless scenarios of how the air war was being fought, and how the ground war would be fought, speculation about Iraqi casualties was conspicuously absent. The coverage created the impression that the war was accurate, antiseptic and, above all, clean. Scholars have noted the celebration of firepower historically, but Desert Storm had taken such narratives to new heights. The celebration of the modern technology of war gave the bombing a kind of moral justification. The smart bombs were so accurate, and there was no intention of targeting civilians, and so those worries were easily set aside.

Civilian Casualties as Enemy Propaganda

When U.S. television did show pictures of dead civilians, viewers were invited not to feel concern because they were part of Hussein's "psychological war against the American public." Over graphic videotape of the charred bodies of dead children, NBC's Faith Daniels said, "What they do show is that Saddam Hussein's propaganda machinery continues to function." And after airing a few moments of civilian casualties, the PBS *News Hour* called the footage "heavy handed manipulation." Some publications went to great lengths to cavalierly abdicate moral responsibility. *Time* magazine defined "collateral damage" as "dead or wounded civilians who should have picked a safer neighborhood."

"Smart" bombs successfully dissociated from human costs became the heroes of the war, but it was primarily the dumb bombs that wiped out the Iraqi forces. Over a period of six weeks, old-fashioned B-52 carpet bombing destroyed "Hussein's war machine." And as Dr. Paul Rogers of the Peace Studies Department at Bradford University in England noted, such bombs also wiped out the Iraqi soldiers in retreat. "There was systematic carpet bombing with B-52s of fleeing troops...and persistent use of anti-personnel munitions such as cluster bombs, and I would guess that there was a level of carnage which we've probably not seen since the First World War." Though no imagery of such bloodshed was aired, the death was often justified through implication and terminology. For example, on February 24, CNN's Brian Jenkins referred to Iraqi prisoners kneeling in the Kuwaiti desert as a "fearsome, warlike" people, while their Saudi captors were "gentle" and "mild-mannered."

YELLOW RIBBONS

Opposing the war became the equivalent of not supporting the troops. The media adhered to that assumption consistently. A proliferation of stories from the homefront featuring flags and yellow ribbons was aired nightly. As we will see in the next chapter, homefront stories were encouraged by advertisers fearful that combat footage would not sell cereal and soda, the staples of broadcast sponsorship. Effective in its demands, advertising's preferred patriotic coverage resulted in public support for a war little understood. Opposition came to mean disloyalty, an assertion articulated at the highest levels of government. The wave of yellow ribbons and American flags that swept across the doorsteps of America became testimonies of the power of the media to generate uncritical national unity when troops are in the field. The orchestrated hyper-patriotism of the half-time entertainment at Super Bowl 1991 was so extreme that some sports writers made critical comments. Some journalists became critical of the media organizations they worked for. Hodding Carter admonished the press to "make sure that from the same newspaper that prints the yellow ribbon" that there also be editorials expressing that "it is absolutely solidly American, that there are those who oppose this war."[4] He also noted that there "ought to be multiplicity of views and diversity of approach." In the grip of a highly unified media approach, David J. Wolbrueck, managing editor of the *Round Rock Leader* in Texas, was fired for publishing a story from the perspective of a Palestinian native working in Round Rock who was against the war. After firing him, the publisher wrote a front-page editorial apologizing to the president for the story.

THE GROUND WAR: THE "MOTHER OF ALL BATTLES"

On February 23, 1991, U.S.-led forces began a long-anticipated ground battle against the recalcitrant leader of Iraq, in spite of the fact that Hussein had already agreed to leave Kuwait under a negotiated peace initiated by the Soviet Union. A matter of days were the difference between what might have been the end of the war and the engagement of soldiers on a battlefield. The morning after the ground offensive began, *CBS Sunday Morning* anchor Charles Kuralt asked White House correspondent Bill Plant why the ground war was necessary, given Saddam's clear indication that he was willing to leave Kuwait. After acknowledging that there was little difference in the U.S. and Soviet proposals, Plant asserted that without the ground war, Bush would not have been able "to humiliate Saddam Hussein. He really wanted to go mano-a-mano with Hussein." Some news analysts might consider it surprising that no follow-up question was posed to Plant, one that might have placed the statement within a reasoned context or tried to draw out the moral implications of such braggadocio.

That the desire "to go mano-a-mano" was left as a plausible explanation for a ground war, for risking U.S. lives and killing thousands of Iraqis without arousing even slight indignation, and that it was inserted into the terrain of legitimate American political discourse, marked one of the lowest points of American news reporting. The iconic phrase, pulled straight out of fictional narratives of conflict, was the most notable indication that, at such a defining historical moment, independent news judgment had been irreversibly compromised. Strategies of press management, together with military successes, had produced an atmosphere equivalent to that of the most triumphant World War II celebrations.

As it turned out, the long-awaited Mother of All Battles was little more than a sweep against a defeated army in retreat. Quoting Pentagon sources, the *Washington Post* estimated that 85,000 to 100,000 soldiers were killed, mostly as a consequence of the air campaign. As allied forces continued to destroy the retreating Iraqi army, still defined as a target, it was characteristically the tabloid press that expressed the most visceral sentiment, "If It Moves, Kill It."[5]

Anticipating possible public criticism of what might be perceived by some as unnecessary slaughter, though not articulating that position, Dan Rather offered this explanation: "Someone might be saying, 'Why wouldn't we let them get out?' Here's the reason. What General Norman—The Bear—Schwarzkopf said from the git go...the plan was from the start to defeat the Iraqi army and liberate Kuwait...." Other explanations offered in the media argued that Hussein had not recognized the U.N. resolutions, showed no remorse and did not personally voice a surrender on the radio.

THE END OF THE VIETNAM SYNDROME

What became clear as the ground war pressed on to "total victory" was that one of the main targets for destruction was actually the specter of the Vietnam War. This theme was openly acknowledged by media organizations. Again, the most direct articulation came from CBS's Dan Rather, as he explained that, for those currently in control of the military, the "defining experience was in Vietnam," where they felt there was "political interference with the military goals." This time "all indications are that it will continue unabated until victory is complete." Negotiations would not be pursued. Only a clearly defined military triumph could overcome America's political inhibitions toward sending U.S. soldiers into foreign lands, now and in the future.

One pilot said the road to Basra, filled with the withdrawing Iraqi army, looked like "spring break at Daytona Beach" as he bombed the congested line. No images from the ground that might have sobered up the college metaphor were provided. After the war, Pulitzer prize-winning journalist Patrick Sloyan, (2001, 60–61) uncovered what was hidden in the last days of the ground war. As artillery bombardment pinned Iraqi soldiers in their trenches, plows mounted on M1 Abrams battle tanks, followed by Bradley fighting vehicles were used to push the desert sand into the trenches. About 2,000 Iraqis were able to surrender, but thousands more were killed by fire or buried alive under tons of sand. No traces of the buried bodies were seen by pool reporters allowed on the scene in the days that followed (Sloyan 2001, 62). Americans were allowed to see only uplifting footage of the liberation of Kuwait and grateful Iraqi prisoners kissing the hands of their "liberators." As Paul Rogers pointed out, only behind-the-scenes international pressure stopped the carnage at that point. It was clear that American public opinion would not have. Utterly insulated from the feelings of human suffering taking place on the ground, as Iraqi forces were being brutally slaughtered from the air as they retreated, America seemed to have finally gotten over the Vietnam Syndrome.

On March 2, 1991, the *New York Times* quoted the president in a "spontaneous burst," saying "By God, we've kicked the Vietnam syndrome once and for all." The victory was indeed complete as television declared, "This will finally be putting Vietnam behind us in so many ways and George Bush will get a lot of credit for that."

The morning after the cease-fire was announced, victory was declared, and networks interviewed the "person-on-the-street," who gloated, "we kicked their butt." Television reports assessing the destruction of once the "fourth-largest Army in the world" listed the numbers of tanks and equipment destroyed but expressed no concern for the loss of human life. Indeed, the public was directed not to care for the largely conscripted army of men referred to consistently in the media as "a machine" or personalized as "him," implying that the destruction of all those soldiers was really only the destruction of the thoroughly demonized embodiment of evil, Hussein himself.

CONCLUSION

Most Americans either never heard or quickly forgot that Ambassador April Glaspie first responded to Saddam Hussein's threat to invade Kuwait with "we have no opinion on...your border disagreement with Kuwait." The war that started in such a fog ended in a crystal-clear vision of American purpose. Reasoned discussions and informed consent were replaced by the celebration of "smart" bombs and yellow ribbons.

Put on the defensive by the military and still struggling for access to combat, the press was willing to acquiesce to military management. Journalists understood that the Pentagon's management of the press in Saudi Arabia was designed to create morale-boosting, uncritical coverage of the military deployment, yet the television networks and papers of record would not join the legal challenge brought by their counterparts. Sloyan noted the "constitutional landmark" set during the Fist Gulf War: "Desert Storm marked the occasion when the world's most powerful media barons gave up their constitutional right to report on U.S. troops in battle by bowing to government censorship" (2001, 63).

Commentators interested in fostering meaningful debate might have asked a series of questions. Now that the cautions of the memory of Vietnam have been swept away, what moral and ethical principles will replace them? If it is now acceptable that highly sophisticated weaponry can be employed to wipe out large numbers of people in the name of the American public, while hiding the consequences from that public, to whom will this New World Order be held accountable? Should the military manipulation of the press and the American public give pause to those who would invest the United States with the moral authority to wield such military might globally?

But censorship and Pentagon press strategies alone could not have vanquished the Vietnam Syndrome. As noted earlier, going to war in the Persian Gulf was not popular with the public. In an attempt to change those attitudes, the American public would become the target of a host of effective new media technologies, public relations strategies and marketing methods. Forms of persuasion would be borrowed from World War I propaganda rhetoric, mixed with opinion-management strategies designed in previous public diplomacy campaigns and combined with new public relations techniques and the latest marketing devices. Exploring the parameters of the new media environment created at the intersection of news and persuasion during the First Persian Gulf War is the subject of the next chapter.

12

Consuming the Persian Gulf War

From Baby Incubators to Patriot Missiles

As the Bush administration struggled to articulate a definitive need to go to war in the Persian Gulf, a variety of different reasons had been offered, from the preservation of American democracy to claims of Iraq's nuclear capabilities. But as Desert Shield continued through the autumn of 1991, another highly persuasive rationale for war began to circulate on Capitol Hill. The stories of Iraqi soldiers throwing premature Kuwaiti babies out of their incubators should have been recognized as a classic propaganda narrative early on. But its thematic structure, visceral impact and successful demonization of a depraved enemy provided the needed rationale for American intervention. The old story from World War I of ape-like German Huns bayoneting babies was reworked and given new life through modern marketing strategies and satellite technology.

THE BABY INCUBATOR STORY

On October 10, 1990, Nayirah, a fifteen-year-old Kuwaiti girl, gave testimony in public hearings to the Congressional Human Rights caucus. With tears in her eyes, and at times barely able to continue, she told of armed Iraqi soldiers storming hospitals in Kuwait, snatching premature babies out of their incubators and leaving them on the floor to die. Adult Kuwaiti men and women by her side cried as she gave testimony.

Hill and Knowlton

A camera crew hired by Hill and Knowlton recorded Nayirah's story, and the film was used to produce a video news release. The VNR was sent to Medialink, the firm that serves some seven hundred television stations around the United States, and eventually reached a total audience of about thirty-five million. Portions of the film were aired that night on NBC's *Nightly News.*

President Bush evoked Nayirah's story six times in one month while explaining the need to go to war: "Babies pulled from incubators and scattered like firewood across the floor." And in another speech, "…they had kids in incubators, and they were thrown out of the incubators so that Kuwait could be systematically dismantled."

Nayirah's story and other VNRs about Iraqi human rights abuses in Kuwait became compelling justifications for U.S. intervention in the Persian Gulf. By January 8, 1991, when the House Committee on Foreign Affairs held a hearing, the alleged incubator murders had risen to 312, a number also cited by Amnesty International in a human rights report widely circulated to Congress during the final months of 1990. Seven senators referred to the deaths of the babies in explaining their reasons for supporting the January 12, 1991, resolution authorizing war.

What many members of Congress and the American public did not know at the time was that Nayirah was the daughter of the Kuwaiti ambassador to the United States, and that Hill and Knowlton had coached her before she gave testimony. Only later would it become public that Hill and Knowlton was working for Citizens for a Free Kuwait, a client financed almost entirely by the Kuwaiti royal family. One Hill and Knowlton executive later interviewed on *60 Minutes* admitted that the campaign was designed to create public support for war. Polls commissioned by Hill and Knowlton from the Republican political consulting firm the Wirthlin Group showed a lack of support for intervention. Wirthlin conducted focus groups to determine a strategy that could change public opinion. They found that atrocity stories stirred anger and encouraged sentiments in favor of war. The babies-thrown-out-of-their-incubators tale was particularly effective.

The editor of *Harper's* magazine, John MacArthur (1992), observed, "The whole country got suckered." Journalists accepted Nayirah's and other stories of atrocities without question, never seeking corroboration. However, the human rights group Middle East Watch investigated the story. Researcher Aziz Abu-Hamad interviewed doctors and staff at neonatal wards of a number of different hospitals in Kuwait. He went specifically to the hospital Nayirah said she worked at. Those interviewed either knew nothing of the story or said it never took place. He also found that many doctors had been employed by the Kuwaiti government to do public relations work. Later, many of them changed their stories. Corroborating Nayirah's original story was testimony from one Dr. Bebehani, who claimed to have buried fourteen newborn babies himself and supervised the burial of over one hundred more. Bebehani turned out to be a dentist, not a doctor, and later admitted that he did not know where the babies came from, how they died, or exactly how many there were. After the war, ABC's John Martin also interviewed key Kuwaiti hospital officials. They acknowledged that some babies had died as a result of chaotic conditions, including shortages of nurses who had fled the country, but said no infants had been dumped from their incubators. Nayirah herself later admitted that her written testimony prepared by Hill and Knowlton was not true.[1]

Had the incubator story been proven a public relations ploy at the time, it most certainly would have affected the decision whether or not to go to war. Had the public and members of Congress known that the Kuwaiti government perpetrated such deceit, the outcome could have been much different.

Robert Dilenschneider, president of Hill and Knowlton at the time, was very proud of the company's role in the war. Speaking on an Australian radio documentary after the war, he said, "I believe we were able to target very precise audiences for a very precise message, and I think launch a communications campaign with an efficiency and economy that has never before been witnessed in the Western World." As we will see, such a claim can be made about many of the media strategies that were highly effective in promoting the First Gulf War. Indeed, Hill and Knowlton maintained their involvement in shaping coverage throughout the war. They worked for the Pentagon and continued to make video news releases using footage from private companies in Kuwait that were given access to the front. Broadcasting companies around the world bought the VNRs, as independent journalists were restricted from the fields of military operations.

THE VIDEO NEWS RELEASE: FROM INFORMATION TO PERSUASION

As discussed in the last chapter, Pentagon restrictions left journalists with few sources for news coming out of Kuwait, and Hill and Knowlton filled the void with the highly produced, widely distributed segments. As Dilenschneider boasted, "With one VNR, we reached 61 million Americans.... We found that the press kits were extremely important because the media couldn't get the information they needed."

But journalists had become accustomed to not getting the news they needed. During the first wave of media mergers that occurred in the late 1980s, news reporting had undergone geologic structural transformations. With the downsizing and even closing of news divisions at small television stations around the country, news was more dependent on centralized sources and newsgathering practices. In the aftermath of media consolidation, journalists found their divisions understaffed and reorganized.

Video news releases became important news fillers for news divisions experiencing the effects of bottom-line cutbacks. For over a decade, VNRs had been the "next big thing" in marketing, developed as a new strategy for product promotion, an advertisement mimicking the format of a news segment. They were being used to sell everything from seat belts to pharmaceuticals. News departments had learned to accept VNRs and present them to their viewers at face value. Indeed, many former journalists found themselves working for public relations firms creating the visually sophisticated segments their news divisions could no longer afford to produce.

Independent newsgathering and fact-checking were rapidly becoming old-fashioned techniques of a bygone era. Journalism was being replaced by media marketing techniques that targeted the public with messages intended to persuade, not inform. At the historical juncture between news and the First Gulf War, enhanced persuasive techniques met war reporting head-on, and the American public would feel the impact. The following analysis of the way the war was presented and understood seeks to further illustrate how changes in media ownership led to practices predisposed to represent the war in a favorable light. Nonfiction programming had already been given over to marketing strategies that targeted consumers with persuasive messages instead of providing information to a democratic polity.

In addition to integrating VNRs into the news frame, broadcast journalism was influenced by a variety of other marketing trends. Advertisers had been making increased demands for promotional-friendly programs for some time, and news was no longer exempt from those pressures. The Persian Gulf War was the first time advertisers were allowed to play a prominent role in shaping the design of war stories. As we will see, such influences on reporting would contribute to the creation of a media environment favorable to war.

Advertising's Influence on Program Design

As soon as the war in the Persian Gulf began, television advertisers made it clear that they were disinclined to sponsor news coverage of the conflict. Executives at all three networks complained, "Advertisers' skittishness about war coverage was costing them millions of dollars" (Carter, 1991).

War specials received high ratings, but they had sold only about 20 percent of their commercial time. Richard Dale, an executive at Deutsch Advertising, told Bill Carter (1991) of the *New York Times*, "Commercials need to be seen in the right environment. A war is just not an upbeat environment." Advertisers worried that the "tone" of most commercials was vastly different than war news that may contain tragic images. "Commercials are full of music and happiness. They have a lot of comedy in them. Everything is upbeat." There was a general reluctance to place such upbeat commercials—for items like soup, sodas and cereals—on programs about the war. The Campbell Soup Company decided to minimize its commercials in news programming during the war. The decision was part of a trend among advertisers to "stay away from programs involving heavy controversy" (Carter, 1991).

The reluctance by advertising CEOs to buy time on war programming underscored two important points. On the one hand, it signaled the degree to which advertisers have become accustomed to programs they consider appropriate vehicles for advertising messages. But it also indicated the steps broadcasters were taking to accommodate the needs of their sponsors. They listened carefully to advertisers' demands for more positive "programming environments." Programming strategies were designed to guarantee that both fiction and nonfiction shows would be profitable—more closely resembling the commercial messages surrounding them.

Pressure from advertisers led to the proliferation of upbeat "home-front" stories of the war as network executives sought to assuage the worries of their sponsors. CBS executives "offered advertisers assurances that the war specials could be tailored to provide better lead-ins to commercials" with "patriotic views from the home front" (Carter, 1991). Postwar critiques of the media coverage point out that during the Gulf War, for the first time television news featured stories of soldiers waving to their loved ones back home. As we will see in part 4, this would become a prominent feature of war reporting in the twenty-first century.

Advertising and Patriotism

CNN, defensive over charges that correspondent Peter Arnett was spreading Iraqi propaganda, often bent over backward to promote the media version of patriotism—i.e., flag-waving and war support. An extreme example was a February 15 "Special Assignment" on patriotism, in which CNN celebrated the images and sentiments of patriotic virtues. "The flags are everywhere and on everything and with everybody," reported CNN's Mark Feldstein. "In Duluth, flags flap in unison—harmony in a fresh breeze. In San Diego, a human flag—a grand gesture, a statement of solidarity."

The segment was openly celebratory of the president as the symbol of national pride, linking lengthy footage of flags to a bunting-draped portrait of George Bush. Used as background music, without identification, was the 1988 Republican campaign song. Amid the festivities there was no suggestion that anyone opposed the war. In fact, the story went so far as to assert that opposition to it was a relic of America's "troubled past," represented by a burning flag superimposed over the Vietnam Memorial as the words were spoken. That was a time in the "bad-ol'-days" when U.S. soldiers were "abandoned." African Americans, who persistently expressed more opposition to the Bush policy than whites, were featured prominently in the pro-war imagery.

When the segment presented a commercial for Boeing as an example of the use of patriotic imagery, it was difficult to tell where CNN stopped and the commercial began—except that Boeing's film quality was higher. As pictures of helicopters, tanks and soldiers giving the thumbs-up sign appeared, Feldstein said, "Those images have fueled America's new outpouring of patriotism."

Defining a Modern Propaganda Environment

As we have seen, Pentagon press restrictions and military censorship had successfully blocked most stories critical of the logistics of troop deployment. The promise of battlefield access and the Pentagon's "Media Support Program" helped foster positive stories about soldiers stationed in Kuwait. Advertisers were demanding upbeat stories, and television responded with feel-good themes of patriotism from the homefront. The government failed to articulate a just cause for war, so a public relations firm representing a foreign government created emotional narratives of murdered babies. Independent media producers and video makers were assembling footage of protests around the country, yet none of that footage was making it onto mainstream television. In the grip of war, the media environment could more accurately be characterized as persuasive than informational. It was certainly not characteristic of a public sphere that encouraged informed and reasoned discussion. Nor could it be described as one characteristic of diverse opinion.

Yet none of that sounds like "war propaganda" in the old World War I sense of the phrase. By the late twentieth century, the battle over hearts and minds was being fought with the latest high-tech communication modalities and marketing tools, with satellite feeds and sophisticated message targeting. But persuasion is also the stuff of culture, and sentimental, ironic literary modes used to make sense of the Great War no longer resonated. The culture that lays the foundations for conceiving of war is now the familiar culture of broadcast narratives and media choreography. A closer look at the language and visual strategies of one of the many television war specials will show how changing reporting techniques in the wake of economic transformations resulted in media representations that redefined war coverage.

THE WAR ON *PRIMETIME*

Diane Sawyer hosted a *Primetime* segment that best illustrates how the language and visual strategies of war coverage reflected the changes taking place in commercial media. The show featured the tank being used in the war in the Persian Gulf. Sawyer begins by explaining, "The army let us use their tank simulator so we could take you to the battlefield inside a tank." In addition to the graphic imagery, the army also supplied the tank itself. Viewers follow Diane, looking through the camera over her shoulder as she climbs onto the military vehicle. As if following a tour guide through an army theme park, we enter right behind her. The extreme subjective perspective gives the viewer the experience of entering the tank as the camera's descent jerks through the narrow compartment on top. The camera lens is our eye. Inside, we move toward the tank's viewfinder to survey the battlefield, the blurred image coming into focus as if our eye itself had approached the lens. The image then turns to video simulation as *we* start driving. The tank vaults over hills. The visual frame shoots up into the sky and then bounces back down as we hit the bottom of a rut.

Experience the News
This mode of address is fundamentally different from conventional news reporting. The newscaster does not convey information through the ritualized language of detachment. Instead, the camera is used extensively to incorporate the viewer into a prescribed subjective position. Diane invites her viewers *to experience* the tank. We do not see someone looking through the lens into the simulated battlespace; we look through it ourselves, and as we do so we lose analytical detachment. No longer allowed to sit on the sidelines and watch or contemplate, we become participants in the battle. The visual language conveys feelings of danger and anticipation. The next moment our tank is under attack. From the cockpit we are aware of being fired at. The military video simulation shows explosions coming dangerously close. As we traverse the rough terrain through ditches meant to stop our trajectory, we continue on, under fire. The camera perspective tells us that our fingers are on the buttons, and we are told, "How fast you sight the target and fire on the enemy can make the difference between life and

death, and death can come very quickly.... You make a mistake, you're dead."

Feel the Power

We have been positioned within the action. We now know what it feels like to push the buttons that control the most modern, efficient, hi-tech "killing machine." We have experienced the thrill of power and the threat of being the enemy's victim. We have been given control of the technology and the justification for its use. By watching we have come to participate in the war, quite literally, from the point of view of the military.

The techniques that convey immediacy, excitement and highly charged emotional experiences are now acceptable as "serious" news. They are also evident in contemporary filmmaking practices. In the *Primetime* segment, we feel the thrill of the battle. We furiously dodge the explosives threatening to blow our tank off the killing field and make us one of the casualties. To feel the tension of being under attack and fighting back in the hi-tech killing machine is the same technique used for depicting contemporary film violence. Even though it was informational programming about a war the public was being asked to support, the visual and textual rhetoric of the *Primetime* segment allowed no space for thought, contemplation and especially "ambivalence" about the war. Instead it offered *virtual reality*. The act of viewing constituted participation, as the format actively worked to deny any contemplative distance from the action and instead make us *feel the experience*. Here we see parallels between news design and filmic techniques. Miller (1990, 209–10) describes visual sequences that are inherently "non-narrative and subvisual" and argues that contemporary movies "force our interest, or reactions, through a visceral jolt." (As we will see, with the release of the film *Black Hawk Down*, these techniques became even more pronounced.)

Such depictions exist within increasingly commercial media. The rise of "product placement" has "damaged movie narratives…through the fundamental shift of power that the practice has wrought within the movie industry: the transfer of creative authority out of the hands of filmmaking professionals and into the purely quantitative universe of the CEOs" (Miller 1990, 198). Product placement demands that movies become vehicles for the display of commodities, and now film language follows the logic of advertising.

Advertising has also asserted itself as an integral part of broadcasting, and similar effects are evident in the way nonfiction narratives are told. As advertising drives media culture, its modes are embedded at every level. Adjectives and language used throughout the *Primetime* segment do not describe or inform; instead, like advertising, they convince and persuade. With Diane's opening lines we are invited to leave the world of information and enter into a realm of illusion, into "a rolling hi-tech fantasy." And in the exaggerated language of advertising, "the U.S. says when it comes to mobility your tank is the best in the world." None of these superlatives conveys information about the design or construction of the tank, or its appropriateness for desert warfare. Instead we are given soft-sell techniques. "This is the M1A1. It's called the king of the killing fields." It's "the fastest" in the world, and in it "you go head to head" with the enemy.

PICTURE-PERFECT BOMBS

The night the bombing of Baghdad began, "unconfirmed" reports from the Pentagon claimed that the Iraqi air force was "decimated." This of course would prove to be false, and even though those were "unconfirmed reports," they served to set the simple, exaggerated and positive *advertising* tone. On CBS, the "rolling thunder air war" was described as "staggering" and "fantastic." Cruise missile footage showed "electronic warfare" and planes that can see for three hundred miles. The night footage of the bombing of Baghdad, presented as a thing of beauty, lit up the night sky and described the destruction of the city. Pictures supplied by the Pentagon were aired and enthusiastically described as "riveting visuals" showing the "astounding accuracy" of "smart weapons systems" with "computer brains." The pilots became the *Top Guns*, just like the movie. Meanwhile, most journalists described the incessant bombing in exultant terms like "a marvel" and "picture-perfect assaults."

The Nintendo War
As the bombing continued, animation footage was used on every network, presenting the war through the visual icons of the video game. The incorporation of video game, entertainment and visual graphic formats created a unity of expression wholly distinct from traditional nonfiction. Views from cockpits showed direct hits fired on imaginary targets. Snippets of infrared video footage released by the Pentagon, taken from cameras mounted on the noses of bombers, were strikingly similar to the animation.

OF VIDEO GAMES AND REAL WARS

The visuals provided by the Pentagon were convenient one-way images, familiar to a generation brought up on video games and commercial television. Real people do not inhabit the interior space of video monitors, so there is no need to give one moment's thought to the consequences on the ground. The seductive visual perspective invites the viewer in, and this engagement creates a type of complicity with the "operation."

No one spoiled the fun by pointing out that these were only a few of thousands of the "sorties" flown, and maybe they were not all so accurate, resulting, of course, in civilian casualties or "collateral damage." Negative information does not fit within the upbeat, simple, positive advertising environment. The coverage of the bombing of Iraq and Kuwait fit the common definition of persuasion, the repetition of one powerful message to the exclusion of all others.

Utterly absent from media discourse was concern for the people of Iraq. The coverage created the desired impression that this war was accurate, antiseptic and, above all, clean, just like the world presented in commercial messages. Very few messy pictures of the thousands of civilian casualties in Iraq muddled the picture, with the exception of those provided by CNN. For his efforts, Arnett was accused of disloyalty and sympathizing with the enemy—accusations which again were meant to poison the debate about U.S. moral responsibility for the death of innocent people. Arnett incurred such criticism because he provided a consistent view of the other end of the war, a view dangerous for the legitimacy of the media as a whole. The celebration of firepower depended on not contradicting the representations of magic and fantasy. Some publications went to great lengths to cavalierly abdicate moral responsibility. As cited earlier, *Time* magazine defined "collateral damage" as "dead or wounded civilians who should have picked a safer neighborhood." At this point, news reporting becomes a cartoon, defined mainly by its commercial viability.

The generational appeal of media representation of a video war was demonstrated by the findings that people between the ages of eighteen and thirty-two supported the war in greater numbers, but knew less about it than any other age group (Lewis, Jhally and Morgan, 1991).

But war casualties, media representations of the real consequences of war, were absent, hidden by the overwhelmingly upbeat environment of persuasion.

Patriot Missiles

As the Patriot missiles entered the war, the discourse evoked to describe their use was also largely metaphoric. In news narratives they were treated as the superior white knights countering the attacks of the dark forces of Saddam's blunt instruments, the Scud missiles. Only after the war was the assessment of the Patriot missile revised. After examining videotapes and the record of damage done by Scud missiles before and after the use of

Patriots, Theodore A. Postol, professor of national security policy at the Massachusetts Institute of Technology, found that the Patriot was highly ineffective. Just as the commodities disappoint when compared to the exaggerated and fanciful promises made in advertisements, so, too, the exaggerated claims of Patriot magic were unfounded. Before Patriot missiles were used, thirteen unopposed Scuds fell in Israel. These Scuds "damaged 2,698 apartments and wounded 115 people" (Postol 1991–92, 140). After Patriot missiles were set in place to defend Tel Aviv and Haifa, there were fourteen to seventeen Scud attacks. After Patriots, "7,778 apartments were reported damaged, 168 people were wounded, and one person was killed…by an impacting Patriot interceptor" (Postol 1991–92, 140). Postol explains that the increased damage after Patriots was a consequence of greater amounts of debris falling to the ground when Scuds were intercepted. Pieces of Patriots were added to the Scud debris. In addition, "it appears that in a high percentage of these cases, the scud warheads fell intact and detonated, but the impact of the large pieces could do considerable damage as well" (Postol 1991–92, 146).

News as Product Promotion

ABC correspondent Beth Nissan reported feeling uncomfortable covering the Gulf War. At a forum assessing the war's media coverage, she said she did not "like the idea of working for an advertising agency." She characterized news coverage as an "American media commercial where everything works perfectly and the viewers are asked to buy the product portrayed."[2]

Patriot Magic
Advertising culture is saturated with the intoxicating assertion that for every problem or need there is a product solution. Indeed the Patriot missiles, the "smart bombs," and the vast array of hi-tech weapons were "incanted" as product solutions to the war. Products routinely perform impossible feats of magic in advertisements. As Jhally (1989, 217) points out, "all normal physical and social arrangements are held in abeyance." So accustomed is the public to this mode of discourse that singular, exaggerated, one-sided claims of properties, almost magical in nature, seem plausible.

Weapons became the magical objects that would in the most simple, clean and easy way solve the problem in the Persian Gulf. As Judith Williamson (1978, 140–42) observed, "Magic…creates a never ending exchange between passivity and action, a translation between technological action and magical action." Advertising offers the individual compensation for inactivity, and in the case of the war, exclusion from public debate and participation. "The only thing we can *do* in fact is to buy the product, or incant its name—this is all the action possible as *our* part of the excitement offered." And the excitement offered by the smart bombs and missiles constituted the public's participation in the war.

The Acceptance of Contradiction

As Ewen (1988) argues, the logic of advertising promotes the unity of opposites and creates a milieu in which contradiction no longer evokes a sense of uneasiness. Because the quality of commodities is conferred through an associational discourse, advertising creates a geography of arbitrary connections devoid of internal coherence and material connections. Nonconformity is sold as a lifestyle, the adherence to which requires conformity. Reverence of nature is evoked to sell a plethora of products whose manufacture, use and elimination destroy the serene beauty of nature depicted in those advertisements.

These discursive strategies allowed the enormous contradictions of Gulf War reporting to go unchallenged. How could Saddam Hussein be likened to Hitler? Was the history of the post-World War I division of the Middle East remotely similar to the history of Europe? How did the United Nations suddenly become the legitimate voice of world unity when previous U.S. involvement with the world body had been contentious? Most striking was the justification that the United States would restore "democracy" for a kingdom with no electoral process and demonstrably lacking in social equity. Lastly, if the war was fought for human rights or humanitarian purposes, and not for the control of oil, why were the devastating effects of the postwar sanctions of so little concern?

In lieu of independent evaluation, the public was enjoined not to seek accuracy in the justifications for war, but rather to enjoy the feeling of national unity, even if that unity was coerced.

Lifestyle and Belonging

Just as lifestyle advertising promises emotional security through a sense of belonging to the consumer group, so, too, did war coverage offer belonging as a psychological gratification. As Fore (1991, 52) points out, media representations invited viewers "to share emotionally charged experiences with others, [and] to gain a sense of identity...." Again, war representations resembled advertising more than depiction of complicated, confusing, often negative depictions of war.

Indeed, the public was enjoined in no uncertain terms to buy the product. Opposing the war became the equivalent of not supporting the troops. The media adhered to that assumption consistently. A proliferation of stories from the homefront featuring flags and yellow ribbons aired nightly. Opposition came to mean disloyalty. Patriotism was the last refuge for support of a war that was little understood by the public. The wave of yellow ribbons and American flags that swept across the doorsteps of America became testimonies of the power of the media to generate a mass psychology of uncritical national unity. The rhetoric of national unity embraces the same promise of belonging asserted in lifestyle advertising.

The Changing Discourse

The aim of contemporary advertising is fundamentally different from reasoned discourse. Its purpose is not to inform but to evoke positive feelings that can be attached to products. Whether by the alleviation of pain or the fantasy of wish fulfillment, advertisements work through affective states, not logical discourse. As an advertising consultant, Tony Schwartz regularly cautioned advertisers "not to make claims that could be proven false, but to concentrate instead on creating pleasurable experiences" (Jhally 1989, 225). War coverage did just that. It created positive feelings, not public debate. Certainly many of the assertions made by the media about the war were debatable, but that was not the point of the coverage. In a persuasive environment, a visceral response becomes the substitute for public debate.

Most of the claims made about the motivations for the war—the efficiency of the smart bombs and their effects on the people of Iraq, the accuracy of the Patriot missiles—could easily have been proven false in an information environment. One moment of critical thought might have sparked the realization that in a small country like Kuwait it would be virtually impossible to have over three hundred premature babies in that many incubators in one place. The closing down of information left a void in media discourse that was filled with the emotional, associative, illogical discourse of persuasion.

Under the influence of advertising, the public becomes a target, not a participant. Controlled information curtailed the public's right to know, but there was a reward for being kept in the dark. The place for civic information was transformed into a realm of fantasy wish-fulfillment. The war coverage offered the thrill of technological empowerment. Positioning the viewer in front of the control panel is a compelling summons, an invitation to control the technology. Media representation of high-tech military weaponry—the tanks and the Patriot missiles—evoked feelings of empowerment through the control of state-of-the-art weaponry. Numerous news programs invited us into video simulators and positioned our hands at the controls, at the same time that real control and political power had been foreclosed by the military. Over the next decade, these representative strategies would become very familiar with the development of videogame warfare as entertainment.

What substitutes for representations that offer distance and critical space is what Fiske calls "voyeuristic pleasure," defined as "the power to...insert oneself into the process of representation so that one is not subjected by it, but conversely, is empowered by it" (Fiske 1987, 236). War coverage allowed the American public to feel powerful. William F. Fore (1991, 52) noted that television representations of the war offered viewers psychological gratifications. "The War coverage met a number of deep-rooted psychological needs: to feel powerful and in control, to experience extreme emotions in a guilt-free and non-threatening environment." The fantasy of hyperrealism protects at the same time that it evokes positive feelings about war and its technology.

Such feelings of empowerment have come to replace the actual political power the public might wield by becoming involved in national debate from an informed perspective. A University of Massachusetts study done by Lewis, Jhally and Morgan (1991) measuring public opinion and public knowledge illustrated the power of persuasive modes to generate support for a war the public knew very little about. The study found that "the more television people watched the less they knew" and the more they supported the war.

The effects of "news" coverage were overwhelming because in covering the Gulf War, journalistic standards were replaced by the more persuasive logic of advertising. The fundamental assumptions of advertising, with its simplified and exaggerated language, its false promises of fantasy wish-fulfillment and empowerment, inspired the design of Gulf War coverage. The war and its media representations met at an historic crossroad where advertising communication practices converged for the first time with international conflict.

Journalists and public relations specialists themselves were surprised by opinion polls that measured the response of the American public to the war coverage. David Colton (1991), Deputy Managing Editor for *USA Today*, said that pollsters had not seen numbers like these before: "85 percent who want to start a ground war, 88 percent supporting Bush. I mean you ask somebody their correct name and you don't get those numbers.... And Saddam Hussein who was known by nobody on August 1st, suddenly was Hitler, and chemical weapons were known.... I'm still stunned by the support on a very complicated issue that isn't as black and white as the numbers are showing."

In the midst of war's consensus, Americans were shielded from critical discussions and the knowledge that tens of thousands of Iraqis were killed in the first month of devastating air attacks, and most remained unaware that Iraqis continued to die in large numbers after the war (Roy 2003, 65). American bombs targeted water treatment plants (Nagy 2001), and half a million Iraqi children died, as a consequence of war and a decade of sanctions, from lack of food, medicine, water, and health care. Amid the silence about dying Iraqi children, U.S. Ambassador Madeleine Albright would tell Leslie Stahl on CBS, *60 Minutes*, "I think this is a very hard choice, but the price—we think the price is worth it" (May 12, 1996).

CONCLUSION

Very early on, the war coverage became so exaggeratedly positive that it seemed to become a caricature of news reporting. The embellished reports of the accuracy and effectiveness of high-tech weaponry employed adjectives so inappropriate for nonfiction programming that it seemed a burlesque. The maudlin narratives of hardship endured by those involved seemed a self-parody of the victims and heroes of tabloid news. Saddam Hussein, scripted as "the enemy" and embodiment of evil, resembled a cartoon character far more closely than a head of state. And the ubiquity of the flag-waving images rendered the lack of media independence unmistakable. In other words, the discourse was not that of information, knowledge or understanding—or any of the social purposes usually associated with news reporting. Instead it was the simplified, exaggerated, upbeat and exciting discourse of persuasion and advertising. The grabby, stimulating, evocative formats led to one sensibility and ultimately to a nod of agreement as the public was asked to buy war—-the product.

13

CNN

24 Hours of War

It is by now well understood that the First Persian Gulf War changed the political geography of the Middle East and U.S. global aspirations into the twenty-first century. But Operation Desert Storm also changed the landscape of the American and international news media forever. The clear winner was Cable News Network—in ratings, name recognition, praise, even envy. CNN became the dominant global channel.

When Iraqi foreign minister Tariq Aziz was asked if he was familiar with a statement made by President George H. Bush, he sarcastically answered, *yes, he also watched CNN*. Dan Quayle boasted that viewers of CNN could see for themselves how successful the air campaign was.

Over a period of years, compelled by the highly competitive domestic market, CNN had chosen to develop an international newsgathering and dissemination network. Its organizational strategies focused on setting up a complex system of foreign bureaus, barter agreements and satellite hook-ups at a time when other major outlets were moving toward corporate conglomeration and cutting back funding for international news bureaus and staff worldwide. By 1990, CNN had established an information flow able to circulate materials from and among many countries, including those traditionally shunned by the established news networks. These practices gave CNN a presence in Iraq that its other American competitors could not match during Desert Storm.

Using this newly established system of two-way communication, CNN correspondent Peter Arnett stayed in Baghdad and continued to report from there, even as other journalists were lining up to board planes out of the country after the U.S. government warned them to leave. Certainly the Pentagon preferred a one-way flow of information, from the U.S. outward, but during the early days of the war, Arnett provided an American voice reporting from the country on the receiving end of the air war. Indeed, he became one of the only reminders that there *was* a receiving end. The journalist-left-behind-enemy-lines became the target for a flood of criticism. For staying in the country, Arnett was accused of becoming a propagandist for Saddam Hussein. But while statements and even images provided by the Iraqi government were easily dismissed, eyewitness reports by a Western journalist were harder for the U.S. military to counter.

While his first reports depicting Baghdad markets functioning normally did not contradict U.S. government assertions that Iraqi casualties were light, Arnett quickly came under fire for his eyewitness accounts of the consequences as the bombing continued. His first controversial story disclosed that an alleged chemical weapons plant hit by U.S. bombs was in fact a baby milk factory that supplied many countries in the Arab world. Arnett reported seeing no barbed wire surrounding the grounds or other indications that the plant had any military purpose. While commentators ridiculed Arnett for being under the spell of the Iraqis, the German architects of the factory indicated it would be impossible for the building to have been used for chemical weapons manufacturing (*Washington Post*, February 8, 1991), and Nestle confirmed that the plant manufactured a competitor to its own infant formula (*Weekend Australian*, January 26, 1991).

Enemy Propaganda

The media began to report that images of the destruction of Baghdad were part of a "campaign of psychological warfare" against the American public designed to "weaken our resolve." The intensity with which news outlets focused on the idea of Iraqi propaganda stood in sharp contrast to the media's silence about the arguably more effective U.S. propaganda campaign detailed in this study. Saddam Hussein's clumsy attempts at displaying friendliness toward the children he was holding hostage were easy to see through, but the U.S. media were nevertheless diligent in alerting the public that propaganda was on their screens. In one report NBC's Bryant Gumbel gazes cautiously at footage of Arnett interviewing Hussein. He has scheduled an NBC "psychological expert" to view the footage with him. Gumbel asks, "Is he saying that for our benefit?" CNN anchors also repeatedly warned about Iraqi censorship. A story aired on CNN by Independent Television Network reporter Brent Sadler is introduced with: "Keep in mind an Iraqi official monitored him." Sadler himself repeats the caveat as the story begins: "All media, including ITN, have to operate under Iraqi control." And when the anchor returns: "And again this reminder: Brent Sadler's report is subject to Iraqi censorship." All these things could also have been said of reporters in Saudi Arabia, who were restricted, monitored and censored by the Pentagon, perhaps to a greater degree than in Iraq. A Western journalist interviewed by Sadler in the segment described above contradicts the anchor's assertions: "Most things, apart from straight military information, you can report from here. Censorship here is exaggerated."

"Arnett Syndrome" and Civilian Casualties

Reports on the destruction of Baghdad earned Arnett vitriolic criticisms, not just from senators like Alan Simpson, but also from mainstream media critics such as the *Washington Post's* Tom Shales, who (February 16, 1991) described "Arnett Syndrome" as "a seemingly inexhaustible concern for the welfare of the Iraqis."

The degree of skepticism contained in reports from Baghdad illustrated the very important point that war correspondents are keenly aware of how reporting can be used as propaganda directed toward domestic populations. Brent Sadler sounded like a psychological warfare expert when he said, "In terms of media imagery, this kind of routine scene at a Baghdad market is important for Iraqi propaganda. The sale of birds...is used to illustrate an atmosphere of calm and resolve." We might pause to note here that if all persuasive war rhetoric, including that which emanates from the Pentagon, were introduced in like manner, its effects would be greatly diminished.

But mainstream journalists, dependent on sources and access, and many times in agreement with their government's action, rarely acknowledge that they are being used by a sophisticated system of opinion manipulation—one, of course, totally outside Saddam Hussein's league. Indeed, the resistance to using the term propaganda to characterize all war rhetoric sets up a profound double standard, since only the enemy uses propaganda.

With the exception of Arnett in Baghdad and the controversy surrounding his reporting, American official and military sources provided the overwhelming bulk of CNN's 'round-the-clock coverage.

24 HOURS OF WHAT?

One of the traditional lamentations on the limits of network news has been the time constraint. Since the mid-1960s, is has been argued that half-hour programs are simply not long enough to explain complex national and international affairs. The short segments are inadequate for the presentation of serious perspectives. Then came CNN. A news organization that had the luxury of 24 hours, time that could presumably be filled with more background and analytical information than the networks ever dreamed of.

But CNN did not present any greater depth of coverage of the Persian Gulf War. The vast majority of airtime was filled with reporting that revolved around a narrowly defined military perspective. Now familiar to twenty-first-century audiences, the hours were filled with minute details of activities in the "theater of operation," anticipation of upcoming confrontations with seemingly endless speculation of battle strategies. The briefings, speeches and addresses by U.S. officials were often carried live, and then excerpted segments were repeated throughout the day with very little additional information. Soundbites punctuated the coverage, such as James Baker asserting that Desert Storm was "a just war in a just way," or President Bush assuring "so that peace will prevail, we will prevail." A critical posture to such pronouncement was abandoned in favor of the official redundancies that were left unchallenged.

Only in rare cases was a historical perspective presented, even with time allotments. It might be argued that analysis and history are inappropriate for CNN's "video wire service" format. However, particular historical perspectives were offered, and the topics are telling. One long segment featured the history and development of military tanks, broadcast live from Fort Knox's World War II museum. In-depth military reporting was also propelled into the future, with an "analytical" report on what the fighter planes of the twenty-first century and the even higher-tech "war of the future" will look like.

The expanded format resulted, in most cases, in the uninterrupted, unchallenged dissemination of longer and more frequent versions of the U.S. government perspective. So it became very clear that CNN presented the world to the world, but through the highly filtered prism of a U.S. lens. Yet a muddled, incongruous view came to characterize CNN coverage during the Persian Gulf War. The viewer must have felt a strange discomfort taking hold after watching this new cable news network for any length of time. Eyewitness reports from Baghdad showed images of the destruction of the bombing and its impact on civilian life. A reporter stood in front of a destroyed bridge and commented, "Its loss will further complicate the lives of civilians here." Later at a press briefing, officers would show aerial photos of hits on the same bridge, now unquestioningly referred to as a military target. Then a later CNN report would state that Iraq is "stepping up its claims" of civilian casualties: one hundred and fifty dead, thirty-five of them children. This would be followed by the disclaimer that "extreme efforts are being made to avoid civilian casualties."

But the alert viewer could no doubt glean that there was a perspective on the war beyond the carefully tailored view of the Pentagon information managers, one more troubling and deadly, not easily hidden from the point of view of the country where the bombs were landing. Ultimately, CNN coverage offered another view of the war by virtue of its perspective, but, as we will see, careful planning by the Pentagon during the second war on Iraq all but erased that view, particularly on American television screens. Over six hundred embedded correspondents would report Operation Iraqi Freedom through the eyes of the American military.

For its coverage of the Persian Gulf War, CNN would be lionized in the years that followed. The HBO film *Live From Baghdad* aired shortly before the second war on Iraq, in December 2002. The movie portrayed the danger and chaos of reporting from enemy territory and the difficulty of keeping the satellite technology up and running. The media became the story, and the war was seen through the eyes of the brave reporters who stayed "in country." The Hill and Knowlton invention would be revisited in the film, depicted as if the story were true, not the discredited propaganda of a decade earlier. Just before another war in Iraq, the public would hear the story of the babies on the cold hospital floor in Kuwait thrown out of their incubators by invading Iraqi forces. The baby atrocity story, first invented as propaganda in World War I would come full circle, perpetuated into the twenty-first century, timed as advanced notice of anther invasion. Only through the efforts of the media watch group FAIR, did HBO executives admit that the story was probably a fiction.

The other earlier films made after the First Gulf War, were ambivalent interpretations of the war and its motivations, disturbing stories that expressed discomfort toward the war.

14

How the War Was Remembered

From Courage Under Fire
to Saving Private Ryan

After the First Gulf War, smart bombs and high-tech weapons became the central commodities around which the culture of war revolved. The iconographic references to obliterated targets blown up on videotape by precision "sorties" would long be recognized by a generation who also tied yellow ribbons around trees for the troops. The war had created heroes for a small screen. General Norman Schwarzkopf gained heroic stature as he stood in uniform before television cameras pointing at maps where he wielded the destructive technological power over Iraq. Televised daily press briefings and military-supplied camera gun footage fueled the celebration of "Stormin' Norman." Only later would this imagery, so successful at the time, be perceived as a Pentagon public relations problem.

Avoidance of a bloody ground battle with few American casualties was considered an astonishing success at the end of the war. President George H. W. Bush proclaimed that the country had arrived at the end of the Vietnam Syndrome. In the years since Vietnam, fighting wars from the air and preventing media coverage of the theater of battle had been the military strategy of choice. Quick interventions with few casualties that no one saw prevent the public from turning against military adventures. Grenada, Panama, the Persian Gulf and Kosovo fueled little opposition. But the military paid a price. While air attacks saved the lives of U.S. military personnel, their imagery replaced depictions of fighting men demonstrating their bravery and courage under fire. These awesome new video modes never translated well into grunt-level narratives of hand-to-hand combat, physical exhaustion and the classic sacrifices made by indomitable foot soldiers—the classic heroes of war.

The celebration of soldiers, bravery and the glories of fighting are elemental aspects of the culture of war, and those things would not be resurrected until Steven Spielberg made *Saving Private Ryan*.

COURAGE UNDER FIRE AND THE REFUSAL OF VICTORY CULTURE

Filmic renderings of the war were troubled narratives, not myths of victory. The first significant film to be set in the Persian Gulf depicting Desert Storm was Edward Zwick's *Courage Under Fire* (1996). Instead of celebrating masculine pilots in heroic fighter jets, the film features Lieutenant Colonel Nathan Sterling (Denzel Washington), the leader of a tank battalion, who during the war had directed fire at a suspected enemy vehicle, only to find that he had destroyed one of his own. After the war he struggles to come to terms with this incident of friendly fire that bears an uncomfortably close resemblance to actual conduct in the war. Sterling is dispatched to investigate events surrounding the death of Captain Karen Walden (Meg Ryan), a Medivac helicopter pilot killed in action. The film's dark cast of the military goes further than friendly fire and portrays the mutiny, cowardliness and incompetence of the soldiers Captain Walden helped save. Unable to accept orders from a woman, one soldier under her command leaves her wounded in the desert, telling the rescue pilot that she is already dead.

The movie ends in success, but it seems a personal victory for Captain Walden, who appears in flashback and receives the Medal of Honor. The main axis of the narrative is gendered, and the movie illustrates the difficulties for women in the male culture of the military. As Robyn Wiegman (1994) argues, during the First Gulf War, women entered the theater of operations as combatants for the first time in history, "threatening to undo war as the privileged location of masculinity's performance" (176). So controversial was this film that the U.S. Army refused to supply equipment unless Zwick changed the script. Refusing to depict the military and the war in a better light, Zwick made the film without assistance from the Pentagon. By the second invasion of Iraq and the daring rescue of Jessica Lynch, the military would learn to control its own fictions confirming the need for combat to save the "soft bodies" of the "weaker sex." The rescue would reaffirm the new culture of militarism by reclaiming the battlefield as the site of masculine prowess and military paternalism, values essential to the language of war being constructed though fear of terrorism. But that would come later.

THREE KINGS

In the years that followed Desert Storm, David O. Russell's *Three Kings* (1999) demonstrated the ambivalence to a war whose motivations were little understood. Though the public had acquiesced to the war, that consent was largely a product of media persuasion of a glorified television spectacle that lost much of its influence once off-screen. So quickly replaced with other programming was the war that a year later the president who proclaimed an end to the Vietnam Syndrome would lose his bid for reelection.

The motivations of the main characters in *Three Kings* are less than noble, as they embark on an adventure to steal Kuwaiti gold taken by the Iraqis during their occupation of Kuwait. Along the way they do help a group of refugees find their way into Iran, but they are also paid in the bargain. The film demonstrates the callousness of racist attitudes toward Iraqis, using language like "rag head," and the shallowness of American foreign policy toward the country and its people. Yet it does try to redeem that policy by rewriting one of the most troubling aspects of the war. In the aftermath of the Gulf War President Bush encouraged Iraqis to rise up against Hussein. When they did, however, the United States did nothing to stop Saddam and his forces from crushing the rebellion. Pollard (2003) notes that the movie tries to rewrite that history. "*Three Kings* encourages the viewer to identify vicariously with a military action that appears to save Iraqi lives. Of course the action is nothing more than a fantasy. U.S. forces did nothing to assist rebels or refugees..." (336). Ultimately the film fails to remember the war as noble, or the Americans as altruistic.

SAVING PRIVATE RYAN: BACK TO THE GRAND NARRATIVE

It was not until 1998 that the military victory in the First Gulf War would be culturally celebrated. Steven Spielberg retrofit the classic Hollywood war movie in the revival film *Saving Private Ryan*, and in so doing reclaimed military heroism by returning to the grand narrative of the Good Fight. The war movie genre had been mocked and challenged by such nihilistic post-Vietnam renderings as *Apocalypse Now* and *Full Metal Jacket*. To reinvent military legitimacy and American triumphalism in the late 1990s, the war movie needed to be recast in a mold where military authority was legitimate and commanding officers were once again noble. By setting the film on the Normandy battlefields and the European theater, the audience could identify with the unquestioned bravery of uncompromised heroes under one of the most vicious attacks by easily recognized enemies.

Captain Miller in *Saving Private Ryan* is a classic war hero. As Auster (2002) puts it, he is "that generic of all Hollywood heroes, the uncommon common man." Miller is able to demonstrate extraordinary abilities only in the context of war. Played by the movie's biggest star, Tom Hanks, the audience is invited to identify with him as he quells the near-mutiny of his men, counsels his young soldiers, worries about the numbers lost under his command and holds up under the pressures of continued battle even as his hand begins to shake. Miller reasserts the legitimacy of military command, breaking with the post-Vietnam treatments in which military authority was derided as contemptible. In an emotionally fraught scene at the end of the movie, he is killed only moments before reinforcements arrive. In one of the most patriotic sequences in American film, Captain Miller's death can only be justified by the words of Abraham Lincoln himself, who speaks of the costs of freedom, as the American flag waves. Conventional World War II treatment shrouds death on the battlefield with an aura of noble sacrifice to the higher cause, civilization itself.

There are films with important cultural significance whose treatments resonate historically in significant ways. *Saving Private Ryan* is one of those films. Indeed, an edition of the *Journal of Popular Film and Television* highlighted the historic revival of the World War II narrative after the First Gulf War. In that volume, John Hodgkins (2002, 77) writes, "If the Gulf War was a military and political attempt to atone for the conflict in Vietnam, then *Saving Private Ryan* is a filmic one." By the end of the 1990s, the legitimacy of the military had been reestablished through the use of a dislocated cultural form that actively denied the highly mechanized modern warfare of aerial bombardment. In doing so, it sought to reclaim a more heroic battlefield where soldiers fought and died for a just cause and were able to demonstrate their courage. These issues would continue to be central to the culture of war and became the subject of one of the first controversies about war's conduct in the aftermath of the September 11 attacks.

Part IV

Terrorism, Censorship and Patriotism

Re-Scripting Victory Culture

15

From Tragedy to War after 9/11

As flames consumed the World Trade Center, framed against the blue sky of a late summer morning, it was difficult to comprehend that the representations were real. Black smoke billowed from both towers, and at times a faint shadow, ghostlike, seemed to fall and twist its way past the gaping hole in Tower One. Yet the studio voices that accompanied the images spoke only of buildings, with little mention that the smoking specters were occupied by human beings. TV anchors, some calm, some excited, repeated that a plane had crashed into the North Tower, and then another hit the second skyscraper. Live footage showed real buildings burning in real time, but the surreal effect of the long camera shots was amplified by the lack of natural sound. As another explosion tore through the second tower and flames silently consumed more floors, the realization that these were actual sequences of real events began to take hold.

The inability to fully grasp events as they occurred in real time was further hindered by the field of images familiar to media culture, the ones most readily available as frames of reference. Fictional narratives of computer-generated action films, the stuff of summer blockbusters, routinely draw on urban mutilation and destruction to entertain audiences sitting in air-conditioned comfort. *Independence Day*, one such cartoon-like filmic adventure, features aliens attacking New York and Washington, the very cities that were now being shown burning on every network channel. Our perceptions have been permanently framed by the sensibilities of those commanding fictions, and television practitioners were certainly under the sway of the techno-hyper-real. Openly awed by the visual spectacle, one television anchor intoned, "This is quite a sight." It seemed as if we were living through "Life—The Movie." Could this be some sort of spectacular sequel? It was hard to bring actual human beings into this zone, which was essentially fictional, uniquely visual and usually without real consequences. After all, we do not mourn for the thousands who die in movies like *Independence Day*. Instead, we are thrilled by the adrenaline rush of excitement and awed by the visual spectacle of American entertainment genius.

Throughout the day there was much concern expressed for the New York skyline. At Newark Airport, one journalist pointed a camera over the tails of a fleet of United Airlines jets to find empty sky where this morning, we were told, stood the World Trade Center. Commentators lamented the loss of the buildings, yet the fact that people had already entered them to start their workdays was rarely mentioned. It became clear that this was deliberate after a police officer requested anonymity for estimating that the loss of life would be in the thousands.

A misguided sense of responsibility might have prevented reporters from attending to those still inside. Was it some desire to prevent mass hysteria?[1] Whatever the reasons, television did not see fit to allow viewers to grieve for the people left trapped in the buildings *at the time they were still alive before the buildings went down*. We will never be able to have that collectively summoned moment of silence they all deserved. One journalist actually used the term "collateral damage" for those killed, diminishing the humanity of the lost.

Millions of people watched as the first, then the second tower collapsed floor by floor, each onto itself, as thick, white dust pushed out from under the rubble into the surrounding area. Cameras caught clouds of debris billowing along the ground, intensified as it was channeled between narrow city blocks. People ran out of side streets screaming, pursued by the threatening clouds. Those sequences, too, were familiar, strikingly similar to visual effects in movies such as *Armageddon*. There, too, people in the film (extras) also run down city streets between tall urban structures, escaping from threatening destruction. Repeating such sequences over and over, many times with no sound, further removed them from the realm of real-time experience. What became endless repetition turned the events of September 11 into a fascination. By day's end, one of the newsmagazines had produced a slick sequence molded into familiar entertainment-enhanced newspeak ending the narration with, "doctors and interns lined up like on a set of a disaster movie."

The people who were featured on news reports that day were the ones out of harm's way—survivors. Some eyewitnesses told how they had fled the buildings, but most who spoke had already been cleaned up, calmed down and seated in television studios, the danger for them well past. Television footage did show some New Yorkers covered in soot, running away from the dust. As one man came into the frame, his lips moved, but studio voices talked over his image. We were told that a storeowner was giving out water but could not view such meaningful moments. In class the following day, many students said they had turned away from American television and watched instead the BBC, which offered more on-the-ground reporting of people in the streets who were allowed to speak for themselves. U.S. television personalities interpreted and explained, described and repeated, a discourse that tended to create distance from the more immediate terror of human experience spoken by the victims themselves.

This was not reporting that positioned viewers in the streets experiencing what New Yorkers were feeling, sharing their struggles for survival and grieving for the ones lost. Instead, it was coverage that was awed by the spectacle, cleverly referenced and calmed with the stories deemed appropriate by gatekeepers. Those who wanted to be thinking, feeling citizens, part of a human community pulling together in a crisis, found themselves instead placed in front of a sight, at a distance. The disaster had no frame of reference in the world of popular culture adequate for its expression, one able to grasp its meanings. Television struggled to find ways to express a sense of reverence for those lost, but the fictional frames are just that: entertainments. The storylines and image styles of commercial culture draw attention away from emotional empathy. We have few words and virtually no visual conventions able to recognize the sadness of death as it happens, while preserving the dignity of those it is happening to.

Ethical battles have been fought, some won, some lost, about airing graphic depictions of human horrors. Many have been deemed too ratings-worthy to be shelved. Presented in short bursts with little context, the images of such human dramas are sensational. Those who find themselves in desperation in front of network cameras are mostly in other parts of the world. The presentation of such horrors is reserved for people outside our own communities. When the media air grizzly pictures of people suffering the consequences of famine, disasters, death and war, they are elsewhere, crowded together, begging in front of the camera, under attack, starving, suffering horrible indignities. Their language, dress and cultural expressions are not commensurate with our own. They are presented as those outside our experiences; they become Othered. As we found with images from Central America during the Reagan years, the news context seldom evokes emotional engagement. We are distracted from compassion, with talk of geopolitical strategies and policy consequences for U.S. interests.

Commercial television did find a footing the day after the attack. As New Yorkers struggled with their grief, even commercial television found a human perspective. Family members began their hopeless search for the missing, and local news featured them holding pictures of the lost. Held by mothers, brothers, daughters, wives and husbands in the throes of grief, they looked back at viewers. Those in pain, as recognizable members of our own community, bridged the gap between empathy and distance.

INDEPENDENT MEDIA AND PUBLIC GRIEF

Within hours of the attacks, another kind of documentation was being carried out in earnest by independent artists, filmmakers and videographers, many residents of New York City. This was documentation of a collective expression of public witness and grieving. New Yorkers seeking to find comfort in the embrace of shared emotional experience had spontaneously found a sense of place and community at Union Square Park, where hundreds of people gathered to mourn, cry, talk and exchange emotional reactions. This collective testimony included poems, candles, banners and songs among strangers compelled to connect to a shared humanity in the face of crisis. All this was documented, and within days videotapes were being distributed outside mainstream media outlets, on the Internet, on college campuses and over public-access television and community broadcasting.[2]

Public expression in the streets of New York and on college campuses, much of it documented by alternative media, included questions, challenges and a commitment to finding the answers to what had motivated the attacks. As Judith Butler observes in her fine contemplative essays in *Precarious Life*, the attacks exposed unbearable vulnerability and were cause for fear and mourning; they were also instigations for political reflection. Students and others began such reflection by posing questions; one of the most recognizable became "why do they hate us?" A reevaluation of foreign policy was at the top of the list of topics. Some wanted to redefine America within a global community. Contradictions emerged with the realization that Americans enjoy democracy and freedom but that the U.S. government supports authoritarian regimes that deny those same rights and rule by force and brutality. Middle East experts and policy critics understood well that U.S. support of authoritarian regimes had led to repression and human rights violations in countries such as Saudi Arabia, where most of the terrorists who piloted the planes had come from. These were the issues raised for debate among people who sought to understand the attacks in a global context. As residents of the First World, the familiar security of American lives had been suddenly shattered beyond the imaginable, and new imaginings were stirred.

Yet those in positions to respond to the attacks would rely on familiar narratives commonly imagined in American culture. The president in power soon imaged himself on the take-charge heroes of popular culture. George Bush asked rhetorically, "Have you heard the saying out West, Wanted Dead or Alive?" Certainly other models were available in that same cultural firmament, but at that moment in history American vulnerability transmuted with lighting speed into military violence and retaliation. The culture of war and the icons of heroism would be drawn upon and redrawn for the genres that would come to represent America's new War on Terror, and blaze the path to victory over the forces of evil. These were the sentiments repeated with increasing ferocity in the media in the aftermath of the attacks. The American mainstream media never paused to ask other questions, such as those posed by Judith Butler and others. If we are interested in arresting cycles of violence, what, politically, can be made of grief instead of a call for war? Instead, war scenarios would set in motion a course of violence that would become all but impossible to halt.

CALLING FOR WAR

With so many possibilities for action and reassessment, the media and their spokespeople immediately directed the country's emotional response toward retribution, presenting war as inevitable. On network television, the call for war started within the first few hours of the attacks and would be repeated with increasing certainty. Within days ABC news featured a montage of voices from Americans across the country, each calling for a military response. One man says, "They can't do this to us, we're Americans." Another warns, "We're going to clean their clock," and a women asserts that "You can't reason with the enemy." Though a small group of people, their sentiments stood unopposed, as representative of the totality of American opinion. Commentators, former officials and news anchors such as Tom Brokaw, steeped in his greatest-generation mythologies, were eager to liken the terrorist attack to Pearl Harbor, an event with very little in common with 9/11. But after Pearl Harbor America declared war, and that would be the inevitable next step in 2001. So many years after Walter Cronkite went to Vietnam to argue for an "honorable" peaceful negotiation to end the war, his successor Dan Rather, in a moment of high emotion, would tell David Letterman that he wanted to follow George Bush into battle.

WAR RHETORIC

Within days President Bush called for a "war on terror" and referred to Osama Bin Laden as the "Evil One." These words were direct quotes from Harold Lasswell's account of effective war propaganda: "All the specific means of conquering the Evil One are, and should be, glorified. The cult of battle requires that killing the enemy should have the blessing of the holy sentiments" (1927, 206). A demonized enemy had been identified within a religious context, asserting that this new battle would be carried out in the name of God. This led the president to explain the War on Terror using the word "crusade." Such psychic agitation removed any reasoned analytical framework from geopolitics and diplomacy and placed it among personal hatreds.

The simple dichotomies of war between good and evil quickly emerged as the president called on the world community to choose between civilization and terrorism. A steady stream of voices framed a "new war" of values between good and evil, between freedom, liberty and "our way of life." Feeling it impossible to oppose such abstract ideals, few felt comfortable voicing a protest against freedom, democracy and our civilized values, especially after the violation of American sovereignty. The rhetoric closed off the debate, its political dimensions and its complexities. There would be no open debate on American foreign policy, especially in the Middle East, especially in the mainstream media. A few commentators would be the ones to raise questions.

Bumpers and Branding the Attack

Ratings for the big three network newscasts had been in a free fall for years, but audiences almost doubled as Americans looked to network television for information. Television capitalized on the commercial advantage by branding the crisis, tying it to their networks logos. The face of American television was redesigned using an array of starkly patriotic and militaristic images that evoked power, force and retaliation. Pulsating targets tagged with bold capital letters heralded "America's New War." Television viewed its role as providing a sense of unity, and of course the redesigned graphic presentation of crisis and response that would keep the ratings high. It failed at the much more important task of providing a multiplicity of voices, information and debate of citizens in a democracy. Unity translated into speaking in a single voice and disseminating executive branch persuasions to get the country ready for combat and the vanquishing of evil worldwide.

Censorship

Those who sought to explain the attacks of 9/11 within the context of American foreign policy and those who argued that changing that policy would make the country and the globe a safer place were labeled "blame America firsters" and charged with being unpatriotic by cable talk show anchors and others.

Writing in the *New York Times* shortly after the attacks, Frank Rich (2001) lamented that this new war had "already whipped up one of the cold war's most self destructive national maladies—a will to stifle dissent." As America was attacked by external forces of long genesis, powerful political and military leaders assured that the public would not hear historical analysis or be allowed to judge dissenting voices. Attempts to control information by the Bush administration led Rich to comment on "its determination to keep us in the dark." Rich lamented the "disproportionate avalanche of invective" leveled against Susan Sontag, Bill Maher and Noam Chomsky. University campuses, along with the Internet, the foreign press and independent media outlets, emerged as the venues for critical debate and alternative information and analysis.

An almost immediate regression to the institutionalization of persecution of university professors sprang up with McCarthyite organizations such as Campus Watch. Karl Rove openly assailed one presidential historian who dared to ask where the president had been during the hours after the attacks.

Corporate media outlets such as Clear Channel, with its vast network of over twelve hundred radio stations, removed over two hundred songs from its play lists, including John Lennon's "Imagine" and Cat Stevens's "Peace Train," and in the months to come would call for the silencing of the Dixie Chicks for criticizing the president. The corporation would use its resources to counter war critics and begin a protracted effort to promote war through such things as sponsoring pro-war rallies and playing "Bomb, Bomb, Bomb" frequently over the airways.

Preparing the Public for the Death of Americans

Bill Maher, on *Politically Incorrect*, created a firestorm of controversy and calls for censorship when he spoke to military issues of bravery and cowardice. Sponsors threatened to cancel their advertising after Maher said, "We have been the cowards lobbing cruise missiles from 2,000 miles away. That's cowardly." Maher was responding to commentator Dinesh D'Souza, who had asserted that suicide terrorists willing to die in service to their cause, whatever else they might be, were not cowards. (Many had characterized the attacks on the Pentagon and World Trade Center as cowardly.) Commentator Arianna Huffington[3] came to Maher's defense, saying, "I've made much the same criticism of a foreign policy that obliges our military to fight at great remove from the theater of battle. It was a mistake when we bombed a pharmaceutical factory in the Sudan, and it was a mistake when we killed the very Albanian refugees we were trying to protect with our indiscriminate carpet-bombing of Kosovo."

As the United States prepared for air strikes over Afghanistan and wider plans for a permanent air war, American military strategies were being characterized as cowardly. White House spokesperson Ari Fleischer told all Americans: "You should watch what you say." Bill Maher was in danger of losing his program, and in fact he did watch what he said. When fellow media professionals came to his defense, their arguments were disturbing. Some said that Maher was actually making the same point President Bush made when he said that the war on terrorism "will not look like the air war above Kosovo two years ago, where no ground troops were used and not a single American was lost in combat." Bush was clearly preparing the public to accept the death of U.S. troops in combat. Some Americans would have to die in this War on Terror.

A little over a month after 9/11, America began bombing Afghanistan.

HIDING THE BODIES

Like censorship, "information management" was part of the war from the outset. On October 17, 2001, ten days into the bombing of Afghanistan, the U.K. *Guardian* reported that the Pentagon spent millions of dollars to prevent Western news outlets from acquiring highly accurate satellite pictures of the effects of the bombing. The advanced civilian satellite, *ikonos*, produces images of such clear resolution that "it would be possible to see bodies lying on the ground after last week's bombing attacks" (Campbell, 2001). The deal the Pentagon made with Space Imaging, the company that manages *ikonos*, guaranteed exclusive rights to all the satellite's images of Afghanistan, retrospectively to the start of the bombing raids. The *Guardian* reported that the decision to bar access to the images had been taken after "heavy civilian casualties" were reported during attacks on training camps near Darunta, northwest of Jalalabad.

Instead of buying the pictures, the U.S. military could have exercised legal means to prevent dissemination of the images. Civilian satellites launched from the United States are subject to "shutter control" by the Defense Department, a provision in place to prevent enemies from using images while America is at war. But "since images of the bombed Afghan bases would not have shown the position of U.S. forces or compromised U.S. military security, the ban could have been challenged by news media as being a breach of the First Amendment" (Campbell, 2001). Nor did the military need the images from *ikonos*. With six "keyhole" satellites in orbit, and another launched as the bombings took place, the military's own images were estimated to have up to ten times the resolution of the *ikonos* pictures.

The Pentagon's attempts to control the images over Afghanistan made it clear that like the previous wars in the twentieth century, "America's New War," as CNN called it, would also be fought on two fronts. The battle over public opinion was waged at the same time bombs—including anti-personnel cluster bombs—were being dropped on urban areas in Afghanistan. But the Pentagon had in the twenty-first-century corporate media willing allies to help make such killing acceptable to the public. CNN chair Walter Isaacson sent a memo to his staff requiring that all reporting on death and hardship in Afghanistan as a consequence of U.S. bombing be carefully scripted. It said that images of civilian devastation in cities should be balanced with reminders that the Taliban harbored murderous terrorists who killed innocent Americans, adding that it "seems perverse to focus too much on the casualties or hardship in Afghanistan." Reporting on the memo, media critic Howard Kurtz (*Washington Post*, October 31, 2001) quotes a follow-up memo from CNN standards and practices that suggested actual language and some alternate wording, adding that "even though it may start sounding rote, it is important that we make this point each time." Thus were the American people subjected repeatedly to such "balance" in the rare instance when fleeting images of Afghan bombing victims were presented. Meanwhile, global audiences, even those watching CNN International, saw "images of wounded Afghan children curled in hospital beds or women rocking in despair over a baby's corpse" (*New York Times*, November 1, 2001). When CNN reported from the site of a bombed medical facility in Kandahar, the network followed with pictures from the rubble of the World Trade Center, and the anchor recalled the deaths of 5,000 people "whose biggest crime was going to work and getting there on time." Though Isaacson told the *Washington Post* he didn't want CNN to be used as a propaganda platform for the Taliban, the media watch organization FAIR (November 1, 2001), noted that his memo "mandated that pro-U.S. propaganda be included in the news." One rare, on-the-ground report aired on NBC (December 3, 2001) saw reporter Mike

Taibbi bear witness to destroyed villages and human deaths. In the face of Pentagon denials, Taibbi referred to a fragment of a U.S. missile with the serial number intact. More often coverage mirrored Thomas Friedman's tone in the *New York Times* (November 23, 2001), suggesting that Afghans did not mind being killed by U.S. bombs: "It turns out many of those Afghan 'civilians' were praying for another dose of B-52's to liberate them from the Taliban, casualties or not."

Repeated media claims that civilian casualties in Afghanistan should be viewed only as troubling Taliban propaganda, and not considered troubling humanitarian consequences of war, solidified as the bombing continued. Claims that Afghan civilians were being killed were "unverifiable," charges in the "propaganda war" made by the "Taliban propaganda machine." CBS's Dave Martin called the Taliban's chief weapon "pictures they say are innocent civilians killed or injured by the bombing" (October 23, 2001). One NBC report on civilian casualties in the Arab media labels it as propaganda, though the description is that of legitimate coverage: "Daily doses of news concerning civilian casualties in Afghanistan. Graphic pictures below front-page headlines. Compelling stories on cable television, as well." Dan Lothain ended the story with "The first casualties of this war were thousands of American civilians," adding that the United States must now fight a public relations war.

Dead civilians presented public relations problems for the Pentagon, not for America's collective conscience. CBS reported that George Bush opened up a new public relations front because "claims of heavy civilian casualties had provoked howls of protest" in the Middle East (November 6, 2001). The network had set the tone weeks earlier (CBS, October 18, 2001) when it quoted Secretary of Defense Donald Rumsfeld saying that visual scenes of civilians apparently killed by American bombs "makes the terrorist hunt more difficult." Indeed, the bombing was expanding the recruiting ground for extremists.

American officials expressed anger toward Al Jazeera and other news outlets that showed the human consequences of dropping bombs, and to counter those images, they enlisted advertising specialist Charlotte Beers. As the war was branded on U.S. network television, similar strategies were employed to alter the perceptions of Muslims. *Advertising Age* quoted Secretary of State Colin Powell who said hiring Beers was "an attempt to change from just selling the U.S.... to really branding foreign policy" (Teinowitz, 2002). Beers oversaw the creation of, among other things, glossy color brochures and posters for distribution in the Arab world depicting images of the tolerance and respect enjoyed by Muslims in America. In their insightful and timely book, *Weapons of Mass Deception*,

Rampton and Stauber discuss the folly of government-sponsored public relation's campaigns that offer superficial image solutions to real foreign policy problems. Unfavorable views toward the United States are based on a history of support for dictatorial regimes, and perceptions of America in the Arab world did not improve with fancy posters in the midst of suffering civilians in Afghanistan. As one commentator wrote in the *New York Times*, "The whole Muslim world is watching this with shock and horror. Among the young, new animosities are created and there are new calls for revenge. This is dangerous; this is the atmosphere that creates terrorism, creates extremism" (MacFarquhar, 2002).

In the midst of the bombing of Afghanistan, Human Rights Watch and Amnesty International issued press releases (October 26, 2001) calling for a moratorium on the use of cluster bombs and an investigation into possible violations of international and humanitarian law for "indiscriminate attacks" on civilians by the U.S. military. Their concerns received little media coverage, and none on ABC, NBC or CBS. University of New Hampshire professor Marc Harold (2002) began a research protocol that recorded civilian deaths reported in international news outlets. His finding of over 3,500 killed was given a Project Censored Award as a major underreported news story that year. Harold's figures were hotly contested, and he would later write an in-depth account of that controversy. His investigation included inventory lists of different bombs and their use, and his findings offered reasons for the high casualty rates. Military facilities in Afghanistan were located in urban areas, a legacy of the fight between the Soviet-supported government and the rural insurgency of the mujahideen. What had been easier to defend during that Cold War battle became deadly for urban Afghanis when intensive American bombing began. His reports argued that so many civilians died, not because of targeting errors or malfunction or faulty intelligence, but from decisions to employ highly destructive bombs on targets populated by civilians, whether in residential neighborhoods or villages. He tells one story of Ghulam and Rabia Hazrat, who lived on the outskirts of Kabul near a Taliban military base. The neighborhood was showered with cluster bombs after a U.S. missile landed in the family's courtyard. "There was no warning. I was in the kitchen making dough when I heard a big explosion. I came out and saw a big cloud of dust and saw my children lying on the ground. Two of them were dead and two died later in the hospital." Harold goes on to say that from the point of view of U.S. policymakers, "the 'cost' of a dead Afghan is zero as long as these civilian deaths can be hidden from the general U.S. public's view. The 'benefits' of saving future lives of U.S. military personnel are enormous, given the U.S. public's post-Vietnam aversion to returning body bags." Harold's criticism echoed the earlier condemned utterance of Bill Maher, that U.S. bombs saved American fighters but killed civilians. Harold also articulated the role of the media in helping employ the policies designed to have such consequences. But Americans would be shielded from information and public debate about the humanitarian consequences of the way the War on Terror was being fought.

The media "ether" seemed to expel a toxic mix that demanded the need for retribution as it denied feelings of empathy while emitting stern warnings that silenced criticism. Television anchors and personalities pre-empted the expression of public compassion for those killed by U.S. bombs. In contemplating such omissions, Judith Butler writes that we are obliged to become "senseless" before the lives we have eradicated and without expressions of grief we lose the capacity to mourn. We are left with only a ritualized expression for those whose loss is considered meaningful and whose deaths are therefore grievable. But even those lives begin to lose their worth when used to stoke national fervor as a counterbalance to more killing. This process of forgetting and evoking, of denying and recalling, carried out in a discourse of warring abstractions, leads to an overall crisis of humanism and the inability to oppose more violence. Thus did America accept and hold dear the time-honored cycle of the victimized becoming the victimizers, and embrace the dry grief of perpetual rage, instead of inventing new narratives of interconnection and a sense of safety born of mutual compassion.

As we now know, retaliation against the Taliban in Afghanistan after 9/11 was a reversal of American foreign policy. Only months before the attacks the U.S. government sent aid to the Taliban in the form of $42 million to fight the war on drugs, even as critics expressed outrage at U.S. support of that repressive regime. War in the place of diplomacy would continue in earnest once the Bush administration had firmly established a war footing. The White House continued its plans for regime change in Iraq.

The September attacks provided the incumbent president with an opportunity to begin a permanent war. Many who felt the attacks were a missed opportunity to redefine America's identity as part of a global community were relegated to the margins, ignored and—worse—silenced. Permanent war required that exclusionary patriotism be evoked in a climate of fear. The movement away from democratic priorities that helped fuel a growing security state has now been well documented by civil liberties groups, former officials, alternative media, writers and citizens' groups. The movement included such antidemocratic activities as the intimidation of dissent, explicit censorship, suspended constitutional rights, extended surveillance mechanisms and the passing of the Patriot Acts I and II.

The war for American opinion would require the continued absence of the human costs of wars and isolation from the global community. The task fell to the media and other entertainment formats to fill those "doxic," or empty spaces with stories that framed the new war as an exciting media event. The job would be to find formats, genres, narratives and styles that would make the war seem real but shield the public from death. Empathy and sadness over the loss of life would be replaced with the excitement of the hyperreal. Like the visual imagery of the 9/11 attacks, real war would intermingle with and become indistinguishable from its fictions.

16

Black Hawk Down

The New Logics of War and Representation

Rushed out to catch the wave of the new bellicosity, Ridley Scott's account of
U.S. troops in Somalia is some kind of accomplishment—the most extravagantly
aestheticized combat movie ever made.
   —J. Hoberman, (2001) *The Village Voice*

The movie based on the best-selling book by journalist Mark Bowden
tells the story of the U.S. military operation in Somalia in 1993 that
left over one thousand Somalis and nineteen Americans dead, among them
Army Rangers and Delta Force commandos. Produced by Jerry Bruckheimer and directed by Ridley Scott, the movie focuses on the heat of
battle, the action/adrenaline rush of a military strike. Movie critic John
Powers (2002, 1) commented on the intensity of the imagery: "Warfare
in the movies has grown more assaultive and spectacular. Hollywood can
now thrust us into the belly of battle, rattling our seats with Dolby-ized
explosions and rattling our sense with jittery camera work and tracer bullets whizzing by our ears."

The release of *Black Hawk Down* in the midst of the U.S. war against the
Taliban raises a number of media concerns. A feature-length entertainment
film succeeded in sitting viewers in the middle of military action, while actual news reporting of the war kept the public at a distance, removed from
the battles that remained hidden from the camera's view. Evidence of this
blackout could be seen on CBS news. As a reporter approaches the scene

at Mazur-I-Sharif, Afghanistan, after an American bomb went off, injuring five U.S. troops, we see an American soldier reach for the camera and pull the lens down as he says, "Hey, there are wounded Americans here."

In *Black Hawk Down* we see not only wounded soldiers, but we hear what they say to each other and their commander (Sam Shepard), who listens at a distance as the mission collapses into chaos. We see the men fatally struck by sniper fire, being blown out of humvees and crashing down in Black Hawk helicopters. But the military kept journalists away from even interviewing wounded soldiers in Afghanistan. Reporters were literally locked in a warehouse at the U.S. base in southern Afghanistan when marines wounded by "friendly fire" arrived for medical care.

The public flocked to the fictional battlefield, however. *Down* was the highest-grossing film the weekend of its release. The story behind this movie seemed to neutralize criticism about the film's timing. Though it is, according to Hoberman (2001, 81), "the most extravagantly aestheticized combat movie ever made," the story is real. *Philadelphia Enquirer* reporter Mark Bowden spent several years reconstructing the incident, a task that took him to Somalia to interview eyewitnesses. The actual blow-by-blow account is told in excruciating detail. The soldiers who died were real ones. Those who survived appeared on *Larry King Live* and other media presentations during the movie's promotion. They repeated their accounts on a two-hour documentary produced by the History Channel. As one movie critic put it, *Black Hawk Down* "plays like a documentary of disaster" (Lemire 2001, 1). NBC's Fred Francis (January 4, 2002) declared that it was Hollywood's most realistic portrayal of modern combat, and the BBC referred to the movie as "the true story of what happened" in Mogadishu.[1] As such, *Black Hawk Down* and its promotion worked together to confirm the existence of an open information environment. Such truth-telling about a failed mission at the very same time another incursion was under way seemed to lend a certain gravitas to the Hollywood establishment, legitimizing the democratic role of the media even in a time of war and censorship.

Yet *Black Hawk Down* was a script the new government/Hollywood alliance deemed appropriate for the post-September 11 information environment. Its original release date was pushed forward, and Sony Pictures sponsored a special screening at the White House attended by the president and other members of his staff. Oliver North attended the Washington premiere. The Pentagon is quite selective in choosing which movies it officially endorses with access to bases and ultra-high-tech weaponry. *Black Hawk Down* was generously supplied by the Pentagon and highly accessorized with military hardware, including the helicopters that carry its name. The stamp of approval from the White House and the military might have caused some critics to ask why *Down* was so appealing to the president's agenda, but it was a question that went largely unasked. In fact, the rhetorical structure and persuasive content of *Black Hawk Down* were all but ignored. To some writers the movie lacked even patriotic fervor. "The movie is almost too exhausted to wave a flag. It tries, but the soldiers (like we) are glad to get out, and back to the wars on television" (Elliott 2002, 3). The Associated Press reviewer insisted that the movie doesn't glorify what happened; "rather, it's a timely, brutally realistic depiction of the potentially devastating results of swooping down in a foreign land to enforce what we perceive as the greater good" (Lemire 2001, 4). After all, the mission in Somalia was "disastrous," "failed," "botched," "miserably chaotic," "fraught" and "doomed," to list a few of the descriptors applied by film reviewers. Even the BBC declared that *Black Hawk Down* "tells the story with surprisingly little U.S. bias" (Youngs, 2002).

National Public Radio critic John Powers (2002, 1) approached an understanding of the movie's true significance when he observed that *Black Hawk Down* "attempts something very strange. In chronicling America's debacle in Mogadishu…it seeks to grab victory from the very bowels of defeat." How can this be done, and why is this particular story important? What accounts for the rhetorical need to reverse the coordinates of this defeat? In the book, and in subsequent interviews, Bowden reveals his motivations and his understanding of the incident and the lessons it teaches. Those lessons are quite distinct from the ones the movie teaches. Illustrating these differences and exploring the implications of intense battlefield realism will reveal the ongoing transformation of the geography of war and culture into one more favorable to the new frontier of a permanent War on Terror.

As we have seen in the case of Oliver North and the Iran/Contra scandal, old myths must be redesigned to fit the new contingencies of global conflict. In 2001 the Bush administration declared a permanent war on terrorism, a war without clear definition, or even national borders. The Delta Force commandos of *Black Hawk Down* are the heroes of this new millennium. The film reinterprets conventional myths of the masculine. It places the collective hero group in the new military and political context of the time. In doing so, *Down* attempts a profound cultural transformation of attitudes and opinions toward fighting and dying, and war in general, and in doing so takes the film far beyond its claim to be entertainment, or even documentary fiction.

Boots on the Ground

Black Hawk Down delivers the field of battle as never before. The movie thrusts viewers into the fighting "with an almost tactile sense of the conflict—the dust of the streets, the reports of the guns, the agony as bullets rip into flesh, the taste of sweat, blood and grime" (Gabler 2002, 4). One reviewer noted that *Black Hawk Down*, "for all its elegant copter views, has its heart on the ground and inside the men" (Elliott 2002, 3). This is not a story told from the air, of bombing raids with puffs of smoke on unseen landscapes. In *Black Hawk Down*, "the experience of war is palpable" (Gabler, 2002, 4).

The detailed, extensive *camera vérité* production leaves the impression that *Down* affords viewers the experience of "what it was really like." This authoritative claim to realism justifies the graphic nature of the imagery and gives purpose to its production. Here we might revisit the observations of one of the early reviewers of the "war record" films of World War II. Writing for *Time* and *The Nation* during the 1940s, film critic James Agee was one of the first who struggled to understand the impact of war footage on audiences, many of whom had friends and loved ones fighting abroad. Concerned with the relationship between soldiers and audiences, Agee asserted that battle footage could give viewers "a part in the proceeding." He believed that the war documentary was the only representation capable of bridging the gap between civilian and soldier, and that certain films could even blur the distinction between actual and vicarious participation. Writing about the 1943 film *Desert Victory*, a film that included piercing natural sounds of battle, Agee wrote, "It is the first serious attempt to make an audience participate in the war. No audience should be spared it" (Youra 1985, 22).

Agee was particularly captivated by *With the Marines at Tarawa*, a film that did not include shots of wounded or dead Americans. Nevertheless, the footage was compelling, and "a boundless sense of death chokes the screen," with nineteen minutes of "unflagging pity and terror" (Youra 1985, 22). He describes one sequence when marines return from battle, "one gaunt man, his face down with sleeplessness and a sense of death, glances up.... In his eyes, in his grimace, he looks into the eyes of every civilian and whatever face that civilian is capable of wearing in reply" (Youra 1985, 23). Accusatory glances, sounds and images that don't spare the audience, reveal Agee's interest and intent: civilians should experience the horrors of war. Better to know what soldiers endured, even if the only conceivable method is watching a film.

But toward the end of World War II, Agee began to reassess the effects of horrific actuality footage. At first believing such images could unite soldier and civilian, he later worried that repeated exposure would desensitize viewers, resulting in a loss of empathy. As Youra (1985, 24) points out, "it becomes clear to Agee that the assault actually constitutes that distance." Grappling with consciousness and conscience, Agee is troubled that "vicarious observation" can evoke sensations quite at odds with empathetic understanding:

> Very uneasily, I am beginning to believe that, for all that may be said in favor of our seeing these terrible records of war, we have no business seeing this sort of experience except through our presence and participation. I have neither space nor mind, yet, to try to explain why I believe this is so; but since I am reviewing and in a way recommending that others see one of the best and most terrible of war films, I cannot avoid mentioning my perplexity. Perhaps I can briefly suggest what I mean by this parallel: whatever other effects it may or may not have, pornography is invariably degrading to anyone who looks at or reads it. If at an incurable distance from participation, hopelessly incapable of reactions adequate to the event, we watch men kill each other, we may be quite as profoundly degrading ourselves and, in the process, betraying and separating ourselves the farther from those we are trying to identify ourselves with; none the less because we tell ourselves sincerely that we sit in comfort and watch carnage in order to nurture our patriotism, our conscience, our understanding, and our sympathies. (Youra 1985, 24)

Agee and other critics such as Berger and Sontag all understood that watching horror degrades the viewer because there is no adequate response to such suffering. Unable to participate or take any action that would mitigate the suffering, viewers are further compromised by the fact that the brutality remains at a safe distance. There seems no way around this, as civilians, by definition, do not go to war. Sitting in comfort watching images of men killing each other, even if to nurture conscience or understanding, became for Agee disturbing, even pornographic. The limits of empathy expressed by Susan Sontag (1977, 20) about the photographic image of suffering still resonate: the image "does not necessarily strengthen conscience and the ability to be compassionate. It can also corrupt them...."

IDENTITY, VOYEURISM AND THE HYPERREAL

But what are we to conclude when the practice of viewing is done not for some higher goal such as conscience, but for entertainment? *Black Hawk Down* compounds this problematic because of the vivid representations not only of dying, but of bodies blown in half while still talking, of arms and limbs detached, the bloody stumps in full view and even handled. Agee felt compelled to caution viewers of the pornographic aspects of war imagery, even when such imagery was real, yet by today's standards far from graphically explicit.[2] But *Down* has escaped the worst criticism, the charge that the ninety-minute conflict sequence is little more than titillation.

The charge of voyeurism has not been leveled primarily because the movie claims to be a realistic (read: "documentary") recounting of a story that is "true." Yet, we are still left with the paradox that when death is real, it cannot be visually rendered. Depicting actual death, especially of American soldiers, in real time, in wars as they happen, has been deemed absolutely taboo in news footage. Returning to the claim that *Down* is like a documentary, it is now time to explore the differences between what is real and what is fiction, and what purpose is served by collapsing the two and denying the distinction.

Though Agee became suspicious of some war films and remained ambivalent to others, he understood that some filmic treatments created more distance, while others evoked empathy. For Agee, empathy could be achieved only when camera technique and visual treatments did not intrude on the viewing experience. A "straight approach" avoided distracting the viewer's attention and creating distance. As Youra (1985, 23) notes, Agee endorsed "manipulations only insofar as they contribute to an impression of artlessness." In his opinion, art and artifice were not appropriate to the war record. The aestheticization of death and horror has long been understood as a transforming process, one able to evoke abstract notions of glory and patriotism even when rendering brutality and disgust. Claims that *Black Hawk Down* is "realistic" or equivalent to a documentary are belied by the recognition that the movie is extravagantly aestheticized. "As grueling as the strewn body parts and staged battlefield surgery are, it's hard to repress the thought of the filmmaker fussing over camera placement—his point of view is the movie's only constant" (Hoberman 2001, 81). In addition, *Down* continually signals the viewer that he is watching a feature film, not a documentary. Intertextual filmic references abound, even with regard to horror. One can't help but think of the opening sequence on Omaha Beach in *Saving Private Ryan*, when one of the Rangers picks up the blown-off hand of a friend and puts it in his pack. The stump of an arm is retrieved similarly in *Down*. Such recognition by the viewer inserts filmic appreciation and a corresponding empathetic distance. As we will see, the message of *Black Hawk Down* is entirely different from the antiwar satire of *Catch-22*, yet Ridley Scott displays his auteur credentials by mimicking the parody just before the pilots take off on their mission. And as the combat sequences begin, it is impossible to hear the rock and roll beat of Guns

N' Roses' *Welcome to the Jungle*, without recognizing post-Vietnam filmic treatments of war as *genre* itself. Such aesthetic devices are far harder to achieve in news footage of actual war, and without them, the distance collapses. But the specter of Vietnam weighs heavily on any attempt to evoke human empathy for soldiers, the kind not shrouded in heroics and fictional flourishes, for fear that the media would be charged with being antiwar, as Frank Capra was so many years ago.

Down's in-the-battle perspective includes other aspects that transform the phenomenology of battle and the viewer's interaction with it. The Rangers and Commandos who dive out of Black Hawk helicopters, as so many film reviewers noticed, are not stand-alone Rambo-types of a previous generation. "It's not about characters," Powers (2002, 2) asserts. "The men tend to seem collective," writes Elliott (2001, 3). And the AP reviewer critiqued the screenplay by "first timer" Ken Nolan, saying it "fails to flesh out the individual U.S. Army Ranger and Delta Force soldiers who were killed and injured—one of the movie's weaknesses. Their collective story, though, is powerful" (Lemire 2001, 2). The loss of the individuality of each soldier is a necessity of *Down*'s message, a key factor in the role the film plays in the War on Terror.

Black Hawk Rangers and Delta Force Commandos work as a team to do "what a man's gotta do." In this war narrative, the myth of the masculine is fulfilled through acts of collective bravery and teamwork, not acts of individual heroism. This is a break from filmic representations of 1980s heroes and the assumed point of view through the eyes of the main character. The popularity of Sylvester Stallone illustrates the source of viewing pleasure: subjective identification with *Rocky*, *Cobra* and *Rambo*, as audiences experience the struggles, danger and battles through the eyes and antics of this exaggerated hero. Such bonds assume the character's longevity. Hollywood convention usually avoids attachments with characters that will not make it to the end of the movie. Individuals are not in focus in *Black Hawk Down*, because so many of them are killed.

Yet soldiers are regularly killed in battle in an older generation of World War II movies, including Steven Spielberg's revival film, *Saving Private Ryan*. The difference is that all of them, especially Captain John Miller (Tom Hanks) die for a cause. Their deaths are given higher purpose through meaningful principles. Audiences have historically accepted fighting and dying for a just cause, but what about a war not so clearly identified as noble? We will return to this point shortly.

Viewers of *Black Hawk Down* are psychically invested in the movie in a way quite distinct from character identification. Individual emotional involvement is replaced with an equally powerful sensation, the experience of combat. With the price of the ticket, the audience becomes part of the action. The soldiers under fire offer no accusatory glances. Instead, the rhetoric of the camera tells us that we are next to our heroes, fighting *with* them, not *through* them. Like them, we are willing to risk our lives. *Black Hawk Down* is a "maelstrom of fighting, retreating, charging, wounding, dying" (Elliott 2002, 2). But we don't grieve for the fallen; there is no time, as another bullet slices the Dolby-ized theatrical air.

The intensified battle sequences offered by Ridley Scott mirror the interaction with a video game. We are outside the game, yet inside at the same time, even directing the action. It is the nature of virtual experience itself, and a culture that offers increasingly real sensations, to deliver those thrills with no consequences. We vanquish so many enemies, and then the game its over. This is experience in which empathy, compassion and responsibility have been thoroughly purged. The perceptual shift from concerned observer to vicarious participant allows the movie to depict the death of American soldiers without viewers recoiling from it. This is the aesthetic hook that hinges this particular movie to a new brand of war pro-motion. As "the tolerance (or taste) for split-second carnage…is taken to a new level," Americans are encouraged to accept the deaths of U.S. soldiers in faraway places (Elliott 2002, 2).

Thus have the deepest concerns of those who seek empathy in battle footage come full circle. Death is accepted, not rejected, and comes not from battle fatigue, but from participating in its intensity. Agee insisted viewers have "a part in the proceedings" but saw the need to arouse empa-thy, not thrills.

DEATH WITHOUT JUSTIFICATION

But the loss of filmic identification, and even the considerable virtual thrills offered by *Black Hawk Down*, is not the only perceptual detour this film takes to achieve its remarkable level of cultural revisionism. Another shift revolves around the failure and nihilism of the mission itself. The heroes of *Black Hawk Down* refuse to contemplate the political explanations and even the military logic of this "failed," "botched" and "doomed" mission in Somalia. As the battle is foregrounded early on, it is made clear that such problematic politics do not matter at all.

> *Delta Force Commando*: You know what I think? It don't really matter what I think. Once that first bullet goes past your head, politics and all that just goes right out the window.
> *Staff Sergeant Matt Eversmann*: I just want to do it right.
> *Delta Force Commando*: Just watch your corner. Get all your men back here alive.

In *Black Hawk Down*, engaging in military conflict has lost all legitimate political justification. Yet in a brilliant turn of phrase, *Down* offers in its place something akin to fighting for fighting's sake, but with a new twist. As one Delta Force Commando asserts, battle is always about the same thing: "It's about the man next to you. That's it." As the articulation of an elevated political purpose for war goes out the window, a new meaning for death on the battlefield is found. This point is acceptable to some viewers, as one commented online: "Every one of the soldiers who were killed died for their friends. None of them died for nothing."[3] It is this sense of individual morality that also led several reviewers to extol the virtues of *Down*: "The film conveys no sense of any noble cause to save humanity. The mission is instead suffused with another kind of morality. The rangers' obligation is to one another—to make sure their friends and fellow troops survive" (Gabler 2002, 4). Herein lies the answer to our first question, which explains the mechanism by which the film grabs victory out of the jaws of defeat. The defeat becomes irrelevant as the film asserts a new "moral high ground" in the representation of war: *no one gets left behind*.

Black Hawk Down works overtime to convince viewers that the political context for war is irrelevant by admitting that the mission in Somalia was a political debacle, yet one that can be justified by the bravery and morality of the men who died there. Winning or losing no longer matter, as no rational political explanation or "noble cause to save humanity" is given. Urging the public to accept the death of American soldiers without political cause or justification certainly benefits the U.S. military and a White House that shifts explanations for war as each one before it is articulated and discredited. The film is a brilliant reflection of the current political atmosphere. To present these new parameters as natural, *Down* must make a radical departure from a genre of war movies. To appreciate this change, recall *Saving Private Ryan*. In one of the most patriotic sequences in American film, Captain Miller's death can only be justified by the words of Abraham Lincoln himself, who speaks of the *costs* of freedom, as the American flag waves. More conventional war genres shroud death on the battlefield with an aura of noble sacrifice.

Black Hawk Down (re)adjusts the genre for a new era. The soldiers' deaths have no great political, humanitarian or enlightenment meanings. "You can't control it. It ain't up to you. It's just war," as the Ranger says acceptingly. But the film accomplishes this reversal through sleight of hand. Even as *Down* asserts the irrelevance of the failed mission, it makes powerful, implicit claims that the cause *was* noble. To do this it must rewrite the history of the Somalia affair. This divergence between fact and fiction is key to understanding why fiction must stand in for real-time witness. The changes the movie made to the historical narrative of Somalia, and to Bowden's (2000) narrative, renders the claim of authenticity most troubling.

A HUMANITARIAN CAUSE?

The opening sequences of *Black Hawk Down* ground the interpretive frame and offer the film's explanation for the military action depicted. The camera pans across a dry, fly-infested landscape littered with the black bodies of Somalis dead from starvation. The text under the images tells of the twenty thousand marines sent to distribute food in the midst of a famine. A U.S. helicopter surveys downtown Mogadishu. The warlord Aidid's militias fire on a hungry crowd at a food distribution center, and the pilot radios headquarters in outrage: "Unarmed civilians getting shot down here at 9 o'clock." In an order of restraint he is told not to return fire because he was not targeted. In another scene, General Garrison interrogates a Somali arms dealer focusing on the issue of starvation. "300,000 dead is not a war, that's genocide." These scenes assert a sense of compassion, measured control and a humanitarian reason for the mission. Aidid is preventing the distribution of food and perpetuating genocide on his own people; "hunger is his weapon." Taking out two of his top lieutenants seems like the right thing to do. Most reviewers ignored these grounding sequences that offered viewers a noble, but false, premise.

In fact, the mission to apprehend Aidid's "henchmen" was not humanitarian. The marines were initially sent to Somalia in 1992 to distribute food, but that humanitarian effort was over. Bowden himself makes this point in a History Channel documentary that illustrates the end of the famine with images of healthy-looking Somali toddlers eating sufficient quantities of food. Major General Garrison arrived in Mogadishu well after the marines, in August 1993, with Army Rangers and Delta Force Commandos, soldiers not trained for humanitarian missions. The subsequent operation, called Task Force Ranger, was a military mission. As Bowden (2002) explains, "Unlike the marines who preceded them, this is not a humanitarian mission. It had nothing to do with feeding people or distributing rice or anything else."

Down makes a show of concern for civilian casualties, yet many civilians in Mogadishu had been killed as the Rangers engaged in close urban conflict with indigenous Somali militia. As a consequence the population began to turn against the U.S. military, which was increasingly viewed as an occupying force. According to Bowden (2002), "Of course there was a tremendous amount of resentment. Imagine if some foreign power swooped into your little suburban neighborhood and at gunpoint started arresting your community leaders. In pretty short order everyone who had a rifle would be in the streets to shoot at them, which is exactly what happened in Mogadishu."

The dishonesty of *Black Hawk Down* is best illustrated by the film's omission of a brutal incident, a massacre of indigenous leaders detailed in the documentary version. As Bowden explains on The History Channel documentary meeting of "intellectuals and elders" was called to discuss the situation with American forces and "Aidid's militant posture." Its purpose was "to try to get Aidid to comply with all U.N. and U.S. demands…when a number of cobra helicopters…surrounded the building…and began pumping tow missiles" into it, killing between fifty and seventy people. An eyewitness explains, "The American helicopters kept shelling and shelling the house, killing everyone. The U.N. human rights office at the time called it a cold-blooded murder." This, of course, helps account for some of the hatred that inspired the defiling of the bodies of two U.S. soldiers killed during the operation. Images of those bodies being dragged through the streets of Mogadishu are part of the photodocumentary record of the event, yet this inauspicious ending was omitted from the film. The humiliating message of that insult would have been hard even for Ridley Scott to reverse, especially with no historical explanation.

In addition, the meaning of the "botched" mission recounted in *Black Hawk Down* cannot be understood outside the context of U.S. policy toward Somalia. The failure exhibited on the big screen did not mirror the true ignominy of American policy toward Somalia. No mention is made of the devastating effects of the Cold War and the role the United States played in the country's economic disruption and decline into social violence. From the late 1970s until early 1991, the United States spent more than $50 million annually supplying arms to Somalia in return for the use of military facilities there. The bases were used to support American military intervention in the Middle East. U.S. arms supported the authoritarian regime of Siad Barre that was responsible for the deaths of thousands of civilians. As one Middle East analyst wrote:

> The consequences of U.S. military support for the Barre regime on the Somali people was deemed of little importance by American policy makers. The U.S. government ignored warnings throughout the 1980s by Africa specialists, human rights groups and humanitarian organizations that continued American aid to the dictatorial government of Siad Barre would eventually plunge Somalia into chaos. (Zunes 2002, 2)

Such predictions came true as the country descended into full-scale civil war in 1988. Barre's regime stayed in power by systematically dismantling traditional leadership structures and pitting different Somali clans against each other. As Barre's misrule splintered the country, Congressman Howard Wolpe, then-chairman of the House Subcommittee on Africa, and a former professor of African Politics, observed: "What you are seeing is a general indifference to a disaster that we played a role in creating" (Zunes 2002, 2).

Over the years, as money for arms poured into the country, the United States offered little economic assistance that would help build a self-sustaining economy able to feed the population. In addition, "the U.S. pushed a structural adjustment program through the International Monetary Fund which severely weakened the local agricultural economy. Combined with the breakdown of the central government, drought conditions and rival militias disrupting food supplies, there was a famine on a massive scale, resulting in the deaths of more than 300,000 Somalis, mostly children" (Zunes 2002, 3). The sad irony of the failed U.S. policy toward Somalia, never alluded to in *Down*, is that thousands of M16 rifles sent to Somalia and paid for by U.S. taxpayers were then used to kill U.S. troops.

The lack of historical context for understanding the economic and political chaos in Somalia causes the country to be branded as contemptible and the people uncivilized and ultimately expendable. The movie mystifies historical processes and blames the culture itself, just as news reporting did in recounting the civil war in El Salvador. As the Somali fighter explains in *Down*, "There will always be killing. This is how things are in our world." Once the violence is decontextualized, it becomes inevitable—that's just the way things are in this (uncivilized) country. America stands apart, morally superior, assuming no responsibility for chaos. One of the most regressive aspects of the film is the portrayal of the Somalis. It offers a classic paradigm of dehumanized enemy hordes throwing themselves at heroes in utter disregard for life itself.

The assertion by critics that the film is not biased in favor of a U.S. perspective derives, no doubt, from the mission's failure. Also significant in making this assertion is the clear friction between the elite forces of the Pentagon and the executive branch of the American government. But the fact that the operation was not fully supported by the Clinton administration only strengthens the position of the current pro-war American government, one more willing than ever to make use of elite forces that operate in secret. Ignoring democratic processes and celebrating military force, even when it is outside civilian control, becomes the message of *Down*. No warnings of the dangers of such force are even alluded to in the movie. But David Halberstam (2001, 260) quotes Les Aspen, Secretary of Defense under Clinton, worrying at the time, "We're sending the Rangers to Somalia. We are not going to be able to control them. They are like overtrained pit bulls. No one controls them."

We are told at the end of the film that over one thousand Somalis were killed in Mogadishu that day, yet few comment on this death toll in any detail. One reviewer observed, "Not since Zulu (1964) have so many whites slaughtered so many suicidal black men," yet the writer offers only mild criticism, referring to an "undertone of implicit racism" (Elliott 2002, 3). How can such an imbalance be acceptable to contemporary viewers? If media debates have taught us anything, it is that context creates meaning, and that even the worst brutality can be justified. One strategy, of course, is to eliminate nuance and present "our guys" as overwhelmingly sympathetic and their foes as singularly demonic. As we have seen, the depiction of the inhabitants of Mogadishu as inherently violent, together with their lack of a civilized sensibility justifies their slaughter. As a director schooled in advertising as well as feature films, Ridley Scott understands that persuasive design entails accentuating the positive and eliminating the negative. The absolute munificence of the Rangers and Delta Force Commandos is another stunning feature of *Black Hawk Down*.

VIOLENCE AS MEASURED RETALIATION

A few minutes after the men hit the ground in *Black Hawk Down*, the danger is palatable. The atmosphere of foreboding began as the copters left the base swinging wide out over the beach below as the Jimi Hendrix song "VooDoo Child" pounds on the soundtrack. A boy (the VooDoo child?) makes a call on a cell phone alerting Aidid's men, and tires are set afire, the smoke signaling the militias to mass for a fight. The battle is imminent and the viewers tense; yet even when the U.S. soldiers are on the ground, they refuse to shoot. "Why aren't you shooting?" one demands. "Because we're not being shot at!" The retaliatory nature of their violence is underscored throughout the film. The most memorable incident, which takes place toward the end of the ordeal, shows the single African American soldier holding off advancing Somalis. He finally kills one sniper and sees a woman in traditional dress heading for the dead man's gun and says to himself, "Don't you do it." He kills her only after she picks up the rifle and fires it at him. Such measured responses folded into the sequential structure validate the need for all that killing.

Examples of compassion and restraint are littered throughout the film in heroic gestures too numerous and magnanimous not to register emotionally with viewers. A lone American soldier furtively moves through a house as a woman holds her frightened children around her. He quiets them and waves goodbye in a gesture of sentimentality utterly at odds with the movie's action. Once outside, he spares the life of another child, who grieves for the father he has just killed, but who tried to kill him first.

NEWS REPORTING AND THE REALITIES OF WAR

If we compare the fictional conduct of soldiers in *Black Hawk Down* to press reports from Afghanistan during the movie's theatrical run, we may flush out the potential differences between propaganda and news. On January 24, 2002, U.S. commandos with eight helicopters and at least two humvees burst into a school in the small hamlet of Uruzgan, north of Kandahar. Unlike the retaliatory violence depicted in *Black Hawk Down*, eyewitness news accounts from Afghanistan say U.S. troops did not wait until they were fired on. At the school "they found Afghan fighters sleeping and began spraying the beds with gunfire." One witness of the aftermath at the Sharzam school "said that Americans shot Afghans as they hid under beds and rushed out of doorways" (Ware 2002, 8). A guard named Hamdullah, who evaded the attack by hiding in a ditch, "told *Time* he heard men inside the school plea, 'For the love of Allah, do not kill us. We surrender'" (Ware 2002, 8). Most were shot at close range, and two were found with their wrists bound. "One soldier left a note: 'Have a nice day. From Damage Inc'" (Ware 2002, 8).

The attack on Uruzgan was reported in detail only after the Pentagon became embroiled in a controversy after mistakenly targeting friendly forces. The U.S. military later agreed to release twenty-seven anti-Taliban fighters held in custody after the raid. The incident illustrates the complexities and ambiguities of war and raises disturbing issues of the conduct of U.S. soldiers in battle. But questioning the orders given by commanding officers that determine military conduct is outside the vision of movies such as *Down*. Certainly both fiction and nonfiction representations are capable of more complex renderings of military behavior and motivations than the simplistic ones offered in *Black Hawk Down*. But the movie is more a product of its own intentions and the agreement between the Hollywood and the executive branch.

When Hollywood agreed to promote the president's agenda on terrorism, the task appeared to many as little more than harmless public relations and patriotism. But the agreement was much more than that. After the Vietnam War, military planners understood that wars must be short with overpowering superiority, resulting in quick victories and few casualties. In addition, the Pentagon learned that media imagery must be strictly controlled, and the First Gulf War was a shining illustration of smart bombs and Patriot missiles. Though Pentagon information strategies were successful, the military paid a price. Devastating air attacks saved the lives of U.S. military personnel, but they also robbed fighting men of demonstrating their bravery and courage under fire. The celebration of soldiers, bravery and the glories of fighting are elemental aspects of the culture of war, and in recent years, hand-to-hand combat has been eliminated from war's lexicon. As we have seen, television news anchors supplied ample war rhetoric immediately after the September 11 attacks, but the cult of the war hero was absent. Some television commentators made offhand remarks that Americans could only drop bombs and had no heart for fighting. In fact, this had been confirmed in Somalia after U.S. casualties led to a withdrawal.

Ironically, the fictional retelling of the story of Mogadishu reaffirms the quality of bravery in the American military. *Black Hawk Down* is a quintessential rendering of battle. Under siege and constantly surrounded by hostile Somalis, the urban setting is a gauntlet of seemingly endless combat that lasts for ninety minutes. It is a nonstop test of bravery, skill and stamina, as "nothing tests a fighting man quite like urban combat in twisting, ruined precincts honeycombed by ambushers" (Elliott 2002, 2). *Black Hawk Down* answered Bill Maher's now-famous remark about high-tech air wars with few American casualties.

There is no doubt that U.S. troops fight bravely in war. The war about to be undertaken in Iraq would, sadly, test fighting skills in a gantlet of urban combat, killing over 2000 U.S. troops by the end of 2005. But Americans would not see real images of men and women fighting and dying in their name, because only fictional and mythic renderings can make those deaths acceptable to the public. Ironically, it is the acquiescence to those same myths of war and combat that makes their deaths possible.

CONCLUSION

At the beginning of the twenty-first century, a new landscape of imagery can convincingly supplant news with fiction, and now the real battle is substituted with a simulation. As audiences experienced a fictional battle, adopting and celebrating the transcendent logic of the military, enemies, civilians and U.S. troops died in Afghanistan in a war made unreal by media and military censorship. The aesthetic simulations of the real drive an age characterized by postmodern representation. So it does not seem strange that Jerry Bruckheimer produced a thirteen-part "reality" series on the war in Afghanistan. It should not be surprising that war can now be rendered in fictional form, even as it remains censored in real time, the fictional allowed to "stand in" for the real. We might even say, in an age of *Life—The Movie*, the existent cultural logic dictates that battlefield bravery be reclaimed by the "most realistic combat movie ever made."

Entertainment fictions are easier to shape, and their messages can be crafted more definitively, while real battles are unpredictable and often ignoble. Images of soldiers dying in real time are harder to embed in narratives able to evoke the desired response. Hollywood is an accommodating and fluid culture where hero myths can change over time, able to adjust to the given historical circumstances and cultural requirements. *Down* gives birth to a new, sadly expendable, hero/soldier in the midst of the hyperreal sensations of battle entertainments.

By reversing the coordinates of the defeat in Mogadishu, *Black Hawk Down* revises history and lays the groundwork for an enduring culture of war. The message of *Black Hawk Down*, understood within the present historical context, offers a cultural attitude of acquiescence to the desires of the U.S. military that continues to prepare for a permanent war on terrorism. *Black Hawk Down* promotes the acceptance of ill-conceived military adventures and the deaths of U.S. soldiers on ill-defined missions with little measurable success.

17

The Iraq "Reality" War

Embeds and Militainment

Major combat operations, as the initial invasion of Iraq is now called, were brought to a close with the president's dramatic made-for-television landing onto the U.S.S. *Lincoln*.[1] It was the choreographed final sequence of a narrative of invasion that turned battle into entertainment in real time, and took the representation of war to a new level—one of stagecraft on a grand scale. Though purporting to be "reality," the television presentation of the invasion featured a Hollywood set design, a theatrical rescue invented by the military and a toppling statue of an iconic demon who fell to "cheering crowds"—the result of psych-ops operatives on the scene. The invasion was a contained, ongoing narrative with distinct plot sequencing, a form of fictionalized nonfiction that forever changed the history of war and television.

WAITING FOR WAR

It can be said that the coverage of the conflict was underway before the fighting started. Though February 15, 2003, shortly before the invasion, marked the first time in history that millions of people around the world demonstrated against a war before it started, Dan Rather and Tom Brokaw were already wearing khakis in the desert, driving humvees, profiling soldiers, hitching rides on helicopters and previewing high-tech weaponry. "With all this firepower and all these forces primed and ready to go, how long can they stay in peak condition?" worried Brokaw (NBC, February 18, 2003), reporting with a "band of brothers" on the northern border of Kuwait.

The media build-up to war presented a military attack on Iraq as an overwhelming natural force whose momentum could not be stopped. "The clock is ticking," NPR reported on March 8, 2003, with soldiers in Kuwait complaining that there was "too much waiting around." Military preparations were like a "huge gun and every day you cock the hammer back a little more."

The "waiting for war" stories that dominated coverage were the result of what was being heralded as a new era of military openness. The Pentagon promised access to the battlefield unseen since Vietnam. "Embedding" was the brainchild of Assistant Defense Secretary Victoria Clark. Clark's public relations experience includes working for Hill and Knowlton, the public relations firm responsible for promoting the false baby-incubator story from the First Gulf War. "We want robust coverage," she told the cable news anchor of the *Capital Report* as she promoted the idea (CNBC, February 19, 2003). Hundreds of journalists were embedding with military units waiting for close-up views of combat. A spate of stories followed, showing "embeds" training at media boot camps, learning about gas masks and running with heavy backpacks, pointing their cameras at soldiers.

Many journalists expressed "hopeful skepticism" about Pentagon promises to accompany troops into Iraq. One reporter, waiting to embed in Bahrain, said, "They're not crapping around this time. Journalists could die."[2] Network anchors prepared audiences for what they said would be an uncensored war. ABC's Peter Jennings told his viewers on March 11, 2003, that the military wanted Americans to "see war as it really is." These pre-embed stories before the battle resulted in highly positive coverage, the best public relations the Pentagon had seen in decades. Indeed, the positive coverage was predictable after the Pentagon learned from the First Gulf War that journalists were unlikely to jeopardize the promise of future access to the battlefield with stories critical of the military operation. Other aspects of the war, such as the potential humanitarian crisis (among many others), remained largely outside the news agenda (Coen and Hart, 2003), dominated as it was by pieces such as CBS's *Profiles of Courage* from the frontlines.

"A MEMBER OF THE TEAM"

Even as it promised a lack of "blanket censorship," the Pentagon did not hide its desire to shape positive coverage. The military went to great expense to produce a media-friendly war. A Hollywood set design was created as the backdrop for official briefings in Qatar. Press restrictions over the years had blocked what the military perceived as positive stories along with the negative. General Wesley Clark, working as a CNN consultant, admitted that restricting journalists during the 1991 Gulf War was a "huge mistake." It was "perhaps the biggest armored battle ever, but not a single image was reported or documented" (CNN, January 3, 2003). An In addition, the military understood the need to enlist the vast resources of the media, in what White House Chief of Staff Andrew Card referred to as the war's extensive "product-marketing campaign" (*New York Times*, March 23, 2003).

Many analysts and journalists understood from the beginning that embedding would create a different dynamic between reporters and soldiers than existed in previous wars. Vietnam has been referred to as the *uncensored* war (Hallin, 1986), largely because of the frontline access afforded war correspondents. Photojournalists and "renegades" covering the war moved freely through the country, found their own units and buddied up with soldiers and officers alike. They covered them for a time and then moved on. "Embeds" in Iraq had no independence, no vehicles, and were required to stay with the assigned unit for the duration of the war. There were lists of restrictions and rules to be followed. Assignments were centrally organized by the Pentagon, and there was no "cutting deals" in the field.

Discussions in the alternative media took on a different, more critical attitude to embedding than those in the mainstream media. Veteran war correspondent Chris Hedges was one of the most outspoken critics of the idea and appeared on Bill Moyers's *Now* as well as the radio show *Democracy Now!* (February 27, 2003) with host Amy Goodman. Hedges told Goodman embedding was "insidious" and predicted that it would produce a "further loss of distance" and a "false sense of loyalty."

Hedges was referring to a commonly held attitude about reporters and officials. Many journalism texts (Bennett, 2003) spend time recounting cautionary tales about how journalists should avoid the loss of professional and emotional distance from their sources. Accurate reporting demands journalistic independence. Certainly journalists covering Iraq were totally dependent on the military, not only for access but also for equipment, medical supplies and their own protection. In addition, journalistic independence was disdained by the military from the beginning. At briefings in Kuwait City, journalists were told, "The idea is by making you a part of the unit, you'll be a member of the team" (*Washington Post*, March 7, 2003). And some journalists indicated a favorable attitude toward the military effort from the start. As one reporter from *U.S. News and World Report*, speaking on CNBC, merged his role with the needs of the U.S. military, saying that the Taliban had lied about civilian casualties in Afghanistan, "so we'll be a kind of truth brigade" for the American military in Iraq (February 19, 2003). Military "minders" made their intentions clear to would-be embeds, that the normal practices of journalism would be viewed as disloyal. "Reporters shouldn't be...independently probing for facts," Lieutenant Colonel Rick Long told the *Washington Post* (March 7, 2003). "If something bad happens, it's the military's job to investigate."

In Afghanistan, American troops showed their displeasure with a *Washington Post* reporter trying to investigate civilian casualties from the aerial bombing. They explained that he shouldn't be there for his own security, as they threatened to shoot him. "That's always the line they are going to feed you," Chris Hedges said (*Democracy Now!*, February 27, 2003). Hedges's doubts about embedding derived from his experiences with censorship and the pool system during the First Gulf War.[3] "If things go wrong the press won't be anywhere in sight." The idea that they will have "unfettered access is ludicrous."

Official military escorts would also accompany embedded journalists, and a long history of information management follows military escorts. In Vietnam, journalists disdained official escorts and military briefings, referring to them as the "5 o'clock follies." Relations between networks and other elite press and military officials had improved since Vietnam, but alternative news outlets took the military to court during the Gulf War. The Center for Constitutional Rights (1991) filed a lawsuit against the Pentagon for censorship during the Desert Shield and Desert Storm operations. The suit documented the ways in which public affairs "escorts engaged in arbitrary censorship of interviews, photography and altered the activities of the soldiers when reporters came into their presence, not for security reasons, but to ensure favorable coverage of the military presence" (10–11).

A HOST OF MYTHIC WARRIORS

One way in which military strategists shaped positive coverage of the First Gulf War was by favoring local television crews over national and print journalists. "Hometowners" were given much freer access to the field because the Information Bureau chief in Saudi Arabia admitted he favored human-interest news (Nathan 1991, 26). Local television excelled in morale-boosting stories by sending words and pictures of the boys to the folks back home.

Network anchors learned the lesson well, and twelve years later much of national network news followed that lead, with feature stories about soldiers and their families. NBC's Tom Brokaw promised his audience (February 18, 2003), "I'll be back later in the broadcast with a touching story of a sergeant with the 3rd Infantry Division who is here, his family back in America, and how we managed to connect them via videotape." Sergeant Charles Weaver waved to his wife and children, who gazed back at him from the screen of Brokaw's digital video camera—all for the benefit of national television audiences.

CBS had its own news segment devoted to the portraits of soldiers. "I'll be back later in the broadcast with a Profile of Courage," said Dan Rather (February 18, 2003), "the story of an American soldier who's risked his life for his country many times and why he does it so willingly." Such profiles were singularly reverent. While they celebrated the individuals who risk their lives, in doing so they offered a uniquely positive attitude to war, one designed to block independent evaluations. The memoirs of soldiers who look back on their experiences of battle, expressed in their own words, offer insights from a different point of view. For example, consider the words of Sergeant Weaver interviewed on NBC (February 18, 2003). "I want to be battle-tested, but the idea of going and destroying someone else's family…. There's nothing good about that." Now compare those to the words of Anthony Swofford, the Desert Storm veteran who wrote the memoir *Jarhead*. Swofford (2003) and his marine sniper unit celebrated being deployed for combat by getting drunk and watching war movies. They loved watching such films because of the "magic brutality" that celebrated the "terrible and despicable beauty of their fighting skills." Swofford writes that "filmic images of death and carnage are pornographic for the military man." In addition, Swofford reveals the structured nature of the relationship between soldiers, who are prepped by their commanding officers, and journalists. As mentioned in chapter 11, when journalists visited Swofford's platoon in the Saudi desert, his sergeant told the troops to take off their shirts, show their muscles and say they believed in the mission.

By 2003, among the many "profiles of courage" on the nightly news, soldiers selected to be interviewed routinely said they joined the military to protect their families and country. In today's volunteer army, much economic analysis explains other incentives for joining the military, but Swofford recounts even less noble motivations. The marine recruiter "gleefully talked to me about buying sex in the Philippines…. He guaranteed me I could book a threesome for 40 American dollars in Olongapo…. I was sold." This was information "my mother would never see in the brochures." When compared to a broader range of human experiences, expressions and emotions, it becomes obvious that television presented a mythic stereotype of the soldiers fighting in Iraq. The presence of the stereotype is as harmful to the soldiers as it is to viewers. A variety of issues regarding salary scales, Gulf War syndrome and the controversy surrounding the uses of depleted uranium in high-tech weaponry, among many others, are all topics too complicated and challenging to stand next to the generic war hero narratives so prevalent in popular culture.

No wonder viewers were not prepared after the war started to see an American soldier face down on the ground, his hands behind his back, subdued after throwing grenades into the tent of his comrades, killing his commander and wounding fifteen others. The media-friendly war provided no context for understanding the complexities of a real war and the effects it has on human beings. Stories suitable as homefront morale boosters profile only camera-ready soldiers, and such stage-managed heroes became the mythic stereotype at the center of the *militainment* genre.

Profiles from the Front Line

Much of the media coverage of the invasion of Iraq was foreshadowed by *Profiles from the Front Line*. A series filmed in Afghanistan and later aired on ABC during the buildup to war in Iraq, *Profiles* was the first program to present war as reality television. As press requests for access to the war in Afghanistan were refused, Jerry Bruckheimer shot *Profiles* with full cooperation from the U.S. military and ABC's entertainment division. As detailed in the previous chapter, Bruckheimer's *Black Hawk Down* was theatrically released during the bombing of Afghanistan and also produced with full cooperation from the military. Bruckheimer's movie posters hang on the walls of the Pentagon. Television news would later take its cues from movie producer Bruckheimer when the war on Iraq began.

The initial scenes of *Profiles* establish the war's justification as needed retaliation for the attacks of 9/11. An officer preps his soldiers on their way to Afghanistan by saying, "How dare they" come to the U.S. and attack American citizens?

Profiles offers a wholesome, sanitized version of war where young men are mothered by a surrogate, tough-talking, African American woman who whips her staff into line to prepare the daily meals. The disproportionate number of nurturing women enlisted on *Profiles* made war fun for the whole family, like the female nurse who was pleased that she was called for duty, not her husband. She found it a good opportunity to lose some weight.

Through television cameras, viewers ride along with the bearded special forces troops who are shown bullying Afghans claimed to be Al Qaeda
members. But the men look the same as villagers, and the viewer has no way
of knowing if such claims were presently or later verified. Indeed, the program contained very little actual information. Speaking on the entertainment news program *Extra* (March 28, 2003), Jerry Bruckheimer admitted
that he was patriotic and wanted to help the war effort. This is entertainment that primes viewers to be receptive to the messages of war through
powerful production qualities, film montages and rousing soundtracks.

An American soldier dies, but we see only grainy, muted-green, night-
vision images (repeated and slowed) of a stretcher being carried into the
surgical unit and, later, long sequences of the wife and mother, who smile
nobly at the camera. Similarly grieving family members of dead or captured
fighters became familiar television images during the invasion of Iraq. But
as we will discuss in later chapters, as the war drug on and soldiers stayed
to fight a brutal counterinsurgency war often with inadequate armor and
equipment, with no Weapons of Mass Destruction to be found, family
members and the soldiers themselves would become the most outspoken
opponents of the Iraq War.

This first "reality show" treatment of the War on Terror made no attempt to cover civilians killed in the bombing of Afghanistan, and certainly
offered no pictures of that reality.

WAR'S CASUALTIES

Amid all the excitement and patriotic, red-white-and-blue graphics that
presented the coming war, one tended to forget that war is about death
and that when smart bombs reach their destination, people die, especially
in an urban center as densely populated as Baghdad. Independent journalists offered a different perspective on some of these issues. Best-selling
investigative reporter Greg Palast said, "We've forgotten about the Iraqis.
Who will document the effects of the bombing?"[4] When another journalist, soon to embed with the U.S. military, was asked if he would be allowed
to take pictures of Iraqi civilian casualties, the response was, "We're telling the U.S. military's story, that will be up to other journalists."[5] Chris
Hedges told Bill Moyers, "We've lost touch with war's essence. And that
essence is death" (*Now*, March 7, 2003).

The Deaths of Journalists

With over six hundred journalists assigned to the military, Hedges predicted that non-embedded journalists, or unilaterals as they were called,

attempting to report independently from Baghdad would "come under great pressure" (*Democracy Now!*, February 27, 2003). Indeed, days before the war, the BBC reported (March 13, 2003) that the U.S. military had threatened to target the satellite uplinks of independent journalists covering the war in Iraq. Under such circumstances the killing of a number of non-embedded reporters by American troops remains suspicious. Though he was traveling in a Jeep clearly marked as a news vehicle, Veteran British ITN reporter Terry Lloyd was severely wounded in cross-fire while driving to Basra in southern Iraq at the start of the war. The bodies of cameraman Fred Nerac and translator Hussein Osman were never found and presumed dead. On September 10, 2003, six months after Lloyd's death, a British paper, the *Daily Mirror*, reported that he was not killed in crossfire, but died later on the way to the hospital when his vehicle was strafed by a U.S. helicopter gunship (*Democracy Now!* September 25, 2003).

On April 8, three journalists were killed in two separate incidents of U.S. attacks on non-embedded reporters covering the war. Two journalists, Taras Protsyuk of the British news agency Reuters and Jose Couso of Spanish network television Telecino, were killed and three others injured when a U.S. tank from the Third Infantry fired into the Palestine Hotel in Baghdad, a well-known base for journalists. Pentagon officials knew that the hotel was full of journalists and had assured the Associated Press that the United States would not target the building. Reporters refuted U.S. claims that troops were being fired upon when they attacked the hotel. Later a tank commander said the camera lenses had been mistaken for binoculars used to spot targets. U.S. forces also said they had come under fire from the offices of Al Jazeera after they launched air strikes killing one of the channel's main correspondents, Tareq Ayoub. In a letter to Defense Secretary Donald Rumsfeld (April 8, 2003), the Committee to Protect Journalists wrote that, given the protection journalists receive under the laws of war, "these attacks violate the Geneva Conventions." Other international journalists and press freedom organizations also condemned the U.S. attacks. Reporters Without Borders (April 8, 2003) declared, "We can only conclude that the U.S. Army deliberately and without warning targeted journalists." Articles critical of the actions against journalists by the U.S. military appeared in the international press, but little reporting and less skepticism appeared in the U.S. media.[6]

WAR AS ADRENALINE RUSH

When the "Final Hour" finally came on March 19, the war was picture perfect. Initial coverage blended excitement and anticipation with firepower and the photogenic bombing of Baghdad. Images of incredible devastation registered as painterly pink clouds when, on March 21, three hundred cruise missiles destroyed two dozen buildings in a matter of minutes. In the city once again, Peter Arnett exclaimed, "An amazing sight, just like out of an action movie, but this is real."

As U.S. troops pressed into southern Iraq, television images merged cinematic references with reality-style camera perspectives. Viewers gazed across the sand from inside army vehicles, a fantasy ride–along with desert warriors as the tanks and armored convoys sped "virtually unopposed deep into the Iraqi desert" (CNN, March 21, 2003).

As with the reality show *Cops*, which adopts the view of law enforcement, camera and journalistic perspectives merged into a point of view united with the military effort. Empowered by riding shotgun with the soldiers, journalists barely contained their excitement. They wore goggles and flack jackets and even reported through gas masks as they adopted military jargon: "There are boots on the ground." They interviewed Top Gun pilots and crawled along the ground with gunfire in the distance, pressing microphones into soldiers' faces as they pointed their weapons. So surreal was the experience that newscasters felt compelled to tell viewers that the images they were seeing were live, not a movie.

Tom Brokaw (*New York Times*, March 23, 2003) understood the effects of such visual and narrative representations: "Television cannot ever adequately convey the sheer brute force of war, the noise and utter violence." This is certainly true when the violence and brutality are edited out, while the excitement and heroics are sensationalized. But Brokaw passed blame to the medium itself. "It somehow gets filtered through the television screen, and that's probably just as well," he said.

Few unpleasant images disrupted the flow, certainly nothing horrific, gruesome, or in "bad taste." This was war as adrenaline rush with no responsibility. Americans interested in the effects on the Iraqi population flocked to websites for news and pictures of wounded civilians, the war's consequences. One diary of a young man from Baghdad, written under the pseudonym Salam Pax, read, "Why does this have to happen to Baghdad? As one of the buildings I really love went up in a huge explosion, I was close to tears."

SHATTERED ILLUSIONS

But by the afternoon of March 23, unmanaged images from Iraqi state television shattered the grand illusion. As the whole world was watching, Al Jazeera aired video footage of the bloodied bodies of dead American soldiers sprawled carelessly on a slab floor. Iraqi interrogators interviewed the POWs. The war that couldn't wait had suddenly become a problem. Alternative information finally rendered the war real, horrible. Though networks censored the footage initially, they showed clips.

Almost overnight, the tone of media coverage flipped from what CNN's Aaron Brown (*New York Times*, March 25, 2003) admitted was a "gee whiz" attitude to a tempered anxiety about "another messy, frustrating combat situation" (CNN, March 24, 2003). The mix of sentimentality and visual sensationalism was wildly successful as long as it remained unchallenged. By Tuesday, March 24, the *New York Times* noted, "An image of awesome American firepower had been replaced by pictures of vulnerability." The thrilling momentum of the Iraq reality war slammed into a different set of cultural references and memories. An overmatched enemy was engaging in guerrilla tactics resulting in American casualties, quagmires, body counts and body bags.

YellowTimes.org, a website displaying images of Iraqi civilian casualties, was shut down on March 24. That night, embedded journalist Phil Ittner (CBS, March 24, 2003) showed pictures of wounded children but provided the acceptable context that justified the war. The videophone story from south-central Iraq showed a soldier rocking a little girl in his arms and another stroking her face. They came "streaming out to give what aid they could. They are here to take down the leadership in Baghdad, which they see as a threat to their families back home.... They wish they didn't have to do it."

As the Pentagon scrambled to control the meaning of its now-unpredictable war, it knocked out the Iraqi television signal. "War as it really is" seemed far too harsh for the Pentagon. Donald Rumsfled called the images a breach of the Geneva Conventions. On Tuesday, Dan Rather announced approvingly that the U.S. military had "pulled the plug" on what CBS called Saddam's "propaganda" channel.

Ironically, those most critical of the Pentagon as the war stalled were not media professionals themselves but their retired military consultants. At that point in the war's coverage, certain embedded reporters overtly served to boost civilian morale. One Fox News embed is of particular interest. Sixteen years after being called before Congress for subverting the Constitution, Oliver North was accepted as a legitimate journalist and became one of the most visible reporters covering the push into Baghdad. A man who had been so skilled at playing to television cameras was now on the field of battle helping create the images of war. "Ollie," as Sean Hannity of Fox News called him, repeated his emotional style (so familiar from the Iran/Contra hearings), now in the Iraqi desert, telling Sean, "I really get emotional about these guys. I just really love them." Hannity (April 1, 2003) fawned over North as he dispelled criticism of the war. "There's a lot of negative reporting out there Ollie." But the marines have gone "so far, so fast, with so few casualties, all the munitions you need, all the supplies you ever wanted, all the gasoline. When people hear it from you, because you're there, it means more than anything I can tell them."

SAVING PRIVATE LYNCH

What the war needed at that moment was a stunning plot reversal to propel the narrative forward. In the wee hours of the morning on April 2, the military provided the much-needed heroic device (with middle-of-the-night footage): the rescue of Private Jessica Lynch was announced to reporters at a 2:00 a.m. briefing at Central Command in Qatar. The young private had been plucked from a Nasiriyah hospital by a crack commando unit that carried her to safety in a waiting Black Hawk helicopter. Greenish night-vision video taken by a member of the rescue team was aired for journalists the following morning. The gripping story was ubiquitously described as a "daring raid" (e.g., CNN, April 8, 2003; NBC, April 6, 2003; ABC, April 7, 2003). For CBS (April 11, 2003), it was "a story for history, Jessica comes home." CNN (April 1, 2003) declared, "it was such a lift"; as *Time* magazine put it (April 14, 2003), the story "buoyed a nation wondering what had happened to the short, neat liberation of Iraq." "Hollywood," the magazine asserted, "could not have dreamed up a more singular tale."

Doubts about the story's authenticity were first raised by the London *Times* (April 16, 2003) that reported Lynch's rescue "was not the heroic Hollywood story told by the U.S. military, but a staged operation that terrified patients and victimized the doctors who had struggled to save her life." Based on interviews with hospital personnel, including Dr. Harith al-Houssona, the doctor who attended Lynch, the *Times* account described a terrifying assault in which soldiers handcuffed and interrogated doctors and patients, one of whom was paralyzed and on an intravenous drip.

By May the British Broadcasting Corporation (BBC2, May 18, 2003) had thoroughly investigated the incident and concluded that "Her story is one of the most stunning pieces of news management ever conceived." Though the assault met no resistance, as Iraqi and Baath leadership forces had fled the city the day before, the action was staged by the U.S. military. "It was like a Hollywood film. They cried 'go, go, go,' with guns and blanks without bullets, and the sound of explosions. They made a show for the American attack on the hospital—action movies like Sylvester Stallone or Jackie Chan" (BBC2, May 18, 2003). No embedded journalist accompanied the raid, and the green night footage was shot by the military. As Robert Scheer (Alternet, May 20, 2003) noted, "The video was artfully edited by the Pentagon and released as proof that a battle to free Lynch had occurred when it had not."

When the footage of the rescue was released in Doha, the words of General Vincent Brooks sounded familiar, similar to the lines delivered in the movie *Black Hawk Down*: "Some brave souls put their lives on the line to make this happen, loyal to a creed that they know that they'll never leave a fallen comrade." The fictional references were hard to miss and led the BBC (May 18, 2003) to observe, "The Pentagon had been influenced by Hollywood producers of reality television and action movies, notably the man behind *Black Hawk Down*, Jerry Bruckheimer." Indeed, is seems more than a coincidence that military spokesmen refer to the movie. One officer quoted in *Time* (April 14, 2003) was pleased that the military's Combat Camera crew had produced a narrative he felt was more favorable than Bruckheimer's movie: the rescue "worked perfectly. It was like *Black Hawk Down* except nothing went wrong."

The irony is that the Iraqi doctors worked hard to save her life, but when they attempted to deliver Jessica to a U.S. outpost the day before the raid, the Americans fired on the ambulance driver, making it impossible to proceed. Following the Central Command briefing in Qatar, the *Washington Post* (April 3, 2003) headlined that "She Was Fighting to the Death" and had sustained multiple gunshot wounds, adding that Jessica was later stabbed by Iraqi forces. The *Los Angeles Times* (May 20, 2003) would later report that, "It has since emerged that Lynch was neither shot nor stabbed, but rather suffered accident injuries when her vehicle overturned. A medical checkup by U.S. doctors confirmed the account told by the Iraqi doctors, who said they had carefully tended her injuries, a broken arm and thigh and a dislocated ankle, in contrast to the U.S. media reports that doctors had ignored Lynch." Nor was Jessica raped as reported in a *New York Post* front-page article.

The incident demonstrates how war propaganda, in its reincarnation as militainment, was reinvented for the wars of the twenty-first century. As the war became problematic, it looked as if the brutal realities might overtake the fictions. The rescue of Jessica, a classic "damsel in distress" story of mythic proportions, is already culturally compelling. With an overlay of more recent war-hero texts and expert timing, the fictional story buoyed the broader war narrative, providing the heroism, patriotism and indignation needed for boosting morale and public support for the war.

The ongoing, made-for-television "reality" war was ready for the next and last plot sequence. It needed the moment of triumph.

"Not Choreographed, Not Stage-Managed"

If Lynch's rescue provided the symbol of America's sacrifice and heroism, the downed statue of Saddam Hussein in Baghdad's Firdos Square became the icon of victory over Iraq. More important, it provided evidence that Iraqis welcomed American troops. In an interview before the war, publisher and author John MacArthur asserted that like the triumphant pictures of the liberation of Kuwait over a decade before, the military wanted embeds with the troops "for the victory pictures, waving flags and cheering Iraqis."[7] Later MacArthur told *Democracy Now!* (April 17, 2003) that the idea of "irrational exuberance" was preposterous. Upending the statue "is Torry Clark's great media moment." It would take more than a year before the truth of the tumbling statue would be known.

At the time, the statue toppling was repeated countless times on television and became the reference for some of the most exuberant media commentary of the war. Its meaning was clear to almost all: "It's a time for rejoicing particularly because of what television cameras clearly revealed—that many Iraqis support the coalition's mission and see the U.S. and its allies not as enemies but as friends and liberators," the *Indianapolis Star* (April 10, 2003) spelled out. "The picture says something about us as Americans," pronounced *USA Today* (April 10, 2003), "about our can-do spirit, our belief in lending a hand." The *Washington Post*'s Ceci Connelly, interviewed on Fox News (April 9, 2003), was one of many to compare it to the tearing down of the Berlin Wall: "Just sort of that pure emotional expression, not choreographed, not stage-managed, the way so many things these days seem to be. Really breathtaking." The *Chicago Tribune* (April 10, 2003) described "a crowd of hundreds of Iraqis" and continued, "This was the day the fog of war lifted. And the whole world could see the truth."

A few reporters indicated that the event was not as straightforward as U.S. media usually presented it. "Whenever the cameras pulled back, they revealed a relatively small crowd at the statue," the *Boston Globe* noted (April 10, 2003); others were struck by the fortuitous appearance on the scene of a pre-Gulf War-era Iraqi flag, as well as crowd members who had been spotted at Nasiriyah just the previous day, suggesting their appearance in Firdos Square might be something other than spontaneous.

On July 3, 2004, more than a year later, the *Los Angeles Times* quoted an internal Army study that found the statue toppling to be one of the many psychological operations maneuvers employed by the military. After a marine colonel decided to do the toppling, "it was a quick-thinking Army psychological operations team that made it appear to be a spontaneous Iraqi undertaking" (Jackson, 2004).

The use of powerful images to mold perceptions of Iraq was stunningly effective and at times, as we have seen, quite at odds with what was real. As Ron Martz, a print journalist for the *Atlanta Journal-Constitution* and a former marine, wrote in *Editor and Publisher* online (May 15, 2003), "When I wrote in one story about 'bloody street fighting in Baghdad,' it appeared the morning television viewers were seeing jubilant marines and Iraqi civilians tearing down statues of Saddam Hussein on the eastern side of the Tigris River. Some readers, believing all of Baghdad was like that, were livid. They did not grasp the fact that, on the western side of the river, pitched battles were still taking place. Because they did not see it on television, it was not happening. And it did not fit their view of the war."

With the media's overwhelming rush to lift the image of the tumbling statue to iconic status, reality was once again overtly ignored. By the end of the day, noted *Chicago Tribune* television critic Steve Johnson (April 10, 2003) stated that "the symbol's power had overtaken the hard facts."

Indeed, twenty-three days after the war started, CBS's *48 Hours* (April 11, 2003) opened its celebratory segment, "After the Fall," with footage of the toppling statue. As Dan Rather observed with evident approval, "Remnants of the regime still stand, but surrounded now by a conquering power." Rather encountered burned-out vehicles and intoned, "In this one there is a body. What happened, who shot him, who knows?" In the world of militainment, the "conquering power" bears no responsibility for the death left in its wake. In the chaos that is Baghdad, where soldiers serve as "police and social workers," Dan Rather offered little more than what has become a cliché to end his story: "Theirs is not to reason why, theirs is but to do or die."

The actual quote from Tennyson's "Charge of the Light Brigade" reads: "theirs but to do *and* die." More important, over the years the quote has lost its source and original meaning. It was intended as a comment on blind obedience to war even in the face of "blunders" by the high command and regardless of the deadly consequences. The poem commemorates the ill-fated cavalry charge by the British at Balaclava during the Crimean War. It may be instructive to offer a longer segment:

> "Forward, the Light Brigade!"
> Was there a man dismayed?
> Not though the soldier knew
> Some one had blundered.
> Theirs not to make reply,
> Theirs not to reason why,
> Theirs but to do and die.
> Into the valley of Death
> Rode the six hundred.

Though certainly not what Mr. Rather meant to imply, the sentiments loom ominously at a time of relentless war, when democracy's critical dialogue is replaced with militainment.

The few print journalists who rejected the militainment spin came under fire from their readers. As Martz (*Editor and Publisher* online, May 15, 2003) noted, "Criticism was not limited to me. They even criticized soldiers for doing what all soldiers do—complain. When I voiced complaints from soldiers about the lack of mail, water, and spare parts, they were called 'whiners' and 'crybabies.' And when I quoted one soldier who had been under fire almost daily for four weeks complaining about faulty intelligence, one reader suggested he be stripped of his uniform and sent home in disgrace."

CONCLUSION

As we have seen, each new war makes use of the latest communication technologies, media formats and marketing strategies to tell its story. The new 24-hour cable news program, CNN, played an essential role in the First Gulf War, just as television brought the Vietnam War into America's living rooms for the first time. The Second Iraq War made use of the popular television genre developed over the decade—the reality show. The hybrid created from the merger of combat footage and reality-style production practices can best be described as *militainment.*

At every phase along the way, the meaning of war with Iraq was systematically shaped and understood through a set of fictional frameworks that rendered the images more convincing and compelling than the unpleasant realities of war. The ongoing narrative sequencing and real-time reporting succeeded in transforming war coverage of Iraq into visual entertainment in a way that had not been previously achieved.

Before the war, with the promise of covering combat, the press corps was abuzz with World War II "band of brothers" camaraderie, evoking the memory of Ernie Pyle, the correspondent famous for his grunt's-eye view of the infantrymen he followed. "Pyle embedded himself among the troops, taking terrific risks to report on 'the boys' on the front lines," the *Washington Post* recalled (March 7, 2003). Veteran and literary scholar Paul Fussell (1989, iv) is highly critical of the uses of World War II analogies and suspicious of the reasons they are evoked: "The Allied war has been sanitized and romanticized almost beyond recognition by the sentimental, the loony patriotic, the ignorant, and the bloodthirsty."

Unarguably influential in shaping public opinion in the short term, the consequences of any new form of persuasion are not always apparent, even to those who propagate it. As Hightower (Alternet, May 20, 2003) points out, in addition to the $1 million spent on the "Top Gun" episode, Bush also spent "the integrity of the American presidency" as he used "our brave soldiers as his political props." For Robert Scheer (*Los Angeles Times*, May 20, 2003), one of the disturbing aspects of the Jessica Lynch story is that "the premeditated manufacture of the rescue…stains those who have performed real acts of bravery, whether in war or peacetime." The president may have experienced a Top Gun moment of fame, but history will not be kind to the creation of the Private Lynch story, and militainment in general, and the consequences of what were written out of those story lines, of death hidden behind the screen and the enduring wounds that remain.

Nor will history be gentle in judgments yet to be passed on the rationales that claimed war was necessary. A series of astonishing allegations about Weapons of Mass Destruction, repeated and legitimized in the media, would provide the main rhetorical justification for attacking Iraq. Only after the invasion, when no definitive evidence could be displayed for the cameras to record, would the allegations be discredited. The *Washington Post* and the *New York Times* would be forced to admit that their reporting on Bush administration claims about WMDs leading up to the war had been woefully inadequate, and that readers were left seriously misinformed. Wealth of evidence that the Bush administration had long planned to oust Hussein and that WMDs were the convenient cover existed well before the invasion. Indeed, former Treasury Secretary Paul O'Neil would later reveal that his first cabinet meeting in the White House, well before the September 11 attacks, was interrupted by generals who came in with maps to plan bombing sites in Iraq (Suskind, 2004).

As we have seen, the invasion of Iraq was viewed favorably by the media and even promoted and augmented as an exciting media event. Successful as entertainment, the war coverage left the public unprepared for the consequences and the death toll to come, or the serious constitutional problems that would emerge in its wake. The international community would note grave breaches of the Geneva Conventions as the occupation took more American and civilian lives. Yet the U.S. media would continue not only to ignore, but discredit reports of civilian casualties. Soldiers who returned to voice criticisms of the invasion and its aftermath would not find themselves bathed in the media spotlight as they had been before the war. From this lamentable trajectory, we turn our attention in the next chapter to the problematic alliance between the media industry and the military enterprise that was solidified over half a century. With an escalating momentum in the 1990s, the economies and technologies of war and media were inextricably bound up to become a major cultural force.

18

The Military-
Entertainment Complex

Permanent War and the Digital Spectacular

"Our industry has contributed to a change in humankind."
—Robert J. Stevens, former marine and chief executive, Lockheed Martin
(*New York Times*, November 28, 2004)

During the buildup to the Iraq War in 2003, a Channel 5 Fox News broadcast in New York City opens a story with "Plan of Attack" lettered over a digitalized pulsing graphic of layers of red targeting crosshairs. The announcer intones over ominous music:

Well the U.S. wants to take on the so-called Butcher from Baghdad, but this plan of attack will require some serious weapons. Fox 5 got a look at some of these weapons and you better believe they're a lot more advanced than what we used the first time around. They're mean Saddam fighting machines. Linda Schmidt gets an up close and personal look....

As Linda speaks we see a grainy, monochromatic field with squares and rectangles transforming into white blurs, "The U.S. Air Force in Afghanistan zeroing in and firing at buildings, trucks and terrorists." Under the coarse satellite field the framed station banner reads "War Games." Linda tells us: "Watch closely and you can see a person running on the ground." We are told to look for "a white dot moving across the center of your screen; they're firing at him, and then, they nail him!" The white dot blurs just as the squares did moments before. Edit to a picture of a large artillery weapon. "It made its debut in Afghanistan in the war on terror, being fired out of an Air Force gun ship." We see more satellite footage supplied by the U.S. Air Force; this time a weapon is fired out of a plane. "The military will also use it in Iraq if we go to war to take out what they call soft targets. In other words, Iraqi soldiers." Edit to a factory setting now, a man with a ponytail saying proudly, "The Air Force soldiers call it the Meat Grinder." Linda nods with a knowing smile, "The Meat Grinder." The man with the ponytail responds, "Yes Ma'am." Linda goes on to marvel at how light and easy the sixteen-pound weapon is to use as she holds it on her shoulder and aims.

Though the footage supplied by the military depicted actual weapons in real war footage, it was labeled "War Games" and looked strikingly similar to first-person shooter video games. Satellite photography offered the blurred images of buildings and human targets as they are destroyed. In addition, by handling and aiming the weapon, or we might say "playing with it," Linda moves the viewer into the zone of gaming and the participatory mode central to a player's experience of an interactive video. This is the new visual rhetoric of war—call it the digital spectacular. As news reporting looks and feels more like entertainment, that entertainment has a particular type of sensibility, a video-game feel and look. Such simulations are now seen across the media spectrum and have become fundamental to news representations of war.

THE MILITARY-ENTERTAINMENT COMPLEX

The stylized imagery of high-tech digitalized weaponry celebrated on television is only the most visible display of a fundamental merger taking place between the military and the media industries. During the 1990s, the military and the media worked together on the research and development of digital, computer-based technologies. At a number of centers, institutes and conferences, designers, artists, and executives from the entertainment industry join with analysts and engineers from the Department of Defense to share expertise in pursuit of digitalized graphics and the 3-D virtual worlds constructed for the fields of entertainment, news, video games and warfare. The digital technologies that drive the most profitable sector of the entertainment industry—computer games—are the shared technologies essential to advanced weapons systems. Computer games have also become key training and recruiting tools for the military. The characters that inhabit virtual game worlds locked in endless battles between good and evil double as "warfighters" and kill targets for military training.

A report by the National Research Council published the findings of a conference held in Irvine, California, in 1996 that brought together the Department of Defense and the media industry. Their report begins:

> Modeling and simulation technology has become increasingly important to both the entertainment industry and the U.S. Department of Defense (DOD). In the entertainment industry, such technology lies at the heart of video games, theme park attractions and entertainment centers, and special effects for film production. For DOD, modeling and simulation technology provides a low-cost means of conducting joint training exercises, evaluating new doctrine and tactics, and studying the effectiveness of new weapons systems…. These common interests suggest that the entertainment industry and DOD may be able to more efficiently achieve their individual goals by working together to advance the technology base for modeling and simulation.

And work together they have. At Irvine, members from DOD's Defense Modeling and Simulations Office (DMSO), and from the Defense Advanced Research Projects Agency (DARPA),[1] together with navy and air force representatives met with industry people from Pixar, Disney, Paramount, and George Lucas's Industrial Light and Magic. Joining this group, as Burston (2003, 164) reports, were other "computer industry executives and academic researchers in computer science and computer art and design. Their collective mission: to investigate the potential benefits of collaboration in creating 'the technical advances upon which future entertainment and defense systems will be built.'"

Taking a look at some of the history of development of the digital spectacular helps illustrate the media/military merger. The military has long dreamed of electronic machines able to simulate human activities and skills. Realizing this goal would require computer generation and Artificial Intelligence (AI). In the early 1980s, the military pioneered the first wave of research into AI. In 1983, DARPA's Strategic Computing Program outlined a five-year, $600 million plan for a new generation of computer applications that would be needed for the creation of "intelligent" machines, including autonomous land, sea and air vehicles. "These vehicles would have human abilities, such as sight, speech, understanding natural language, and automated reasoning" and be capable of reconnaissance as well as attack missions (Kellner 2003, 230). Gray (1997, 56) quotes a former employee, declaring "DARPA is responsible in large part for the existence of applied AI." These research priorities led to the establishment of AI divisions within the defense industry in such weapons manufacturers as Martin Marietta, Lockheed, Boeing, Rockwell International, and General Electric among many others (Gray 1997, 56).

In addition to intelligent machines, human skills and responses are necessary for convincingly rendered computer-generated characters (CGCs), key components of simulated training exercises and video games. The media and the military have found common ground in their interest in CGC. As the 1996 NRC report points out, both the military and the entertainment industry would like to develop CGCs "that have adaptable behaviors and can learn from experience" (Burston 2003, 164).

Another advanced computer technology essential to both video games and military training is flight simulation and imaging. The military took the lead in developing this technology as well, a technology that has become so much a part of the visual imaging of war across the media landscape. Computerized flight simulation was a crucial point in the history of computer generation and interactive electronic gaming. James Davis (1993), writing in *Aerospace America*, notes that the image generator component designed initially for military flight simulation modeling is at the heart of any computer-based visual system. Flight simulation became one of the basic models for interactive media. As Crogan (2003, 276) observes, popular games such as Microsoft's *Combat Flight Simulator 2: World War II Pacific Theater* (2000) are direct descendants of military research and represent "the passage of military-driven technological innovations into the heart of contemporary computer visualization and simulation."

The media industry excelled at turning the military's computer research into popular entertainment and handsome profits. However, by the 1990s the military began to understand "that if they wanted to take it to the next level, it was time to get a little help from Hollywood" (Burston 2003, 164). Calling on the magic of Hollywood marked a new phase in the development of advanced digital technologies. As it became clear that video games were bringing about an "entertainment revolution" (Poole, 2000), the media industry picked up the pace of R&D[2] and took the next research steps in computer gaming with highly profitable results. The flow of networking and software innovations began to even out and, in some cases, even reversed direction. Important advances made by commercial researchers in the entertainment industry were appropriated by the military (Richard, 1999). Cyberlife Technology's *Creatures 2.0* offered the cutting edge of artificial life simulation and helped realize the dream of smart weapons systems such as pilotless fighter aircraft. Another essential technological advance useful to the military, particularly for recruitment and training, is interactive first-person shooter technology developed by id Software in 1994 with its game *Doom 1.9*. "The U.S. Marine Corps Modeling Simulation Management Office has adapted *Doom 1.9* for the purposes of tactical combat training exercises" (Crogan 2003, 279).

Now this trans-sector reciprocity is a stable, ongoing, mutually beneficial industrial relationship. Military funding remains essential to the technologies of the digital spectacular, with a $45 million grant awarded to the University of Southern California's Institute for Creative Technology, a research center with the stated mandate to "enlist the resources and talents of the entertainment and game development industries and to work collaboratively with computer scientists to advance the state of immersive training simulation" (ICT, sited in Burston 2003, 166). In 1999, when military leaders set up simulation training centers, they decided they could use "a shot of Hollywood magic." In an interview with the *New York Times* (Hart, 2001), ICT's creative director James Korris explained the military's interest in collaborating with Hollywood when he said they wanted some "fairy dust." They found it at ICT in Los Angeles while working with such dream-makers as Paul Debevec, creator of the "trailing bullet" in *The Matrix*, who was charged with "improving the richness of the photorealistic detail in the computer-generated animations" used for military training. A number of producers, directors and writers of feature films specializing in special effects are also part of ICT's talent pool.[3] ICT's multilayered office complex (laid out by Herman Zimmerman, a *Star Trek* production designer) houses a staff of forty-five, including "a cadre of rumpled techies intent on constructing training scenarios that deliver a visceral wallop." Military training without the stardust was dull, as Korris put it; "When they put people in these simulators, they kept getting bored." With ICT's Digital Walls, that doesn't happen anymore. Simulating immersion training is created by converting "flats," a standard of Hollywood set design, into a "convincing 3-D effect of a rugged mountain landscape." In addition, Jacquelyn Morie, ICT's manager for creative development, explained that sound is also a key stimulus. "And so the 'whup, whup' of a helicopter swoops across the ceiling...while a rumble floor vibrates" to approximate the battlefield. The long-awaited Mission Rehearsal Exercise (MRE), a curved screen simulation in front of which officers-in-training are presented with a number of different options for emergency action, allows trainees to interact with digital actors, who themselves 'listen' and 'respond' with instantly variable 'emotions'" (Burston 2003, 167).

Hollywood has now become a full partner in new weapons training and development. At ICT the management skills of former media executives from NBC, Paramount and Disney can direct designers from Silicon Valley to help adapt the same digital effects used for movies, amusement parks and video games to military platforms. When synthetic characters, becoming known as "synthespians," can act and react in realistic ways to numerous stimuli, they make video games more challenging. In military training, synthespians make better "warfighters." Both benefit from the other's expertise. The video game *America's Army* boasts the most authentic rendering of combat, because real soldiers are the consultants.

Orlando, Florida, is another important site in the new military/entertainment trans-industrial formation. The well-known home of Disney's teams of R&D imagineers, the DOD's Simulation Training and Instrumentation Command (STRICOM) is also headquartered there. In addition, the University of Central Florida's Institute for Simulation and Training, together with other virtual-reality designers such as Real3D, adds "sub-woofer power to the formidable node of the North American military entertainment establishment that STRICOM's own website likes to call 'Team Orlando'" (www.stricom.army.mil). Last, but certainly not least, is another major player in Team Orlando; the complex across the street from STRICOM houses the nation's largest military contractor, Lockheed Martin. With this assembled money, talent and technology, STRICOM can accomplish what Der Derian (2001) explains as "the twenty-first century warfighter's preparation for real world contingencies."

Cyborg Soldiers on a Virtual Battlefield

In press conferences and promotional materials, army visionaries lay out plans for the battlefields of the future; they are digitalized and "Net-ready." As Kellner (2003, 231) observes, "with the complex communications systems now emerging, all aspects of war—from soldiers on the ground and the thundering tanks to pilotless planes overhead—are becoming networked with wireless computers providing information and exact locations of all parties." The computerized helmets worn by soldiers will receive signals from the Global Positioning Satellite system, allowing precision mapping of enemy terrain. Data from numerous sources will be networked and integrated into a central command system monitored by computers. Robot scouts will send surveillance imagery to commanders instantaneously. Der Derian witnessed such a simulated battlefield in action in 1994 in California's Mojave Desert, during the army training exercise Desert Hammer VI. At Fort Irwin, the U.S. Army's National Training Center, the exercise "served as the testing ground of the first fully digitalized task force." He describes the soldiers of the 194th brigade as "digitally enhanced, computer-accessorized, and budgetarily gold-plated from the bottom of their combat boots to the top of their kevlars." The training exercise took the troops "as close to the edge of war as technology of simulation and the rigors of the environment" allowed. The war game combined real-time airborne and satellite surveillance, digitalized battlefield communication, helmet-mounted displays, and a computer for every warrior. They rode atop the latest M1A2 Abrams battle tanks, each carrying an information system that collected real-time battlefield date from airplanes, satellites and unmanned vehicles. Day and night vision scopes were mounted on their M-16s, and the twenty-first-century "land warriors" carried video cameras, computers in the rucksacks, with one-inch LED screens attached to their helmets. They were connected by radio communication to a battle command vehicle coordinating the attack through a customized Windows program. Using SIPE (Soldier Integrated Protection Ensemble), the physical state of the soldier can be monitored in the same way video games register the breathing and movement of players.

Though, as Der Derian describes, the digitalized army's combination of brute force and high tech appeared "formidable," the Americans did not win the simulated battle against their "Krasnovian" opponents.

WEAPONS FOR A NEW AMERICAN CENTURY

Connections between the digital spectacular and the political and economic realities of military spending and planning are profound. By the end of 2004, national security spending had surpassed $500 billion a year in the United States, with Lockheed Martin the major recipient of the largess. Much of this money is dedicated to the quest for the smartest, "Net-ready," electronic digitized weapons designed for military domination on a global scale including Star Wars II.

It might be assumed that military spending escalated only after the terrorist attacks of September 11, 2001, but the plan for vast increases was already articulated in the run-up to the 2000 presidential race by a conservative think tank founded in 1997 and calling itself the Project for a New American Century. In a document serving as its statement of principles, entitled *Rebuilding America's Defenses*, PNAC envisioned a new, more aggressive role for America as the single super power. It pictured an America with unlimited military might, its global power based on state-of-the-art weapons systems, including the revival of missile defense. This founding document carries the signatures of Paul Wolfowitz, Dick Cheney, Donald Rumsfeld "and numerous others who have gone on to become major players in the Bush administration" (Hartung and Ciarrocca, 2003, 18). When President Bush took office, his military budget equaled the exact amount outlined by PNAC. According to Hartung and Ciarrocca (2003, 18), *Rebuilding America's Defenses* "served as a blueprint for the Bush-Rumsfeld-Pentagon military strategy."

The connections between PNAC, the Bush administration, the military and weapons contractors are a multi-channeled nexus of policy, technology and funding flows, and as we have seen, the media industry is structurally invested in this complex. Lockheed Martin hired Thomas Donnelly, principal author of *Rebuilding America's Defenses*, and former deputy director of PNAC in 2002. Bruce Jackson, a founding member of PNAC, was a Lockheed Martin executive who left the corporation to work full-time on military policy issues. Robert Stevens, current CEO of Lockheed Martin, told the *New York Times* (November 28, 2004) that Lockheed is at "the intersection of policy and technology." At the "heart of America's arsenal," it puts its "stamp on the nation's military policies, too." He went on to say that that "requires thinking through the policy dimensions of national security as well as technological dimensions" (November 28, 2004). This Team Orlando associate maintains its ongoing interconnections with the Bush administration. Former executives serve on the Homeland Security Advisory Council, the Defense Policy Board and the Defense Science Board. Currently E.C. Aldridge, Jr., is a member of Lockheed's board of directors and is also the Pentagon's chief weapons buyer.[4] Those who make the weapons now help articulate the policy justifications for their use. And as we can see, major sectors of the media industry are part of that nexus.

The media have also played a leading role in legitimizing the new foreign policy directives of PNAC, a stance most likely to result in the need for high-tech weapons systems. The same sprawling media conglomerate that produces television reports on lethal weapons that resemble Arms Expos more than news helped influence the Bush administration to adopt military and foreign policies rejected by previous administrations as too hawkish.

PNAC and the Weekly Standard

It is doubtful whether the opinions of such a small group at PNAC could have had such impact without the influence afforded them by the *Weekly Standard*, a neoconservative journal edited by William Kristol, a founding member of PNAC. Bankrolled by Rupert Murdoch, the same conservative media tycoon who owns the Fox network (including New York's Channel 5, mentioned above), the *Standard* promoted the sweeping new vision for American foreign policy and became one of the most influential journals in Washington. "The *Standard* may have a circulation of just 55,000, but it has aimed successfully at policy-makers rather than average readers" (Murphy, 2003). John Hulsman, a fellow at the Heritage Foundation, was critical of the doctrine of preemptive attacks, believing they would lead to "endless war," but as he notes, under the younger Bush administration the more traditional conservatives who were influential in the first Bush White House lost favor in the halls of power (Murphy, 2003).

The yearnings for a more aggressive U.S. foreign policy, long simmering among neoconservatives at PNAC, was finally realized on September 20, 2002, when the Bush administration set forth its plan for America's global future. The National Security document defined America as the single superpower and detailed the reasoning behind "preemptive strikes." A key concept was "counterproliferation." As Kellner points out, the clumsy Orwellian concept was offered as a replacement for "nonproliferation." A variety of phrases, some pulled from PNAC documents—such as "regime change"—and others often repeated—such as "anticipatory self-defense"—became the new rhetoric of the "preemptive strike," language that justified unilateral actions against countries declared dangerous to the U.S. policy designed by PNAC was chosen over more conventional thinking represented by other elite factions at the Heritage Foundation. According to Kellner (2003, 240), in effect Bush "renounced the global security, multilateralism, and rule by international law that to some degree had informed U.S. thinking since World War II, and that appeared to be an emerging consensus among Western nations during the era of globalization." Other critics viewed this historic shift as the end of the system of international institutions and laws that had been built for half a century.

THE NEW ELECTRONICALLY MEDIATED CULTURAL MILIEU

It should come as no surprise that the convergence between the media and the military as both pursue mutually beneficial goals would have cultural implications with alarming consequences. Mapping the media landscape of the digital spectacular we see from press reports to television coverage, and from movies to video games, a profound alignment between the executive branch, the military and media coordinates. During the buildup to war in Iraq, the highly positive nature of the news coverage was inescapable. Military officials and a bevy of "consultants" and former generals dominated television screens "explaining" the strategies, logistics, preparations and weapons of war. Television networks and cable channels featured patriotic graphics and promotional bumpers that adopted the military's terms of engagement. We might ask, under this new confabulation between the military and the media, how the media could possibly adopt an independent stance toward an enterprise they are so integrally connected to. Contemporary news coverage can best be understood as part of a new geography of war, one defined and dominated by the merger between the media and the military. Under this partnership, those who promote war can be transformed into journalists, such as NBC's legal correspondent Pete Williams, who held the position of press secretary at the Pentagon under Dick Cheney during the First Gulf War.

A Bradley Tank on Saddam's Bunker

Retired General Barry McCaffrey is only one of many ex-generals now paid as a television analyst. On MSNBC (March 31, 2003), McCaffrey openly idolized the weapons of war in Iraq: "Thank God for the Abrams tank and the, you know, the Bradley fighting vehicle. The war isn't over until we've got a tank sitting on top of Saddam's bunker." Like the media industry, McCaffrey has financial interests in war. As *The Nation* (March 21, 2003) discovered, he sits on the board of Integrated Defense Technologies, a company that in one month "received more that $14 million worth of contracts relating to Abrams and Bradley machinery parts and support hardware." In the twenty-first century, America is a brave new world where those who profit from weapons are now also paid to persuade the public of their virtues.

THE NEW WAR FILMS

Nowhere is message compatibility so apparent as in feature films released after September 11, 2001, a crucial point at which the military called for a more open alliance with Hollywood, enlisting the talents of the entertainment industry to promote what President Bush termed the War on Terror. While some resisted, most notably Robert Redford and Oliver Stone, the effects of this alliance were direct, and its legacy will be felt for years to come.

Behind Enemy Lines

As we have seen, entertainment values have long been applied to military realities, but new versions of "Hollywood stardust" are continually required to fashion the evolving rationales and standard of conduct for warfare into the culturally recognizable.

As Burston (2003, 164) notes, there is a "Join the Navy" feel to blockbuster military spectaculars like *Behind Enemy Lines*, (2001) one manifestation of the media/military merger. But in addition to exciting atmospherics and powerful heroics, the film's action sequence moves to confirm a military and foreign policy consistent with the Bush administration. In addition, its special effects and extravagant visuals also celebrate war's new sensibility as the digital spectacular.

On a routine mission on Christmas Eve, an American pilot, Captain Burnett (Owen Wilson), is shot down over Bosnia during the U.N. action in Yugoslavia. When Burnett is trapped behind enemy lines, Admiral Leslie Reigart (Gene Hackman) is told by his NATO commander, Admiral Piquet (Joaquin de Almeida), that Burnett must be sacrificed. A rescue mission will threaten "peace talks." Admiral Reigart bucks NATO command and carries out a secret and daring rescue mission to save Burnett after a French team fails. As Fuchs (2001) notes, "if you want something done right, you (assuming you're the U.S. military) need to go on and do [it] your own self." Successful and dangerous actions carried out by tough, independent military heroes are no doubt the kind of plots the Pentagon had in mind when it approached Hollywood. Along the way the film seems to offer a perfect illustration of what Vice-President Dick Cheney meant (in August 2002) when he defended the unilateralist doctrine arguing for a preemptive strike against Iraq: "The risks of inaction are far greater than the risks of action." As Pollard (2003, 339) rightly observes, "The film is anti-NATO peacekeeping operations, which are depicted as ineffectual and contrary to U.S. interests." The movie affirms that the United States has every right to act unilaterally, independent from the international community because it is the right and most efficient thing to do.

In fact the heroic actions taken by Admiral Reigart result in Captain Burnett being able to document Serbian war crimes, including soldiers killing and burying innocent civilians. This seems proof in itself that the action was worth the risk. In alignment with the new unilateralism, the film nevertheless carries a reassuring message that the truth will be revealed, that independent information about the horrors of war will reach the public through the mass media. Captain Burnett and the truth both triumph.

High-tech digital war jazzes up the plot as Admiral Reigart tracks the missing soldier using satellite systems reminiscent of the destruction of a terrorist camp in *Patriot Games* (1992). In addition, both the director John Moore and cinematographer Brendan Galvin worked on Adidas and SEGA commercials before this film and use spectacular visual rhetoric to wow the audience. As Fuchs (2001) describes: "The action is considerably amplified by incredible camera tricks: Those speedy zooms in and out, freeze frames, all-shook-up shutter speeds, and exciting-to-the-max editing." The film's most exhilarating scene: "The out-top-gunning-Top Gun effects are breathtaking, with the F-18 zooming and zipping through the sky, the camera swish-panning and smash-cutting like there's no tomorrow." The audiovisual atmosphere that celebrates the weapons of the twenty-first century is an exciting place to be, whether in a movie theater or playing a video game. Now in the realm of the Digital Spectacular, these two mediums have begun to merge.

Video Games

Video games have positioned warfare at the center of high-tech digital culture. War now enjoys the popular buzz that always surrounds the celebration of "the new." As simulated combat scenarios multiply in virtual worlds, warfare becomes inseparable from the latest innovations in entertainment technology. New modes of war representations are transfiguring cultural practice at the individual as well as social level. Depictions of war are no longer confined to the two-dimensional spaces of film and television with passive viewers who follow predetermined storylines. Video games create virtual worlds of action and combat that engage players as participants. The movement from narrative, either fictional or documentary, to interaction has created new spaces for war.

FROM NARRATIVE TO INTERACTIVE SIMULATION

To explore the distinction between narrative and simulation, let's begin with the game that uses the air war in the Pacific during World War II as its setting. The player can pick and choose missions, select aircraft and even opt for different characters or "skins" to depict an enemy. Players can make modifications to games, substituting jet planes for World War II fighter planes. (In many games Osama bin Laden became a popular substitute skin after 9/11.) Once in the game world, the player's interaction becomes more skilled as he/she masters increasing levels of difficulty while overcoming threats and challenges in a process that, according to Crogan, leads to "personal discovery."

Another theorist, Espen Aarseth, appropriates the Greek term used in physics—*ergodic*—to explain the interactive process. Ergodic combines two words, *ergo*, "work," and *hodos*, "path," to define the process of working and progressing in video game play. But the player does not process along a single, direct path in preset amounts of time. The game generates a cybernetic feedback loop of different sequences from the one before it. The interactive game is goal oriented, but the goal is to learn to respond better, faster and more accurately to a changing set of complex stimuli. While the narrative form is concerned with the time of the story and its telling, gametime concerns the time of the gamer's interactive process.

Crogan describes the interaction created in the game *Doom*, as the player adopts a "first-person perspective of the game's virtual world and attempts to survive frequent deadly attacks by a variety of monsters while navigating labyrinthine environment in level of increasing complexity and difficulty." It becomes clear why the marines use this game as a training tool. The cognitive multitasking of gametime is coterminous with the process of tuning the perceptions to the needs of war. Succeeding in combat, virtual or real, depends on anticipating contingencies, advanced skill levels and increased proficiencies, all with the goal of surviving the battle by controlling the event space and destroying or otherwise neutralizing the enemy. Engaging and learning in game time and space, with all contingent threats neutralized in order to win, results in a sense of power and control over a simulated battlefield. The process is fundamentally different from the act of viewing a feature film with a conventional plot that moves from beginning to end.

HISTORY, FILM AND VIDEO GAMES

Though they are quite distinct as entertainment modes, there is a growing interconnection between video games and narrative film, with significant cultural implications. Like movies, video games often call upon World War II as the preferred narrative of war. The manual for *Combat Flight Simulator 2: World War II Pacific Theater* is packed with historical reproductions and documentary materials that attempt to authenticate the reconstruction of well-known missions of the Pacific Theater. The material features actual quotations from diaries and flight instruction manuals, and summaries of major conflicts and biographies of famous aces. However, the game belies this historical authenticity by significantly changing the historical narrative of the air war in the Pacific. It does not start with the bombing of Pearl Harbor, nor does it end with the ultimate climax, the bombing of Hiroshima.

CFS2 shares some spectacular digital effects with the movie *Pearl Harbor* (2001). The movie features extraordinary combat simulations that one reviewer called "Zap Happy." Images of the attack, particularly of a bomb hitting the U.S. ship *Arizona*, are imbued with a sensibility akin to video games. The point of view of the falling bomb could not have been depicted before digital simulation. It was achieved with the aid of computer-generated imaging. As Crogan puts it, "The audiovisual combat spectacle presents an extraordinary view of the action such as the bomb POV and shots that portray aerial dogfighting maneuvers in a way that is not possible with a real camera" (185).

Like the packaging of *CFS2*, the film *Pearl Harbor* is also packaged through the powerful rhetoric of historical reproduction. The film's website features interviews with veterans from the attack and includes a special section titled "the documentary," complete with an oral history project with veterans. Yet consider the film's narrative divergence from the historical record. In the film, bystanders see the action, though the attack took place in the very early morning, making that highly unlikely. During the surprise attack by the Japanese, the film's two young flying heroes, Rafe McCawley (Ben Affleck) and Danny Walker (Josh Hartnett) manage to change from their Hawaiian shirts into their uniforms, commandeer two fighters and launch a fierce, though contrived, counterattack. As Pollard (2003, 335) puts it, "U.S. flyers were unable to mount any serious defense against the attack, which makes the heroic aerial scenes quite implausible." The culture of the digital spectacular speaks with persuasive rhetoric about a world it claims is real, while constructing an implausible present and rewriting history to suit current attitudes and sensibilities.[5]

PURE WAR

There are considerable consequences to the new military-entertainment complex outlined here. As we have seen, the boundaries between war and peace begin to lose distinction in an age when so many resources, technologies, creative talents and cultural practices are devoted to the anticipation, preparation, planning and imaginings of warfare. As Virilio and Lotringer (1997) argue in the concept of "pure" war, spatial, temporal and logistical distinctions that once separated war from peace have lost their defining power. The "logistics" of war, the broad nexus of military planning in preparation for armed conflict, including transportation and training, overflow into civilian society and become integral to that society.

The idea of permanent war preparation and its social effects has long been articulated, especially with regard to a military-dominated economy. Most notably, Seymour Melman (1988) and others have extensively detailed the social costs of an economy based on war. They have demonstrated how many school buses each F-18 fighter jet could buy. They have posited a visionary plan of an economy converted to civilian well-being and made convincing arguments that society might be better served if public money were redirected toward improving basic economic infrastructure, from bridges to schools. Others have argued, in an age of terror, that improving such failing infrastructures as the public health system, currently incapable of providing the population with flu vaccine, would provide more safety and security than more fighter jets. And on a global scale, Jeffrey Sacks (2002), at Columbia University's Earth Institute, argues for weapons of mass salvation to end global poverty instead of calling for war. When the vast majority of the earth's population lives in dire poverty without basic health and immunization services, spending $87 billion on global health would create a world community far more able to promote peace and stability than weapons of war. Virilio's notion of pure war advances our understanding of the relationship between military priorities and civilian society by including the media-cultural component and arguing that media developments have become fundamental to the social transformation into pure war. Following Virilio, Crogan (2003) argues that digital technologies and virtual abstractions are major steps toward "the merging of the military and the domestic spheres in the realm of audiovisual cultural forms" (279–80). We have seen how video games have become central components of the unity between culture and military logistics. In the age of pure war, America's new culture of militarism has entered the home as recruitment, training, planning and perceptions are managed at the site of domestic digital entertainment centers.

Policy formulations, weapons technology and war have merged with entertainment culture as weapons displays thrill moviegoers and television audiences. Such visions of virtual war are no doubt in the minds of those who plan and execute combat operations in foreign lands, but just as the television coverage of war is often entertaining fiction, so, too, are futuristic battlefields. Just as one young soldier recounts in the film *Fahrenheit 9/11*, "it's not like a video game when real people die"; the battlefields of virtual war games have little in common with occupying a foreign country. It is a long perceptual leap from the gold-plated war games that Der Derian visited to Iraq, where soldiers have refused missions because their humvees have not been bullet-proofed. Media industries help create the virtual simulations of weapons systems even as they portray war through digitally entertaining formats; both technologies share the fictional sensibilities of games, not reality. The reality of war remains hidden, especially the deadly consequences of bombs not contained within computer screens and virtual worlds.

19

Of Smart Weapons, Civilian Casualties and the Crimes of War

The Whole World (except the United States) Is Watching

As Operation Iraqi Freedom burst onto television screens with red, white and blue enthusiasm in beat with pulsating drums of invasion, the Pentagon quietly issued a directive forbidding news coverage of "deceased military personnel returning to or departing from" air bases. Nor would Vietnam-era body counts be part of the military's public relations lexicon. Nor would the Department of Defense make any attempt to document the war's "collateral damage." Death would not be a player in the televised reality war, and the Pentagon would be successful in keeping it almost totally off-camera.

The Pentagon continued to report the deaths of U.S. soldiers and personnel in Iraq, but it would not keep track of civilian deaths caused by American troops or bombs, or record the numbers killed as a consequence of invasion and occupation. Instead, the U.S. military repeatedly reiterated that it tried to prevent civilian deaths as best it could. By 2005, a British study of civilian casualties in Iraq compiled the recorded deaths from published sources and arrived at an admittedly conservative figure of 25,000 dead. A U.S. military spokesperson responded to the study, saying, "We do everything we can to avoid civilian casualties in all of our operations." Lieutenant Colonel Steve Boylan told Reuters, "Since the start of Operation Iraqi Freedom until now, we have categorically not targeted civilians. We take great care in all operations to ensure we go after the intended targets." For the Pentagon, since civilians are not targets, their deaths are *accidents* and killing them is *unintentional*. (As we saw with the image of nine-year-old Kim Phuc running from napalm in Vietnam, the accidental victim is rendered somehow less horrific.) Accepting such official reassurances also depends on accepting some fundamental assumptions about high-tech warfare: that state-of-the-art weapons are deadly accurate and lethal only to those who appear in the crosshairs. During the war in Iraq, the twin military logics of unintended victims and high-tech weapons were uniformly accepted and repeated in the media. But consider the coherence and values of such language and assertions.

As the military planned a massive aerial bombing campaign in the densely populated city of Baghdad, the Pentagon phrase "Shock and Awe" was repeated with enthusiasm on television, part of the celebration of the power of modern warfare. Smart bombs contain within their tracking systems almost magical properties, a theme celebrated in American culture since the First Gulf War. As we have seen, the rhetoric and imaging of high-tech is the preferred language of modern warfare, and it spans the media spectrum from video games to news reporting, with heavy doses appearing in commercial feature films. When the "good guys" wield this mythic technology, it treats of precision, necessity and empowerment. The state of the art of American weaponry confers, ironically, a moral legitimacy on the battlefield because the bombs are "smart," "precise" and "deadly accurate," but only to the intended targets.

Infrequently, on the news, the truth of real bombs and their actual consequences challenge the language of these myths. Before the invasion, an occasional story warned that, as an unfortunate consequence of the air war, some innocent people might be killed. Consider the words of NBC correspondent Jim Miklaszewski (February 9, 2003) as he reported that the Pentagon was worried about the possible "thousands" of Iraqi civilians that may "be killed entirely by accident in an intensive bombing campaign." Reassurances to audiences that civilian casualties are "unintentional," while at the same time bombs are "precise," stand awkwardly side by side. Juxtaposing the chatter reveals some logical contradictions. One month after explaining that accidents could happen, Miklaszewski (NBC, March 21, 2003) used the military phrase "surgical strike," saying, "Every weapon is precision-guided—deadly accurate, designed to kill only the targets, not innocent civilians." Rachel Coen and Peter Hart, writing in the media criticism journal *EXTRA!* (2003, 17) point out: "The view that all the U.S.'s weapons are 'precise' would seem to be at odds with the notion that all civilian deaths caused by U.S. attacks are 'accidents,' but both claims were equally popular with the U.S. press."

The 2005 British investigation into Iraqi civilian deaths provided documentation on the accuracy of modern weapons. Independent investigators at Iraq Body Count (IBC) published the analysis in conjunction with Oxford Research Group, a U.K.-based public interest organization. The accounting method required that each death be reported by at least two reputable English-language publications before being included in the database.[1] By the authors' own admission, the report's count of 24,865 civilian dead in the first two years underestimates the total loss. These are only the bodies that English speakers have been able to document. In many cases the documentation also recorded how they were killed.

BOMBS KILL CHILDREN

IBC's data included the type of weapon responsible for the death recorded, and that data was used to assess the accuracy of high-tech weapons. The study shows that aerial weapons are not at all smart, particularly with regard to war's smallest victims. "If it is assumed that adults, not children, are the intended targets in war, the proportion of children to adults killed by different types of weaponry can be used as a measure of the indiscriminateness." Using this data to evaluate various weapons, the group found that explosive devices, especially ones in which aircraft are involved, killed a significantly higher proportion of children. The authors conclude, "It appears that whatever their military advantages and benefit to soldiers, 'stand off' weapons, which put a substantial distance between soldiers and their intended targets, are the most likely to cause unintended harm to bystanders." Hand-held firearms are far "smarter" and usually result in low child lethality, "which suggests that clearly identifiable civilians are more likely to be spared when combatants are able to personally control and direct their fire."

Telling viewers that civilians were not targets and that the Pentagon is concerned about casualties is a comfort. It seems a humane sensibility, but it hides a fundamentally antihumanitarian reality. When an intensive bombing campaign named Shock and Awe is planned, celebrated and carried out in an urban area, how can the deaths of civilians be accidental? When bombs are dropped on a city, many of the people living there will be killed. It is a logical consequence of aerial bombardment. This is revealed in the contradictory assertions, simultaneously articulated, that bombs are smart yet death is accidental. The advantage of aerial warfare is fewer American casualties, which allows war to be fought as long as numbers stay low and combat ends quickly. Yet the cost to civilians is high. This "collateral damage" adds another set of image requirements for the continuation of war.

The age of "stand off weapons" coexists in a culture of media distraction. The new video-game sensibility through which American culture now offers the "experience" of war presents digital thrills dissociated from the killing of real people. Looking through the elevated eyes of the warriors is antithetical to concern for the victims on the ground. Entertainment models make the absence of death hardly noticeable. But speaking of death is at times unavoidable. To do so, the media still draw on a variety of conventional strategies recognizable after a century of war. When death is presented, it is contextualized in ways that dull the senses, eliminate compassion and avoid accountability.

"Impossible to Determine the Cause"

During the Shock and Awe bombing campaign, over sixty people were killed when a missile crashed into a heavily populated open-air market in the Shuala section of Baghdad. The media avoided assigning blame for the deaths. The *New York Times* (March 29, 2003) reporting was typical: "it was impossible to determine the cause." By May 2003, no U.S. news outlets had reported investigations into the bombing, but British war correspondent Robert Fiske found a serial number on a missile fragment at the scene of the explosion. The London newspaper *The Independent* traced the number to the Raytheon Corporation. The number corresponded to the HARM anti-radar missile or a Paveway laser-guided bomb—both American weapons used in the bombing. *The Independent* determined that the damage to the market was consistent with a HARM missile, which has a tendency to go off-target.

As Enemy Propaganda

One U.S. news magazine (*Newsweek*, April 7, 2003) asserted that it did not matter who was responsible. "In at least one respect, it doesn't make much difference who bombed the two markets. Either way, Iraqis are blaming the Americans, and Saddam Hussein is reinforcing his position among his people." In this view, people killed "unintentionally" by the not-so-smart weapons gain significance only as pawns of the "enemy" in propaganda strategy. The same article declares, "When it comes to manipulating the minds of his countrymen, Saddam Hussein is a malevolent genius." As we saw in chapter 6, these same strategies provided the context for images of the dead in Central America. When Radio Venceremos reported the massacre at El Mozote, State Department official Elliott Abrams asserted it was little more than enemy propaganda. But in Central America, the

United States only supplied the weapons and advisors. As a culture we have become accustomed to such antihumanistic reporting, so often repeated over the years that it serves as a callused shorthand for victims, now of direct American military power. As citizens of a democracy, war is carried out in the name of the public, yet every aspect of the reporting of the victims denies empathy and responsibility for death. When the public is invited to deny and justify the human cost of war, it comes at an increasing psychic and spiritual cost.

Bombing One Bad Guy

Another way in which the rhetoric of war shrouds the consequences of death and destruction is the discourse of a singular, demonized enemy. The bombs dropped will somehow seek out only one man, Saddam. Recall the pre-invasion Fox News broadcast discussed in chapter 18 that began by bragging, it's a "mean Saddam-fighting machine." The fantasy that this instrument is bent on destroying an individual is easily exposed, particularly when coverage includes the aftermath of a bombing campaign. Those representations, however, appear only in the alternative media to small audiences.

Consider an interview done in February 2003 by independent filmmakers for the Deep Dish video network that distributes primarily to educational, community and public access venues. One program features a dignified Iraqi woman whose home in Baghdad is transformed into a folk-art gallery containing treasures from antiquity and other lost traditions, as well as the work of contemporary artists. Dressed in Western garb and speaking fluent English, she is an impressive individual, one impossible to present as Other. She possesses enormous cultural capital. Viewers are able to superimpose recognizable identities over hers, even their own. Along a public dimension, she could be someone's art teacher, a curator, even a diplomat. Along personal lines, she could be one's mother, aunt, even wife. It would be virtually impossible to present this woman's death as justified; her presentation resists codes of danger and maliciousness. As she speaks she reminds us that bombs are not "clever" (smart), that they fall everywhere. The constant bombing, day and night during the First Gulf War, destroyed art galleries, after which she offered her home as a shelter.

In another sequence taped in July 2003, after the invasion and bombing of Baghdad, we meet her again as she walks through the rubble of her once-beautiful home. No longer calm and reassuring, she appears pale and annoyed at the camera. "This is not bombing Saddam," she says, looking down and pushing crumbled concrete with her foot. "This is not one man. This is Iraq." She stands amid barren walls where once we saw the beautiful art displayed. There is no color, just the gray of concrete dust that covers the scene. Identities such as hers are not presented on American television, for the viewer would have to come to terms with understanding that Baghdad is full of people like her, like us. Television presents no one coded "like us" standing accusingly in judgment of the American destruction of his or her home.

100,000 DEAD

Les Roberts laid down flat on the bed of an SUV to sneak across the Lebanese border into Iraq. He had done this kind of work before, recording the human costs of war in Bosnia, The Congo and Rwanda. He would work with Richard Garfield, professor of nursing at Columbia University, who had documented the humanitarian crisis in Iraq since the mid 1990s. They were joined by Riyadh Lafta from Al-Mustansiriya University in Baghdad. Together the three trained investigators made door-to-door surveys of nearly 8,000 people in 30 homes in 33 randomly selected neighborhoods across Iraq. Using a statistical method with a significant sample size of 3 percent, they extrapolated civilian deaths in Iraq from the time of the invasion. When deaths were reported, in 63 of the 78 houses the deaths were confirmed with a death certificate.

Their work was dangerous, and two doctors conducting interviews were detained, but they completed the study for the Johns Hopkins Bloomberg School of Public Health unharmed, and the findings of pre- and post-invasion mortality in Iraq were published in *The Lancet* (October 29, 2004) just before the U.S. presidential election. The public health study of Iraq concluded that the death toll associated with the invasion and occupation of Iraq was about 100,000 civilians, and might have been higher. "Violence accounted for most of the excess deaths and air strikes from coalition forces accounted for most violent deaths." Helicopter gunships, rockets or other forms of aerial weaponry were responsible for 95 percent of the deaths, of which more than half were women or children.

The European news media took the report very seriously, and many newspapers published front-page articles. The American press greeted the report with unusual skepticism and published mostly short, dismissive news briefs. The *Los Angeles Times* and the *Chicago Tribune* ran short stories on inside pages of about four hundred words. On page 8, the *New York Times* compared the Johns Hopkins study to figures recorded by Iraq Body Count that totaled 17,000 at that time, noting that the report would be controversial. No follow-up stories about the controversy were published. Hostile commentators used words like "politicized" and "worthless." Neither the State Department nor the Department of Defense responded to the finding, though other studies done by Roberts using similar methods in The Congo for the International Rescue Committee received a great deal of official attention. Roberts told the academic journal *The Chronicle of Higher Education*, "Tony Blair and Colin Powell have quoted those results time and time again without any question as to the precision or validity" (Guterman, 2005).

The most damaging coverage came from the *Washington Post* in a story that included a comment from Marc E. Garlasco, an intelligence officer at the Pentagon until 2003, who was then a senior military analyst at Human Rights Watch. Without having read the report, Mr. Garlasco is quoted as saying, "These numbers seem to be inflated." He later explained to the *Chronicle* (Guterman, 2005) that he told the *Post* reporter he had not read the paper and could not comment, but "like any good journalist, he got me to." Garlasco said he had misunderstood the journalist's description and the paper's result, and his published comment was "really unfortunate."

The negative reception of such a significant public health report prompted an evaluation by *The Chronicle of Higher Education*. It found that the scientific community accepted the paper's methods and the significance of the results and in many cases was troubled by the media treatment. Bradley A. Woodruff, a medical epidemiologist at the U.S. Centers for Disease Control and Prevention, said the report made use of the "best possible methodology." Comparing the study to Iraq Body Count, Woodruff asserted, "[Roberts] has the most valid estimate." Offering an explanation for why a *Slate* writer characterized the study's statistical range of possible deaths (from 8,000 to 194,000) as not an estimate but a "dartboard," Woodruff said they misunderstood the science. "They thought, 'Well, it's just as likely to be 18,000 as 100,000.' That's not true at all. The further you get away from 100,000, the probability that the number is true gets much smaller."

The U.S. military maintains that it is not trying to kill civilians, but as Marc Garlasco points out, the consequences on the ground contradict Pentagon assurances. "They're using all these precision weapons, so one would expect that if you're striving to minimize casualties, you'd have very low casualties. In Iraq we've seen the exact opposite, so one has to wonder why." An effective way to prevent innocent people from being killed (besides not dropping bombs) would be to quantify their deaths and the causes, and use that information to minimize future casualties. Such monitoring could trace effective protection, but the Pentagon keeps no records. Indeed, the refusal to measure the war's effect on innocent people has led international organizations to question the legality and the nature of the war. Though Roberts's report was all but ignored in 2004, it will remain a valid historical accounting of the human cost of the war on Iraq. As Dr. Meddings of the World Health Organization notes, accurate information "shifts the burden of proof onto militaries to substantiate why what they're doing is worth this humanitarian cost" (cited in Guterman, 2005). In the face of 100,000 deaths, articulating a moral high ground of lofty principles such as democracy begins to call those principles into question, as it persuades fewer and fewer people.

OCCUPATION, INSURGENCY AND THE SPIRAL OF VIOLENCE

In rare moments of transparency, when journalists provide analysis and documentation that clarify what has been clouded in an authentic and candid manner, it finds its way to the public. Such was the case when Farnaz Fassihi, a correspondent for the *Wall Street Journal* in Baghdad, sent an email to about forty friends at the end of September 2004. Instead of shaping a story according to the constraints of news reporting, she told the truth about what she saw, the conditions under which she worked and how she felt. Bypassing the qualified, muted language required by editors, her words spread like wildfire over the Internet. Her experience in Baghdad was like "being under virtual house arrest." It was too dangerous for her to walk in the street or go grocery shopping, much less look for news or be curious about what people were saying, doing or feeling. Fassihi could only travel by heavy armored vehicle and could not "go to scenes of breaking news." But her most critical words were reserved for the bigger picture of how the insurgency had spread to every part of Iraq, saying, "despite President Bush's rosy assessments, Iraq remains a disaster. If under Saddam it was a 'potential' threat, under the Americans it has been transformed to 'imminent and active threat,' a foreign policy failure bound to haunt the United States for decades to come.... The genie of terrorism, chaos and mayhem has been unleashed onto this country as a result of American mistakes and it can't be put back into the bottle" (Massing, 2004a).

Her words echoed an article, published in the *New York Review of Books* (August 28, 2003) only six months after the invasion, when even then it was clear that Iraq was spiraling into chaos. After a trip there, Mark Danner wrote: "It may be that the United States, with its overwhelming military power, has succeeded only in transforming an eventual and speculative threat into a concrete and immediate one." As the Downing Street memos would later confirm, the Bush administration had no plans for post-invasion Iraq. They did protect the oil fields, but the antiquities that carried the heart of five thousand years of history were allowed to be looted and destroyed.

Unprepared for a growing and deadly insurgency, with far too few soldiers to defend themselves, much less provide security and stability to the country, Americans came under increasing attack.[2] In a follow-up article in the *Review* (May 12, 2004), Danner quotes an Iraqi who says, "The attacks on the soldiers have made the army close down. You go outside and there's a guy on a Humvee pointing a machine gun at you. You learn to raise your hands, to turn around. You come to hate the Americans." Iraqis lived under an occupation that grew increasingly more brutal. Indeed this is the inevitable progress of counterinsurgency warfare. Fighting against overwhelming military power, insurgents rely on ambush and suicide bombs in unexpected places and in city neighborhoods, and Americans respond by wounding and killing civilians. Danner noted that the consequences of the increasing violence kept "overworked American troops under constant fear and stress so they will mistreat Iraqis on a broad scale and succeed in making themselves hated." The continued fighting in urban areas succeeds in turning the population against the Americans and recruiting more insurgents.

The brutal tactics of occupation did succeed in nurturing hatred toward coalition forces. Consider the effects of constant home invasions detailed by the International Committee of the Red Cross, practices later confirmed by U.S. Army investigations:

> Arresting authorities entered houses usually after dark, breaking down doors, waking up residents roughly, yelling orders, forcing family members into one room under military guard while searching the rest of the house and further breaking down doors, cabinets and other property. They arrested suspects tying their hands behind their backs with flexi-cuffs, hooding them, and taking them away. Sometimes they arrested all adult males present in the house, including elderly, handicapped and sick people...pushing people around, insulting, taking aim with rifles, punching and kicking and striking with rifles.

Throughout the autumn of 2003, increasingly desperate to find "actionable intelligence" that would prevent rebel attacks, Americans conducted many such night raids, carting away hooded prisoners who ended up in places like Abu Ghraib. Those digital pictures seen around the world were of only some of the eight thousand Iraqis imprisoned there under stinking, vile conditions. At that time the ICRC quoted anonymous military intelligence officers, estimating that between "70 and 90 percent of the persons deprived of their liberty in Iraq had been arrested by mistake" (Danner 2004, 3). Consider one of the hooded men pictured at Abu

Ghraib. He stands naked, hands above his head. With a malicious grin and a cigarette hanging from her mouth, Lynndie England points to his genitals and gestures a thumbs-up. This is prisoner number 13077, a thirty-four-year-old Shiite from Nasiriya named Hayder Sabbar Abd, who had served eighteen years in the Iraqi army. He was picked up at a checkpoint because he tried to leave the taxi he was riding in. From there his odyssey through different prisons began and ended at Abu Ghraib. He was never interrogated or charged with a crime. He described his sexual abuse to Ian Fisher of the *New York Times*, which included being beaten so badly that his broken jaw still troubles him. Speaking of himself and the six other prisoners at the "hard site" the night the pictures were taken, he says, "The truth is we were never terrorists. We were not insurgents. We were just ordinary people."

THE DESTRUCTION OF FALLUJAH

The study done by Roberts and his colleagues on civilian casualties did not include casualty rates for the city of Fallujah, because averaging in the higher numbers would have skewed the total upward. After four U.S. contractors had been killed in Fallujah and their bodies mutilated, U.S. troops had attempted to "pacify" the mostly Sunni inhabitants of Iraq's third largest city in April 2004, but failed to hold it. Only days after Bush won reelection, he escalated the war and sent the military back into Fallujah. Arguing that it was necessary to root out the "insurgency" in order to hold fair elections in January 2005, the military laid siege to the city for the second time in November 2004. Before the attack they warned civilians to leave, and about fifty thousand families, or two hundred and fifty thousand people, fled to camps or houses of relatives around the country. About fifty thousand residents remained in the city, which was estimated by the military to hold from five hundred to two thousand insurgents. Men between the ages of fifteen and forty-five were denied safe passage out. Many civilians were killed in what the international media would call a massacre. Casualties were compounded when U.S. forces seized the main hospital and denied the wounded access to medical care. Writing in the *New York Times*, Richard Oppel (2004) said the hospital was shut down because it was "considered a refuge for insurgents and a center of propaganda against allied forces." Oppel fails to explain that the "propaganda" referred to by the military was documentation done by doctors of the dead and wounded they treated during the first battle in April. Photographs of dead and wounded civilians were disseminated worldwide but were little seen by Americans.

Civilian Deaths as Propaganda in Fallujah: April 2004

During the April offensive, Dr. Abdul Jabbar, an orthopedic surgeon, struggled to treat the wounded as the first bombs fell. U.S. troops had sealed off the main hospital, and doctors were forced to provide emergency medical treatment from small clinics around the city. He describes horrific conditions and shortages of supplies and medications only periodically alleviated when the Red Crescent and other NGOs managed to make deliveries during the siege. Dr. Jabbar gave estimates to international organizations of at least seven hundred people killed in Fallujah. He told reporter Jamail (2004a), "I worked at 5 of the [clinics] myself, and if we collect the numbers from these places, then this is the number. And you must keep in mind that many people were buried before reaching our centers." Explaining the high number of civilian deaths, Dr. Jabbar said, "many people were injured and killed by cluster bombs, and we treated them at the clinics." Another surgeon, Dr. Rashid, confirmed, "I saw the cluster bombs with my own eyes. Most of these bombs fell on the families. The fighters—they know how to escape, but not the civilians." He estimated that "not less than 60 percent of the dead were women and children." A photo gallery of the destruction of Fallujah can still be accessed online.[3] A young child, clothed in rags and covered in blood and dirt, lies crying on a clinic bed, her dark hair matted around her face. Other pictures show men holding "flechettes" used by the U.S. military, the body of an elderly man, and another old man who lies on a hospital cot without a leg. Another picture shows a little boy on a cot without a leg. The pictures are indeed persuasive documents, attesting to the inhumanity of bombing. It is no doubt easier to claim that they are propaganda, and many will accept such an offering rather then believe such devastation occurred in their name. But they do little more than bear witness to the human cost of weapons so routinely celebrated. When received by the American public, so accustomed as it is to only the accolades of precision bombing, the pictures might better be called counterpropaganda.

Documentation by the doctors in Fallujah and the international response put the Pentagon on the defensive, and in November 2004, Operation Phantom Fury began by targeting Fallujah's main hospital. The second siege would be far more brutal than the first, with resulting civilian casualties ten times as great. Though the mainstream media would not bring the destruction to the attention of the American public, the alternative and international media documented the devastation, which continues to be widely disseminated on the Internet and to the global public.

November 2004

Though non-embedded reporters were barred from the city, some journalists were in Fallujah, and many stayed on the outskirts of the city to interview survivors who fled. Accounts from refugees, aid workers and independent reporters have described some of what happened. American Friends Service Committee representatives Mary Trotochaud and Rick McDowell published a detailed account of the attack for the journal *Peacework* in January 2005. In the months that followed, a number of documentaries were also made.[4] This body of work bears little resemblance to the coverage by journalists embedded with U.S. forces, which rarely mentioned that civilians were in the city. In the aftermath of the fighting, preliminary estimates of civilian casualties were as high as six thousand people, yet reports from embedded reporters included only the numbers of dead American and Iraqi soldiers, and "insurgents."

Even though the U.S. military estimated at most two thousand insurgents in the city, they treated the remaining fifty thousand inhabitants as enemy combatants. Speaking on the documentary *Fallujah: The Hidden Massacre*,[5] American soldier Jeff Englehart, who escorted a commander into Fallujah for Operation Phantom Fury, said "we were told going into Fallujah, into the combat area, that every single person that was walking, talking, breathing was an enemy combatant."

A doctor who was inside the city as the attack began recounted the instructions from U.S. and Iraqi forces as they entered the Fallujah General Hospital: anyone who disclosed information about the raid would be arrested. They stopped medical procedures in progress and handcuffed the doctors (Jamail, 2004b). Daily aerial bombardment and the use of cluster bombs cut off water and electricity "and people quickly ran out of food as they were trapped in their homes by sniper fire" (Trotochaud and McDowell, 2005). Jamail's interviews with journalists and residents who fled Fallujah give accounts of U.S. troops killing unarmed and wounded people. Burhan Fasa'a, an Iraqi journalist who works for the popular Lebanese satellite television station LBC, was there for nine days during the most intense combat. During that time, none of the wounded, "women, kids and old people" were treated or evacuated. He reported that unarmed residents in homes were also killed:

"They entered the house where I was with 26 people, and [they] shot people because [the people] didn't obey [the soldiers'] orders, even just because the people couldn't understand a word of English" (Jamail, 2004b).

Many refugees say they witnessed American armored vehicles crushing people still alive, throwing Iraqi bodies into the Euphrates and shooting unarmed Iraqis who waved white flags. An Associated Press photographer,

Bilal Hussein, witnessed similar events. After running out of basic necessities, he ran to the Euphrates to escape.

"I decided to swim," Hussein told colleagues at the AP, who wrote up the photographer's harrowing story, "but I changed my mind after seeing U.S. helicopters firing on and killing people who tried to cross the river." Hussein said he saw soldiers kill a family of five as they tried to traverse the Euphrates, before he buried a man by the riverbank with his bare hands (Jamail, 2004b).[6]

When U.S. soldier Jeff Englehart is asked by an Italian reporter what he will tell his child about the battle of Fallujah, he responds by saying, "It seemed like just a massive killing of Arabs. It looked like just a massive killing."[7]

White Phosphorous Bombs

Englehart watched most of the firefight in Fallujah sitting atop a Humvee parked on the outskirts of the city. He said he heard U.S. forces call over the radio for white phosphorus bombs. They'd say, "In five, we're going to drop some Whiskey Pete. Roger. Commence bombing... Whiskey Pete, that's the military slang."[8] Doctors reported seeing patients whose skin was melted from exposure to phosphorous bombs.[9] Documentary images show graphic photos of burned bodies, faces melted away, with clothing that is still largely intact. Englehart explains how this can happen with white phosphorous, "when it makes contact with skin, then it's absolutely irreversible damage, burning of flesh to the bone. It doesn't necessarily burn clothes, but it will burn the skin underneath clothes." [10]

On November 28, 2004, in an interview with investigative reporter and news anchor, Amy Goodman, on the program *Democracy Now!* Dahr Jamail noted:

> I have interviewed many refugees over the last week coming out of Fallujah, different times from different locations within the city. The consistent stories that I've been getting have been refugees describing phosphorus weapons, horribly burned bodies, fires that burn on people when they touch these weapons. And they're unable to extinguish the fires even after dumping large amounts of water on the people. Many people are reporting cluster bombs, as well. And these are coming from different camps [and] different people.

By December 23, the International Committee for the Red Cross reported that three of Fallujah's water purification plants had been destroyed and the fourth badly damaged. The humanitarian relief crisis caused by destroying the infrastructure of a city of three hundred thousand residents was all but ignored in the American press. As temperatures dropped, two hundred thousand people were living as refugees, with shortages of food and cooking fuel (Trotochaud and McDowell, 2005).

THE MARLBORO MAN

It is instructive to compare these eyewitness accounts to U.S. mainstream media coverage of the siege. The image that became the icon of the assault on Fallujah was featured on the front page of the *New York Post*. The huge, bold headline, "SMOKIN'," and below, "Marlboro men kick butt in Fallujah," frames the close-up shot of a soldier, his face covered in dirt, as a cigarette hangs carelessly out of the side of his mouth. The classic shot of the helmeted fighter bears a striking resemblance, noted by many commentators, to depictions reminiscent of World War II. In the text, filed from Washington but sounding as if he experienced the Good Fight himself, Niles Latham heralds high-tech weapons and the heat of battle. "The thugs were quickly overwhelmed by superior American firepower as unmanned aircraft tracked the movements of the rebel bands." Citing U.S. commanders and embedded reporters, he describes "intense" fighting with "small bands of terrorists. The enemy quickly was killed or fled when they encountered U.S. firepower." He lauds the "massive intelligence-gathering operation over the terrorist-held city," using dozens of "unmanned Global Hawk and Predator drone aircraft" that took "instant video images." They also "intercepted terrorist communications" using "sophisticated electronic eavesdropping equipment" that allowed the military to "call in precision airstrikes that killed hundreds of insurgents." No mention is made of civilians, nor are phosphorous or cluster bombs discussed. Troops killed thousands and flattened seventy percent of the city, but the details of battle provided by Latham are filled with the familiar assurances that only very high-tech weapons can provide. Journalists never mention the effects of phosphorus bombs or anti-personnel devices used in civilian areas, or question the military's use of such devices.

The papers of record wrote in different, yet equally antihumanitarian, genres. Theirs was not the thrill of precision but reasoned arguments about the consequences for U.S. interests. The *New York Times* noted that the attack was "not a textbook way to conduct a counterinsurgency campaign" and warned that the city's decimation could be a "very costly victory." Such writing implicitly acknowledges that civilians are being brutalized, but the killing raised for the *Times* no humane, moral or legal questions. The *Washington Post* lauded the military effort with these words: "The prospective restoration of government rule and the elimination of an open haven for terrorists is a significant step forward." The *Los Angeles Times* editorial assured readers that the marines opted for a bad solution instead of a worse one, "assaulting the city with the understanding that civilians as well as fighters would be killed...the worse option was to do nothing."

Operation Phantom Fury left in its wake of bloody trial of evidence that has been recorded and documented worldwide. Yet each new release of information and documentation is met with silence from the U.S. media. When the *Denver Post* did report the release of the Italian Documentary, *Fallujah: The Hidden Massacre*, it was largely to refute the testimony of the soldier Jeff Englehart, a resident of Colorado (Emery, 2005). Two different military officials are quoted at length assuring readers that civilians were not targeted, and that white phosphorous was not used on civilians.

By the first invasion of Fallujah in April 2004, the refusal of the U.S. press to report and investigate civilian deaths in Iraq had turned to open hostility toward news outlets that were reporting casualties. One CNN host, Daryn Kagan, criticized the Al Jazeera network's editor-in-chief, Ahmed Al-Sheik for airing images of civilian deaths in Fallujah. After Al-Sheik defended the broadcasts as "accurate" and representative of what was taking place on the ground, Kagan pressed on in a convoluted justification for killing civilians:

> Isn't the story, though, bigger than just the simple numbers, with all due respect to the Iraqi civilians who have lost their lives—the story bigger than just the numbers of people who were killed or the fact that they might have been killed by the U.S. military, that the insurgents, the people trying to cause problems within Fallujah, are mixing in among the civilians, making it actually possible that even more civilians would be killed, that the story is what the Iraqi insurgents are doing, in addition to what is the response from the U.S. military? (Hollar, 2004)

With such an openly demonstrated acceptance of innocent death on the part of the U.S. media, it is no wonder that Operation Phantom Fury could be carried out in November with the assurance that there would be no public protest. The American public would not see the pictures of horribly charred bodied burned to the bone underneath the civilian cloths that remained intact.

U.S. FEDERAL LAW AND THE GENEVA CONVENTIONS

The moral outrage expressed over press coverage of the siege of Fallujah consisted of the charge that the *New York Post* photograph of the soldier, because he was smoking, presented a negative role model to children. As the country debated this moral outrage, the international community received news of Fallujah with open concern. The U.N. High Commission for Human Rights' Louise Arbour called for an investigation into charges that Americans and their allies had engaged in "the deliberate targeting of civilians, indiscriminate and disproportionate attacks, the killing of injured persons, and the use of human shields" (Trotochaud and McDowell, 2005). Such conduct violates the Geneva Conventions against crimes of war that target noncombatants, and they violate United States federal law. The U.S. signed the war crimes act in 1996, making crimes against civilians illegal under United States statutes. Marjorie Cohn (2004), a professor at Thomas Jefferson School of Law and the U.S. representative to the executive committee of the American Association of Jurists, called the U.S. invasion of Fallujah a violation of international law that the U.S. had specifically ratified: storming and occupying the Fallujah General Hospital is a direct violation of the Geneva Conventions.[11]

Transforming the Imagery of War

The *New York Times* published a series of iconic photographs of war. Down the page the disquieting images register each war, their cumulative signature an indelible mark on the human psyche. At the bottom, from the war in Iraq, stands George W. Bush cradling a huge turkey, in a symbolic gesture that hides the visual register of the death and horror of Iraq, of all the civilians, the fighters on all sides and those locked naked and hooded in places across Iraq and the world.

Something must replace the empty void where the icons of war's human costs reside. On Thanksgiving Day 2003, the White House supplied a substitute image. Air Force One left Washington, DC, on a secret trip that would carry a small group of aides with the president to the Baghdad Airport for a two-and-a-half-hour visit and photo-op with six hundred U.S. troops lucky enough to be stationed in the Green Zone. November 2003 had been the bloodiest month for occupation forces, with seventy-eight Americans and thirty other coalition soldiers killed. But there were no images of flag-draped coffins returning home, no sound of taps playing as soldiers in formal dress carried the remains of their brothers across the tarmac, and the new war president was not there to greet them.

The widely published image from this trip shows a beaming president wearing an Army flight jacket, cradling a bountiful golden-brown turkey generously garnished with grapes and all the trimmings. He appears to be serving dinner to the grateful soldiers who surround him. A moment of high patriotism, the picture was ubiquitous in the days that followed, and the president's poll numbers shot up five points as criticism for his seeming indifference to the suffering of American troops was quieted, at least for a time.

It would take a week for the *Washington Post* to report that the president was not actually serving the soldiers, who were eating pre-sliced turkey from canteen-style hot plates. It was six o'clock in the morning, and the turkey Bush held was inedible. White House spinners rebuked those who called the turkey fake, insisting it was not a presidential prop, but a standard decoration supplied by contractors for the chow hall. In a burst of spontaneous enthusiasm, the president had raised the platter and the shutter clicked. If we suspend disbelief for the claims that the moment was not entirely choreographed beforehand (as was claimed when the White House insisted it had not hung the "Mission Accomplished" banner that perfectly framed the president on the U.S.S. *Lincoln*), we must then assume that, like Oliver North, the president is a master at self-coding. His ability to stand in at Norman Rockwell moments comes naturally, just as he can mimic the scripts of so many Westerns where the man with the badge says, "Wanted: Dead or Alive."

Is this the face of the banality of evil, or is it the banality of a militarized culture that succeeds by placing war in the warmth and security of the American domestic hearth, recognizable and accepted as part of the landscape of America, a mythic fantasy all are asked to believe? To the company that produced a limited-edition Turkey Dinner Action Figure for $34.95, it does not matter that some viewed the secret trip as a "cowardly act." It has become "a piece of our nation's history."

Persons Under Control

But what was actually happening in Iraq in November 2003 could not have been further from American mythic narratives. Almost two years later, the *New York Times* (September 24, 2005) would report the stories of three former members of the army's 82nd Airborne Division who told Human Rights Watch how soldiers in their battalion routinely beat and abused Iraqi prisoners at Camp Mercury, a forward operating base near Fallujah. A Captain Fishback and two sergeants described systematic death threats, beatings, broken bones, murder, exposure to extremes of hot and cold, forced physical exertion, stripping, stacking in human pyramids, sleep deprivation and degrading treatment taking place between September 2003 and April 2004.

Much of the abuse of "persons under control" [PUCs] had nothing to do with intelligence: "Some days we would just get bored, so we would have everyone sit in a corner and then make them get in a pyramid. This was before Abu Ghraib but just like it. We did it for amusement."[12] One sergeant told Human Rights Watch that he had seen a soldier break open a chemical light and use it to beat detainees. "That made them glow in the dark, which was real funny, but it burned their eyes, and their skin was irritated real bad." These stories had been ignored for months by the time they were released.

> Captain Fishback, who has served combat tours in Afghanistan and Iraq, gave Human Rights Watch and Senate aides his long account only after his efforts to report the abuses to his superiors were rebuffed or ignored over 17 months, according to Senate aides and John Sifton, one of the Human Rights Watch researchers who conducted the interviews. Moreover, Captain Fishback has expressed frustration at his civilian and military leaders for not providing clear guidelines for the proper treatment of prisoners. (*New York Times*, September 24, 2005)

THE SOLDIERS' STORIES

The ones who stop believing the stagecraft are the ones who see for themselves and the ones who do the fighting, killing and dying. Neither video games nor boot camp can prepare them for what they find "in country." Hidden from the camera's eye, brought in under cover of night, wounded Iraqi veterans struggle to make sense and meaning out of the war and their role in it. As we saw in chapter 17, news stories featured soldiers as mythic warriors before the war, but when they returned television showed little interest in their postwar narratives. These are not the mythic tales of World War II fantasies. Instead, veterans tell of their battles with post-traumatic stress; of nightmares, anxiety, paranoia and a sense of exhaustive guilt. Jeff Lucey was a 23-year-old Marine Lance Corporal who came home after serving a 12-month tour of duty in Iraq. He lost his battle with war's demons and hung himself with a garden hose from the rafters of his parents' cellar.[13] Jeff Lucey is featured with other Iraq combat veterans in the 2004 documentary *The Ground Truth: The Human Cost of War*, by independent filmmaker Patricia Foulkrod. The short documentary is a collection of interviews with men and women who recount their experiences in Iraq and Afghanistan without interruption or prompting. Like the World War I soldiers who discovered the gap between war persuasions and the realities of the battlefield, these veterans speak of the gap between media representations and what they know to be true. One marine sergeant, Rob Sarra, is haunted by the memory of shooting an elderly burkha-clad woman he thought was a suicide bomber. He had not seen the white flag she carried. When Rob Sarra sought help for the psychological trauma, he was ostracized at Camp Pendleton. Another marine cannot dislodge the sight of a soldier driving over an Iraqi child who had walked into the roadway. Soldiers are under orders to take such actions to protect their own lives against roadside bombers.

The brutal realities of war have led to decades of global negotiations, treaties, agreements and laws that seek to restrict war, by international consensus, to retaliation and self-defense. Understanding that there is no greater violation of human rights than war, signatories to the United Nations Charter have agreed that aggressive war, carried out without provocation is against international law. In signing the United Nations Charter, the United States agreed not to violate the sovereign territory of other nations. Invading another nation without cause would be a violation of international law. The Bush administration would base the legality of its invasion of Iraq in 2003 on the claim that Saddam Hussein had weapons of mass destruction and that they endangered the United States. Those claims would turn out to be false. Further, in 2005 a report by the Carnegie Endowment for International Peace concluded that the Bush White House "systematically misrepresented" the threat posed by Iraq (Mooney 2005, 30). The *Columbia Journalism Review* (Mooney, 2005) examined the nation's leading newspapers and concluded that they were far too accepting of the dubious claims of WMDs and failed to hold the Bush administration to an "adequate standard of proof." Especially when it came to launching "not a just war, but a preemptive war opposed by most of the world" (30). In the following chapter we will examine some key moments of the failure of the press to adequately report on the Bush administration's dubious claims about WMDs.

20

The "Entertainer-in-Chief" and the Downing Street Memos

A year after the invasion of Iraq, with five hundred Americans dead and no Weapons of Mass Destruction discovered, the front page of the "Style" section of the *Washington Post* referred to George W. Bush as the "Entertainer-in-Chief." The date was March 24, 2004, and the president was the invited speaker at the annual black-tie dinner of the Radio and Television Correspondents Association. In front of fifteen hundred journalists, President Bush showed a series of slides of himself looking under papers, behind drapes and out the window of the Oval Office. A smiling Bush narrated, "Those weapons of mass destruction have got to be somewhere," followed by, "Nope, no weapons over there," and "Maybe under here?" The transcript shows that this stand-up routine was greeted with "laughter and applause." News coverage of the event was equally jovial and expressed no outrage at the performance. As Greg Mitchell *of Editor and Publisher* (June 21, 2005) observed, "It is hard to find any immediate account of the affair that raised questions over the president's slide show." Mitchell called Bush's performance and its reception "one of the most shameful episodes in the recent history of the American media, and presidency, yet [it] is rarely mentioned today." Shortly after the president entertained the national press, in April 2004, Sherwood Baker would be killed in Baghdad while providing security for the group looking for WMDs. It was a flagrant waste of human life and resources at a time when U.S.

troops were flailing in the midst of an impossible and increasingly brutal occupation. By then, of course, as David Key had reported months before, no WMDs existed.

Laughing with the president seems to indicate knowledge of a shared amusement, a mutual understanding that the threat of Weapons of Mass Destruction was always mythic, little more than a contrived persuasion from of a focus-group enquiry. (Indeed, this very fear was exploited as a last resort in order to transform Desert Shield into Desert Storm.) This jovial applause may help explain one of the most curious media failures regarding coverage of the war in Iraq, about a secret meeting finally brought to the light of day, but not by the American media.

THE DOWNING STREET MEMO

On May 1, 2005, the *London Sunday Times* printed secret, leaked minutes from a meeting Prime Minister Tony Blair held with close advisors on July 23, 2002. Blair and his cabinet discussed the Bush administration's plans for war in Iraq and the political and military contingencies for British support for an invasion. Richard Dearlove, head of M16, the British Intelligence service, reported to the group what he learned during a visit to Washington: "Military action was now seen as inevitable. Bush wanted to remove Saddam, through military action, justified by the conjunction of terrorism and WMDs. But the intelligence and facts were being fixed around the policy."

British coverage of the document was thorough. In addition to analysis, the *Times* also published the meeting minutes in full. Press reports rocked Blair's reelection campaign. The document was seen as clear evidence that the decision to go to war had been made fully eight months before the invasion, and that making the case for war came later as the "facts were being fixed." The United States had shaped intelligence to support the drive to war, and Blair had gone along with it. Elections in Britain took place a week after the *Times* published the memo. While Tony Blair won reelection, largely understood as a consequence of the country's strong economy, his majority in Parliament fell from 161 to 67.

In the United States, press coverage of the Downing Street Memo was hard to find. Some reports mentioned it as a tie-in to British election coverage, but no front-page headlines or exposés appeared in the papers of record or on network television. On May 6, CNN's Jackie Schechner observed that the document was a hot topic on the blogosphere but wondered why it didn't get more coverage in the U.S. media. By May 8, *Washington Post* ombudsman Michael Getler noted that readers had complained about the lack of coverage, though no explanation for the omission was offered. Noting the missing media reports, Joe Conason of *Salon* referred to "fresh and damning evidence of lies" and a media "simply too timid" to report.[1] By May 10, FAIR issued a media advisory entitled "Smoking Gun Memo? Iraq Bombshell Goes Mostly Unreported in the U.S. Media." They lauded Knight Ridder wire service reporting that provided the only widely circulated story in the mainstream press. The story quoted an anonymous U.S. official who said that the memo contained "an absolutely accurate description of what transpired" during Dearlove's meeting in Washington.

Serious analysis of the memo, its meaning and importance did not come from any mainstream news organization in the United States. It came instead from Mark Danner on May 16, in a piece entitled, "The Secret Way to War" for the *New York Review of Books*, which also published the original memo in its entirety for the first time in the United States. Danner begins by taking readers back to October 16, 2002, just after the 107th Congress voted to authorize the president to go to war with Iraq. President Bush is addressing the American people from the East Room of the White House "in a somber mood befitting a leader speaking frankly to free citizens about the gravest decision their country could make." Bush declares, "Though Congress has now authorized the use of force, I have not ordered the use of force. I hope the use of force will not become necessary." Bush claimed that Iraq had the power to prevent war by "declaring and destroying all its weapons of mass destruction." But if those weapons were not destroyed, the United States would "go into battle, as a last resort." Bush's speech, widely viewed by Americans, was easily compared to the contents of the memo, illustrating that even by October 2002, the president claimed war was a last resort, when invading Iraq had actually been a priority for months.

Danner's feature offers the most widely circulated post-invasion discussion of exactly how the United Nations was cynically used by Bush and Blair. The secret minutes reveal the calculated strategy behind building a "political context" through a "U.N. route." Danner tracks the behind-the-scenes maneuverings essential for understanding the process by which the war was sold. The British were inclined to go to war with Bush, but as signatories to international law, the war was illegal. "The Attorney-General said that the desire for regime change was not a legal base for military action." Of three possible justifications, two were dismissed. Self-defense was not plausible, as British Foreign Secretary Jack Straw argued. "The case was thin. Saddam was not threatening his neighbors, and his WMD capacity was less than that of Libya, North Korea or Iran." Nor would humanitarian intervention make the case: Saddam was not engaged in genocide. The Foreign Secretary solved the puzzle when he said, "We should work up a plan for an ultimatum to Saddam to allow back in the U.N. weapons inspectors. This would also help with the legal justification for the use of force." At this point Blair agreed that such an ultimatum could be politically critical, but only if "Saddam refused to allow in the U.N. inspectors." As Danner points out, "Thus, the idea of U.N. inspectors was introduced not as a means to avoid war, as president Bush repeatedly assured Americans, but as a means to make war possible."[2]

But Saddam did let the weapons inspectors in, and though the United States insisted it knew that Saddam had such weapons, and even where they were hidden, American officials were never compelled to say where. Yet even then, had the inspectors been able to finish their job and complete the search, there would have been no war, at least not one justified by WMDs. Demonstrating the propaganda efficacy and power of the United States, the inability to find WMDs before the war confirmed not that the threat was fabricated, but that Saddam was hiding weapons.

Much of the misinformation about WMDs that found its way into the U.S. press, especially the reporting of *New York Times* correspondent, Judith Miller, came from the Iraqi National Congress headed by Ahmad Chalabi, a group with close ties to neoconservative war planners, such as Douglas Feith. Feith set up the Office of Special Plans at the Pentagon in 2002. As Maureen Dowd (*New York Times*, March 31, 2005) put it, the office functioned as a "shadow intelligence agency to manufacture propaganda bolstering the administration's case." This parallel intelligence agency overrode much of the more professional information produced at the CIA, and served as the Iraq war equivalent to the Office of Public Diplomacy detailed in chapter 7.

The Joint Press Conference
Though initially ignored in the United States, the Downing Street Memo would not be forgotten. On June 8, 2005, Dan Froomkin wrote in the *Washington Post*, "After six weeks in the political wilderness, the Downing Street Memo yesterday finally burst into the White House—and into the headlines."[3] The document that wouldn't go away confronted Bush and Blair when they gave a joint press conference at the White House on June 7. A reporter asked, "On Iraq, the so-called Downing Street memo from July 2002 says intelligence and facts were being fixed around the policy of removing Saddam through military action. Is it an accurate reflection of what happened? Could both of you respond?" Bush was visibly angered and gave a confused and rambling response. "And somebody said, well, you know, we had made up our mind to go to use military force to deal

with Saddam. There's nothing farther from the truth." He insisted that facts had not been manipulated, rehashing the now-dated message that the war was a last option. He cut the press conference short.

At this point another opportunity presented itself for thorough coverage of the British documents, yet the American media missed another chance to expose the falsities that led to war and to correct the historical record. The delayed coverage of the memo that finally "burst into the White House" reveals the current complexities of media failures. With the Iraq invasion, we see the reinvention of a war's history even before it has ended.

The Memo Was "Not News"

The media, particularly the papers of record, now on the defensive for a lack of coverage, adopted a unified theme: the memos contained no news. A *Washington Post* (June 15, 2005) editorial asserted: "The memos add not a single fact to what was previously known about the administration's prewar deliberations. Not only that: They add nothing to what was publicly known in July 2002."[4] The *New York Times* (June 14, 2005) claimed the documents were "not shocking," asserting that "Three years ago, the near unanimous conventional wisdom in Washington held that Mr. Bush was determined to topple Saddam Hussein by any means necessary." NBC's Andrea Mitchell agreed that you would have to be "brain dead not to know" what the White House was doing then. Yet this knowledge and understanding did not inform reporting. For example, Mitchell presented the president's prewar remarks as truthful articulations of his intentions, that Bush's dealings with the U.N. were part of "the diplomatic campaign to avoid war" (March 16, 2003). If the media knew the "U.N. route" amounted to nothing more than a public relations campaign to sell the war, then why, as FAIR posed the question, "were reporters not exposing this bad faith at every turn?"[5] And even after the post-Downing Street joint press conference, when the president said that "Nobody wants to commit military into combat. It's the last option," if this is known to be a manifest lie, why not identify it as such in news reports in 2005?

What becomes clear from this case is that journalists know and understand something quite different from what they actually report. For the most part, the known and the reported are two very different narratives. With a "nothing new" defense, reporters and editors are making astonishing admissions of complicity and redefining the role of journalism. Admitting to understanding *at the time* that justifications for war were a ruse, yet not challenging such claims, leaves them not only complicit, but compelling actors in promoting war. Without the dissemination of official pronouncements and speeches presented in legitimizing fashion, the public could not be convinced to commit their sons and daughters to the war. Parroting a president known to be inventing justifications for war does not fulfill the mandate of the First Amendment, the Fourth Estate, or even their own professional canons that emphasize the obligation to the public, not to the president or the executive branch.

In fact, there is a compelling body of evidence indicating that the news media did know quite well that claims of WMDs were unfounded. Investigations into alleged WMDs had already been carried out and greeted with critical skepticism by many independent reporters, academics, U.N. investigators and former government officials. That material was readily available in books and on the Internet, and presumably of interest to those trained in newsgathering. Further, news organizations actively omitted material and censored sources refuting the Bush administration's pretense for war. As noted earlier, MSNBC cancelled *Donahue* shortly before the invasion of Iraq. When an internal MSNBC memo was leaked to the TV industry website www.allyourtv.com on February 25, 2003, it offered dramatic evidence of the media's refusal to present alternative views. The memo explained that Donahue presented a "difficult public face for NBC in a time of war," because he "seems to delight in presenting guests who are antiwar, anti-Bush and skeptical of the Administration's motives." The network needed to censor the "anti-war agenda" because competitors were "waving the flag at every opportunity." The refusal to question the war was equally evident in reporting information obtained from Saddam Hussein's weapons chief and son-in-law Hussein Kamel.

Hussein Kamel's 1995 Revelations

Kamel defected from Iraq in 1995 and was debriefed by the CIA. He also talked at great length with U.N. weapons inspectors about Iraq's unconventional weapons programs. Kamel became a major source for the Bush administration's claims that Saddam had WMDs, even though he told officials that *all the weapons had been destroyed*. In 1995 he told *CNN*, "Iraq does not possess any weapons of mass destruction." He did admit that Saddam had concealed WMD-related activities, and that Iraq's chemical, biological and nuclear weapons programs had been more advanced than the Saddam Hussein regime had admitted to inspectors. But he also said they had been destroyed. The administration used Kamel's remarks selectively. In addition, on March 3, 2003 Newsweek published key statements from the transcript of Kamel's 1995 debriefing by officials from UNSCOM, the U.N. inspections team, and the International Atomic Energy Agency

(IAEA). *Newsweek* reported that Kamel told the same story to the CIA, "All weapons—biological, chemical, missile, nuclear—were destroyed." They also said his account had been "hushed up." Shortly thereafter, Cambridge University's Glen Rangwala made the complete transcript of Kamel's discussions with inspectors available on the Internet.

F.A.I.R.[6] noted shortly after the *Newsweek* report that this crucial information went largely unreported in the mainstream media. Unfortunately, *Newsweek* diminished the story's news value by placing it in the miscellaneous "Periscope" section with a generic headline, "The Defector's Secrets."[7] The *Chicago Tribune* (September 10, 2002), did publish an opinion piece by former head of the U.N. weapons inspection team Scott Ritter, who pointed out that speeches made by Bush officials, including Dick Cheney, omitted critical parts of Kamel's story: "Throughout his interview with UNSCOM, a U.N. special commission, Hussein Kamel reiterated his main point—that nothing was left. 'All chemical weapons were destroyed,' he said. 'I ordered destruction of all chemical weapons. All weapons—biological, chemical, missile, nuclear—were destroyed.'" Scott Ritter, as a former UNSCOM official, was one of the most knowledgeable sources on the topic and spoke widely on the issue refuting administration claims, yet he was largely ignored by the mainstream press. Before the invasion of Iraq, CNN taped an hour-long interview with Ritter in which he detailed Kamel's testimony. CNN declined to air the interview.[8]

THE BASEMENT HEARING

But the press would fail yet again, this time with a willful disregard for constitutional checks on the executive branch by the legislature. Reporting on congressional hearings on the memos called by Rep. John Conyers, Dana Milbank (*Washington Post*) reported that House Democrats "took a trip to the land of make-believe." He was mocking Conyers and his "hearty band of playmates" for attempting to make a basement conference room look like an official hearing room by adorning it with American flags and white table cloths. Objecting to Milbank's characterization, the congressman wrote that the meeting was there because "despite the fact that a number of other suitable rooms were available in the Capitol and White House office buildings, Republicans declined my request for each and every one of them." At a moment in American history when all branches of government are dominated by a single party, an attempt to assert some congressional influence over the declaration of war was mocked as "illegitimate ravings" by the *Washington Post*.[9] No other reporting on the hearing appeared in the pages of the *Post*.

One panelist at the hearing was former CIA analyst Ray McGovern, who evaluated the memos and detailed the trajectory of spurious claims of WMDs made by the president and his staff. McGovern also took the opportunity to remind journalists of the R&T Correspondents' dinner (the night the president became the "entertainer-in-chief") saying accusingly: "You all laughed with him folks. But I'll tell you who is not laughing. Cindy Sheehan is not laughing." The president and the media would soon discover Cindy Sheehan.

21

The Unraveling

The Ghost of Vietnam and the Soldiers "Over There"

On August 12, 2005, during an oppressive summer heat wave in New York City, and as the Bush administration refused to release additional pictures from Abu Ghraib even under a court order to do so, an independent distribution company theatrically released a film featuring U.S. soldiers admitting, and in many cases detailing, the horrible atrocities they had committed "in country." Though their narratives were sometimes halting, at other times the words poured out like poisons they needed to expel. That night at the Walter Reade Theater at the Lincoln Center Performing Arts complex, only steps away from the expressive heights of civilized culture, the soldiers in the film explained that in Vietnam, conduct such as the rape of young women, the indiscriminate killing of civilians (as long as the body count recorded a dead Vietcong) and the strafing of villagers from the air were all "SOP"—standard operating procedure. One sequence showed a still photograph bearing an uncanny resemblance to one from Abu Ghraib. A young American stands grinning over dead bodies at an interrogation site. The words he speaks over the image warn: "Don't ever let your government do this to you." The film was *Winter Soldier*, shot in Detroit between January 31 and February 2, 1971, during a gathering of over two hundred Vietnam veterans who needed to tell their stories and who were trying to stop the war they now considered brutal and immoral. Network television refused to air *Winter Soldier* then, and few Americans had ever seen the film that was now thirty-four years old, but a document more relevant that summer than the vast majority of television programming.

CINDY SHEEHAN

During that same summer of 2005, the heat in Crawford, Texas, could not stop Cindy Sheehan from camping out near the president's ranch and demanding to speak to him about the son she lost in Iraq. She said her question to the president would be a simple one. If he thought the war in Iraq was such a noble cause, would he consider sending his own daughters there?

As the president spent time clearing brush and riding bikes with Lance Armstrong, the politics of the personal began to play out in the press, directed now at a president who—like his father before—seemed detached and isolated from the rest of the country and the spiraling violence in Iraq. *New York Times* columnist Maureen Dowd referred to him as the "boy in the bubble," and later the cover of *Newsweek* illustrated her point showing the president trapped in a bubble. As Iraq continued to unravel, and the model democracy that neoconservatives had promised morphed instead into a government heavily influenced by Iran, public support for the war continued to slide. A mid-June Gallup Poll showed that those still confident in the president and his war had dropped to 40 percent, and 60 percent no longer believed the war was worth the cost. By the first week in August, *Newsweek* reported that Bush's approval rating for handling the war had slid even lower, to 34 percent, virtually the same as the 32 percent rating LBJ received for his handling of Vietnam after Tet. The two presidents' overall approval ratings were also equivalent: 41 percent for Johnson during Vietnam, 42 percent for Bush, the new war president. Recall that when LBJ's war had so little public support, he declined to run for reelection.

Bush was feeling the understandable resentment evoked for what had now clearly become a quagmire in Iraq. Essayist Thomas Lynch wrote eloquently in the op-ed pages of the *New York Times* (August 17, 2005) about the president's character flaws:

> And maybe this is the part I find most distancing about my president, not his fanatic heart—the unassailable sense he projects that God is on his side—we all have that. But that he seems to lack anything like real remorse, here in the third August of Iraq, in the fourth August of Afghanistan, in the fifth August of his presidency—for all of the intemperate speech, for the weapons of mass destruction that were not there, the "Mission Accomplished" that really wasn't, for the funerals he will not attend, the mothers of the dead he will not speak to, the bod-

ies of the dead we are not allowed to see and all of the soldiers and civilians whose
lives have been irretrievably lost or irreparably changed by his (and our) "Bring it
On" bravado in a world made more perilous by such pronouncements.

Indeed, columnist Bob Herbert (*New York Times*, June 30, 2005) had already noted the president's "intemperate speech" and the goad, "bring 'em
on," uttered shortly after Bush landed the fighter jet onto the U.S.S. *Lincoln*. After the completion of "major combat operations," about two hundred American troops had died, and the president remained in the potent
grip of a victory narrative. Yet even then—July 2, 2003—as the growing
insurgency was evident, and military planners began to realize that troop
strength was woefully inadequate, Mr. Bush told White House reporters,
"There are some who feel that the conditions are such that they can attack
us there. My answer is, Bring 'em on." Two years later, as the number of
military coffins (blocked from public view) approached two thousand (with
many thousands wounded and disfigured), Herbert called the *bring 'em
on* phrase "an immature display of street-corner machismo that appalled
people familiar with the agonizing ordeals of combat." *Bring 'em on* is a
stance and bravado that invites attack by hordes of inferior enemies who
dare challenge the superior power of the victor. It is the stuff of movie dialogue, a fantasy boast suitable only for fictional narratives of war.

THE UNREALITY SHOW

But George W. Bush is a president of his media age. Like Oliver North's in
the summer of 1987, his self-coding fit the entertainment genres by which
his culture defines and admires the champion. Either as a tie-in product
for an action hero, an immature street tough or, as David Corn of *The
Nation* noted, a "comic book" figure, all are recognizable, and all display
acceptable, even positive cultural attributes that can be substituted for real
courage and integrity in an age when media culture places little value on
such qualities. By the fifth August of the Bush presidency, America had begun to confront the limits of this culture, of the various forms of militainment and counter-branding, of silencing dissent and attacking critics, and
all the other staged events and information strategies that made the war
possible. The reality of death and destruction was beginning to overtake
the fantasy world of high-tech weaponry, cyber soldiers and video-game
conquests in virtual worlds where no one ever really dies. The ultimate
admission of this fact came on August 14, when the *Washington Post* quoted
a "senior official" involved in policy since the 2003 invasion as saying, "We
are in a process of absorbing the factors of the situation we're in and shed-

ding the unreality that dominated at the beginning." He said further that "What we expected to achieve was never realistic given the timetable or what unfolded on the ground." This quote echoed through the media as reality suddenly became relevant again.

THE VOICES OF SOLDIERS

Those who testified in *Winter Soldier* seemed to be explaining to themselves as much as to the cameras the reasons for their conduct. They described the brutality of boot camp, the beatings and humiliation, the chants to "Kill, Kill, Kill," the marine hymn that lulled them to sleep. Over and over again they repeated how their training and battle context taught them to regard the Vietnamese as less than human. *They were just gooks, they weren't human.* Only that could explain the blood sport described by Scott Camil as a daily "hunting" expedition. Another story about the stoning of a three-year-old boy seemed inexplicable by the time it was recounted, yet in Vietnam the company of GIs collected rocks so huge they demolished the boy's little hut as well as him. Another order from a lieutenant in charge to "kill everything in sight" resulted in nineteen women and children being rounded up and executed. Only after a young girl had been raped by many was she added to the pile of bodies. So difficult was it to tell these stories that some could not. They stopped, too choked up to continue. Only a few months out of Vietnam, their disorientation was obvious, as one seemed to ask himself out loud: *How could we be doing these things, we were supposed to be the civilized ones?* It became abundantly clear that My Lai was not an isolated incident and was in fact a consequence of policy, of the way the war had been fought, with the highest body counts rewarded with three-day leaves, and "free fire zones" designated across civilian areas. To survive in an impossible war against an enemy indistinguishable from civilians, soldiers were forced to kill or be killed. In a constant state of fear and anger at being shot at, they shot first and questioned later.

Young Iraqi veterans were also at the long-awaited showing of *Winter Soldier*, and after being invited on stage by their older brothers in arms, one veteran who had served as a medic told of seeing dead and wounded Iraqi civilians at a checkpoint guarded by American soldiers. He told a story with eerie similarity to what the audience had just heard from Vietnam, about the way U.S. soldiers would string and wear the ears of the Vietcong they had killed.[1] The young man who had served in Iraq said an American soldier picked up the empty shell casings from the bullets that had found their way into Iraqi civilians and strung them into a bracelet that he wore proudly. Soldiers returning from Iraq had begun to tell their stories, and families of veterans were speaking when soldiers could not. These accounts, spoken so often in pain, unvarnished and straightforward, cut to the heart of war's rhetoric. Consider the words of the mother whose son was on his third tour with the 82nd Airborne and has been in Iraq for 60 percent of the total fighting:

> He knew the war was based on lies as soon as he got to Iraq. He doesn't know who the enemy is. He shoots anybody who looks like they might be an enemy. It's me or them he says. Our Administration has turned our soldiers into terrorists, but I don't blame them. They must stay alive. I blame the administration; it is a consequence of the invasion. It's chaos there. We must get our troops out. They were sent on a lie and the war is creating terrorism and an unsafe world for our children and grandchildren.[2]

With this Iraq narrative, so similar to those from Vietnam, history began to play the same cards dealt so many times before. The long road home is a journey taken by those who fight. Along the way they expose the realities of war, so long hidden from the public. As another soldier in Iraq asked his mother: "What is the media doing? Why haven't the public stopped this war?[3] At the same time that the public is silenced (because criticism, it is said, will demoralize the troops), the troops themselves find their voices. They discover that the rhetoric is false, the training is dehumanizing and the killing cannot be justified. They are the voices of the boys in the trenches on the Western Front who knew for themselves that Germans were no worse than other soldiers. They are veterans-turned-writers like Paul Fussell, who deconstructed the grand narrative of World War II, and Joseph Heller, who understood the insanity of a *Catch-22*. From Vietnam, they are the Winter Soldiers and Ron Ridenhour, who cried when he thought of My Lai, and Ron Kovic and all the others who wrote memoirs filled with guilt, fear, anger and hopelessness, to Micah Ian Wright, the brilliant poster artist who looked out over Panama City as it burned and wondered why, to Anthony Swofford, who saw brutality and excess and wrote about them in *Jarhead*, and Captain Fishback from the Army's 82nd Airborne Division who told Human Rights Watch how soldiers routinely beat and abused Iraqi prisoners at Camp Mercury, near Fallujah. They are the future veterans, able to break the prevailing constraints, who will speak out against the conduct of the next war.

Narratives that confirm the loss of humanity as an inevitable consequence of war and explain that killing can only be accomplished by dehumanizing the enemy are the silenced narratives. So dangerous to war's project is this expression that they are conveniently forgotten as the next generation is thrown into the maelstrom of killing. Over the course of the twentieth century, those voices have been hushed to expedite conflict, but at no time have they been more viciously attacked than in the midst of the occupation of Iraq during the reelection campaign of George W. Bush.

THE SWIFT BOAT VETERANS FOR "TRUTH"

Though the American public was not allowed to see *Winter Soldier*, its content would be shaped and distorted by political strategists working to give the president another term in office. Testimony from the Winter Soldiers' conference was entered into the *Congressional Record* in April 1971, and it included the words of a young Vietnam veteran named John Kerry. This act of conscience would be used by the Swift Boat Veterans for Truth to discredit Kerry's bid for the White House.

The attack against Senator Kerry told a story so wrought with inconsistencies as to be incomprehensible. The group's political strategies included accusing Kerry of lying about his experiences in Vietnam and even inflicting his own wounds. Yet the media gave credibility to the attack in spite of the long historical record documented by official sources. Many cable news talk-show hosts kept the story on the nightly agenda, featuring the Swift Boat veterans, their charges and assertions.

The animosity toward John Kerry was a consequence of his opposition to the war he fought, not the way he fought it. Counter-branding a U.S. senator as unpatriotic, especially one who earned combat medals, was an attempt to cast a negative aura around the idea of opposition itself. As the number of American troops being killed in the permanent War on Terror was beginning to escalate, the rhetoric of fear was losing its persuasive force. What was known was becoming far more frightening than the unknown, and opposition to the war in Iraq was building. But in the political culture of the twenty-first century, the debate about the war in Iraq was displaced, and emerged in the contended memories of Vietnam.

(Re)Writing Vietnam

The media strategies of the 2004 presidential election are best understood as part of an ongoing political contestation over the meanings and memories of the Vietnam War. As we saw in chapter 4, Vietnam was a bloody, lingering conflict that took many lives. As the war became unwinable and more brutal, the public recoiled and turned against the war. Pentagon planners often blame the war's opponents for the military failure. Though most credible journalists ultimately discounted the assaults on Kerry in 2004, the media moved closer to adopting the perspective that opposition to Vietnam was divisive and unpatriotic. David Broder, writing in the *Wash-*

ington Post (August 24, 2004), asserted that the country was still "divided" over the Vietnam War, and that this divisive battle has raged for over three decades. As the national media embellished the theme of a country "divided" it took on increasingly negative connotations in the post 9/11 era where patriotism had become equivalent to unity. In this new mix, Kerry's opposition to the Vietnam War was unpatriotic, but this association can only be achieved by rewriting the actual history of American attitudes toward the Vietnam War.

There is no doubt that the country was torn apart by Vietnam, but in his book, *The End of Victory Culture*, Tom Engelhardt details the complexity of that unraveling. Americans were disillusioned by Vietnam in discordant ways. The draft disgusted and terrified students, and the war's illogic drove them to challenge authority. Enraged political subgroups, such as the Weather Underground, wanted to turn the hypocrisy of violence back onto America itself. Parents felt their children had been stolen from them, and African Americans, 25 percent of U.S. forces, felt the sting of racism with their disproportionate numbers sent to fight. Most telling were the arguments that sought to explain My Lai. Good American boys had been turned into killers by the military, or worse, they were driven to insanity by something foreign, in Vietnam itself. Government officials such as Robert McNamara, who asked historians to write what came to be called the Pentagon Papers, felt victimized by the war's incomprehensibility. Even President Nixon, as he tried to talk to demonstrators in the early morning light of the Washington Monument, seemed betrayed that Vietnam had not turned out like World War II.

It was not opposition to the war that left the country disillusioned and stunned, that was a consequence of the war itself. Opinion polls tell a story of American unity, clearly opposed to the war. The public has been steadfast in its opposition to the Vietnam War since 1968. The Gallup organization has tracked opinion over the years, and this long-term record shows the consistency with which the public views the war. In the years 1985, 1990, 1993, 1995 and 2000, Americans were asked whether the United States made a "mistake" in sending troops to fight in Vietnam. The public consistently characterizes the war as a mistake by a margin of more than 2 to 1; in 1990, for example, by 74 percent to 22 percent, and as recently as the year 2000, 69 percent still called it a mistake, with only 24 percent saying it was not. As to whether the war was just, vast majorities still believe it was not. In 1990, 68 percent said it was not, with only 25 percent willing to assert that the Vietnam War was just.[4] Indeed, in another question about the morality of Vietnam posed by Gallup in 1995, 52 percent of Americans were willing to express a devastating criticism of their country by agreeing that the Vietnam War was "fundamentally wrong and immoral."[5]

THE GHOST OF VIETNAM

For America, Vietnam is more than an era, a country or a war; it is the most potent sign of military breakdown. It is a narrative of war's debacle. It has become the symbol of brutality. And most important, it represents the historic moment when public opinion turned against the leaders of a misguided and inhumane war. Just as the Good Fight is the grand narrative for the just war, Vietnam is the canon for its opposite. References to Vietnam contain within them devastating criticisms from which war planners rarely recover. The word quagmire itself is a call for war's end. Erasing this searing memory is essential for those who seek to continue war. Twisting the history of opposition to Vietnam helps silence those who would oppose war's future, especially those in the media. The most trusted and influential newscaster of his day, Walter Cronkite, openly called for an end to the war.

In the summer heat of 2005, dissent had begun to summon the ghost of Vietnam. News reports now covered expressions of antiwar sentiment, and The *New York Times* referred to "a time of rising protest." The interpretive field was shifting. Vietnam narratives, references and explanatory frames began to emerge, displacing those of the Good Fight in many different forums. When George W. Bush finally left his Texas ranch in the fifth August of his presidency, he struggled to (re)embed the war in Iraq within the uncontested memory of the Good Fight. He told a gathering of fifteen thousand V.F.W. members in Salt Lake City that the sacrifices of Americans in Iraq would be remembered just as the heroism shown in World War II and Korea was commemorated. But Henry Kissinger was writing in the *Washington Post* (August 12, 2005), comparing the difficulties of exiting Vietnam with those of Iraq. He also offered an object lesson from Vietnam: "Military success is difficult to sustain unless buttressed by domestic support."[6] Gary Hart opened an op-ed piece in the *Post* (August 24, 2005) by quoting the Pete Seeger anti-Vietnam War song, "Waistdeep in the Big Muddy, and the big fool said to push on." In the *New York Times*, Maureen Dowd's August 27 opinion piece brought those lyrics up to date with "Bike Deep in the Big Muddy." And Frank Rich entitled his August 28 piece "The Vietnamization of Bush's Vacation." Cindy Sheehan, the middle-aged woman in the funny hat, was teaching the lessons of Vietnam to a reluctant new war president.

Other antiwar expressions reminiscent of the Vietnam era were also in full swing that summer. The most requested music video on MTV was the antiwar song "Wake Me Up When September Ends," by Green Day, about the pain of soldiers. Dan Harris noted (ABC News, August 24, 2005) the mood change from when the Dixie Chicks were pilloried for criticizing the president. The N.F.L. did not cancel its sponsorship of the Rolling Stones tour, even though Mick Jagger made entertainment headlines by confirming lyrics critical of the president in a song entitled "Sweet Neo Con."[7] As the ground began to shift, and every major poll indicated that a majority of Americans were now against the war in Iraq, in a stunning denial, ABC News (August 25, 2005), purported to take a "reality check" on the "depth of sentiment against the war" and claimed that opposition to U.S. troop presence was "relatively small," only 13 percent. As FAIR noted, the network managed this by using dated poll numbers arrived at with misleading questions.

WHERE HAVE ALL THE SOLDIERS GONE?

The war's lack of popular support was reflected in recruiting shortfalls. Finding more young people to fight the wars of the twenty-first century was becoming a major problem. The *Los Angeles Times* wrote that army officials predicted that the recruiting shortfall in 2005 would be even worse in 2006 (Rich, 2005). Though the Pentagon failed to release the findings of the Mental Health Advisory Team for six months, a report released in July 2005 found that 54 percent of the troops stationed in Iraq felt that morale in their individual units was "low or very low" (Rampton, 2005).

The army began to fight back with the most extensive marketing and advertising campaign ever targeted at America's youth. The same media marketing strategies that turned the war into entertainment were being deployed to convince the next generation that fighting is fun, and also a great career choice. The Pentagon hired the Leo Burnett advertising agency at a cost of $350 million to sell the army to new recruits. Ads would make no mention of Iraq. Corporate media conglomerate Clear Channel also helped with recruitment by partnering with the U.S. Navy to sponsor a popular Summer Jam weekend in the Bay Area, an event attended mainly by young people of color and promoted heavily on the airwaves at KMEL.

But the most important recruitment tool remains *America's Army* and the creation and promotion of war as a fun, empowering game. The online website sponsored by the U.S. Department of Defense expanded its offerings of games available for kids to download or play online. The game

Overmatch: Few soldiers, certain victory promises "a contest in which one opponent is distinctly superior...with specialized skills and superior technology...," expressing the same fantasy high-tech message of war that drove the military adventure into Iraq.

As we saw in chapter 18, the collaboration between the military and the gaming industry is a potent promotional force. Continuing that merger, the DOD contracted with the company Ubisoft to help market and distribute *America's Army*. At a computer gaming conference in early 2005, Ubisoft continued the traditional gendered associations of war, deploying the Frag Dolls, a group of young women gamers with names like Jinx and Eekers, who demonstrate *America's Army*. But these "booth babes" not only pose for pictures, they also play the games, inviting young men to enter and occupy the gaming space. Eekers's promotional blog about her Combat Convoy Experience can be found on the *America's Army* website.

> You have this gigantic Hummer in a tent loaded with guns, a rotatable turret, and a huge screen in front of it. Jinx took the wheel and drove us around this virtual war zone while shooting people with a pistol, and I switched off from the SAW turret on the top of the vehicle to riding passenger with an M4.

Sheldon Rampton noticed the particular combination of violence and fantasy observing, "Although the games are violent, with plenty of opportunities to shoot and blow things up, they avoid graphic images of death or other ugliness of war, offering instead a sanitized, Tom Clancy version of fantasy combat" (Rampton, 2005).

But like the soldier who speaks on camera in Michael Moore's *Fahrenheit 9/11*, saying *when real people die, it's not like a video game*, the volunteer army was beginning to understand that real war is different from the recruitment fantasies, video games and the compelling advertising. As the army struggled to secure reluctant warriors for the twenty-first century, other fictional and commercial formats would be offered to an uneasy public.

TELEVISION AND THE CULTURE OF WAR

Throughout the occupation of Iraq, the silencing of critical moral debate led to a disturbing number of unspoken, though troubling, contradictions. How could Americans be vanquishing Evil and liberating Iraqis when images of Abu Ghraib existed? Though denied, justified and ignored, it was impossible not to know that civilians were being killed in Iraq. Mothers of American soldiers and soldiers themselves were beginning to be noticed;

though they were downplayed, they were impossible to ignore completely. Indeed, as the leak of CIA agent Valerie Plame's name became a scandal, leaving a *New York Times* reporter in jail, the country knew in atmosphere if not in detail that officials prevaricated and retaliated in less-than-noble ways. The sullied unpleasantness hung uneasily over America in what Mark Danner calls "frozen scandals" such as Abu Ghraib, where no official investigation exposes the truth or punishes those truly culpable.

In these discursive voids fictional narratives fill in the blanks by speaking in alternative modes. They offer not coherent counter-arguments but associations, implications and sensibilities that struggle to make the unpalatable, if not inevitable, then grudgingly acceptable. This was the role that prime-time television played in the dramatic series *24* on the Fox network, incorporating scenes of torture within the popular imagination of what is tolerable in America. On *24*, torture is a featured interrogation tactic carried out by the main protagonist Jack Bauer (Kiefer Sutherland), the hero whom audiences have come to know, rely on and admire. While under interrogation, Jack and his Counter Terrorist Unit shoot a suspect in the leg, subject the son of the defense secretary to sensory disorientation, stun gun an innocent colleague and use a lamp cord to shock a businessman. They do all this to thwart a terrorist plan and save the world in one day.

The plot sequence offers the most unlikely scenario, but the one most accepting of the practice of torture. Recall that at Abu Ghraib, 70 to 90 percent of the eight thousand Iraqis who passed through the prison gates were citizens simply caught up in raids, searches and checkpoints who could offer no "actionable intelligence." Nevertheless, on *24* torture becomes the primary way to save lives. Executive Producer Howard Gordon understands that *24* taps into the public's "fear-based wish fulfillment" of having protectors who will do whatever is necessary to save society from harm. Indeed, promoting fear, then playing the role of protector, mirrors the public relations strategy of the War on Terror. As producer Gordon says, "In some ways, [Jack] is a necessary evil" The program perpetuates the myth that torture results in accurate information. But such practices only make U.S. soldiers more vulnerable, and further isolates America from the global community.[8] Ultimately, they continue to chip away at the humanity of the American public, a loss that only perpetuates danger by acquiescing to the deadly culture of belligerent warfare.

The most significant indication that torture had become the latest fashion in media culture was its appearance in an advertisement for Sprint long-distance service. Agony washes across a man's face. He is tied in a chair as his tormenters extract information from him by using his cell phone to drive up his long-distance bill. In the next scene he enters the

Sprint office to sign up for a better, cheaper service plan, his hands still tied behind the chair he carries as he walks. Though suffering clearly registers on his face, the comedic gag denies the horror. As a joke, torture becomes recognizable, depicted in a void of moral indignation. Now familiar, it can be incorporated as part of the everyday world of a militarized culture, not as the sickening, grotesque physical violence that it is, in a culture that refuses to label it as such.

OVER THERE

Operation Iraqi Freedom became the first "reality show" invasion, and the occupation of Iraq made entertainment history by inspiring the first dramatic series about a war to air on television while that war was still being fought. It should not be a surprise that *Over There* aired on the Fox cable service, FX. The program contains the same twenty-first-century war themes and messages that Bruckheimer forged in *Black Hawk Down*. Like *Down*, the series capitalizes on war as entertainment, thrilling audiences with the excitement of combat punctuated with horrific yet highly aestheticized violence.

While the series offers war stories of actual battle conditions in Iraq, complete with visual references to the reality style coverage of the invasion itself, the theme song, "Ours Is Not to Reason Why," makes it clear that *Over There* is committed to avoiding the politics, prevarications and controversies of the war in Iraq. In a promotional video, producer Steven Bochco said he didn't want the show to have "a political point of view" (Franklin 2005). But like *Down*, presenting the "apolitical view" glorifies thrilling combat for no good reason and accepts war for war's sake.

Claims of being devoid of politics notwithstanding, narrative sequencing and plot structures in *Over There* reinforce the justifications and conduct for the war in Iraq. While each explanation for the real war was methodically discredited, violent sequences in *Over There* confirm that any killing done is justified, only retaliatory and most necessary. From the beginning, the unit is plunged into desert combat under attack by insurgents who had agreed to surrender peacefully, but who—after negotiating an agreement—continue to fight. Within this context comes graphic violence so startling it certainly falls within the type of imagery that Philip Agee identified as pornographic during World War II. An Iraqi is torn in half by a grenade, and though his severed torso falls to the ground, his legs continue to walk independently before collapsing. Bochco clearly follows in the footsteps of the stunning violence of *Saving Private Ryan* and *Black Hawk Down*. Viewers assume the privileged position of detached spectators, entertained by war, yet secure, distant observers of its titillating violence. Alessandra Stanley (2005) notes this in the *New York Times* online, referring to it as a "show business atrocity, a commercial abuse of a raw and unresolved national calamity." But in the sentence that follows, Stanley asserts that it might bring the reality of war home to the public. "'Over There' dramatizes wartime slaughter and suffering that all too often go unnoticed. For all the lives lost and billions spent, the Iraq conflict has raged on with surprisingly little impact on most Americans." But the failure of the media to show Americans the burned and brutalized corpses of civilians, and the dead and maimed bodies of U.S. soldiers can not be corrected with the graphic hyperrealism of fictional narratives that turn war into entertainment.

As Iraq is turned into a television fiction, the program rewrites actual events making them more palatable. In the real war in Iraq, American soldiers have killed innocent civilians at checkpoints, including one incident that became an international embarrassment. An Italian government agent, Nicola Callpari was escorting journalist Giuliana Sgrena,[9] who had just been released by kidnappers when American troops fired on their convoy, killing Callpari. A checkpoint incident is depicted in *Over There*. But in the fiction, a murderous insurgent is hiding in the trunk of the slain Iraqi's car. On the fictional representation, an "interrogation" is portrayed as strictly above board. And after questioning the suspect reveals "actionable intelligence," that is used to save lives by revealing where twenty Stinger missiles are hidden. In the real war, anonymous suicide bombers kill American soldiers without warning and the bodies of U.S. soldiers are sent home in "transfer tubes" under cover of darkness.

After *Black Hawk Down* and *Profiles from the Front Line*, *Over There* is the next inevitable step toward the logic of militainment. Writing in *The New Yorker*, Nancy Franklin (2005, 87) observed "There's an overall pointlessness to the show that's rather shocking, considering the outrageous lies and arrogance that got us into the war." But that is surely the point. *Over There* is tailored to forget the lies that created it and instead to sit comfortably next to all the other forms of pointless violence so prevalent on television. Iraq is lost in this landscape, no longer unusual, its violence now part of the unexceptional where shoot-to-kill is simply a video game command or entertainment dialogue. Its exceptional nature disappears as it is folded into mainstream culture, contained now as part of the familiar. It has become the banal culture of militarism.

As war is woven into popular media culture, its entertainments serve to suppress the realities and support the fantasies of war. As fact is transmuted into fiction, and fiction is as easily substituted for fact, it is no wonder that the term "truthiness," coined by political satirist Steven Colbert, has resonated so strongly through political culture. It is an apt expression for a media environment no longer capable of telling the truth, or representing the real.

Conclusion

War, Humanism and Democracy

In 1975, Paul Fussell wrote that World War I left us with an enduring ironic sensibility that "has become an inseparable element of the general vision of war in our time" (33). This vision was crafted through the writings of Siegfried Sassoon and other post-World War I poets who turned to literature to illuminate the unbearable loss of war. Unable to make sense of the astonishing horrors of the Great War, they used codes of irony and contrast to comprehend war's meanings. The idyllic, pastoral beauty of Britain's golden summer of 1914 was utterly at odds with the unexpected shock of winter's barren landscape of war. In the post-war outlook, hope and progress had given way to horror and barbarism. But what has remained of this critical view of war and the overriding sense of loss? By the twenty-first century, the literary codes of irony are no longer the interpretive frames that make sense of war and give its history meaning. A variety of media, steeped in advertising, marketing and persuasive methods, ever more closely tied to government and military objectives, now give form to the landscape of war's culture. A century later, the language of war interacts with commercial media discourse, television formatting designs and digital imaging that constitute contemporary popular tastes, and these have become the vision of war in our time.

After the "war to end all wars" the weapon implicated in the killing of millions, the machine gun, was seen from the view of those it slaughtered, an entire generation of the youth of Europe cut down in its prime. This loss and the tragedy of death were evoked through binary metaphors—the "naked swimming soldiers contrived by the post-Great War imagination to register the supreme pathos of flesh menaced by hurtling iron" (Fussell 1975, 309). Over the course of the century, even as Americans die in foreign lands, the pathos of weapons that tear through flesh is replaced by aestheticized hyperrealism contrived to entertain audiences sheltered from the true dreadfulness of battle. Fast-action narratives leave no time or sensibility to contemplate the humanity of obliterated bodies and severed limbs. Twenty-first century viewers have been invited to view the weapons of war, not as the destroyers of frail bodies, but as the empowering technology of avenging angels reigning down destructive force on evil enemies. Ignoring the bodies left in the rubble on the receiving end has been an active process of forgetting. On occasion over the course of the century, the humanity of the dead has become present, impossible to ignore, but only to be forgotten again as the battle over memory and meaning carries on from one war to the next.

The view of war seen through cross-hairs ready to strike the target is the preferred perspective for those who plan and implement war. This picture of empowerment is made possible by extraordinary technologies capable of transmitting images from the nose of smart bombs through the use of computer-based imaging. Those digital technologies that create the exciting images also drive the weapons systems. The power and the sight is the result of enormous human effort, resources and creativity marshaled to realize the goal of such technological proficiency. The largest economy the globe has ever known, indeed a "super-power," at the height of its progress, has directed its astonishing advancements toward the creation of the ultimate forces of destruction. The atmosphere that nurtures war and weaponry could not have been realized without the exhilarating perspective that invites viewers into their digital virtual worlds. This has now become the social sensibility of war in the twenty-first century.

Detached from consequences, sheltered from horrors, positioned as victims and agitated through demonization, this view is strikingly devoid of compassion. The contemporary loss of empathy was eloquently expressed by critic Bob Mondello, (NPR March 3, 2006) who noted the change in sensibility from wars past. He reviewed the French film *Joyeux Noel*, that tells the story of the Christmas truce of 1914. Soldiers crossed the no-man's-land between the trenches in at least a dozen spots along the Western Front. For a few hours it became common ground as they ate, sang, smoked and celebrated mass together. Mondello observed that the camaraderie depicted in *Joyeux Noel* feels almost "fairy taleish" today, "because humanity being so human in war time seems so clearly to belong to another time." His observations are reinforced by filmmaker Patricia Foulkrod, who explored the shattered humanity of twenty-first century soldiers in her documentary film, *The Ground Truth: When the Killing Ends.*[1] *The Ground Truth* is offered as an alternative to "the sanitized images found on the nightly news," as Foulkrod's camera records the "broken hearts" devastated psyches of soldiers that are otherwise "invisible." When images of broken soldiers are blocked to prevent protest, that absence also blocks the presence of their humanity.

Yet there have been times when Americans have declined the invitation to adopt this inhumane point of view. Their eyes were cast instead to the ground where children ran burning and soldiers lay dying. The American public rejected the vision of war once confronted by the seemingly endless images of human destruction. Appraised of war's devastation, they averted their gaze and rejected its justifications. For the government and the military, the return to a pre-Vietnam public sensibility was a long hard battle with the Constitution, the First Amendment and with journalists willing to bear witness to war's human costs. At the beginning of a new century, the country finds itself learning the lessons of war once again, yet also presented with an opportunity to prevent future lapse of memory.

REFRAMING MEMORY

Commenting on the *News Hour* (May 31, 2000) about the controversy over reporting the massacre at No Gun Ri during the Korean War, respected media critic Marvin Kalb asserted that the role of the press was not to function as historian but to stay focused on what is timely. Kalb seemed to forget that historical references are fundamental to journalistic interpretations and views of the world, especially those of war. For Tom Brokaw, the 9/11 attacks were a repeat of Pearl Harbor, and for the press corps, embedded reporters had returned to the practices of World War II and Ernie Pyle. So replete with historical references to the Good Fight is war news and imagery that they become invisible even to critics. Those who call for war know well that persuasions must ignore and deny the memory of past horrors and the inhumanity contained in war's counter-narratives. No mention can be made of No Gun Ri, My Lai, El Mozote or the brutality that forms the major part of the actual human experiences of military interventions. When memories are summoned they emerge as fleeting and fragmentary, a type of shallow sympathy unable to get to the heart of comprehension or find a path to more humane policies and sensibilities. One such fragment of memory from El Mozote illustrates these points.

ANOTHER HALLOWED TERROR GROUND

On January 13, 2002, the *New York Times Magazine* featured a 2-page color photograph taken in El Salvador by Susan Meiselas. The picture shows a solemn procession of men, each carrying a small coffin on his shoulder. At the front of the line a man grips a wooden cross adorned with wild flowers as he leads the group toward the graveyard. In a story titled *Another Hallowed Terror Ground* the massacre at El Mozote merits one column, a little over 500 words. Writer Tina Rosenberg draws connections between what happened twenty years before in El Mozote and the September 11th attacks on Americans. She explains that all victims of terror share similar needs, the "desire to name and acknowledge those who died...the need to bring the guilty to justice, the families' urgency to possess a shard of bone to bury—these things Americans understand, instinctively, as the foundations of healing." She acknowledges that the victims of El Mozote have been denied such a healing process "in what is probably the largest act of terror in recent Latin American history, the massacre at El Mozote, El Salvador." The story is about the six-hour ceremony in December 2001, to bury some of the remains of the smallest victims of the massacre. Excavations of the site had yielded more bones and children's skeletons, and those remains were being reburied on the occasion pictured in the magazine.

In drawing emotional connections between the families of victims in El Salvador, and those in America, the story offers a shared sense of mutual loss and empathy, a welcome reversal from the news depictions of death in Central America in the 1980s. Acknowledging the massacre as an act of terror is also a departure from the history of denials and the story speaks of the need to identify those who are guilty and seek justice. Yet the text offers few facts about the perpetrators of the El Mozote massacre. Readers are told that the massacre was perpetrated by the "American-trained, American-financed Atlacatl Battalion" but little else, and not that U.S. taxpayers paid for the M-16s that killed the children with ammunition made in Missouri. Though the act is identified as terrorism, the military junta (termed "moderate" by the press at the time) that perpetrated the crime is not identified as "terrorist." Nor are readers reminded that official thanks and recognition were given to the Salvadoran military after the findings of the Truth Commission at a ceremony presided over by Colin Powell.[2]

Fleeting reference is made to the American government when Rosenberg tells of Rufina Amaya, the survivor of the massacre. "Her account, and eyewitness reports of the bodies, were dismissed by the Reagan administration and the government of El Salvador as guerrilla propaganda." Blame for the cover-up is placed at the feet of the Salvadoran government, which for eleven years, Rosenberg explains, "insisted that no massacre had taken place at El Mozote" (26). No further details of Reagan administration actions cloud the tone of the story, even though U.S. government officials both in Washington and the American embassy also covered up the massacre. Readers are not told of Mark Danner's interview with former U.S. Marine John McKay, who admitted being too scared to go into the mountains and confirm the deaths. Forgotten are other embassy officials who actively denied a massacre they knew had happened.

The paper also omitted its own history with regard to El Mozote, making no reference to Raymond Bonner's reporting or the fact that he was taken off the story, even though he and Susan Meiselas also provided "eye-witness reports of the bodies." The *Time's* remembrance of the El Mozote massacre is an encouraging impulse toward humanism, but it fails to provide any details that might lead to more humanistic policies through an understanding of the past. The larger history of U.S. sponsored terrorism in Central America is left buried with the remaining bodies at El Mozote, never to be unearthed.

The Cold-War activities of the Reagan White House seem part of a distant past with little relevance to the present. But much of current U.S. policy was prefigured in Central America, and drawing out the ways in which that history continues to influence United States policies would allow the paper to come to terms with its own history and fulfill its mandate to its readers. Tracing some of those buried strands will clarify the need for a journalistic mandate to include historical background.

Recall the U.S. official who denied the massacre before Congress and prevented its investigation—Elliott Abrams. After the Iran/Contra hearings, Abrams was convicted of lying to Congress, but in 1992 was pardoned when George H.W. Bush left office. Abrams went on to join the team at the Project for a New American Century and from there was able to help promote the idea of "regime change" in Iraq. By 2001, in spite of Abrams's stated preference for military policies over humanitarian concerns, George W. Bush rehired Elliott Abrams as senior director for democracy, human rights and international operations at the National Security Council. Later he would be transferred to become the director of Middle Eastern affairs at the NSC.

Another public official from the period who continues to have enormous influence is former U.S. ambassador to Honduras in the 1980s, John Negroponte. He was responsible for coordinating aid to the contras from the mountains that bordered Nicaragua. Honduran generals and the notorious Battalion 3–16, another U.S. trained unit, were responsible for hundreds of assassinations and disappearances in Honduras, including the murder of Joseph Carey, a Jesuit priest (Brouwer 2004, 181). According to numerous sources including human rights workers and investigative reporters, Negroponte kept silent about military atrocities at the same time he sent supplies to the contras. In 1986, the International Court of Justice found the U.S. guilty of terrorism for its war against Nicaragua. In 2001, John Negroponte became the U.S. ambassador to the United Nations, and when it passed a resolution against terrorism, Negroponte's words to the assembled delegates on September 28, 2001, must have sounded ironic. He reminded delegates that the U.N. action "obligates all member states to deny financing, support, and safe haven for terrorists" (Hallinan, 2001).[3]

Negroponte should also be remembered in future discussions of democracy and open society for his work as the director of national intelligence at a time when intelligence agencies were discovered systematically removing thousands of previously declassified historical documents from public access. Historians were alarmed to find that decades-old reports had disappeared from open files, and National Archivist Allan Weinstein said he knew little of the secret operation until 55,000 pages had been confiscated. Among the documents removed was "a report that the CIA and the rest of the U.S. intelligence community badly botched their estimates as to whether or not Communist China would intervene in the Korean War in the fall of 1950" (Aid, 2006). It is difficult to imagine how such documents could harm U.S. national security, but with their removal, the American people are denied their own history. On March 2, 2006, Weinstein called for a moratorium on the reclassification scheme (Shane, 2006).

As the war in Iraq began, revisiting the history and players in the Iran/Contra scandal might have offered the public a context for judging official claims and the veracity of sources in the Bush administration with their long participation in some of America's most unpleasant history. For example, Colin Powell, as an assistant to Secretary of Defense Caspar Weinberger, signed the paper ordering the transfer of about four thousand antitank missiles from the U.S. Army to the CIA for delivery to Iran at a time when all government officials actively denied such activities. [4] The American public was left uninformed about the geopolitical effects of selling missiles to Iran at the same time that the administration was arming Saddam Hussein. It prolonged the Iran/Iraq war and led to thousands more deaths. Left in the dark as to the global consequences of American foreign policy, the American public remains unprepared for the current costs of those policies, both globally and at home.

But Powell's history goes even further back, to Vietnam, where as a young officer at the Pentagon he denied claims that a massacre had taken place at My Lai, an action that helped delay the investigation for months.

That history might have shaded Powell's claims before the United Nations that Hussein possessed Weapons of Mass Destruction. Indeed, as the *Columbia Journalism Review* noted, Powell's visual presentation at the United Nations was the single most influential event that persuaded editorial writers at the country's major newspapers of the need to go to war with Iraq (Mooney, 2005). Had those editors remembered the deceptive interpretations of satellite imagery when Ronald Reagan justified the invasion of Grenada, they might have considered Powell's U.N. images with a degree of skepticism. As historian Howard Zinn (2003, 2) noted in an essay titled, *The Specter of Vietnam*, such falsities were easily predictable: "The so-called 'drones-of-death' turned out to be model airplanes. What Colin Powell called 'decontamination trucks' were found to be fire trucks. What U.S. leaders called 'mobile germ labs' were found by an official British inspection team to be used for inflating artillery balloons."

JUSTIFYING TORTURE

Though the public overwhelmingly opposed the military adventures in Central American during the 1980s, their desires were circumvented by the secret actions and arguments of public officials. Those same officials continue to play key roles in advancing new arguments, equally unpopular and imperious in the twenty-first century. During the Reagan years, Dick Cheney was a representative from Wyoming and ranking Republican on a House select committee investigating the Iran/Contra scandal. David Addington was an aide working with Cheney's committee and helped write a report for the Republican minority arguing that the law banning funding for the contras was an "unconstitutional infringement on of Presidential prerogatives" (Mayer 2006, 36). With the administration of George W. Bush, David Addington became the vice-president's chief of staff, a highly influential position in the White House.[5] Writing in the *New Yorker*, investigative reporter Jane Mayer (2006, 36) observed, "Both men continue to embrace an extraordinarily expansive view of executive power," and though the vice-president's office has no statutory role in the military chain of command, Addington "played a central part in virtually all of the Administration's legal strategies, including terrorism and detainee policies." Mayer provides this information while profiling Alberto J. Mora, former navy general council, who tirelessly campaigned against torture with dissenting legal opinions. Mora frequently warned his superiors at the Pentagon that the president's February 2002 decision to circumvent the Geneva conventions, which specifically prohibit torture and "outrages upon personal dignity," and "humiliating and degrading treatment," was an invitation to abuse. He also argued that such actions could leave U.S. personnel open to criminal prosecution. Arguing against institutionalizing torture, Mora's confronted the Cheney/Addington view of extraordinary executive power in matters ranging from interrogations to wiretapping. He described as "unlawful," dangerous," and "erroneous" the novel legal theories they supported that granted the president the right to authorize abuse (Mayer 2006, 32).

After promoting illegal, unconstitutional and unpopular views in Central America, Dick Cheney and others, rose to power and attempted to make their views the laws of the land, and they succeeded in doing so, at least temporarily. This could only have been accomplished in a media atmosphere that hides the histories, actions and actual political philosophies of government officials.[6]

WHEN PRESIDENTS LIE: GOVERNMENT DECEPTION AND WAR

Legendary journalist I.F. Stone once said, "Every government is run by liars, and nothing they say should be believed." Stone's views were formed covering the Korean War, Blacklisting, the Cold War and Vietnam. His famous dictum is quoted in a comprehensive treatment about government lying written for the *Columbia Journalism Review* by Anthony Marro in 1985. In it, Marro detailed episodes of deception as silly as the release of a fake recipe for Trisha Nixon's wedding cake, to ones as serious as the lies told about the invasion of Grenada. Over the years, the press has had to grapple with governmental dishonesty, a problem particularly troubling in a system based on trusting the informed consent of the governed.

What has become evident over the years is that deception, secrecy and war are inseparable. Deception was an essential component in carrying out the Reagan Doctrine during the 1980s and analyst Morton Halperin explained Reagan White House secrecy this way, "These guys came here straight out of nineteen forty-six. They came out of World War Two, when the government lied all the time, and it was all right to lie. The whole Normandy invasion, and the covert operations that surrounded it, are an important part of that mind-set...They still think fundamentally that foreign policy should be left to the executive branch and that people shouldn't even try to find out what they're up to" (Marro 1985, 31). After World War II deception escalated in the 1960s with the massive amounts of misinformation released by the government during the Vietnam War and Watergate. The manipulative strategies used to create favorable attitudes toward war invariably seep into civilian life and over the years lying has become the political status quo. A qualitative leap in this direction was made evident when Reagan administration aides argued that it didn't matter whether some of Reagan's stories were literally true because they contained a larger truth. As Bill Kovach, the Washington news editor of the *New York Times* noted, "This is the first time I've heard that literal truth is not important to the presidency" (Marro 1985, 31). During this time reporters also complained that officials made unprecedented moves to keep them from getting behind the false claims.

Over the years it has been said that secrecy is essential in war for national security reasons—information must be kept out of the hands of the enemy. Yet with every war we find that maintaining homefront morale and public resolve are far more plausible reasons for lying. News of civilian casualties, footage of wounded soldiers and images of flag draped coffins have nothing to do with battlefield strategies, but they do sour the public's enthusiasm for conflict. Viewed not as citizens to be informed, but as targets to be persuaded and deprived of expressing judgment, the public loses its sense of citizenship. When dissenting voices are ignored, silenced and attacked by the media and government officials, the ties that bind the democratic process are broken. As cycles of persuasion continue, advances in marketing research and promotion are enlisted into the next war effort. In a society characterized by continual war preparations, democratic institutions heave under the weight of new forms of censorship and propaganda and the public is habitually locked out of the important debates about matters of state. As Orville Schell, dean of the Graduate School of Journalism at Berkeley points out, the failure to hear the people's voice also cripples political leaders. "The crucial synapses which normally transmit warnings from citizen observers to government increasingly freeze shut" (2004, x).

Presently, distrust of the public is consistent with official dishonesty, and the principle of deception is a disturbing aspect of the neoconservative intellectual outlook now ascendant in governing spheres. Like the theories devised to condone torture, qualitative leaps in the uses of deception and stagecraft are being undergirded through seriously flawed intellectual reasoning. The progenitor of neoconservative thought is the late political philosopher Leo Strauss, mentor to the war's primary intellectual architects and planners, including Under Secretary of Defense Paul Wolfowitz. Abraham Shulsky is another neoconservative who headed the Pentagon's Office of Special Plans, whose work helped override professional CIA analysis to justify the war in Iraq. Shulsky together with Gary Schmitt, leader of the Project for a New American Century, elaborated on Strauss's idea of "hidden meaning," in political life. "Indeed it suggests that deception is the norm in political life, and the hope, to say nothing of the expectation, of establishing a politics that can dispense with it is the exception" (Alterman 2004, 24). In a fascinating admission of the neocon-servative principle of political deception, Paul Wolfowitz revealed that the justification for war in Iraq was a fabrication. In an interview with *Vanity Fair* (May 2003) he said "for reasons that have a lot to do with the U.S. government bureaucracy, we settled on the one issue that everyone could agree on: weapons of mass destruction."

Deception is now a primary problem in politics and it is not a contriv-ance to say that it threatens the heart of American democracy. The manner in which the press has dealt with contemporary government deception is even more troubling.

In a thoughtful essay titled *When Presidents Lie*, media critic Eric Alter-man (2004) considers the lack of consequences for present-day presidential dishonesty compared to the past. He notes that when President Johnson lied about the Tonkin Gulf incident it became a significant factor in his political demise. President Reagan admitted to his Cabinet officials that he feared if the secret weapons sale to Iran were exposed in the media, "We'll all be hanging by our thumbs in front of the White House" (22). Yet when the scandal broke, with the help of Oliver North and the icons of entertainment culture, White House deceptions were revealed without serious consequences.

In recent history, as we discovered with media coverage of the Down-ing Street Memos, press attitudes toward official dishonesty have become even more accepting. The claims that accompanied the call to war were received with little skepticism and more to the point, promoted with en-thusiasm. Take for example, newscaster Connie Chung who challenged a guest opposed to the war in Iraq with, "Who are you going to believe, the president or Osama Bin Laden?" Chung's question makes the expression of misgivings over war equivalent to heresy. The media now often function more often as inhibitors to free expression, not promoters of it. Equally disturbing is the fundamental assumption contained within Ms. Chung's question that because George W. is the American president, he cannot lie. In his book *War Made Easy*, Norman Solomon agrees with the docu-mentation compiled in these pages. In the long history of conflict, there is no single war that the government did not lie about. Yet there have been times when the media told the truth about war. The most troubling aspect of the twenty-first-century media is the assertion, clearly demonstrated by Chung and coverage of the Downing Street Memos, that telling the truth and demanding that public officials do the same are not what media are mandated to do anymore. With the failure to keep elected officials ac-countable to the public they serve, the media have broken the bond that ties their organizations to a democratic polity.[7]

THE CRISIS OF DEMOCRACY

Writers and critics have attempted to come to terms with the democratic crisis of the media outlined here. In exploring the relationship between the press and the public, Eric Alterman (2004, 24) refers to the work of Walter Lippmann as "visionary." Lippmann rightly believed that the necessary precondition for democracy is a civic-minded public with ready access to information. Only then, he argued, could citizens understand public policy. But Lippmann became disillusioned that such a citizenry was possible and concluded that the idea was unrealistic. Lippmann proposed instead that a group of elites should help the public make sense of the world. Alterman asserts that because education has not lived up to the demand for civic literacy, "Lippmann's critique of the inherent inability of democracy to cope with complexity remains salient."

Positing, as Lippmann did, that the general public is too feeble to understand events of the day, and that such matters be left to the minds of elites, abandons the possibility of democracy and allows those in power to condone dishonesty and secrecy. As Alterman concludes, because of the complexities of international diplomacy, even presidents with "the best of intentions come to view deception as an unavoidable consequence." Alterman's nuanced argument does not condone presidential lying, but in general, it can be said that those who admire Walter Lippmann believe that because of the complexity of global realities and international relations the world remains outside of the public's ability to comprehend it.

It is true that influential elites make complicated, even convoluted arguments often referencing abstract principles. But they do so more often to justify unpopular policies than to explain the world. The war in Iraq has demonstrated most clearly, the failures of political leaders, neoconservative intellectuals and the elite few, to understand or articulate the military adventure in ways that comprehend the complexities of international politics. Consider Orville Schell's (2004, ix) observation that President Bush has often spoken of trusting "visceral reactions" and acting on the basis of "gut feelings." Schell argues that the president's decision-making process is not based on evidence: "Reading, facts, history, logic, and the complex interaction between the electorate, the media, and government seem to play a somewhat subsidiary role" in the president's policy formations.

THE HIDDEN CONSEQUENCES

Theories that discount democratic citizenship also naïvely assume that leaders are motivated by altruistic and democratic diplomacy, not by ideologies, power and economic interests that are often at odds with the goals and identities of most Americans. Consider the words of Micah Ian Wright, soldier turned citizen and artist who researched the results of the invasion he was part of and found that it violated his values and visions of America's role in the world. With the U.S. military controlling Panama, conditions in that country deteriorated:

> Unemployment, already high because of the U.S. embargo against Noriega's regime, climbed to 35 percent as drastic layoffs were imposed on the public sector. Pension rights and other work benefits were lost. Newspapers and radio and television stations were closed by U.S. occupation authorities. Newspaper editors and reporters critical of the invasion were jailed or detained, as were all the leftist political party leaders. Union heads were arrested by the U.S. military, an some 150 local labor leaders were removed from their elected union positions. Public employees not supporting the invasion were purged. Crime rates climbed dramatically, along with poverty and destitution. Thousands remained homeless. Corruption was more wide spread than ever...It returned Panama to a Third World client state whose land, labor, resources, markets, and capital were again completely accessible to corporate investors on the best possible terms. (2003, 21–22)

Most Americans are not aware of the conditions left in the wake of their interventions. During the Cold War, the United States fought the Soviet Union by proxy, over terrains and bodies in El Salvador, Nicaragua, Afghanistan and Somalia, just to name a few that are recounted here.[8] But those countries were left with a legacy of horrible violence, destroyed cultures and infrastructures. As Afghanistan and Somalia descended into chaos after the Cold War, they became what analyst refer to as "breeding grounds" for terrorists. After $6 billion was spent on war in El Salvador, no rebuilding effort alleviated that country's pain and chaos, and in the years that followed, America offered about $500 million in aid. The country now suffers from a 50 percent unemployment rate. Understanding the true lack of compassion in American militarized policies toward other countries would make remembering the massacre at El Mozote more than a hallow exercise is fleeting sympathies.

The strategies of war and violence have not helped the movement toward global peace and social justice. Indeed, the military devastation of Central America in the 1980s left the region crippled and impoverished, but friendly to corporate globalization. Multinational companies are more easily able to exploit the region for cheap resources and its peoples as cheap labor markets. Such results benefit multinational corporations but do economic harm to most Americans in the form of low wages and unemployment. These realities are more likely to be the reasons why presidents lie about the wars they call for. By the twenty-first century the media have become full partners in the corporate structures that also benefit from such global policies. Governments deceive, not because their thinking is too complex to explain, but because the policies they insist upon are unpopular and undemocratic.

MYTH AND HISTORY

Lippmann asserted that public judgment was based not on valid criteria, but on the images of the world people hold in their heads, often based on misconceptions, stereotypes and emotional associations. Following Lippmann, Alterman says the public needs to "educate itself" about complicated international politics to expel the "nation's caricatured notion of itself as an innocent and benevolent force throughout the world" (2004, 24). If the media were to provide the public with the actual history and consequences of war, the simplistic caricature of a benevolent force would be a thing of the past. Yet this caricature is promoted by presidents and repeated across the media spectrum in video-game entertainment, news reporting and fictions in every format.

But coming to terms with its own history cannot be done when American historical documents are removed from public shelves or when less information, particularly about global policies, is available from the media. In the book *The News about the News, Washington Post* editors, Leonard Downie and Robert Kaiser (2002, 7), point out, "Although Americans are more globally connected than ever, most news media steadily and substantially reduced their coverage of foreign news during the last years of the twentieth century, depriving Americans of the opportunity to follow the world around them." They also agree with Hickey (1998) that national television networks have trimmed their reporting staffs and closed foreign reporting bureaus to cut their owners' costs (Downie and Kaiser 2002, 10).

By the 1990s, amid increasing demands that news be more profitable, news of war was no exception. As coverage of the world began to shrink, what little remained was augmented through the use of persuasion and entertainment. In the long process that turned foreign news into entertainment, the public has been (re)placed and (re)positioned in front of the empowering images that tell a different type of story. As news is gathered in the commercial borderlands between politics and entertainment, with no evaluative criteria as to its veracity, the movement of history is obscured and rewritten in the first draft, making it harder still to understand what is real.

In *Mythologies*, Roland Barthes (1976) noted the ability of myth to transform the meaning of history. First, through the restricting of information, it must be drained and emptied of its historical truth. Then the hollow shell can be transformed into something else, repackaged according to the cultural mythologies of the day. Throughout his presidency, George W. Bush used the images and icons of American commercial culture to repackage the meaning of war. This feat could only have been accomplished in the historical void left by the media presentation of the world. Only without a history and politics of war could Bush-era stagecraft have succeeded in distracting the press and the public from the truths hidden behind its appealing surfaces.

MILITAINMENT AND BUSH-ERA STAGECRAFT

The long history of commercial media culture helped fashion the president's mythic persona. As presidential historian Douglas Brinkley noted on msnbc.com (December 5, 2003), "He's adopted all the image making that our Hollywood and Madison Avenue society has given us; he's the Marlboro Man." Bush has merely played the role of a cowboy in a white hat out to destroy evil. Such American icons have been the stuff of media culture for decades, but in recent years, employed as presidential stagecraft, they have become indistinguishable from political leadership and accepted by the media establishment as legitimate. Every aspect of the image creation of George W. Bush was accepted and celebrated, discredited only after it had achieved its purpose to such ill effects. Just as militainment is now a feature of establishment media, it serves to hide the realities of war through the controlled fictions it offers. Presidential stagecraft serves the same function. It supplants a discussion of unpopular policies and increasingly undemocratic governing practices. The image has triumphed over substance, because substance has been removed from democratic discourse. Nowhere was this more evident than during the presidential election, when challenger John Kerry tried to compete with his own hero imagery while never mentioning Abu Ghraib, civilian casualties or the global economics of oil that has led to war in the Middle East.

It is an appealing proposition to lay the entire debacle for the war in Iraq at the doorstep of George W. Bush. So intemperate and belligerent a personality, and so uniquely devoted to his failed project, blaming him and moving on will no doubt become increasingly appealing to political media analysts. But George W. Bush did not write this history on his own, or create the confabulations between the military and the media developed over the last half of the twentieth century.[9]

The media celebrated the president's western mystique and his "wanted dead or alive" bluster and believed it was leadership, the mission-accomplished flight was accepted as victory, and the Norman Rockwell turkey moment substituted for authentic expression. Only the reality of death and the true failure of leadership revealed those images to be false, and only when Cindy Sheehan camped outside the Crawford ranch, did she transform its meaning from strength to weakness.

DEMOCRACY AND HUMANISM

It is understandable living through the Great War and supporting it, that Walter Lippmann could became disillusioned with the democratic process. He saw a public persuaded into supporting something previously unimaginable. Yet the war was far more a failure of elected leaders and the press than the democratic process. Information was turned into persuasion, and like today, the checks and balances of institutional and governing structures were redirected toward autocratic theories and practices. Journalist George Seldes also lived through World War I, and looking back, he came to a different conclusion about the people, the press and democracy. In his autobiography, *Witness to a Century* (1987, xxi), Seldes quotes Abraham Lincoln, and reaffirms an unabashed dedication to democratic principles and faith in the public to determine its own history, "I am a firm believer in the people," said Mr. Lincoln; "if given the truth, they can be depended upon to meet any national crisis. The great point is to bring them the real facts."

The American press has broken its sacred bond with the public by not reporting the facts or checking the veracity of official pronouncements. But they have failed the people in another, equally important way. They have silenced the voices of the people themselves. When members of the public are featured, their opinions are either discredited or used to confirm the predetermined points made in the news. From across the country, those who occupy different social positions, those who work in vastly different settings, those of different faiths who make up the majority of people in this country, have not been heard.

Most profound has been the silencing of the voices of dissent. Activists, teachers, artists, intellectuals and citizens from all walks of life have opposed the war in Iraq—loudly, eloquently, visually and verbally. They have organized vigils, taken bus tours, made independent documentaries and sent packages to soldiers, among many other things. Some accepted the president's invitation to the European Union—to take a look at the conditions of the tortured detainees—and they walked to the U.S. prison in Guantanamo Bay, Cuba. Public interest lawyers have worked at the Center for Constitutional Rights, the American Civil Liberties Union and human rights organizations all over the globe to try and stop the inhuman practices of torture that make the world a more dangerous place. Women's organizations have brought women from Iraq to speak of what life is like living under occupation. They tell stories of delivering babies at home without access to medical treatment because of military curfews. They speak in compelling ways that evoke empathy for individuals, such as the young Iraqi who will never stand again, maimed for a lifetime by a stray bullet. These are stories far different from the tale of Jessica Lynch.

The media fail the American public in another tragic way. As the world watches the images of mutilated bodies and listens to debates and condemnations from across the globe—from the Middle East, to Europe and Great Britain—Americans hear almost nothing. They know little of people like Craig Murray, the British diplomat who quit his post as Ambassador to Uzbekistan after learning that the servitude demanded by the country's economic structure was kept in place by horrific acts of torture supported by the American government, "I would rather die than have someone tortured to save my life," Murray said after leaving his post.[10] Instead of engaging the country in a discussion able to pose the dignity of the human person against the politics of fear in a manner worthy of a great nation, the media invite Americans to sit passively entertained, watching a trusted television character engage in torture to purportedly save the world.

As Iraq begins a descent into civil war as a consequence Operation Iraqi Freedom, American film culture has begun to reflect the war and the national atmosphere created by it, in the works most notably of George Clooney. As producer of the Edward R. Murrow biofilm, *Good Night and Good Luck* (2005), Clooney returned to the story of a courageous journalist who exposed the worst excesses of the repressive culture of McCarthyism and the Cold War. While there are journalists who risk their lives and challenge the censorious environment of the War on Terrorism, the film reminds us that Murrow has no contemporary equivalent in network television. Clooney received the Academy Award for best supporting actor for his role as the CIA agent in *Syriana*, a film whose dark and confusing story mirrors the black world of Middle Eastern foreign policy and the politics of oil. As a notable first attempt to begin the feature-film counter-narratives of the war in Iraq, the movie nevertheless portrays the CIA agent as the victim of gruesome torture. The courage to tell the story of Iraq in the way filmmakers came to terms with Vietnam will require a narrative perspective able to express the experiences of Iraqi victims of American torture. This will be left to future filmmakers.

By the twenty-first century, news outside the misleading debates of Washington is found predominantly on alternative media outlets, in art galleries and public forums and on the Internet. Mainstream commercial media exclude the vast majority of these multiple publics, or relegate them to the margins, buried in the back pages, or flashed across screens as bits of fleeting images and confused sound bites. The media no longer listen to the people they are mandated to serve. They rarely register opposing opinions or respond to the sound of public voices and they seem to have forgotten what the face of democracy looks like.

Most tragically, they have forgotten the soldiers. As filmmaker Patricia Foulkrod found, the silent suffering of soldiers was profound and pervasive: "I knew I had to show just how insidious the effects of killing in combat are—whether in self-defense or not—and to create a dialogue about how we can change our 'consciousness of killing.'" She wanted to create a work that encourages people to "wrap their arms around our soldiers and their families...so we can take responsibility for their suffering, that is being experienced in our name." There is little room for reflection, compassion or responsibility in the world created by American commercial media. The culture that creates militainment also creates an atmosphere devoid of real empathy, humanity or responsibility. These are precisely the voices that form the heart and soul of American democracy. Only if such voices are commonly invited into the debate and taken seriously will the media be able to claim it has fulfilled its mandate to the public.

With decisions of war and peace, democracy and humanity are inseparable. If America is to live up to its democratic principles, the process of war must be made transparent. If seeing "war as it really is," turns the public against war, then a democratic process will put an end to war. Those who wish to perpetuate war have also declared war on freedom of thought, expression and emotional autonomy. Cindy Sheehan's words to George W. Bush reverberated so sharply through the social fabric because they began to expose the economics and fictions of war. America pays too high a price when soldiers are recruited through video-game persuasions from the ranks of the economically disadvantaged with promises of economic security. If war is so essential, then leaders who make the call must also be willing to send their children to fight. By the twenty-first century, humanity and democracy demand that if the threat posed by any enemy is not great enough to merit also sending the sons and daughters of elites, then negotiation and diplomacy will have to take the place of war. When media call for war, they must take some degree of responsibility for its consequences and they are obligated to report truthfully on its outcomes. Militainment does not fulfill the media's democratic mandate, any more than does the simple dissemination of government proclamations.

Notes

Introduction

1. Subsequent reports on prisoner abuse based on testimonials from prisoners were printed only after the pictures were released, even though journalists were aware of their stories earlier.
2. See, "Chain of Command: How the Department of Defense Mishandled the Disaster at Abu Ghraib," *The New Yorker* (May 17, 2004).
3. Cited in the *New York Times* (May 16, 2004), sec. 2, p. 1.
4. See "Hollywood Victory," distributed by Paper Tiger Television, New York.
5. On June 1, 2004, *America's Army: Special Forces* was introduced, the latest release in the series that—according to the Army's web page—"continues to focus on the crucial, specialized role of the Army's special forces...as they fight the Global War on Terrorism."
6. Personal communication with the author (August 24, 2004). New York City.

Chapter One

1. Clark's research is cited in Sproule (1997, 11).
2. A favorite mailing list was compiled from *Who's Who in America*, resulting in over two hundred thousand names.
3. As Knightley (2002, 112–13) points out, "knowing the reverence of the Chinese for ancestors and the uncertainty of Chinese opinion toward the Germans, he sent the photographs to Shanghai for release, hoping the story would be 'played back' to Europe."
4. The most notable example was the Reverend Hillis of Plymouth Church Brooklyn, an orator in high demand who spoke frequently at Liberty Bond rallies, reciting a litany of German atrocity stories. Yet in late 1914 he had been a champion of the

League to Limit Armaments, a peace group fighting the increase in U.S. military spending.

5. Miller would go on to establish the Institute for Propaganda Analysis in 1937. For a fascinating discussion of the interactions between Miller and Debs, see Sproule (1997, 1–6).

6. "In July 1914, 30 percent of the front page news from Europe originated in German sources as contrasted to 4 percent during the last half of August" (Sproule 1997, 6).

7. CPI also distributed soft news from the division of Syndicated Features written by a staff of literati that included Booth Tarkington and Wallace Irwin. Ironically, one regular column, "The Daily German Lie," made undocumented accusations about the Germans' use of propaganda.

8. Gibbs would later offer in his defense a now-familiar explanation for keeping the truth from the public: that reporting the deaths of soldiers would be detrimental to the families of the victims.

9. *The History of The Times*, Vol. 4., p. 232.

10. This quote is cited in a footnote in Knightley (2002, 117).

11. *The History of The Times*, Vol. 4, p. 345.

12. One memoir by French author René Naegelen reads, "Three of us were crouching in a hole under the barrage of artillery fire. My two friends…were bleeding. The bowels of one were oozing out. The other had a broken leg; there was a red spot spreading on his breast, and he was rolling his panic-stricken eyes" (1968, 170).

13. For an interesting discussion of Bernays, see Stauber and Rampton (1995).

Chapter Two

1. This point is consistent with Ambrose's view of World War II, as demonstrated in the HBO series *Band of Brothers*, and from his book of the same name.

2. Munro told Knightley (2002, 348) in an interview that "I was committed to the war completely and utterly, right from the start…. We felt that the Germans were going to wreck this world of ours and that we would have to stop them. The troops were committed to it and I think the correspondents were—I certainly was."

3. The defeat was so great and the story so bleak that some journalists were grateful to have been censored. AP reporter Wes Gallagher wrote in a cable to his office, "What would have been an unholy mess was saved by the good sense of front line field press censors" (Oldfield 1956, 172).

4. The text of Murrow's CBS radio broadcast of April 15, 1945 is reprinted in Reporting World War II, published in 2001.

5. The text of this report was reprinted in Reporting World War II, published in 2001.

Chapter Three

1. But CBS insiders asked at the time, "How could the piece help the enemy? *They* knew what was going on" (Sperber 1998, 347).

2. Also deleted from one of the programs aired by WGBH were well-documented statements that both sides—not just North Koreans, but Americans and South Koreans—killed prisoners in the field.

3. Meray lived in Paris, having left Hungary and renounced communism after the failed revolution of 1956, in which he played "an important" role (Cumings 1992, 157).

4. Brian Duffy, Executive Editor at *U.S. News & World Report*, spearheaded criticism of the reporting.

Chapter Four

1. Cited in Aronson (1970, 243), this account was published in the alternative magazine *Ramparts*. Aronson argues that *Newsweek's* coverage was better than most, though it was irregular and confused.

2. Ellsberg (2002, 210) also states: "Tet had simply confirmed, spectacularly, much of what I had been trying to tell the government since I returned [from Vietnam]. The war was an endless, hopeless bloody stalemate. The President seemed finally to have gotten the message."

3. This quantitative measure of success grew out of the close relationship developed between the military and industry during and after World War II. Bibby (1999, 158) argues: "the government's endowment of military contracts to the largest industrial firms led to a virtual conflation of the state, industry, and the military. The military, in turn, took on the scientific views of research and production that privileged performance models." What the military produced was a high number of dead bodies. "Consequently, the literal signification of the human body, and by extension, subjectivity, collapses into a catalogue of integers" (Bibby 1999, 158).

4. Ironically, Aronson (1970, 244) argues that battle fatigue "was increasingly in evidence among United States officials in both Saigon and Washington in 1968, and there were signs of shell-shock," especially after Tet.

5. See Engelhardt (1995, 218). For this account of My Lai, a subhamlet of Son My village, I have drawn heavily from Tom Engelhardt's account of the massacre that appears on pages 215–27.

6. This term is used by Daniel Berrigan (2004) in his play *The Trial of the Catonsville Nine*.

7. Aronson (1970, 232) documents other journalists such as Hanson Baldwin and Joseph Alsop, who also criticized their peers' coverage of Vietnam in 1966, warning that the war was being lost at home, like the Algerian war. He also notes that after David Halberstam stopped reporting for *Time*, "the Press corps in Vietnam became much more acceptable to American officialdom."

8. While it may be true, as some critics argue after looking at the context of the director's overall work, that Kubrick holds a dark, Hobbesian view of human nature, *Full Metal* is also specifically about how war brings out that side of human destructive force.

Chapter Five

1. This well-recognized criticism of news coverage inspired the title of a book by journalist Mort Rosenblum (1979).

2. This terminology was used during the time the author did field research with a freelance network-news crew on assignment in El Salvador at the beginning of 1980.

3. There are numerous articles and books that discuss the topic of television news as entertainment. See Altheide (1976), Postman (1984) and Rapping (1987). The news crew the author worked with would often acknowledge that they were looking for exciting footage.

4. Law-and-order news, as Bazalgette and Paterson (1980–81, 63) have also noted, makes use of "a particular kind of narrative in which the disruption is unmotivated."
5. Americas Watch Committee and the American Civil Liberties Union (1982, xxxiii).
6. Cited in Armstrong and Shenk (1982).
7. Americas Watch Committee and the American Civil Liberties Union (1982, xxiv).
8. The archbishop was interviewed shortly before his death, and these words appear on the documentary videotape *Enemies of War* (1999), produced and directed by Esther Cassidy.

Chapter Six

1. Former *New York Times* reporter Chris Hedges tells of small pieces of paper stuffed inside the mouths of corpses addressed to journalists as a warning.
2. He was afraid they might be ambushed by the military, as four Dutch journalists would be two months later as they traveled with the guerrillas. I am indebted to Mark Danner for his excellent book *The Massacre at El Mozote*, on which I draw heavily for this account.
3. Cited in Danner (1994).
4. Cited in (Danner 1994, 101).
5. As Bonner reported, "A spokesman from the Salvadoran armed forces, Col. Alfonso Cotto, called the reports about 'hundreds of civilians' being killed by government soldiers 'totally false.' Those reports were fabricated by 'subversives,' he said." The *Post* included a statement by the Salvadoran Ambassador in Washington: "I reject emphatically that the Army of El Salvador was engaged in killing women and children. It is not within the armed institution's philosophy to act like that."
6. After the massacre, most peasants who did not join the guerrilla forces fled the country to become refugees in Honduras.
7. And on his way shortly after to a congressional prayer breakfast in Washington, when told by Ambassador Hinton to be prepared to respond to questions about a massacre at El Mozote, he said, "I'll deny it and prove it fabricated." As it turned out, the American government helped him attempt to do just that.
8. In fact, the guerrillas had also offered Todd Greentree, the junior recording officer at the embassy, safe conduct to the site. "I knew the guerrillas would never have masqueraded something like this, would never have fabricated it, if they were offering safe conduct. I was convinced that something had gone on and that it was bad." From an interview done by Mark Danner (1994, 95).
9. True but misleading, this assertion refuses to acknowledge that both Bonner and Guellermoprieta, as well as Greentree and McKay, had talked to survivors from the towns in the surrounding area. El Mozote was the main killing arena, but not the only one, and peasants from other places had fled there in the belief that they would be protected.
10. Personal communication with photojournalist John Hoagland, 1982.
11. One PR strategy was to initiate recreational baseball games between the embassy staff and reporters.
12. A quote from Jim McGovern, then-aide to Congressman Joseph Moakley (D-Mass.), in *Enemies of War* (1999).
13. Among them, General Juan Bustillo, head of the Air Force, and General Emilio Ponce, Minister of Defense.

14. By November 1991, Tutela Legal, the Salvadoran human rights organization, had published the first comprehensive investigation of El Mozote and included the name of the 794 murdered persons.

15. It goes on to state: "In this case, we cannot accept the excuse that senior commanders knew nothing of what had happened."

16. In 1971, while the British government was still supporting official policies toward Northern Ireland, British newspapers began to carry explicit pictures of the war there, prompting the media critic John Berger (1980, 38) to ask the same question.

17. From discussions the author had with photojournalists covering Central America.

18. The camera was heralded as the tool that could deliver scientific data without subjective interference. It was viewed as the most accurate mechanism for revealing the physical world, the lens of the camera being considered more accurate than the lens of the human eye. For a complete discussion of the history of photography, see Newhall (1982) and Kracauer (1960).

19. John Berger (1980, 1982) and Susan Sontag (1977, 2003).

20. For a discussion of how the media coverage from El Salvador during 1982 focused on the pragmatic military concerns of the U.S.-backed Salvadoran army and its ability to win the war, see Massing (1983). The cover of the journal also has, interestingly, the image of a helicopter gunship.

21. This idea is grounded in an analysis done by John Berger, who has observed that the paintings of Francis Bacon contain the message that "the worst has already happened" (1980, 117).

22. Sontag (1977, 19).

23. For a discussion of the aggressive attitude of the frontal pose, see Sontag (1977, 35–36).

24. See, for example, Mattison, Meiselas and Rubenstein (1983).

25. Photojournalists working for the agencies do take these types of pictures. As Helen Hoagland, John's mother, commented, "You can't believe the horror. I call them his gruesome...pictures. And yet his best pictures are of the children. But they're not the ones that get published, the children that are in the camps and the hospitals, the loving pictures." (From an interview with Helen Hoagland in a video documentary on the life of John Hoagland, *John Hoagland: Front Line Photographer*.)

26. It was published in a book entitled *Listen, Companero*, analyzing the war in El Salvador (CENSA and Solidarity Publications, 1983).

Chapter Seven

1. For a more detailed discussion of American public opinion toward Central American policy, see LeoGrande (1984).

2. Walter Raymond officially resigned from the CIA in April 1983, and he continually tried to get William Casey "out of the loop" in an attempt to bypass restrictions placed on the CIA from engaging in the manipulation of American public opinion and political processes.

3. Mayer and McManus (1988, 43) report that Wirthlin's "services cost the Republican National Committee, which shared the polls with the White House, an estimated $1 million per year—far more than had ever been paid to a pollster before."

4. NSC Intelligence Document (1985).

5. Such strategies are now commonly employed, but were only beginning to be developed in the 1980s.

6. A few attending Latin Americanists challenged his characterizations, pointing out that Mr. Leiken was not providing independent analysis and background but was simply repeating unsubstantiated allegations that had already appeared in the press.

7. Interview with the author, January 1987.

8. One of the most interesting cases of the misuse of photojournalism involves an image of Miskito Indians. The picture of Indian corpses being burned was presented to Congress as evidence of Sandinista human rights violations during the 1980s. The picture was actually taken earlier, under the Somoza regime that was responsible for persecution of the Indians.

9. Interview with the author, October 2, 1986.

10. See *The Nation*, June 20, 1987, 855, and after the *Times* article, though not reported subsequently, *The Nation*, October 17, 1987.

11. Analysis of the *New York Times* and *Christian Science Monitor* coverage included the four-month period beginning on January 1 and concluding on April 30, 1986. The time period included the initiation of the request and the first House and Senate vote on aid to the contras.

12. In contracting with outside groups, the General Accounting Office also found that the head of the OPD, Mr. Reich, violated "federal regulations governing contractual procedures" (United States General Accounting Office, 1987).

13. See FAIR, Action Alert: Reviving Cold War Reporting on Nicaragua, (April 5, 2005).

Chapter Eight

1. For the full text see *State Department Bulletin* 76 (December 1983): "Ambassador Kirkpatrick's Statement, UN Security Council. October 17, 1983." This quote appears on page 83.

Chapter Nine

1. Coverage of the Christic Institute lawsuit was judged one of the ten most censored stories of 1986 by Project Censored at Sonoma State University. For an account of the substance of the Christic Institute's lawsuit against the "secret team," see Cockburn (1987).

2. The "super-troopers" portrayal of the central characters Elias and Barnes in *Platoon* is part of Hollywood's myth of the masculine, an image mirrored by Oliver North. Elias and Barnes are proficient warriors with martial arts skills that afford them the ability to survive while others less skilled perish. As Vietnam veteran Cawley observed, the sobering war experience tends to change attitudes toward tough-guy myths. They can die from an ambush or artillery fire as easily as anyone else. Certain skepticism replaces the mythology of toughness in face of the horror of the indiscriminate destruction of human life in war.

3. As Browne (1979, 8) points out, "Smith confronts his central problem: the direct conflict between his role dictated by a theory of representation rooted in popular democracy and a commitment to a more individualized and personal ethic.... The commitment that sustains him and that justifies his turning away from the *vox popula* is the belief in his power to animate the dead words of the legendary figures of

the American Political Tradition.... He assumes the role of speaker, with full self-presence, in command of the lessons or spirit of the tradition."
4. Testimony given to the Iran/Contra Investigating Committee televised live on July 14, 1987. Robert McFarlane had testified earlier but requested to testify again on this date in order to refute some of the testimony given by Oliver North.
5. NBC News/*Wall Street Journal* poll broadcast on July 13, 1987.
6. For example, it is known that the public diplomacy operations were headed by a longtime veteran of CIA overseas-propaganda work, Walter Raymond. Iran/Contra investigators retrieved Oliver North's diary and found that he had held over seventy strategy sessions with Raymond.

Chapter Eleven
1. Study done by Fairness and Accuracy in Reporting, New York, NY.
2. Cited in the *Los Angeles Times*, January 12, 1991.
3. Cited in the *Los Angeles Times*, January 10, 1991.
4. Panel on "The Media and the Gulf War," Suffolk University, aired on C-SPAN, February 23, 1991.
5. Headline, *New York Daily News*, February 27, 1991.

Chapter Twelve
1. On-camera interviews were included in a videotape entitled *Counterfeit Coverage*, made by independent media producer David Shulman.
2. Cited in *Ann Arbor News*, February 16, 1991.

Chapter Fifteen
1. Later that night, when I finally got through to my friends in SoHo, I heard their sorrow at seeing dozens of people crowded at the windows on the floors with no exit routes. A man very near the top had waved a white cloth through a broken window for at least forty-five minutes. He never got out. After seven hours of watching television, I had not heard any such stories.
2. See "9/11," by Deep Dish Television, 2001, New York City; and "From Tragedy to War," Paper Tiger Television, 2001, New York City.
3. See Arianna Huffington, "Land of the Free?" September 24, 2001. Alternet.org.

Chapter Sixteen
1. BBC News online, www.news.bbc.co.uk/hi/english/entertainmnet/reviews.
2. As part of our daily diet, we are far less sensitive to images of violence than we were in the 1940s, a stunning confirmation of the notion of desensitization.
3. BBC News online, www.news.bbc.co.uk/hi/english/entertainmnet/reviews.

Chapter Seventeen
1. In the words of Jim Hightower, "Imagine Eisenhower, or Kennedy, or even Bush the Elder—all of whom were real war heroes—resorting to such a political stunt" (Alternet, May 20, 2003).
2. Personal telephone communication with the author, February 26, 2003.

3. For a thorough discussion of the role of the pool journalists during the First Gulf War, see MacArthur (1992).
4. Personal communication with the author.
5. Personal communication with the author.
6. London newspaper *The Independent*'s Robert Fisk said the deaths "look very much like murder."
7. Personal communication with the author.

Chapter Eighteen

1. DARPA is the DOD agency responsible for the development of the Internet.
2. For production perspective, one of the biggest companies in this industry, Electronic Arts, makes one in every four video games, and has "twice as many in-house game developers as Disney has animators" (Burston 2003, 164).
3. John Milius, scriptwriter for *Apocalypse Now*, and Randal Kleiser, who directed *Honey, I Shrunk the Kids*, have also worked with the team (Hart, 2001).
4. AT $258 million apiece, that makes the F-22 "the most expensive fighter jet in history" (*New York Times*, November 28, 2004). By January 2005, some cuts were made to the defense budget and the F-22.
5. One advertisement for the new breed of video games featuring the war on terrorism, *Tactical Ops: Assault on Terror*, features the question written in white lettering over a black background: "Dad, where is Afghanistan?"; below, the answer: "Level 4, son."

Chapter Nineteen

1. This method was designed by Marc Harold, who meticulously documented the deaths of Afghan civilians in a study also discredited by the U.S. press. See chapter 15.
2. Nor could the Americans provide even basic services to the population, some of whom did welcome the end of Saddam's rule.
3. See Dahr Jamail Iraq Dispatches http://dahrjamailiraq.com/gallery/view_album. php?set_albumName=album28
4. See *Fallujah*, produced by Deep Dish TV and Code Pink 2005. www.deepdishtv. org.
5. *Fallujah: The Hidden Massacre*, produced by Sigfrido Ranucci and Maurizio Torrealta, and broadcast on Italian state television network, RAI in November 2005.
6. Many bodies were not being buried, as Jamail (Sunday Herald, November 12, 2004) quoted eyewitness Ahmed Abdulla, a 21 year-old student whose father has been denied exit from Fallujah like all other civilian men of "fighting age," described that "shops had even been bombed; bodies with arms and legs lying near them were tossed about on the sidewalks in places just after the bombs fell. I still can't get the smell of dead bodies to leave me."
7. *Fallujah: The Hidden Massacre*
8. From the video documentary *Fallujah: The Hidden Massacre*.
9. Dr Salem Ismael, who led an aid convoy into Fallujah in February 2004, photographed the dead, including children, and interviewed remaining residents. He said to reporters, "The accounts I heard ... will live with me forever. You may think you know what happened in Fallujah, but the truth is worse than you could possibly have imagined (Porter, 2005).

10. Englehart goes on to say "And this is why protective masks do not help, because it will burn right through the mask. It will manage to get inside your face. If you breathe it, it will blister your throat and your lungs until you suffocate, and then it will burn you from the inside. It basically reacts to skin, oxygen and water. The only way to stop the burning is with wet mud. But at that point, it's just impossible to stop."

11. But the United States refused to be a signature to Protocol III of the 1980 Convention on Certain Conventional Weapons that prohibits use of the substance as an incendiary weapon against civilian populations and in air attacks against military forces in civilian areas. Ironically, these chemical weapons of mass destruction have now been used on Iraqis by the United States.

12. As the *Times* (September 24, 2005) reported, "Some soldiers beat prisoners to vent their frustrations, one sergeant said, recalling an instance when an off-duty cook showed up at the detention area and ordered a prisoner to grab a metal pole and bend over. 'He told him to bend over and broke the guy's leg with a mini-Louisville Slugger that was a metal bat.'"

13. Before he committed suicide he told his sister Debra, "Your brother's a murderer." His mother believes he took his life because, "He did something, or saw something, that destroyed him" (Moses, 2004).

Chapter Twenty

1. Conason asked, "Are Americans so jaded about the deceptions perpetrated by our own government to lead us into war in Iraq that we are no longer interested in fresh and damning evidence of those lies? Or are the editors and producers who oversee the American news industry simply too timid to report that proof on the evening broadcasts and front pages?" Cited by Jackie Schechner on CNN, May 6, 2005.

2. It would be up to Tony Blair to convince George W. Bush that only by going to the United Nations and having the Security Council pass a resolution would war become acceptable. Cheney and other pro-war officials in the U.S. were against this, because they understood correctly that it might backfire if no weapons were found. Blair succeeded in persuading George W. Bush to take the "U.N. route."

3. The same day, *USA Today* reported that "A simmering controversy over whether American media have ignored a secret British memo about how President Bush built his case for war with Iraq bubbled over into the White House on Tuesday." Certainly "building a case" for war is quite different from fabricating justifications for one. Such downplaying of the significance of the mendacity revealed by the memo was endemic in the U.S. media.

4. Though, with the memo, the head of British intelligence was now on record as saying in 2002 that the invasion was inevitable, "but the intelligence and facts were being fixed around the policy," a *Washington Post* (June 15, 2005) editorial nevertheless made the following claim: "The memos provide no information that would alter the conclusions of multiple independent investigations on both sides of the Atlantic, which were that U.S. and British intelligence agencies genuinely believed Iraq possessed weapons of mass destruction and that they were not led to that judgment by the Bush Administration." Not only were the memos "new, damning information," the investigations referred to by the *Post* were inconclusive documents, a fact the *Post* (July 10, 2005) had reported a year before. The investigation of the Senate Select Committee on Intelligence was limited in scope and made "no judgment on whether the administration distorted the intelligence it was given." And then only a month

before the minutes were leaked, the *Post* (April 1, 2005) reported similar restrictions on another investigation: "The panel that Bush appointed under pressure in February 2004 said it was 'not authorized' to explore the question of how the commander in chief used faulty information to make perhaps the most critical decision of his presidency." These politicized investigations are highly flawed and will most certainly be defined historically as the first post-invasion public relations strategies and official obfuscations. The *Post* editorial is an attempt to solidify a favorable historical interpretation of the war and its coverage using official reports as a foundation, but with full knowledge that those reports were little more than post-invasion cover-ups.

5. FAIR Media Advisory (June 17, 2005). "Justifying the Silence on the Downing Street Memos."

6. See FAIR Media Advisory (February 27, 2003). The date of FAIR's preceded the date of the Newsweek article because the material was published by *Newsweek* before the publication date list on the magazine.

7. The *Newsweek* online version added a subhead that undercut the critical point of the story: "Before his death, a high-ranking defector said Iraq had not abandoned its WMD ambitions."

8. Interview with the author, January 20, 2006.

9. See FAIR Activism Update, "Post Explains Wing Nuts Label." http://www.fair.org/index.php?page=2561

Chapter Twenty-One

1. This was done to create fear in the Vietnamese, who believed that their souls would be lost if their bodies were mutilated.

2. A member of Military Families Speak Out, she spoke in New York City on September 19, 2005. Recorded by the author.

3. Military Families Speak Out, September 19, 2005.

4. Not surprisingly, these numbers diverge dramatically from other wars of the twentieth century. The largest majority of the public, 90 percent, believes World War II was a just cause.

5. By the end of 2004, the Bush administration had gained ground in establishing its vision of war. Noting this phenomenon, Michael Tomasky, writing in *The American Prospect*, put it this way: "Only in 2004—after September 11, with American soldiers engaged in combat on two fronts, and with martial rhetoric for the incumbent administration a daily feature of national life—did the numbers change. But even then, they changed just a little: 62 percent still consider Vietnam unjust, while 33 percent defend it" (2004, 19).

6. Kissinger's piece, entitled "Lessons for an Exit Strategy" (A19), is significant in its entirety as a comparison between exiting Iraq and Vietnam. In it he offers glossy interpretations of the war and—hardly surprisingly—omits his role in the bombing of Laos and Cambodia.

7. The song "Sweet Neo Con," appears on the LP *A Bigger Bang*, and includes the following lines: "You call yourself a Christian, I call you a hypocrite/You call yourself a patriot, well I think you're full of sh*t.

8. And torture makes Americans more vulnerable, as military strategist Anthony Cordesman told the Council on Foreign Relations, terrorists are going to use the images of Abu Ghraib "for years to come...and find ways of tying this to all their

conspiracy theories and hostile images of the West. And the end result is that they will be tools for insurgents and extremists and terrorists" (cited in Danner 2004, 48).

9. Sgrena had covered the battle of Fallujah. U.S. Army accounts assert that the convoy was given ample warning before troops opened fire. Sgrena, who was seriously wounded, denies those claims.

Conclusion

1. The film is an expanded feature from Foulkrod's first film, *The Ground Truth: The Human Cost of War*, and was featured at the Sundance Film Festival in January 2006. Information on the film can be found at: http://www.thegroundtruth.org/film.html

2. Visuals of this military ceremony that show Colin Powel shaking hands with and thanking Salvadoran Military officials after the Salvadoran Armed Forces they were found guilty of atrocities against the Salvadoran people, including those massacred at El Mozote, can be seen on the documentary, *Enemies of War.*

3. Hallinan (2001) reports that Negroponte's words were met with a "studied silence" by Latin American Delegates. "It is hard to cheer when you're gritting your teeth."

4. Such revelations were only reported in the Alternative Press. See Sudetic, 2001.

5. Dick Cheney became the Secretary of Defense in 1989 and presided over the First Gulf War with David Addington as his special assistant. Cheney later appointed Addington to serve as his general council.

6. Indeed, thousands of people marched in New York City on August 29, 2004 CNN presented a profile of Richard Cheney that sounded so similar to promotion that it could have been produced as a celebrity puff piece. In spite of this media deference to undeserved civic stature, the American people have been able to evaluate the actions and attitudes of the vice-president for themselves, and they hold opinions of Richard Cheney that are among the lowest of any elected officials in the history of America. Yet Cheney's unfavorable ratings were registered even before he shot Austin lawyer Harry M. Whittington in a hunting incident that became a proxy debate on the vice-president himself.

7. Fear of the further loss of credibility may be another reason media organizations refuse even now to correct the deceptions that propelled the war in Iraq. To do so would implicate them as well.

8. For an excellent discussion of America's role in the Middle East, see Resurrecting Empire by Rashid Khalidi (2004).

9. Though when he assumed, office George W. Bush promoted and escalated the interconnections between military contractors and the executive branch as public money flowed into the funding of military technologies.

10. Statements made at Session 2, International Commission of Inquiry on Crimes Against Humanity (January 20–22), The Riverside Church, New York City.

References

Aid, Matthew (2006). "Declassification in Reverse." (February 21) The National Security Archive. http://www.gwu.edu/~nsarchiv/NSAEBB/NSAEBB179/

Alterman, Eric (2004). "When Presidents Lie." *The Nation*, (October 25) pp. 20–26.

Altheide, David L. (1976). *Creating Reality: How TV Distorts Events*. Beverly Hills: Sage.

Ambrose, Stephen E. (2001). Preface. *Reporting World War II: American Journalism 1938–1946*. New York: The Library of America. pp. xv–xvii.

Americas Watch Committee and the American Civil Liberties Union (1982). *Report on Human Rights in El Salvador*. New York: Random House.

Amnesty International Report (1980). *Report on El Salvador*. London: A1 Publications.

Armstrong, Robert, and Janet Shenk (1982). *El Salvador: The Face of Revolution*. Boston: South End Press.

Armstrong, Robert, and Philip Wheaton (1982). *Reform and Repression: U.S. Policy in El Salvador 1950 through 1981*. San Francisco: Solidarity Publications.

Aronson, James (1970). *The Press and the Cold War*. New York: The Bobbs-Merrill Company.

Auster, Albert (2002). "Saving Private Ryan and American Triumphalism." *Journal of Popular Film and Television* 30,2 (Summer) pp. 98–104.

Auster, Albert, and Leonard Quart (1988). *How the War Was Remembered: Hollywood and Vietnam*. New York: Praeger.

Barnouw, Erik (1975). *Tube of Plenty: The Evolution of American Television*. New York: Oxford University Press.

———(1993). *Documentary: A History of the Non-Fiction Film*. New York: Oxford University Press.

Barthes, Roland (1976). *Mythologies*. New York: Hill and Wang.

Bayley, Edwin (1981). *Joe McCarthy and the Press*. New York: Pantheon Books.

Bazalgette, Cary, and Richard Paterson (1980–81). "Real Entertainment: The Iranian Embassy Siege." *Screen Education* 37 (Winter): 55–67.

Beck, Robert (2004). "Grenada's Echoes in Iraq: International Security and International Law." *The Long Term View* 2,6: 73–87.

Beidler, Philip D. (1999). "The Last Huey." In *The Vietnam War and Postmodernity*, ed. Michael Bibby. Amherst: University of Massachusetts Press. 3–16.

Belli, Humberto (1984). *Nicaragua: Christians under Fire*. Garden City: The Puebla Institute.

Benaim, Daniel, Priyanka Motaparthy, and Vishesh Kumar (2003). "TV's Conflicted Experts." *The Nation*, April 21.

Bennett, W. Lance (2003). *News: The Politics of Illusion*. New York: Longman. Fifth Edition.

Berger, John (1980). *About Looking*. New York: Pantheon Books.

Berger, John, and John Mohr (1982). *Another Way of Telling*. New York: Pantheon Books.

Berrigan, Daniel (2004). *The Trial of the Catonsville Nine*. New York: Fordham University Press.

Bibby, Michael (1999). "The Post-Vietnam Condition." In *The Vietnam War and Postmodernity*, ed. Michael Bibby. Amherst: University of Massachusetts Press. 143–71.

Black, George (1991). "Rolodex Army Wages a Nintendo War: TV's Deskbound Generals Tune Out on the Crucial Issues--Morality, Economics, Values." *Los Angeles Times*. (January 27). p. 7.

Boggs, Carl (2003). "Outlaw Nation: The Legacy of U.S. War Crimes." In *Masters of War: Militarism and Blowback in the Era of American Empire*, ed. Carl Boggs. New York: Routledge. 191–226.

Bonner, Raymond (1984). *Weakness and Deceit*. New York: Times Books.

Bowden, Mark (2000). *Black Hawk Down: A Story of Modern War*. New York: Penguin Books.

Bowden, Mark (2002). "The True Story of Black Hawk Down." The History Channel. Documentary directed by David Keane. Produced for the History Channel by 44 Blue Productions and Wild Eyes Productions. Aired January 21, 2002.

Boyer, Peter J. (1987). "North Outdraws the Top Show on Daytime TV." *New York Times*, July 11.

Braestrup, Peter (1978). *Big Story: How the American Press and Television Reported and Interpreted the Crisis of Tet 1968 in Vietnam and Washington*. New Haven: Yale University Press.

Broadcasting (1987). "Media Follow the North Star." 113(2), July 13, pp. 23–26.

Brouwer, Steve (2004). *Robbing Us Blind*. Monroe: Common Courage Press.

Brown, Ken (1982). "The Last Just War: How Just Was It?" *The Progressive*, August, pp. 18–19.

Browne, Nick (1979). "The Politics of Narrative Form: Mr. Smith Goes to Washington." *Wideangle* 3,(3) pp. 114–21.

Burston, Jonathan (2003). "War and the Entertainment Industries: New Research Priorities in an Era of Cyber-Patriotism." In *War and the Media*, eds. Daya Kishan Thussu and Des Freedman. Thousand Oaks, CA: Sage.

Butler, Judith (2004). *Precarious Life: The Powers of Mourning and Violence*. New York: Verso.

Calder, Angus (1969). *The People's War*. London: Jonathan Cape.

Campbell, Duncan (2001). "U.S. Buys Up All Satellite War Images." *Guardian Unlimited*. www.guardian.co.uk/Archive/Article/0,4273,427 8871,00.html, October 17.

Carter, Bill (1991). "Few Sponsors for TV War News." *New York Times*, February 7, pp. D1, D20.

Carter, Hodding III, (1990). "U.S. Played God in Panama and Created Its Own Devil." *The Wall Street Journal*, January 4, p. A13.

Cawley, Leo (1987). "An Ex-Marine Sees 'Platoon.'" *Monthly Review* 39,(2) pp. 6–18.

CENSA and Solidarity Publications (1983). *Listen, Companero*. San Francisco: Solidarity Publications.

Center for Constitutional Rights (1991). Federal Lawsuit, U.S. District Court: Southern District of New York, January.

Chamorro, Edgar (1987). *Packaging the Contras: A Case of CIA Disinformation*. New York: Institute for Media Analysis.

Chinnery, Philip (2000). *Korean Atrocity!: Forgotten War Crimes 1950–1953*. Annapolis: Naval Institute Press.

Chomsky, Noam (1987). *On Power and Ideology: the Managua Lectures*. Cambridge: South End Press.

Cobb, Irving, (1918). *Paths of Glory*. New York: Grosset and Dunlap.

Cockburn, Leslie (1987). *Out of Control: The Story of the Reagan Administration's Secret War in Nicaragua, the Illegal Pipeline, and the Contra Drug Connection*. Boston: Atlantic Monthly, Little Brown Co.

Coen, Rachel, and Peter Hart (2003). "Brushing Aside the Pentagon's 'Accidents': U.S. Media Minimized, Sanitized Iraq War's Civilian Toll." *EXTRA!*, May/June, pp. 17–18.

Cohn, Marjorie (2004). "Aggressive War: Supreme International Crime." Truthout.org (November 9).

Colton, David (1991). Panel on "The Media and the Gulf War." Suffolk University. (Aired on C-Span, February 23.)

Committee on Foreign Affairs, U.S. House of Representatives (1988). "Staff Report, State Department and Intelligence Community Involvement in Domestic Activities Related to the Iran/Contra Affair," September 7, p. 34.

Comptroller General of the United States to Dante Fascell, Chairman of the Committee on Foreign Affairs, House of Representatives (1987). "Legal Opinion on Issue of Alleged Lobbying and the Development and Dissemination of Propaganda," September 30, p. 10.

Conlon, James (1989). "Making Love, Not War: The Soldier Male in Top Gun and Coming Home." *Journal of Popular Film and Television*, pp. 18–27.

Creel, George (1920). *How We Advertised America*. New York: Harper & Brothers.

Crogan, Patrick (2003). "Gametime: History, Narrative, and Temporality in Combat Flight Simulator 2." In *The Videogame Theory Reader*, eds. Mark J. P. Wolf and Bernard Perron. New York: Routledge. pp. 276–301.

Cumings, Bruce (1992). *War and Television*. London: Verso.

Danner, Mark (1994). *The Massacre at El Mozote*. New York: Vintage Books.

———(2004). *Torture and Truth: America, Abu Ghraib, and the War on Terror*. New York: New York Review of Books.

———(2005). "The Secret Way to War." *The New York Review of Books*, vol. 52 no. 10, June 9.

Davis, James (1993). "Virtual Systems: Generating a New Reality." *Aerospace America* 31, (August) pp. 33.

Der Derian, James (2001). *Virtuous War: Mapping the Military-Industrial Media-Entertainment Network*. Boulder, CO: Westview Press.

Dickey, Christopher (1985). *With the Contras*. New York: Simon and Schuster.

Doob, Leonard W. (1935). *Propaganda: Its Psychology and Technique*. New York: Henry Holt.

Dower, John W. (1986). *War Without Mercy: Race and Power in the Pacific War*. New York: Pantheon.

Downie, Leonard, and Robert Kaiser (2002). *The News about the News: American Journalism in Peril*. New York: Alfred A. Knopf.

Easthope, Antony (1986). *What a Man's Gotta Do: The Masculine Myth in Popular Culture*. London: Paladin Grafton Books.

Ebert, Roger (1986). "Platoon." Rogerebert.com http://rogerebert.suntimes.com/ apps/pbcs.dll/article?AID=/19861230/REVIEWS/612300301/1023

Elliott, David (2002). "Maelstrom of War Exhausts the Heart of Fighting Men." www.msnbc.com, January 17, pp. 1–4.

Ellsberg, Daniel (2002). *Secrets: A Memoir of Vietnam and the Pentagon Papers*. New York: Penguin Books.

Emery, Erin (2005). "Incendiary Killed Ccivilians. An ex-GI Who was in Iraq Says in a Film That White Phosphorus Used by U.S. Troops Killed Women and Children in Fallujah." *Denver Post*, November 18.

Engelberg, Stephen (1987). "Aide Says North Was to Take Blame." *New York Times*, August 28.

Engelhardt, Tom (1995). *The End of Victory Culture: Cold War America and the Disillusioning of a Generation*. Amherst: University of Massachusetts Press.

Epstein, Edward J. (1975). *Between Fact and Fiction: The Problem of Journalism*. New York: Vintage Books.

Evans, Harold (1980). *Eyewitness: 25 Years through World Press Photos*. New York: William Morrow.

Eviatar, Daphne (2003). "The Press and Private Lynch." *The Nation*, July 7, pp. 18–20.

Ewen, Stuart (1988). *All Consuming Images: The Politics of Style in Contemporary Culture*. New York: Basic Books.

Federal Lawsuit (1991). U.S. District Court, Southern District of New York, January, filed by the Center for Constitutional Rights, 666 Broadway, 7th Floor, New York, NY 10012–9985, pp. 10–11.

Ferguson, Niall (1999). *The Pity of War: Explaining World War I*. New York: Basic Books.

Fiske, John (1987). *Television Culture*. New York: Methuen.

Fore, William F. (1991). "The Shadow War in the Gulf." *Media Development*, October, pp. 51–52.

Fosdick, Raymond (1932). "America at War," *Foreign Affairs*, January, pp. 316–26.

Franklin, Nancy (2005). "The Yanks Are Coming." *The New Yorker.* pp. 86–87.

Frasca, Gonzalo (2003). "Simulation Versus Narrative: Introduction to Ludolgy." In *The Videogame Theory Reader*, eds. Mark J.P. Wolf and Bernard Perron. New York: Routledge. 221–35.

Fuchs, Cynthia (1999). "What Do We Say Happened Here?" In *The Vietnam War and Postmodernity*, ed. Michael Bibby. Amherst: University of Massachusetts Press. 49–86.

———(2001). "War Games." www.Poppolitics.com.

Fulbright, J. William (1971). *The Pentagon Propaganda Machine.* New York: Vintage Books. Fussell, Paul (1975). *The Great War and Modern Memory.* Oxford: Oxford University Press.

———(1989). *Wartime: Understanding and Behavior in the Second World War.* New York: Oxford University Press.

Gabler, Neal (2002). "Seeking Perspective on the Movie Front Lines." *New York Times*, January 27, p. 4.

Gans, Herbert (1979). *Deciding What's News.* New York: Pantheon.

Gellhorn, Martha (2001). "The Battle of the Bulge." *Reporting World War II: American Journalism 1938–1946.* New York: The Library of America.

Gerson, Allan (1991). *The Kirkpatrick Mission: Diplomacy Without Apology, America at the United Nations 1981–1985.* New York: Free Press.

Gibbs, Philip (1917). *The Battle of the Somme.* London: Heinemann.

———(1920). *Now It Can Be Told.* London: Harper.

Gibson, James William (1986). *The Perfect War: The War We Couldn't Lose and How We Did.* New York: Vintage.

Goodman, Walter (1987). "At the Hearings, a Whiff of 'Déjà Vu.'" *New York Times*, July. 19 p. 27.

———(1990). "'The Unknown War,' On the Korean Conflict." *New York Times*, November 12.

Gopnik, Adam (2004). "The Big One: Historians Rethink the War to End All Wars." (August 23). *The New Yorker.* http://www.newyorker.com/critics/atlarge/?040823crat_atlarge

Gray, Chris Hables (1997). *Postmodern War: The New Politics of Conflict.* New York: Guilford Press.

Guterman, Lila (2005). "Researchers Who Rushed into Print a Study of Iraqi Civilian Deaths Now Wonder Why It Was Ignored." *The Chronicle of Higher Education*, http://chronicle.com/free/2005/01/2005012701n. htm

Halberstam, David (2001). *War in a Time of Peace: Bush, Clinton and the Generals*. New York: Scribner.

Hallin, Daniel C. (1986). *The "Uncensored War": The Media and Vietnam*. Berkeley: University of California Press.

Hallinan, Conn (2001). "Caesar's Wife: Negroponte and the War on Terrorism." *San Francisco Examiner*, (October 20).

Harold, Marc W. (2002). "Truth About Afghan Civilian Casualties Comes Only Through American Lenses for the U.S. Corporate Media." *Censored 2003: The Top 25 Censored Stories*. Peter Phillips (ed) New York: Seven Stories Press. pp. 265–94.

Hart, Hugh (2001). "Bringing Hollywood Pizzazz to Military Training." *New York Times*, November 15.

Hartung, William, and Michelle Ciarrocca (2003). "The Military-Industrial-Think Tank Complex: Corporate Think Tanks and the Doctrine of Aggressive Militarism." *The Multinational Monitor* 24,1–2 (January/February). pp. 17–20.

Hedges, Chris (2002). *War Is a Force That Gives Us Meaning*. New York: Anchor Books.

Herr, Michael (1977). *Dispatches*. New York: Vintage.

Hersey, John (1987). "The Story of Lieutenant Colonel Oliver North," by the Editors of *U.S. News and World Report*. Washington, DC.

Hersh, Seymour (2004). "Chain of Command: How the Department of Defense Mishandled the Disaster at Abu Ghraib." *The New Yorker*, (May 17)

Hertsgaard, Mark (1988). *On Bended Knee: The Press and the Reagan Presidency*. New York: Farrar, Straus & Giroux.

Hibbs, Mark D. (1991). "Dropping Saddam's Bomb." *Dateline*, A Bulletin from The Center for War, Peace, and the News Media 6,1 (January/ February).

Hickey, Neil (1998). "Money Lust: How Pressure for Profit Is Perverting Journalism." *Columbia Journalism Review*, (July/August) pp. 28–36.

Hightower, Jim (2006). "Pentagon Says Troops Unprotected." *The Hightower Lowdown*, vol. 8 no.2, February, p. 4.

Hoberman, J. (2001). "Fight Songs: Ali; Black Hawk Down; The Majestic." *The Village Voice*, (December 26) p. 81.

Hodgkins, John (2002). "In the Wake of Desert Storm: A Consideration of Modern World War II Films." *Journal of Popular Film and Television* 30, 2 (Summer) pp. 74–84.

Hollar, Julie (2004). "CNN to Al Jazeera: Why Report Civilian Deaths." *FAIR Action Alert* (April 15).

Huffington, Arianna (2001). "Land of the Free?" OverthrowTheGov.com, September 24, pp. 1–3.

Independent Commission of Inquiry on the U.S. Invasion of Panama. New York, (January 1990).

Iraq Body Count (2005). "A Dossier of Civilian Casualties in Iraq 2003–2005." http://www.iraqbodycount.net/press/pr12.php

Ireland, Doug (1990). "Press Clips: Jingo Bells." *The Village Voice*, (January 2) p. 8.

Irving, David (1963). *The Destruction of Dresden*. London: Kimber.

Jackson, Janine (2004). "War's Iconic Image a PSYOPS Creation." *EXTRA! Update*, August, p. 3.

Jamail, Dahr (2004a) "Atrocities Continue to Emerge from the Rubble of Fallujah." (May 11). http://dahrjamail.com/weblog/archives/dispatches/00002.php.

———(2004b). "Fallujah Refugees Tell of Life and Death in the Kill Zone." *The New Standard*, (December 3).

Jameson, Fredric (1991). *Postmodernism, or, The Cultural Logic of Late Capitalism*. Durham, NC: Duke University Press.

Jeffords, Susan (1989). *The Remasculinization of America: Gender and the Vietnam War*. Bloomington: University of Indiana Press.

———(1994). *Hard Bodies: Hollywood Masculinity in the Reagan Era*. New Brunswick, NJ: Rutgers University Press.

Jhally, Sut (1989). "Advertising as Religion: The Dialectic of Technology and Magic." In *Cultural Politics in Contemporary America*, eds. Ian Angus and Sut Jhally. New York: Routledge. pp. 217–29.

Keegan, John (1999). *The First World War*. New York: Alfred A. Knopf, Inc.

Kellner, Douglas (1995). *Media Culture*. New York: Routledge.

———(1999). "From Vietnam to the Gulf: Postmodern Wars?" In *The Vietnam War and Postmodernity*, ed. Michael Bibby. Amherst: University of Massachusetts Press.

———(2003). "Postmodern Military and Permanent War." In *Masters of War: Militarism and Blowback in the Era of American Empire*, ed. Carl Boggs. New York: Routledge. pp. 229–44.

Kempley, Rita (1987). "Platoon." (January 16). http://www.washingtonpost.com/wp-srv/style/longterm/movies/videos/platoonrkempley_a0cb05.htm

Kenworthy, Eldon (1987). "Selling the Policy." In *Reagan Versus the Sandinistas*, ed. Thomas W. Walker. Boulder, CO: Westview Press.

Khalidi, Rashid (2004). *Resurrecting Empire: Western Footprints and America's Perilous Path in the Middle East*. Boston: Beacon Press.

Kirtley, Jane (2001). "Enough is Enough: Journalists Should Draw the Line in the Sand to Limit the Military's Attempts at Absolute Secrecy." *Media Studies Journal: Front Lines and Deadlines, Perspectives on War Reporting*. Arlington, VA: The Freedom Forum. 15.1. (Summer) pp. 58–63.

Knightley, Phillip (2002). *The First Casualty: The War Correspondent as Hero and Myth-Maker from the Crimea to Kosovo*. Baltimore: The Johns Hopkins University Press.

Koop, Theodore (1946). *Weapon of Silence*. Chicago: University of Chicago Press.

Kornbluh, Peter (1987). *Nicaragua: The Price of Intervention*. Washington: Institute for Policy Studies.

———(1987). "The Contra Lobby." *The Village Voice*, October 13, p. 23.

Kracauer, Siegfried (1960). *Theory of Film*. New York: Oxford University Press.

LaFebre, Walter (1978). *The Panama Canal*. Oxford: Oxford University Press.

Lasswell, Harold D. (1927). *Propaganda Techniques in the World War*. New York: Kegan, Paul, Trench & Co.

Lears, Jackson (2004). "Why the Vietnam War Still Matters." *In These Times*, December 13, pp. 26–27.

Lee, Andrew (2002). "Stars and Stripes." *Talk*, (February) pp. 62–67.

Lemire, Christy (2001). "Timely, Brutal 'Black Hawk Down.'" Associated Press, www.mnnbc.com/news/678348.asp, December 27, pp. 1–5.

LeoGrande, William (1984). "Central America and the Polls: A Study of U.S. Public Opinion Polls on U.S. Foreign Policy toward El Salvador and Nicaragua under the Reagan Administration." Washington Office on Latin America.

———(1987). "The Contras and Congress." In *Reagan Versus the Sandinistas*, ed. Thomas W. Walker. Boulder, CO: Westview Press.

Lewis, Justin, Sut Jhally, and Michael Morgan (1991). *The Gulf War: A Study of the Media, Public Opinion and Public Knowledge*. University of Massachusetts, Amherst: Center for the Study of Communication.

Lippmann, Walter (1997). *Public Opinion*. New York: Free Press. (Original work published in 1922).

Lopez Vigil, Jose Ignacio (1994). *Rebel Radio: The Story of El Salvador's Radio Venceremos*. Latin American Bureau: Curbstone Press. Translated by Mark Fried.

MacArthur, John (1992). *The Second Front: Censorship and Propaganda in the Gulf War*. Berkeley: University of California Press.

MacDonald, J. Fred (1985). *Television and the Red Menace: The Video Road to Vietnam*. New York: Praeger.

MacFarquhar, Neil (2002). "Many Arabs Say Bush Misreads Their History and Goals." *New York Times*, January 31.

Mahajan, Rahul (2003). *Full Spectrum Dominance: U.S. Power in Iraq and Beyond*. New York: Seven Stories Press.

Marro, Anthony (1985). "When the Government Tells Lies." *The Columbia Journalism Review*, (March/April) pp.29–41.

Martz, Ron (2003). "Embed Catches Heat: TV Sanitized the Iraq Conflict, but a Paper Gets the Hate Mail." *Editor and Publisher.com*, pp. 5–15.

Massing, Michael (1983). "About Face on El Salvador." *Columbia Journalism Review* 22, (November/December) pp. 42–49.

——— (2004a). "Iraq, the Press, and the Election." Tomdispatch.com, (Nov. 24) htttp://www.alternet.org/story/20569/

——— (2004b). *Now They Tell Us: The American Press and Iraq*. New York: New York Review of Books.

Mattison, Harry, Susan Meiselas, and Fae Rubenstein (eds.) (1983). *El Salvador: Work of Thirty Photographers*. New York: Writers and Readers Publishing Cooperative.

Mayer, Jane (2006). "The Memo." *The New Yorker*, February 27, pp. 32–41.

Mayer, Jane and Doyle McManus (1988). *Landslide: The Unmaking of the President, 1984–1988*. Boston: Houghton Mifflin.

McNally, Terrence (2006). "Battlefield Iraq." *AlterNet*. (January 20). http://www.alternet.org/story/32053/.

Melman, Seymour (1988). *The Demilitarized Society: Disarmament and Conversion*. Montreal: Harvest House.

Miller, Johnathan (1985). (Office of Public Diplomacy) to Pat Buchanan, Director of Communications, The White House, "White Propaganda Operation," March 13, Confidential, p. 3.

Miller, Mark Crispin (ed.) (1990). *End of Story, Seeing Through Movies*. New York: Pantheon.

Mitchell, Greg (2005). "Yucking It Up in the Post." *AlterNet*, June 21. http://www.alternet.org/story/22278/.

Mitgang, Herbert (1999). "Blood and Tears," *Newsday*, July 4, B1, 11.

Montague, C. E. (1922). *Disenchantment*. London: Chatto and Windus.

Mooney, Chris (2005). "Did Our Leading Newspapers Set Too Low a Bar for a Preemptive Attack?" *Columbia Journalism Review*, (March/April) pp. 28–34.

Moorehead, Caroline (2003). *Gellhorn: A Twentieth Century Life*. New York: Henry Holt and Company.

Morganthau, Tom, and Richard Sandza (1987). "North: Felon or Fall Guy?" *Newsweek*, July 15.

Morley, Jefferson (1987). "The Paradox of North's Popularity." *The Nation*, August 15, p. 22.

Moses, Tai (2004). "Soldiers Once...And Young." *AlterNet*, (October 12). http://www.alternet.org/asoldierspeaks/20140/

Murphy, Bruce (2003). "Neoconservative Clout Seen in U.S. Iraq Policy." *Milwaukee Journal Sentinel*, April 5.

Murrow, Edward R. (2001). "Buchenwald: April 15, 1945. For Most of It I Have No Words." *Reporting World War II: American Journalism 1938–1946*. New York: The Library of America. pp. 625–29.

——— "Bombing Raid over Berlin: December 2, 1943. 'The Target Was to be the Big City.'" *Reporting World War II: American Journalism 1938–1946*. New York: The Library of America. pp. 363–70.

Naegelen, René (1968). "A Doctor's War." In *Promise of Greatness*, ed. G. A. Panichas. London: Cassell. p. 170.

Nagy, Thomas J. (2001). "The Secret Behind the Sanctions: How the U.S. Intentionally destroyed Iraq's Water Supply." *The Progressive*. 65: 9 (September).

Nathan, Debbie (1991). "Just the Good News, Please." *The Progressive*, (March). p. 26.

National Research Council (1997). *Modeling and Simulation: Linking Entertainment and Defense*. Washington, D.C.: National Academy Press. http://bob.nap.edu/html/modeling/

Newhall, Beaumont (1982). *The History of Photography*. New York: Museum of Modern Art.

NSC Intelligent Document, Oliver North to Robert C. McFarlane (1985). "Timing and the Nicaraguan Resistance Vote." March 20, p. 8.

Oldfield, B. (1956). *Never a Shot in Anger*. New York: Duell, Sloan and Pearce.

Oppel, Richard Jr. (2004). "U.S. Target of Offensive Is a Hospital," *New York Times*, (November 8).

Parry, Robert, and Peter Kornbluh (1988). "Iran-Contra's Untold Story." *Foreign Policy* 72, (Fall) pp. 3–30.

Phillips, Peter (2005). *Censored 2006: The Top 25 Censored Stories*. New York: Seven Stories Press.

——— (2004). *Censored 2005: The Top 25 Censored Stories*. New York: Seven Stories Press.

———— (2003). *Censored 2004: The Top 25 Censored Stories*. New York: Seven Stories Press.

Pollard, Tom (2003). "The Hollywood War Machine." In *Masters of War: Militarism and Blowback in the Era of American Empire*, ed. Carl Boggs. New York: Routledge. pp. 311–41.

Poole, Steven (2000). *Trigger Happy: Video Games and the Entertainment Revolution*. New York: Arcade Publishing.

Porter, Adam (2005). "Journalists Tell of US Fallujah Killings." Common Dreams News Center (March 17). http://www.commondreams.org/headlines05/0317-02.htm

Postman, Neil (1984). *Amusing Ourselves to Death*. New York: Elisabeth Sifton Books, Viking.

Postol, Theodore (1991–92). "Lessons of the Gulf War Experience with Patriot." *International Security*, 6,3 pp. 119–71.

Powers, John (2002). Review of *Black Hawk Down*. *Fresh Air*, National Public Radio, from the transcript of January 11.

Prager, Emily (1987). "Full Metal Jackoff." *The Village Voice*, July 21, pp. 43–44.

Pratt, Fletcher (1947). "How the Censors Rigged the News." *Harper's Magazine*, February, pp. 97–105.

Pyle, Ernie (2001). "The War in Tunisia," *Reporting World War II: American Journalism 1938–1946*. New York: The Library of America. pp. 288–305.

Rampton, Sheldon (2005). "War Is Fun as Hell." Alternet.org.

———— and John Stauber (2003). *Weapons of Mass Deception: The Uses of Propaganda in Bush's War on Iraq*. New York: Tarcher/Penguin.

Rapping, Elayne (1987). *The Looking Glass World of Nonfiction Television*. Boston: South End Press.

Ratner, Michael, and Ellen Ray. *Guantanamo. What the World Should Know*. White River, VT: Chelsea Green Publishing, 2004.

Reagan, Ronald (1982). "Remarks at Bridgetown, Barbados," Weekly Compilation of Presidential Documents 463, April 19.

Reeves, Dan (2004). Dan Reeves Biography. *Electronic Arts Intermix*. http://www.eai.org/eai/biography.jsp?artistID=375

Reiter, Dan, and Allan Stam (2002). *Democracies at War*. Princeton: Princeton University Press.

Rendall, Steve and Tara Broughel. "Amplifying Officials, Squelching Dissent: FAIR Study Finds Democracy Poorly Served by War Coverage." *EXTRA!* (May/June) pp. 12–14.

Rich, Frank (2001). "No News Is Good News." *New York Times*, October 13, p. A23.

——— (2005). "The Vietnamization of Bush's Vacation." *New York Times.* (August 28).

Richard, Birgit (1999). "Norm Attacks and Marine Doom." In *Ars Electronica: Facing the Future: A Survey of Two Decades*, ed. Timothy Druckrey. Cambridge, MA: MIT Press.

Richstad, Jim, and Michael Anderson (1981). *Crisis in International News.* New York: Columbia University Press.

Rosenberg, Tina (2002). "Another Hollowed Terror Ground." *New York Times Magazine.* (January 13) Sec. 6. p.26

Rosenblum, Mort (1979). *Coups and Earthquakes.* New York: Harper & Row.

Roy, Arundhati (2003). *War Talk.* Cambridge MA: South End Press.

Sacks, Jeffrey (2002). "Weapons of Mass Salvation." *The Economist.* (October 24). http://www.economist.com/opinion/displayStory. cfm?story_id=1403544

Sandlin, Lee (2001). "Losing the War." http://thislife.org/pages/trax/text/ sandlin.html.

Scheer, Robert (2001). "Many a U.S. President Pays the Pardon Piper." *Los Angeles Times*, (March 6).

Schell, Jonathan (1968). *The Military Half.* New York: Vintage.

Schell, Orville (2004). Preface. *Now They Tell Us.* New York: New York Review Books.

Schiller, Herbert I. (1973). *Mind Managers.* Boston: Beacon Press.

Schindehette, Susan (1982). "Stills: The Life and Times of Journalism's Middle Child." *Washington Journalism Review* 4, (October) pp. 18–25.

Schwarzkopf, General Norman, with Peter Petre (1992). *General H. Norman Schwarzkopf: The Autobiography: It Doesn't Take a Hero.* New York: Linda Grey, Bantam Books.

Seldes, George (1987). *Witness to a Century.* New York: Ballantine Books.

——— (1937). *Freedom of the Press.* New York: Garden City Publishing Co., Inc.

Shane, Scott (2006). "Archivist Urges U.S. to Reopen Classified Files." *New York Times*, March 3, pp. A1, 18.

Sills, Murry (1981). *News Photographer*, September, p. 30.

Sloyan, Patrick (2001). "The Real War: The News Media's Complicity in Government Censorship Dismays a Reporter Who Covered the Persian Gulf War," *Media Studies Journal: Front Lines and Deadlines, Perspectives on War Reporting.* Arlington,VA: The Freedom Forum. 15.1. (Summer) pp. 58-63.

Smith, Terence (2000). Incident at No Gun Ri, Newshour with Jim Lehrer, from the online transcript, www.pbs.org/newshour/bb/media/jan-june00/nogunri_5-31.html.

Soderlund, W.C., et al. (1988). "Constructing the Agenda: The President and Aid for the Nicaraguan Contras, January–April 1986." Paper presented at the Intercultural Communication Conference on Latin America and the Caribbean, University of Miami, February 1988.

Solomon, Norman (2005). *War Made Easy: How Presidents and Pundits Keep Spinning Us to Death*. New York: John Wiley & Sons, Inc.

Sontag, Susan (1969). *Against Interpretation*. New York: Dell.

——— (1977). *On Photography*. New York: Farrar, Straus & Giroux.

——— (2003). *Regarding the Pain of Others*. New York: Farrar, Straus & Giroux.

Spanos, William (1993). *Heidegger and Criticism: Rewriting the Cultural Politics of Destruction*. Minneapolis: University of Minnesota Press.

Sperber, A.M. (1998). *Murrow: His Life and Times*. New York: Fordham University Press.

Sproule, J. Michael (1997). *Propaganda and Democracy: The American Experience of Media and Mass Persuasion*. Cambridge: Cambridge University Press.

Stanley, Alessandra (2005). "The Drama Of Iraq, While It Still Rages." *New York Times*, July 27.

Statement of Mutual Understanding Between the United States and the Republic of Korea on the No Gun Ri Investigations (2001). Online, January 11, www.pbs.org/newshour/media/media_watch/jan-june01/state.

Stauber, John, and Sheldon Rampton (1995). *Toxic Sludge Is Good for You: Lie, Damn Lies and the Public Relations Industry*. Monroe: Common Courage Press.

Stone, I. F. (1952). *The Hidden History of the Korean War: 1950–1951*. Boston: Little Brown & Co., 1988. First published in 1952 by Monthly Review Press.

Sudetic, Chuck (2001). "The Betrayal of Basra." *Mother Jones*, November/December, pp. 46–51, 90–92.

Summers, Col. Harry G., Jr. (1991). "Fighting the War in the Press." *Dateline*, A Bulletin from The Center for War, Peace, and the News Media 6.1 (January/February).

Suskind, Ron (2004). *The Price of Loyalty: George W. Bush, the White House, and the Education of Paul O'Neil*. New York: Simon & Schuster.

Swofford, Anthony (2003). *Jarhead: A Marine's Chronicle of the Gulf War and Other Battles*. New York: Scribner.

Tedesco, Richard (1987). "The Nation Tunes in for Ollie North." *Electronic Media*, July 13. pp. 1, 39.

Teinowitz, Ira (2002). "Charlotte Beers and the Selling of America." *Advertising Age*. (September 23). http://adage.com/news.cms?newsID= 36106.

Tennyson, Alfred (1895). "The Charge of the Light Brigade," *A Victorian Anthology, 1837–1895*. Edmund Clarence Stedman (ed.) Cambridge: Riverside Press, 1895; Bartleby.com, 2003. www.bartleby.com/246/. First written and published in 1854.

Thompson, Ginger (2005). "Old Foe of U.S. Trying for a Comeback in Nicaragua." *New York Times*, April 5. p. A 3.

Thompson, Reginald (1951). *Cry Korea*. London: Macdonald.

Times Mirror News Interest Index (1991). "The People, the Press and the War in the Gulf, January 31.

Toland, John (1968). *The Last 100 Days*. London: Mayflower.

Tomasky, Michael (2004). "Long Division: America Is *Not* Split over the Vietnam War. But Karl Rove Needs You to Believe That It Is." *The American Prospect*, October, pp. 18–21.

Trotochaud, Mary, and Rick McDowell (2004–5). "The Invasion of Fallujah: A Study in the Subversion of Truth." *Peacework* (December–January).

The Twentieth Century Fund (1985). *Battle Lines*. New York: Priority Press Publications, p. 4.

United States General Accounting Office, Report to Congressional Requesters (1987). "State's Administration of Certain Public Diplomacy Contracts," October, p. 14.

Viereck, George S. (1930). *Spreading Germs of Hate*. New York: Liveright. pp. 115–16.

Virilio, Paul, and Sylvere Lotringer (1997). *Pure War*. New York: Semiotext(e).

Ware, Michael (2002). "How the U.S. Killed the Wrong Soldiers." *Time*, February 11, p. 8.

Weiner, Tim (2004). "Lockheed and the Future of Warfare." *New York Times*, November 28.

Wiegman, Robyn (1994). "Missiles and Melodrama (Masculinity and the Televisual War)" in *Seeing through the Media: The Persian Gulf War*, eds. Susan Jeffords and Lauren Rabinovitz. New Brunswick: Rutgers University Press. pp. 171–187.

Williamson, Judith (1978). *Decoding Advertisements*. London: Marion Boyars.

Wise, John (1989). "The Ideological Significance of the Hero in the 'Star Wars Trilogy.'" Paper presented at the Seventh International Conference on Culture and Communication. Philadelphia, PA.

Wren-Lewis, Justin (1981–82). "The Story of a Riot: The Television Coverage of Civil Unrest in 1981." *Screen Education* 40, (Autumn/ Winter) pp. 15–33.

Wright, Micah Ian (2003). *You Back the Attack! We'll Bomb Who We Want!* New York: Seven Stories Press.

Wright, Robin, and Ellen Knickmeyer (2005). "U.S. Lowers Sights on What Can Be Achieved in Iraq: Administration Is Shedding 'Unreality' That Dominated Invasion, Official Says." *Washington Post*, August 14, p. A–1.

Youngs, Ian (2002). "Black Hawk Down." January 21, BBC news online.

Youra, Steven (1985). "James Agee on Films and the Theater of War." *Film Criticism*, (Fall) pp. 18–31.

Zimmerman, Patty (2000). "States of Emergency: Documentaries, Wars, and Democracies," The Video History Project. http://www. experimentaltvcenter.org/history/people/ptext.php3?id=96.

Zinn, Howard (2002). *Terrorism and War*. New York: Seven Stories Press.

——— (2003). "The Specter of Vietnam." TomPaine.com, (June 26)

Zunes, Stephen (2002). "The Long and Hidden History of the U.S. in Somalia." www.alternet.org/story.html?StoryID=12253, January 17, pp. 1–5.

Index